Popular Myths about Memory

Popular Myths about Memory

Media Representations Versus Scientific Evidence

Brian H. Bornstein

LEXINGTON BOOKS
Lanham • Boulder • New York • London

Published by Lexington Books
An imprint of The Rowman & Littlefield Publishing Group, Inc.
4501 Forbes Boulevard, Suite 200, Lanham, Maryland 20706
www.rowman.com

Unit A, Whitacre Mews, 26-34 Stannary Street, London SE11 4AB

British Library Cataloguing in Publication Information Available
The hardback edition of this book was previously catalogued by the Library of Congress
as follows:

Library of Congress Cataloging-in-Publication Data Available

ISBN 9780739192184 (hardback : alk. paper)
ISBN 9781498560801 (pbk. : alk. paper)
ISBN 9780739192191 (ebook)

∞™ The paper used in this publication meets the minimum requirements of American
National Standard for Information Sciences—Permanence of Paper for Printed Library
Materials, ANSI/NISO Z39.48-1992.

Printed in the United States of America

*To my sisters, Susan and Joan, sharers of my earliest memories,
the true ones and the false ones.
And to David, brother in spirit and deed.*

Contents

Contents

List of Figures

List of Tables

Acknowledgments

I have been teaching courses on human memory for 25 years, first at Louisiana State University and then at the University of Nebraska-Lincoln, with roughly 1,000 students over that time. For the past decade or so, one of the class assignments has been to choose two movies dealing with memory and critique them from a scientific and cinematic perspective. Realizing from those papers the large number of movies that address memory—and the varying degrees of scientific accuracy with which they do so—was one of my main motivations in writing this book. I owe a great debt to these students for helping me to organize my thoughts, pushing me to defend my ideas and present them clearly, and recommending relevant case studies, news articles, books and movies. There is a great deal of misinformation about memory out there. If this book helps to educate future students and interested readers about how memory works, and how it doesn't, I will be well satisfied.

My teaching on memory has benefited from the efforts of a number of dedicated teaching assistants over the years: Ani Aharonian, Kimberly Dellapaolera, Lori Hoetger, Sean McCabe, Elina Pierce, and Timmy Robicheaux. Three students assisted with collection and analysis of the data presented in chapter 2: Heather Bryden, Christopher Kimbrough, and Samantha Viola. My apologies if I have left anyone out—but as everyone knows and this book amply shows, memory is fallible—mine no less than anyone else's.

Writing a book on how the entertainment media perpetuate myths about memory required me to consume a lot of material produced by those media, especially novels, movies, and television shows. Indeed, the book gave me a convenient excuse to watch and read things that I would not ordinarily watch and read. Many people recommended relevant books or movies, and several gave generously of their time in attending movies or discussing novels with me. In this vein I am grateful to several Bornsteins (Joan, Lillian, Melissa,

xiii

and Susan), Eve Brank, Carolyn Brown Kramer, Christie Emler, David Fox, Heath Hodges, Randy Mercural, Mary Munter, Greg Page, Timothy Scholl, and Sandi Zellmer. Again, I apologize for leaving anyone out. I also found several relevant movie recommendations in works by Baxendale (2004) and Seamon (2015).

Midway through my work on the book, I came across a recently published book by John Seamon (2015), *Memory and Movies*, that covers some of the same material as this one (thanks to Jonathan Golding for bringing Seamon's very interesting book to my attention). Although we share a fascination with how movies portray memory phenomena and a belief that movies can be used as a vehicle for teaching students and others about memory, the present book differs from Seamon's in three crucial respects. First, the present book uses movies about memory for illustrative purposes, but its focus is on the myths about memory that are widespread in society. Thus, it presents data on the prevalence of memory myths and seeks to explain how the myths clash with scientific evidence. Second, it covers novels, television shows, and theater, as well as cinema, giving it a somewhat broader scope. Third, and perhaps most importantly, Seamon's book focuses primarily on films that portray memory *accurately* (while acknowledging that some get it wrong), whereas mine focuses mainly on films and other popular media that portray memory *inaccurately* (while acknowledging that some get it right). This difference in perspective might reflect a difference in authorial dispositions, with me being the pessimist—and I would not argue with that characterization. But the evidence I present on the widespread myths and misunderstandings about how memory works suggests that there is a relationship between those myths and popular (mis)representations of the underlying cognitive phenomena. The heart of the book is an examination of that relationship.

During part of the time I spent working on the book, I was supported by a faculty development leave from the University of Nebraska-Lincoln. The leave freed me from my usual teaching and administrative duties, allowing me to spend more time writing. Without the university's generous support, I would have completed the book even more behind schedule than I ultimately did. I am also grateful to the interlibrary loan department at the University of Nebraska-Lincoln Libraries. The material for this book required me to range far and wide, often well beyond my usual sources, and the ILL staff promptly tracked down everything I needed. Special thanks to Amy King and Kasey Beduhn, my editors at Lexington Books, who saw the value in the project and were helpful and supportive throughout the writing, revising, and publication process.

Christie Emler was an extraordinary medical consultant on the amnesia chapters, though that assistance pales next to her other jobs of being wife, mother, and boon companion *par excellence*. Kylie Key also provided helpful feedback on several chapters. Edie Greene was unfailingly patient with my delays in our writing a different book together because of my work on this one at the same time—writing two books at once turned out not to be the brightest idea I have ever had. Edie also made substantive contributions to chapters 9 and 10, and if I have managed to present scientific research in an approachable manner, it is in no small part from following her example from our many years of writing together. Jeff Neuschatz went above and beyond the call of friendship in reading and commenting on the entire book. It is much better for his insights, but he is blameless for any shortcomings that remain. Jeff, beer and bourbon are on me for the next decade. My amazing daughters, Lillian and Melissa, were supportive as always while I worked on the book, and they provided several first-person examples that I included to make various points. Nothing makes you appreciate the miracle that is memory, and its limitations, like having children. I lament the everyday parent-child memories that have already faded from my grasp, and I cherish the ones that remain. Most of all, I look forward to forming many new ones. Finally, thanks to my siblings, to whom this book is dedicated—for a lifetime of memories, nearly all of them good ones.

Introduction

Memory, Metamemory, Media, and Myth

Alice Howland, the main character in *Still Alice*, by Lisa Genova (2007), is a 50-year-old woman with Alzheimer's disease. As her memory rapidly deteriorates, she goes from being a highly intelligent, successful, and accomplished Harvard psychology professor to being timid, angry, scared, and dependent on her family for even the most basic daily tasks. Within about eighteen months of her diagnosis she can no longer recognize her family and needs constant care. *Still Alice* was a New York Times bestseller; the film adaptation was one of the most popular and critically acclaimed movies of 2014, earning an Academy Award for its star, Julianne Moore. Alice's story is poignant and all too real. But is it realistic? Do most individuals with Alzheimer's have an experience like Alice's?

The novelist Paul Auster (1982, p. 81) defines memory as "the space in which a thing happens for the second time." When that happens, memory "works"; yet our memories fail us all the time, even in the absence of pathology like Alzheimer's disease. Students are unable to remember material that they studied for an exam; we go shopping and forget where we parked the car; we neglect to take our daily medication; and some individuals even "remember" a former life or being abducted by aliens. Indeed, the workings of memory are most salient on the occasions when it fails; it is therefore important to keep in mind that most of the time it works just fine. In addition to helping us function, this generally smooth operation leads us to take memory for granted. Although it is hardly a uniquely human skill—unlike, say, language, analytic geometry, symphonic composition, or dunking a basketball (and whether other species might also have any of these abilities is, to some extent, debatable)—it is fair to say that human memory is unusually complicated, powerful, and well developed. Consequently, this book will focus on memory in humans. Memory is many things: a repository of information, a sense of self, a process. As the Paul Auster quotation indicates, memory is both a "space" and where a thing "happens."

Alice's illness vividly and realistically illustrates what can happen when a disease affects memory. Although Alzheimer's disease can and does afflict people as young as Alice, the overwhelming majority of Alzheimer's patients are significantly older than 50 years. Like other Alzheimer's sufferers, Alice is a sympathetic character in large part because she is, through no fault of her own, so clearly suffering. Unlike humans, other species do not appear to be aware of, or distressed by, their memory lapses. If I introduce myself to someone at a party whom it turns out I have met three times before, I feel embarrassed and berate myself. But if my dog sniffs another animal as if they were meeting for the very first time, whereas they have actually had several previous encounters, no harm is done (unless the other dog was aggressive, and then my dog should have remembered to keep his distance)—he just goes on his merry way. Unlike dogs, humans routinely form opinions about how their memory, and memory in general, does and should work.

The general public endorses a number of psychological "myths," including mistaken beliefs about memory and other cognitive processes (see, generally, Della Salla, 1999, 2007; Lane & Karam-Zanders, 2014; Lilienfeld, Lynn, Ruscio & Beyerstein, 2010). That is, "students and laypersons in general 'know' many things about memory that are complete nonsense" (Banaji & Crowder, 2000, p. 22). These myths can negatively influence people's performance in a wide variety of everyday, educational, and interpersonal domains (Banaji & Crowder, 2000; Nelson & Narens, 1990), as well as in more specialized situations like healthcare and legal proceedings. For example, believing that memory normally declines with aging could lead someone like Alice to postpone diagnosis and treatment for incipient dementia; and believing that eyewitnesses who are very confident at trial have much better memories than less confident ones could lead jurors to overweigh the testimony of a confident eyewitness.

My thesis in this book is that laypeople's intuitive understanding of memory phenomena is not very accurate in many respects, and that often these misconceptions, or myths, go hand-in-hand with popular misrepresentations about memory functioning. The book examines a number of these memory myths by summarizing research on what they are and how they clash with scientific research findings. The remainder of this introduction presents the concept of *metamemory* as a way of thinking about memory myths. It then discusses the relationship between popular media and individuals' knowledge and behavior in general, followed by a discussion of why memory myths are dangerous. The introduction concludes with an overview of the remainder of the book.

METAMEMORY

Metamemory refers to "our knowledge and awareness of our own memory processes" (Schwartz, 2014, p. 260). It is a type of metacognition, which means knowledge and awareness of cognitive processes more broadly—literally, cognition about cognition (e.g., Beran, Brandl, Perner, & Proust, 2012; Dunlosky & Metcalfe, 2009; Fleming & Frith, 2014). For example, we have an idea of our own language skills, problem-solving ability, and decision-making capacity, as well as our memory processes. Interestingly, people's awareness of their abilities across these different cognitive processes can vary substantially. I have observed this firsthand by conducting an informal experiment over the years. As an experimental social-cognitive psychologist who conducts research on both memory and decision making, I vary what I tell new acquaintances when they ask about my research specialization. Sometimes I say, "I teach and do research on memory." Other times I say, "I teach and do research on decision making." Roughly 75 percent of the time, people will reply to the former statement with something like "I should take your class; my memory is terrible." But not once in roughly 25 years has someone said, in response to the latter statement, "I should take your class; I make terrible decisions." This example, anecdotal though it may be, shows that people do form an opinion of their memory abilities, and that they are less likely to form an opinion of their decision-making abilities—even though human decision making is just as prone to error as human memory (e.g., Baron, 2008). And the example tells us nothing at all about whether their opinion of their memory (or decision-making) abilities is accurate.

As the words "our own" in Schwartz's definition of metamemory make clear, it is primarily personal and self-referential. It involves a self-assessment, or monitoring, of one's own mental states. Is my memory better or worse than most people's? Have I learned the course material well enough that I will be able to remember it on tomorrow's exam? Is some piece of information that I cannot retrieve at the moment, such as a word or name on the tip of my tongue, likely to be in memory? Is my memory worse than it used to be? How do I learn best? These kinds of evaluations that people make of their own memory abilities are often referred to as *memory self-efficacy* (Beaudoin & Desrichard, 2011).

However, there is also an impersonal, broader component of metamemory, which concerns people's knowledge about how memory generally works, such as knowing that mentally repeating information over and over is a good way to maintain it in short-term memory, but not a very effective way to store it in long-term memory. These two components of metamemory necessarily interact (Lane & Karam-Zanders, 2014): One's general beliefs about memory both derive from and influence one's observation and sense of one's own memory performance, as well as the strategies one chooses to implement in efforts to store and remember information more effectively.

Metamemory judgments often, but not always, involve explicit reflective awareness (Fleming & Frith, 2014). There is much debate over whether nonhuman animals and very young children, who presumably lack a highly developed capacity for self-reflection, demonstrate knowledge of their own memory functions, but some research suggests that they do (Beran et al., 2012). One way of inferring implicit metamemory is from neurological activity. Specific regions of the brain, such as the prefrontal cortex, are associated both with the making of metamemory judgments and metamemory accuracy (Chua, Pergolizzi & Weintraub, 2014; Fleming & Dolan, 2014). Not surprisingly, then, brain damage not only can cause memory loss in the form of amnesia (covered in chapters 5–7), but it can also lead to impairments in metamemory (e.g., Cosentino, 2014).

As the examples given above illustrate, one critical application of metamemory is learning in educational settings. Students can tailor their course selection and studying strategies based on their understanding of how they best store information in memory (e.g., visual vs. verbal presentation, lecture vs. interactive classroom exercises, solitary vs. collaborative studying); they can allocate their studying efforts efficiently (i.e., judging when they have sufficiently mastered the material); and they can make strategic decisions when taking tests (e.g., it might make sense to spend additional time trying to remember something you cannot immediately recall if you judge that it is likely to be in memory, but not if you are sure that you don't know it). Metamemory is equally relevant in many other kinds of situations. I know that I am terrible at remembering the performers of music my teen-age daughters like or how, exactly, my myriad cousins are related to me; but that I am good at spelling (not solely a memory phenomenon, but one that has a large memory component) and recognizing actors. Metamemory is also implicated in aging and many forms of amnesia. The awareness that one's memory is deteriorating is one of the most distressing things about amnesia, and it (or family members' awareness of the decline) is a necessary precursor of seeking treatment.

There are also situations where the concern is with others' metamemory rather than our own (Spellman, Tenney & Scalia, 2011). For instance, we rely on others' judgments of their own memory when taking advice from a physician, relying on input from a coworker, trusting a spouse's recollection of a shared event more than our own, or evaluating the testimony of an eyewitness. In general, people believe that their own metamemory judgments are more reliable than those of others (Spellman et al., 2011), although they are willing to defer to others when the others have special expertise (MacCoun, 2015).

In all of these situations, especially when the concern is with one's own memory, the metamemory judgments lead to appropriate behaviors to alter or improve memory functioning, which are often referred to as *control processes* (Nelson & Narens, 1990, 1994; Schwartz, 2014). Students spend more time studying material that they feel they do not know well than material that they believe they have already mastered; when listening to music with my younger daughter, I guess "Taylor Swift!" at every opportunity (a strategy that is only occasionally successful); at family gatherings I make sure one (and preferably both) of my sisters is nearby; and patients who suspect a decrement in memory functioning seek medical advice.

There is a significant, but far from perfect, correlation between memory self-efficacy and memory performance (Beaudoin & Desrichard, 2011). Consequently, metamemory judgments are usually fairly accurate, but by no means always. For example, students not infrequently believe that they have stored some information while studying but are subsequently unable to retrieve it on an exam, especially if they make their judgments of learning immediately after studying (Dunlosky & Nelson, 1992). Conversely, students and others often believe that their memory has let them down (e.g., that they did poorly on a test), whereas in fact, their performance demonstrates that they remembered the material correctly. In part, these errors reflect an inability to predict future changes in memory; people anticipate that their memories will remain stable, and they are not very well-informed about the factors that influence memory, leading them to underestimate both future forgetting and future learning, depending on the circumstances (Kornell, 2011). And amnesia patients are notorious for believing that their memory is working just fine, in large part because the memory deficit prevents them from remembering the occasions when their memory failed. Even in the absence of brain damage, metacognitive accuracy varies substantially both across and within individuals, depending on factors such as the type of task, the kind of material, and even the time of day (e.g., Fleming & Dolan, 2014; Hourihan & Benjamin, 2014). Metamemory judgments are also dissociable from the accuracy of memory itself (e.g., Fleming & Dolan, 2014); that is, having a reliable memory does not necessarily imply having good insight into one's memory performance.

As mentioned above, one aspect of metamemory that is related to an awareness of one's own memory abilities is a general knowledge of how memory works. Surveys of this kind of metamemory show that much of what people think they know about memory turns out to be erroneous, such as the belief that "flashbulb" memories are unusually accurate (see chapter 2) or that a blow to the head can restore memories lost due to amnesia (see chapter 5). There is clearly a relation among these general metamemory beliefs, specific metamemory awareness, and memory performance. For example, someone who believes that rote rehearsal is an effective means of encoding information in memory probably believes that he can remember material that he has rehearsed but not thought about deeply; as rehearsal has limited effectiveness, especially compared to activities that involve deeper processing, his retrieval is likely to suffer. As described below in the section on "The Danger of Memory Myths," general beliefs about memory also influence our perception of others and matters of public policy.

MEDIA

Where do memory myths come from? No doubt they have a number of origins, but Lilienfeld et al. (2010) identify misleading media portrayals (e.g., film, television, popular literature) as one of the leading sources of psychological misconceptions. "Media" is a broad term that has been defined differently when used in various contexts and for various purposes. Media formats include (but are not limited to) the Internet, television, radio, newspapers, films, videogames, smartphones, magazines, live theater, and literature, and they transmit both factual (i.e., nonfiction, such as news) and fictional information. There are more formats today than there were a century ago, and no doubt there will be even more formats a century from now.

Although my emphasis is on fictional/entertainment media, such as novels, movies, and television shows, news media are hardly immune from misrepresenting psychological and other scientific phenomena (Howard & Donnelly, 1999). One well-known example is the Mozart effect—the notion that listening to classical music enhances intelligence. Despite an absence of reliable scientific evidence supporting the Mozart effect (Chabris, 1999), it has attained the status of a "scientific legend," which Bangerter and Heath (2004, p. 608) define as "a widespread belief ... that propagates in society, originally arising from scientific study, but that has been transformed to deviate in essential ways from the understanding of scientists." Distorted media coverage of the Mozart effect has played no small part in perpetuating the legend (Bangerter & Heath, 2004). Other misrepresented psychological phenomena range from sexual behavior (Barron & Brown, 2012) to additional variations on the theme of music enriching cognitive skills (Mehr, 2015). Popular beliefs about the phenomena then become skewed accordingly.

History contains numerous examples of how popular false beliefs about psychological processes, such as the power of magic, witchcraft, and astrology, can influence thinking and behavior (Thomas, 1971). It is tempting to dismiss such beliefs as the product of a scientifically unenlightened age, but cultural forces continue to contribute to the popular acceptance of psychological notions that lack an empirical foundation. For example, within just the last couple of centuries, "claims about one's inability to remember trauma amount to a culturally shaped idiom of distress arising in Europe in the climate of Romanticism" (McNally, 2012, p. 123; for more on memory for trauma and repression, see chapter 3). More recently still, popular culture, fueled by sensationalistic media coverage and fictional portrayals in literature, television, and cinema, has perpetuated a belief in the reality and "repressibility" of phenomena like alien abduction and past lives (Clancy, 2005; Clark & Loftus, 1996; Meyersburg, Bogdan, Gallo, & McNally, 2009). Thus, the media have always had the capacity to influence popular understanding of psychological and other scientific phenomena. The media have enormous potential to influence public perceptions and opinions, whether those perceptions and opinions are about politics, history, current events, the arts, or science.

Perhaps nowhere is the disparity between reality and art as great as in the popular representation of science, likely because of the difficulty of distilling complex scientific processes and theories into an easily digestible visual format (i.e., TV, film) or short soundbytes (i.e., news) with mass appeal. Consequently, popular portrayals of science are often inaccurate and unrealistic (Griep & Mikasen, 2009). Here it is important to distinguish between explicit portrayals of scientists, the scientific process, or stories grounded in science (e.g., movies about scientists working in a lab, dinosaurs, or space exploration), and fictional representations that implicitly reflect scientific phenomena. Authors and film and television producers who are telling science-based stories often do research and hire consultants to make their work scientifically plausible and realistic, which benefits the artistic product as entertainment and can even benefit science by encouraging innovation and the dissemination of ideas (Griep & Mikasen, 2009; Kirby, 2011). The natural sciences, in particular, lend themselves to this sort of explicit treatment (Kirby, 2011). Although psychological research and practice have also been depicted in this manner (e.g., the use of psychoanalysis in Alfred Hitchcock's *Spellbound*, and Jung and Freud's research and treatment methods in the film *A Dangerous Method*; see, generally, Packer, 2012), more often the depiction of psychological phenomena is more subtle. Perhaps this is because the media, like psychology, deal with the wide range of human behavior as a matter of course. But it provides nearly limitless opportunities for not only representing, but misrepresenting, the way people normally act and think.

What makes today's media unique, compared to previous generations, is their variety and the wealth of information they convey and our easy access to it. With the advent of smartphones and tablets, people can now consume media virtually anywhere at any time. Because of the rapid increase in access to information over the last couple of decades, the media play an increasingly central and important role in people's lives (Giles, 2010; Okdie et al., 2014). Our heightened use of and reliance on information obtained through various media means that media have an enormous capability to influence our thinking and behavior (Okdie et al., 2014). This capability confers considerable power to effect positive social change. For example, televised serial dramas have been used to promote prosocial behaviors relating to health, literacy, environmental sustainability, family planning, and civic engagement (Bandura, 2006; Giles, 2003; Shah, Rojas, & Cho, 2009; Walsh-Childers & Brown, 2009). However, the flip side of that power is that media portrayals can entail negative consequences, as in unrealistic representations of beauty and thinness that can contribute to distorted body image and eating disorders (Hausenblas et al., 2013), or depictions of media violence that can contribute to aggression (e.g., Anderson et al., 2003; Giles, 2010). In light of these and other relationships between media and people's cognitions and behavior, it is hardly surprising that media portrayals of memory contribute to erroneous beliefs about how the mind works.

In addition to helping shape what the public knows about various topics and events, the digital technologies that underlie much of contemporary media also make it possible for the media to function as memory repositories. For example, blogs, social media sites, and digital scrapbooks can store a wealth of visual and textual information that in previous generations would have been only in the memories of the individual experiencers. The availability (some would say ubiquity) of such digital media is arguably changing the ways in which we store information in, and retrieve information from, memory (Garde-Hansen, Hoskins, & Reading, 2009). Some evidence suggests that relying on external memory aids, such as writing, can paradoxically have an adverse impact on memory ability when those aids are not available (e.g., Dube, 2000; Foer, 2011). Hence, as electronic devices like smartphones become smaller, cheaper, and more adept at serving mnemonic functions, they might inadvertently detract from the very functions they are designed to serve. This is not to argue that such "memory prosthetics" are undesirable; they can be incredibly practical and effective, especially in individuals with normal or mildly impaired cognitive functioning (see chapters 5 and 6). However, it does suggest that their benefits come with a cost; the more we rely on external devices to remember for us, the less we are training and developing our minds to help us remember things on our own. This unintended consequence of digital media has more to do with media process than content. The present volume focuses on the role of media content in perpetuating memory myths—specifically, popular media's portrayal of memory phenomena.

THE DANGER OF MEMORY MYTHS

There are a number of reasons why we should care about psychological myths and the sources of those myths. Lilienfeld and colleagues (2010), who along with Sergio Della Salla (1999, 2007) are probably the leading debunkers of psychological myths, list three main reasons. First, the myths can be harmful: to the myth-holder, to others, and to society as a whole. At the individual level, someone who believes in repression and recovered memory might come to believe she was abused as a child when she was not actually abused, with all the attendant consequences of believing such victimization occurred; someone who believes that memory abilities are static might not take advantage of techniques that would improve his memory; and someone who believes that Alzheimer's disease frequently afflicts 50-year-olds might experience needless worry over normal memory lapses. Others can be affected in myriad ways, such as the alleged abuser accused on the basis of a false memory, the defendant convicted because jurors were too believing of a mistaken eyewitness or a false confession, or the friends and family members who cannot understand why Johnny has such a hard time retaining new information after that concussion he received playing football. And misconceptions about memory can influence policy making in the areas of law (e.g., the admissibility of expert testimony about eyewitness memory), healthcare (e.g., services for amnesic patients), and medical research (e.g., appropriations for research on amnesia). The potentially negative consequences of myths about the mind are substantial and pervasive.

The second reason we should care, according to Lilienfeld and colleagues (2010), is that the myths can cause indirect damage, in the form of opportunity costs. For example, imagine someone who is so depressed—in the everyday meaning of the term, and possibly in a clinical sense as well—that his routine functioning is being affected. He decides to seek the help of a mental health professional. Whom to consult? If he believes that repression and related unconscious defense mechanisms play a large part in producing mental illness, then he is more likely to go to a psychodynamic therapist than to another kind of practitioner, and the therapist might use techniques like recovered memory therapy. Although he might benefit to some extent, since any psychotherapy is generally better than none, he could experience actual harm (Lilienfeld, 2007); and more importantly, he would miss out on more effective treatment approaches.

The third reason why we should care about psychological myths is that an uncritical acceptance of these myths can spill over to critical thinking in other areas (Lilienfeld et al., 2010). In large part because of the proliferation of media in the current age, we are barraged with more information than ever before. The sheer volume of information increases the need to be able to separate myth from reality, the wheat from the chaff. Relying on myths about the mind could make one more likely to accept myths about other things, such as climate change (e.g., the myth that it is not really happening), healthcare (e.g., the myth that vaccines cause autism), and the like, which carry their own potentially dangerous consequences. Myths imply unquestioning belief. Skepticism is healthy.

Thus, accurate metamemory, in terms of both knowledge of one's own memory abilities and how memory works in general, is adaptive. It leads individuals to allocate their cognitive resources efficiently, to implement encoding and retrieval strategies that are likely to be effective (Nelson & Narens, 1990), and to evaluate others' memory reports properly. In the case of severe memory impairment, accurate metamemory can also lead to the adoption of effective compensatory behaviors (Hertzog & Dixon, 1994). Misconceptions about memory can affect behavior in practically any aspect of life: education (both teaching and learning strategies), healthcare (e.g., how patients respond to early signs of dementia), law (e.g., eyewitness reports, procedures used in questioning witnesses and conducting identifications, jurors' and judges' evaluations of eyewitness and confession testimony), and psychotherapy (both patients' expectations and clinicians' therapeutic techniques). An appreciation of these misconceptions is important because of the many ways in which they can influence not only individual and group behavior but also public policy and legal outcomes.

OVERVIEW OF THE BOOK

Prior research has investigated what people believe about a variety of memory phenomena. Although these beliefs are accurate in some respects, they often conflict with the scientific evidence. Except for chapter 1, which focuses broadly on how researchers study laypeople's memory beliefs, each of the book's substantive chapters examines the clash between media representations of a specific memory topic and scientific research on that topic.

Experimental research on memory has been going on for approximately 140 years, producing a wealth of empirical information. Yet as in most scientific domains, that research has yielded some inconsistent findings, and the literature on some aspects of memory is more conclusive than it is on others. Moreover, some memory topics (e.g., repression) are contentious both within the field and in society at large. In evaluating a body of research, my stance on these topics reflects what I perceive, based on many years of my own research and teaching and a close reading of the literature, to be the majority position in the field and the one that is best supported by the data. These conclusions are necessarily generalizations and, as such, need to be taken in context. In the interest of trying to draw general conclusions for readers, I generally avoid getting too far down into the weeds of conflicting studies, but I do make an effort to acknowledge the existence of competing views.

As described above, an important element of metamemory has to do with individuals' beliefs about how memory works. Chapter 1 reviews previous studies on the sorts of beliefs—accurate and erroneous—that people have about memory (e.g., Della Salla, 1999, 2007; Lane & Karam-Zanders, 2014; Lilienfeld et al., 2010; Magnussen et al., 2006). Most of these surveys focus on a relatively small number of topics, such as memory and the brain, repression and recovered memory, or eyewitness memory. The chapter includes original data from a broad memory myth survey, covering a number of different topics. Laypeople's knowledge of how memory works varies considerably depending on the topic.

Each of the remaining chapters (except for the conclusion) is devoted to a specific myth, some of which have multiple components, or related myths. Each chapter has the same format. After first describing the myth and presenting examples drawn from popular media representations, the chapter substantiates the existence of the myth with survey evidence documenting the incorrect beliefs that many people hold about that particular aspect of memory. The heart of each chapter then consists of a scientific review of the myth and its various components. This review includes a discussion of relevant research findings debunking the myth. In some cases the myth contains a kernel of truth, but even then, the popular representation typically distorts or exaggerates the empirical evidence. Throughout the book, examples from popular culture and the media, such as films, television shows, novels, and highly publicized legal cases, are used to illustrate the myths.

Chapter 2 addresses beliefs about memory accuracy and the permanence of memory, specifically, the belief that memory is like a video recorder or similar mechanical device that has high fidelity and ease of retrieval (e.g., a DVD player, computer hard drive, etc.). Implicit in these metaphors is the idea that we have the capacity to store vast amounts of information and to retrieve that information, on demand, in pristine form. Memories of emotional events, such as "flashbulb" memories, are presumed to be especially accurate. Yet in many circumstances emotion does not confer much of a memory advantage, if any, and flashbulb memories are often inaccurate.

Although the popular view of the relationship between emotion and memory is that emotion enhances memory, the relationship tends to be viewed as nonlinear. That is, some emotional content presumably benefits memory, but many people assume that extreme emotion—especially extreme negative emotion associated with traumatic experiences—can have the opposite effect. The concept of repression, popularized by Sigmund Freud and his followers, holds that remembering traumatic events can be so disturbing that the mind unconsciously pushes those memories out of awareness. Associated with this belief is the notion that the repressed memory is still available and that one can "recover" the repressed memory, which—in large part because of its strong emotional content—is highly accurate. Certain techniques, such as hypnosis, are believed to be particularly effective at recovering repressed memories. Yet contrary to the popular view, there is little evidence that repression occurs; recovered memories very often contain errors and in some cases are entirely false; and hypnosis, while arguably beneficial in some respects, increases the risk of certain kinds of memory errors and is legally suspect. Chapter 3 considers the "unholy tetrad" of repression, recovered memory, false memory, and hypnosis.

Chapter 4 extends the discussion of false memory by further exploring beliefs about implanting memories in the brain, as well as the possibility of transferring memories from a donor to a host organism or selectively erasing memories. Implanting knowledge from a donor's neural tissue to a recipient, or selectively erasing memories, has served as the premise for a number of science fiction films (e.g., *Total Recall*); beliefs that these are plausible and realistic occurrences persist despite an absence of supporting evidence (Della Salla & Beyerstein, 2007). Other movies on the implantation theme, such as *Inception*, raise legitimate psychological issues such as source monitoring (i.e., the ability to identify the source of one's memories). There is a kernel of truth in *Inception*'s portrayal of dream phenomena, in that people routinely have difficulty determining whether they thought of something themselves, obtained it from an external source, or dreamt it (Johnson, Raye, Mitchell, & Ankudowich, 2012; Mitchell & Johnson, 2009). With respect to the erasure of unwanted memories, although it does not work as cleanly as portrayed in popular media representations (e.g., films like *Eternal Sunshine of the Spotless Mind*), some drugs are capable of essentially erasing memories of negative emotional events while leaving other memories relatively intact (Eichenbaum, 2012). Thus, this is an area where in some respects, reality is beginning to imitate art.

Although repression is suspect as a cause of retrograde amnesia—severe memory loss for the past—such memory loss occurs all too often in cases of brain damage. This prevalence is reflected in media portrayals: Retrograde amnesia is probably the favorite memory topic of both Hollywood (e.g., the *Bourne Identity* films, based on the popular novels by Robert Ludlum) and daytime TV (e.g., virtually every soap opera ever made). Many of these depictions involve a protagonist who has no memory whatsoever of his or her former life and who suffers no cognitive deficits other than the profound memory loss (Baxendale, 2004; Seamon, 2015). Such extreme and neatly compartmentalized retrograde amnesia has been documented but is exceedingly rare. Most often, retrograde amnesia is accompanied by anterograde amnesia, which refers to difficulty encoding new information since the brain injury. Anterograde amnesia is as common, if not more common, than retrograde amnesia, and it can occur without any significant retrograde impairment (Parkin, 1997). It is often played for laughs (e.g., the character

Dory in the films *Finding Nemo* and *Finding Dory*) but can be devastating to those who have it and their loved ones. Fictional portrayals of anterograde amnesia also present characters who can remember events of the day just fine for eighty minutes (e.g., Yoko Ogawa's novel *The Housekeeper and the Professor*) or until they go to sleep (e.g., the film *Fifty First Dates* and the novel *Before I Go to Sleep*, by S.J. Watson). The vast majority of individuals with anterograde amnesia forget information within just a few minutes, and the "forgetting while asleep" motif runs counter to scientific research on memory consolidation during sleep. Chapters 5 and 6 examine myths related to retrograde and anterograde amnesia, respectively.

Alzheimer's disease is the leading (but far from the only) cause of pathological memory loss, afflicting millions of people a year, and the incidence is growing as the average life expectancy increases. There is now a sizeable nonfiction literature on Alzheimer's, including books on etiology, treatment, and memoirs by both patients and their caregivers (e.g., John Bayley's book *Elegy for Iris*, about his wife Iris Murdoch's struggle with Alzheimer's). Fictional portrayals of Alzheimer's disease include films (e.g., *The Notebook* [based on a Nicholas Sparks novel], *Away from Her*), television shows (e.g., *Grey's Anatomy*), novels (e.g., *Still Alice*), and theater (e.g., *The Memory Show*, by Sara Cooper). Many of these works are reasonably accurate in depicting the toll of Alzheimer's on others, and the attention—as well as public figures' disclosure that they suffer from Alzheimer's or similar forms of dementia (e.g., President Ronald Reagan, British Prime Minister Margaret Thatcher, and University of Tennessee basketball coach Pat Summitt)—has demystified Alzheimer's and removed some of the stigma associated with the disease. Indeed, Alzheimer's disease has come out of the closet to such an extent that it now runs the risk of being perceived as more prevalent than it really is and an inevitable consequence of aging. Many portrayals of Alzheimer's patients do little to show either the abilities that many patients maintain until the disease is quite advanced, or the cognitive abilities that elderly individuals without Alzheimer's retain at a fairly high level. Chapter 7 summarizes research on the relationship among Alzheimer's disease and related disorders, "normal" aging, and memory impairment.

As noted above, one of the main reasons for studying metamemory is that beliefs about how memory works can have important real-world consequences. Chapters 8 and 9 explore some of those consequences in one particular domain, namely, the legal system. For example, people generally believe that eyewitnesses are highly accurate and that individuals could not "remember," and confess to, a crime they did not commit; whereas in fact, eyewitnesses frequently make errors, and it is entirely possible for a suspect, in the course of a suggestive or coercive interrogation, to create a false memory of having committed a crime. Due to these (and other) factors, false identifications and false confessions are among the leading causes of erroneous convictions (e.g., Simon, 2012).[1] Problems associated with eyewitness testimony and confessions have received a fair amount of media scrutiny, but both forms of evidence remain highly influential, in large part because people—legal professionals as well as the laypeople who serve as jurors—harbor misconceptions about them. Chapters 8 and 9 cover myths dealing with eyewitness memory and confessions, respectively.

Just as there are misconceptions about basic memory processes and memory loss, so too are there misconceptions about superior memory. There are a number of cases in the literature of people with extraordinarily good memory (e.g., Neisser & Hyman, 2000), as well as fictional portrayals, such as David Baldacci's novels *Memory Man* and *The Last Mile*, the movie *Rain Man*, and the recent television show *Unforgettable*, some of which are based on actual persons (e.g., the late Kim Peek inspired the main character in *Rain Man*). Many people expect that photographic memory is not that uncommon, but these individuals are actually quite rare, and there is considerable debate over whether their unusual abilities constitute photographic memory or what, exactly, that term even means. Some of the most amazing feats of memory are performed by individuals who otherwise have significant intellectual or developmental disabilities—that is, persons with *savant syndrome*. Despite the existence of such cases, research shows that most persons with autism or intellectual impairment do not have unusually good memories or any special skills (Treffert, 1989, 2010). Yet even though superior memories are quite rare, memory improvement, often of a dramatic nature, is well within the capacities of most people (e.g., Foer, 2011; Worthen & Hunt, 2011). Chapter 10 discusses myths related to individuals with unusually good memories and the implications of superior memory for understanding normal memory processes and how to improve memory functioning.

The conclusion revisits the book's major themes introduced here, especially the concepts of metamemory and memory myths and the question of how popular culture and the media influence public perceptions of memory and vice versa. This concluding chapter also highlights the consequences of memory myths and possible strategies for debunking them. Finally, the Appendix contains a list of movies that deal with some aspect of memory (other popular media, such as novels and television, are too varied to compile a list that would be anywhere near comprehensive, but numerous examples drawn from literature and television series are included throughout the book).

NOTE

1. See, generally, https://www.innocenceproject.org.

Chapter 1

Memory Myths

A Review and New Data

As discussed in the introduction, "people appear to know many things about how memory actually works, and yet also have beliefs that are mistaken" (Lane & Karam-Zanders, 2014, p. 362). What people know—or think they know—about memory can influence their behavior, at times adversely, in a number of contexts. What, exactly, do people believe about how memory works? Relatively few systematic studies of the topic exist. Several studies of psychological myths touch on memory while treating a variety of cognitive and other phenomena (e.g., Della Salla, 1999, 2007; Levin & Angelone, 2008; Lilienfeld et al., 2010). Although several studies have assessed laypeople's beliefs about specific memory topics, especially eyewitness memory (see chapter 8) and issues related to repression, recovered memory, and hypnosis (see chapter 3), few have focused on memory processes more broadly. It is difficult to compare across previous studies that have assessed knowledge of different topics. In addition, many studies have used different response scales and participant samples. People might also know more than they can demonstrate under narrowly constrained laboratory conditions; for example, performance can vary depending on the manner in which questions are asked (Read & Desmarais, 2009).

Another limitation is that prior studies have generally not examined the relationship in individuals' knowledge and expectations across various memory phenomena. A broader assessment of laypeople's knowledge of memory issues could determine whether stability exists across domains. Some evidence for such stability exists; for example, people who are overconfident when remembering one type of information (e.g., a witnessed event) tend to be overconfident when remembering other types of information (e.g., general knowledge; Bornstein & Zickafoose, 1999). Such an investigation is theoretically important because of its implications for how metamemory develops and is maintained, while identifying individuals who are especially likely to be misinformed about specific memory phenomena has practical implications in a variety of real-world contexts (Lane & Karam-Zanders, 2014).

The present chapter has two components. First, it reviews previous surveys measuring laypeople's beliefs about memory. The review concentrates on "general" memory surveys, leaving those dealing with specific topics (e.g., eyewitness memory) to the relevant chapters. The second part of the chapter summarizes the results of a study I conducted measuring participants' beliefs about a wide variety of memory topics.

MEMORY SURVEYS: A REVIEW OF THE LITERATURE

In a recent large-scale memory survey, Simons and Chabris (2011) asked a diverse sample of 1,838 Americans (demographically weighted to create a nominal sample size of 1,500) their beliefs about six different memory topics. Respondents indicated whether they agreed or disagreed with (or didn't know) the following statements: (1) "People suffering from amnesia typically cannot recall their own name or identity"; (2) "The testimony of one confident eyewitness should be enough evidence to convict a defendant of a crime"; (3) "Human memory works like a video camera, accurately recording the events we see and hear so that we can review and inspect them later"; (4) "Hypnosis is useful in helping witnesses accurately recall details of crimes"; (5) "People generally notice when something unexpected enters their field of view, even when they're paying attention to something else"; and (6) "Once you have experienced an event and formed a memory of it, that memory does not change." All of these statements represent memory myths—that is, they run counter to the weight of the empirical evidence and to the consensus among experts, based on a summative evaluation of the literature.[1]

Nonetheless, each was endorsed by a substantial proportion of the sample (37–83 %, depending on the question). The highest agreement rates were for the statements about amnesia (82.7 %) and unexpected events (77.5 %). Intercorrelations among the various items were low and mostly nonsignificant (i.e., agreeing with one myth was not a good predictor of agreement with other myths). Only 1.5 percent of respondents answered all six questions correctly, and the median number correct was two. Knowledge of memory topics varied as a function of several demographic variables. Younger participants (i.e., <50 years old) outperformed older participants, and Whites, Asians, and members of "other" races/ethnicities outperformed Blacks and Hispanics. Men and women did not differ significantly.

Better performance was also associated with a higher income, more education, taking more psychology classes, and reading more psychology books. As Simons and Chabris (2011) point out, this does not necessarily mean that either education in general or studying psychology (formally or informally) in particular directly increases understanding of how memory works, as these variables are all associated with many other factors (e.g., socioeconomic status and intelligence). However, it would not be surprising if psychology, specifically, and higher education more broadly—especially in the arts and sciences—were a dispeller of myths. Other research has found that psychologists are more skeptical about memory myths even compared to other professionals (e.g., lawyers; Niedzwienska, Neckar, & Baran, 2007). Yet despite these demographic differences, Simons and Chabris (2011) found that none of the demographic subcategories obtained an average greater than three (of six) items correct.

In a study focusing on beliefs about repressed memory (discussed in greater detail in chapter 3), Patihis and colleagues (2014) also included a few items about general memory processes, such as "memory can be unreliable," "memory is constantly being reconstructed and changed every time we remember something," and "memory of everything experienced is stored permanently in brain, even if we can't access all of it." Although the last of these statements appears to contradict the other two—if memories are unreliable and constantly being changed, then they are not really stored permanently, at least not in their original form/content—large majorities of undergraduate participants agreed with all three statements (85.9 %, 90.8%, and 66.7 %, respectively). Significant numbers endorsed other memory myths as well. Consistent with the findings of Simons and Chabris (2011), those with more education, training in psychology, and higher SAT scores (used as a proxy for intelligence) were less likely to endorse erroneous beliefs.

Most of the memory myths included in memory belief surveys, such as those conducted by Simons and Chabris (2011) and Patihis et al. (2014), are plausible, albeit erroneous; that is, they are widely popularized beliefs for which some anecdotal evidence may even exist (e.g., hypnosis, repression), although empirical support is largely lacking. However, significant numbers of laypeople also ascribe to beliefs that are, simply put, ludicrous. For example, Garry, Loftus, and Brown (1994) found that 16 percent of respondents (who were university graduate students) believed that it is possible to remember things that happened in the womb, and 47 percent believed that memories of trauma can be stored in the muscles. Some people also believe—as evidenced by their own sincerely held memories—that it is possible to remember being abducted by space aliens or events from a former life (e.g., Clancy, 2005; Meyersburg et al., 2009). It should therefore not be surprising that even greater numbers hold more "conventional" memory myths, such as a belief in repression of traumatic events or the efficacy of hypnosis.

Americans are not the only ones who suffer from misconceptions about memory. Memory belief surveys conducted in South America (Alvarez & Brown, 2002), the United Kingdom (Conway, Justice, & Morrison, 2014), Poland (Niedzwienska et al., 2007), and Norway (Magnussen et al., 2006) have yielded comparable results. In the largest of these studies, Magnussen and colleagues surveyed 2,000 Norwegian adults about their beliefs about various aspects of memory, such as emotion and memory, memory and aging (i.e., memory functioning in children and the elderly), individual differences, and the possibility of improving memory. One thousand participants answered one of two sets of questions (13 items total), each presented in a multiple choice format (e.g., "When small children recount events they have experienced, do you think they remember better, as well as, or worse than adults?"). Participants also judged the quality of their own memory (e.g., "Do you think your memory is better, as good as, or worse than most people of your own age?" "How good are you at judging the reliability of your own memory?").

Participants' beliefs were in agreement with scientific research findings on some topics but not others. For example, they were fairly knowledgeable about childhood amnesia and the inefficacy of collaborative memory. However, large proportions of the sample had misconceptions about other aspects of memory, such as believing that memory can be trained like a muscle, memory has a limited capacity, and olfactory memory is as good as or superior to visual and auditory memory. The relationship between education and knowledge of memory was less consistent than found in other studies (Patihis et al., 2014; Simons & Chabris, 2011). More educated participants were less likely to endorse some memory myths (e.g., limited storage capacity), but they were more likely to endorse others (e.g., genuinely forgetting frightening events, which the authors used as a proxy for a belief in repression). To some extent, participants' knowledge about memory was interconnected; individuals who knew that memory does not function like a muscle were less likely to believe that memory has a limited capacity, and they also had more accurate beliefs about children's memory. Some other researchers likewise have found that erroneous beliefs about memory tend to cluster together (Garry et al., 1994; Niedzwienska et al., 2007), although others have not (Simons & Chabris, 2011).

A NEW SURVEY OF MEMORY BELIEFS

Previous surveys of laypeople's memory beliefs suggest that laypeople are somewhat knowledgeable about some topics but have misconceptions about others. However, most prior research has concentrated on specific areas of memory or used a relatively small number of questions to assess knowledge of general memory processes. To address these limitations, I conducted a survey of beliefs about a broad array of memory topics. The survey had two objectives: first, to assess knowledge of memory issues in a lay (college student) sample and, second, to examine the relationship among common sense beliefs across a variety of memory domains.

There were two hypotheses. Previous studies show substantial variability in how much people know about the ways memory works, with a majority demonstrating accurate knowledge about some topics but endorsing myths about other topics. Thus, hypothesis 1 was that across all memory phenomena, there would be considerable variability, with beliefs relatively accurate for some topics but relatively inaccurate for others. Some research also shows that "there are distinct groups of memory believers in the adult population" (Magnussen et al., 2006, p. 610; see also Garry et al., 1994). In other words, memory beliefs cluster together, such that individuals who are knowledgeable about some topics are more likely to be knowledgeable about other topics. Thus, hypothesis 2 was that performance across domains would be positively correlated.

Survey Method

Participants were 185 undergraduate students (72.6 % women) who participated in exchange for extra course credit. The survey consisted of 49 statements about memory processes, taken mainly from previous peer-reviewed work on lay beliefs and memory myths (Della Salla, 2007; Garry et al., 1994; Magnussen et al., 2006; Read & Desmarais, 2009). They covered six topical categories: eyewitness memory (16 items; e.g., "When an eyewitness is questioned about an event, the wording of the questions can influence the testimony"), general memory processes (9 items; e.g., "Sensations of smell are remembered better than visual and auditory impressions"), age differences (9 items; e.g., "If you live long enough, you will get Alzheimer's Disease"), biological basis of memory (6 items; e.g., "Damaged brain tissue cannot repair itself the way other body tissues can"), hypnosis and recovered memory (5 items; e.g., "When people undergo hypnosis, they are more easily influenced by leading and misleading questions"), and mnemonics (4 items; e.g., "Chunking is an effective way to store information in memory").

Participants rated their (dis)agreement, on 5-point Likert scales, with each item (1 = strongly disagree, 2 = disagree somewhat, 3 = unsure/don't know, 4 = agree somewhat, 5 = strongly agree). As mentioned in the introduction, a degree of disagreement exists with respect to the "right" answer with respect to some aspects of memory (e.g., the reality of repression and recovered memory). As with the surveys described earlier in the present chapter, correct answers for the present survey were determined by referring to expert consensus and the author's own independent reading of the literature (subsequent chapters will examine some of the nuances underlying these generalizations). The items are shown in Table 1.1, which indicates whether the correct response, based on expert consensus, is Disagree (D) or Agree (A).

Three metamemory questions, mixed in with the knowledge items, concerned self-appraisal of one's own memory ability (modified from Magnussen et al., 2006): "Your own memory has become better during the last five years," "Your own memory is better than most people of your own age," and "You are good at judging when your own memory is accurate and when it is inaccurate"). The first two items, which both deal with a judgment of how good one's memory is, were highly correlated ($r > .4$), so they were averaged to create a single "subjective memory ability" index ($M = 3.36$, $SD = .85$). The third item, which was significantly correlated with the other self-appraisal items but more weakly ($r = .3$ and $.16$, $p < .05$), deals more with subjective memory calibration (i.e., distinguishing accurate from inaccurate memories) than ability to remember. It was therefore retained as a separate item.

A subset of participants ($n = 69$) also indicated whether they had seen a number of movies dealing with memory phenomena (see Appendix).

Table 1.1   Memory Knowledge Survey Items and Percent Correct

Item	% Correct
Eyewitness Memory	
When an eyewitness is questioned about an event, the wording of the questions can influence the testimony. (A)	92.4
The instructions given to an eyewitness by the police during an identification procedure can influence the eyewitness's willingness to make an identification. (A)	85.4
The confidence an eyewitness has in his or her identification decision can be influenced by factors that are unrelated to identification accuracy, such as police instructions, feedback from the police about the identification and time spent thinking about the crime event. (A)	88.6
If a "mugshot" photo of a suspect has been previously shown to an eyewitness, there is an increased chance that the eyewitness will later choose that suspect from a lineup. (A)	85.9
Eyewitnesses' testimony about an event reflects not only what they actually saw but also often includes information they acquired after the event. (A)	83.2
An eyewitness's perception of and memory for an event may be affected by his or her attitudes and expectations. (A)	90.3

Eyewitnesses are more accurate when identifying members of their own race than members of other races (e.g., Whites identifying Whites compared to Whites identifying Blacks). (A)	60.0
The presence of a weapon held by a criminal makes it more difficult for the eyewitness later to identify the person's face accurately. (A)	69.7
An eyewitness's confidence in his or her identification is not a good indicator of the accuracy of the identification. (A)	50.8
Witnesses are more likely to misidentify someone when presented with a simultaneous lineup (all members shown at once) than when presented with a sequential lineup (members shown one at a time). (A)	42.2
Eyewitnesses sometimes mistakenly identify as a culprit someone they have seen in another situation or context. (A)	73.5
The presentation of a single person or photo instead of a selection of people or photos increases the risk an eyewitness will identify the wrong person. (A)	50.3
The more that all lineup members match a witness's description of a culprit, the more accurate an eyewitness's decision is likely to be. (A)	36.8
The more members of a lineup resemble the suspect, the more likely that the witness's decision is accurate. (A)	24.3
Very high levels of stress impair the accuracy of eyewitness testimony. (A)	85.4
The more quickly a witness identifies someone in a police lineup, the more accurate he or she is likely to be. (A)	35.1

Age Effects

Young children are more easily influenced than adults by interviewer suggestions, peer pressure and other social factors. (A)	81.1
Young children are less accurate as witnesses than are adults. (A)	40.5
Elderly witnesses are less accurate as witnesses than are younger adults. (A)	41.1
When small children recount events they have experienced, they remember worse than adults. (A)	23.8
When talking about memories from their early childhood years, people generally cannot remember events before age three. (A)	89.7
Age-related memory decline usually starts around age 65. (A)	52.4
Remembering past events gets worse with age, especially in elderly adults. (A)	71.4
Remembering things we have to do in the future (e.g., appointments) gets worse with age, especially in elderly adults. (D)	9.2
If you live long enough, you will get Alzheimer's Disease. (D)	78.9

General Memory Processes

Of the total information that a person will eventually forget about an event, the greatest amount of forgetting will occur relatively soon after the event, followed by less and less forgetting over time, eventually leveling off. (A)	65.9
The less time a person has to observe an event, the less well he or she will remember it. (A)	63.8
Sensations of smell are remembered better than visual and auditory impressions. (D)	21.1
"Flashbulb" memories—memories of an occasion when we heard an important piece of news, such as the September 11 attacks or the death of a loved one—are more accurate than memories for ordinary events. (D)	16.8

(Continue)

Table 1.1   Memory Knowledge Survey Items and Percent Correct   (Continued)

Item	% Correct
People can remember information presented to them while they are asleep. (D)	42.2
People who are better at remembering past events are also better at remembering things they have to do in the future (e.g., appointments). (D)	18.9
People can remember information that they perceive subliminally (i.e., without realizing it). (D)	9.7
Subliminal information affects the way people act (e.g., a subliminal message in advertising can influence consumer behavior). (D)	11.9
Photographic memory is a real phenomenon. (D)	11.9

Biological Basis

Alcohol intoxication impairs one's later ability to recall persons and events. (A)	95.1
Just as physical exercise makes the body stronger, it is possible to train memory like a muscle. (D)	10.3
There is a limit to the amount of information the brain is able to store. (D)	52.4
Damaged brain tissue cannot repair itself the way other body tissues can. (A)	40.0
It is possible to "implant" memories in a person's mind, for things that they did not actually experience, by brain surgery. (D)	50.3
People who receive organ transplants (e.g., heart, liver, cornea, etc.) can have memories for things that the organ donor experienced. (D)	69.2

Hypnosis/Recovered Memory

When people undergo hypnosis, they are more easily influenced by leading and misleading questions. (A)	50.3
Memories people recover from their own childhood are often false or distorted in some way. (A)	66.5
Hypnosis increases the accuracy of a person's reported memory. (D)	35.7
It is possible to tell the difference between true and false memories. (D)	45.4
Traumatic experiences can be repressed for many years and then recovered. (D)	7.6

Mnemonic Techniques

Mentally repeating something (e.g., an address or phone number) over and over is a good way to keep it in *short-term memory*. (A)	80.5
Mentally repeating something (e.g., an address or phone number) over and over is a good way to store it in *long-term memory*. (D)	35.7
Chunking (i.e., grouping items together) is an effective way to store information in memory. (A)	85.9
Imagery (i.e., forming a mental picture) is an effective way to store information in memory. (A)	95.1

Source: Brian Bornstein.
Note: Participants rated each statement on a 5-point scale, ranging from strongly disagree to strongly agree. (A) and (D) indicate whether the correct response (i.e., most in line with empirical research) is agree or disagree. $n = 185$ for most items.

Survey Results

Table 1.1 shows the percentage of participants answering each item correctly. Performance varied substantially within the content categories. Accuracy rates ranged from 24.3 to 92.4 percent for questions about eyewitness memory; 9.2 to 89.7 percent for age effects; 9.7 to 65.9 percent for general memory processes; 10.3 to 95.1 percent for biological basis; 7.6 to 66.5 percent for hypnosis/recovered memory; and 35.7 to 95.1 percent for mnemonics. Knowledge also varied across the different topical categories (see Figure 1.1). As can be seen in the figure, participants were most knowledgeable about mnemonics ($M = 74.32$ % correct, $SD = 21.24$ %) and least knowledgeable about general memory processes ($M = 29.13$ % correct, $SD = 14.03$ %).

The correlations among the various categories were mostly positive but small. Several of the correlations were statistically significant. Knowledge about age effects on memory was the most predictive category, as it was significantly correlated with knowledge about hypnosis/recovered memory ($r = .17$, $p = .02$), mnemonics ($r = .17$, $p = .02$), and eyewitness memory ($r = .17$, $p = .02$); knowledge of hypnosis/recovered memory was also correlated with knowledge of general memory processes ($r = .26$, $p < .001$) and (marginally) with knowledge of the biological basis of memory ($r = .12$, $p = .09$). Knowledge of biological factors was significantly correlated with knowledge of general processes ($r = .18$, $p = .01$).

The correlation between the two metamemory measures (subjective memory ability and subjective memory calibration) was statistically significant ($r = .28$, $p < .001$), but their correlation with performance on the various

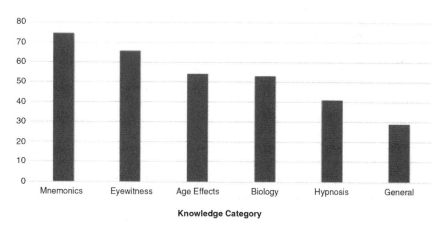

Figure 1.1 Mean Percentage Correct for the Different Memory Knowledge Categories.
Source: Brian Bornstein.

Table 1.2   Movies Viewed by More Than 10% of Participants

Movie	% Viewed	Movie	% Viewed
Finding Nemo	92.8	Rain Man	33.3
The Notebook	81.2	Vantage Point	33.3
50 First Dates	76.8	Overboard	24.6
Inception	69.6	Paycheck	20.3
Shutter Island	65.2	The Forgotten	17.4
Bourne Identity	62.3	The Majestic	15.9
Bourne Ultimatum	58.0	Eternal Sunshine of the Spotless Mind	14.5
Bourne Supremacy	55.1	The Machinist	10.1
X-Men Origins: Wolverine	53.6		

Source: Brian Bornstein.

knowledge measures was negligible. Subjective ability was correlated only with knowledge of age effects on memory ($r = .17$, $p = .02$), and subjective calibration was not significantly correlated with knowledge of any of the topics.

Although some of the movies had been seen by few, if any, of the participants, a number of others had been viewed by a substantial proportion of the sample. Seventeen films had been viewed by at least 10 percent of the sample (see Table 1.2). More than half of the participants had seen nine of the films; over 75 percent had seen *50 First Dates*, *The Notebook*, and *Finding Nemo*. These and most of the other films in Table 1.2 did very well at the box office, suggesting that the present sample is representative of the population as a whole, and that large numbers of people watched these movies that deal with memory.

Summary

Overall, participants knew more about some topics than others (see Figure 1.1). They were most knowledgeable about mnemonics and eyewitness memory (means of 74 % and 65 % correct, respectively). It is hard to say what chance performance would be on a measure where participants rated their (dis) agreement with various statements and could respond "don't know," but it is nonetheless noteworthy that on two topics, general memory processes and hypnosis/recovered memory, performance was below 50 percent (means of 29 % and 41 %, respectively). This finding is consistent with other research showing that knowledge of how memory works is not much better than chance (Simons & Chabris, 2011).

Although some prior research has not found evidence of interrelations among laypeople's memory beliefs (Simons & Chabris, 2011), other studies have found that holding an erroneous belief about one aspect of memory is predictive of holding other erroneous beliefs, at least about closely related topics (Garry et al., 1994; Magnussen et al., 2006; Niedzwienska et al., 2007). There is stability in other kinds of metamemory judgments as well. For example, individuals who are overconfident in their memories in one domain of knowledge tend to be overconfident in other domains (Bornstein & Zickafoose, 1999). The present study examined relationships not among closely related memory topics or for a particular type of judgment (e.g., confidence), but for beliefs across broad categories of memory phenomena. When measured in this broader fashion, participants' knowledge of specific memory topics was somewhat, albeit weakly, predictive of how much they knew about other memory topics. There were significant positive correlations across knowledge for some of the different content categories, but all of the correlations were modest in size (none exceeded an r of .3). Thus, there does not appear to be a strong tendency to endorse memory myths across the board, for diverse types of memory phenomena; rather, memory beliefs might cluster into relatively narrow thematic categories.

Where do these mistaken beliefs about memory come from? Large numbers of participants had seen movies dealing with memory phenomena. As will be discussed in the remaining chapters, many of these movies—as well as television shows and novels that treat similar topics—portray memory in a superficial or misleading manner. Although the present study cannot establish a clear causal connection between inaccurate media portrayals and memory misconceptions, the media's role in contributing to popular misconceptions cannot be discounted.

Participants' self-appraisal of their memory abilities was largely uncorrelated with their actual knowledge. Neither participants' evaluation of their own memory ability nor their capacity to judge whether or not their memory was accurate was a very good predictor of how much they actually knew about diverse memory topics. This finding is consistent with theories of metacognition indicating that metacognitive judgments in general tend not to be terribly accurate (e.g., Beran et al., 2012; Metcalfe & Shimamura, 1994; Nelson & Narens, 1990).

CONCLUSIONS

The present study, along with prior research on laypeople's beliefs about memory, offers four general conclusions. First, laypeople are not very knowledgeable, overall, about how memory works. They subscribe to a number of false beliefs, some of which are completely devoid of any evidentiary basis (e.g., prenatal memories). Second, laypeople know more about some memory phenomena than others. On some topics (e.g., basic mnemonic techniques, understanding that memory can be unreliable), their beliefs are fairly accurate. However, false beliefs about other phenomena, such as hypnosis, recovered memory, and repression, are particularly pervasive (as discussed in depth in chapter 3). Third, beliefs about certain memory topics tend to cluster together (e.g., beliefs about repression and hypnosis), but the relationships across broad categories of memory phenomena are relatively weak. And fourth, there is little correlation between people's assessment of their own memory and their knowledge about memory's workings in general. On the whole, laypeople's metamemory awareness is limited, which has potentially adverse implications for their functioning in a variety of contexts.

The results of memory surveys have a number of practical implications. As discussed in the introduction, memory beliefs are relevant to behavior in a large variety of real-world contexts (e.g., everyday interactions, educational settings, medical treatment, courtrooms, etc.). Mistaken beliefs about memory can have significant and potentially adverse consequences not only for one's own behavior (e.g., studying material for a class, remembering important information at work, obtaining psychotherapy), but also for others (e.g., dealing with one's children, being cognizant of elderly relatives' declining cognitive abilities, evaluating eyewitness testimony as a juror). Thus, erroneous beliefs about memory are hardly, to borrow a term from the courts, "harmless errors."

Can these errors be rectified? The concluding chapter will explore possible strategies for reducing the prevalence of mistaken beliefs about how memory works (or, framed more positively, for increasing laypeople's knowledge about memory). It is noteworthy that individuals who have higher levels of education in general, as well as those with greater exposure to training or literature in psychology, are less susceptible to memory myths (Niedzwienska et al., 2007; Patihis et al., 2014; Simons & Chabris, 2011). A major strategy for improving lay knowledge of memory, therefore, is education. But before addressing remedial strategies, the remaining chapters cover a number of specific memory myths in greater depth.

NOTES

1. As the items from the Simons and Chabris (2011) study make clear, the statements are generalizations. It is easier to determine the "correct" answer for some of the items on these surveys than others. In describing the surveys, as well as the one

I conducted for purposes of this chapter (see below), I rely on the researchers' judgments and my own assessment of the empirical data. The particularities of specific memory phenomena are examined in the following chapters.

Chapter 2

Memory Accuracy and Permanence

Myth: Memory Is Like a Video Recorder—If Not Perfectly Accurate, at Least Pretty Close to It

Related Myth: Emotional Memories Are Especially Likely to be Accurate

One of the more common memory myths is a belief in memory's overall high degree of accuracy (Clifasefi, Garry, & Loftus, 2007; Simons & Chabris, 2011). The nature of the storage metaphor changes with the prevailing technology, such that memory has variously been viewed as a wax tablet, a tape recorder, a video recorder, and now a computer hard drive. All of these metaphors imply a permanent capacity both to store vast amounts of information and to retrieve that information, on demand, in pristine form.

A prime example of the accuracy/permanence myth is *Inside Out* (2015)—the latest animated movie to deal with memory. Although this highly entertaining film deserves credit for accurately portraying memory in some respects, such as memory's large emotional content and the possibility that some unused memories disintegrate and decay, other aspects of the movie perpetuate the myths. The main character, Riley, stores each of her memories in a hermetically sealed glass bubble; each time she retrieves a memory, it plays exactly the same way on the screen of her mind. Moreover, she takes no active role in memory storage or retrieval; it is all done by headquarters with no effort on her part—the memories are stored effortlessly and reappear as if by magic. Now, it might seem unfair and even a bit mean-spirited to criticize the scientific inaccuracies of a film geared toward children (albeit with much of its humor targeting adult viewers). However, assuming that children are more scientifically naïve than adults, then they are more likely to accept misleading depictions unquestioningly.

To be sure, the capabilities of humans' (not to mention other animals') memories are striking. Yet if approximately 130 years of experimental research on memory have taught us anything, it is that memory is notoriously fallible. Not only do we fail to remember some things and misremember other things: we but also "remember" full-blown events that did not, in fact, occur (e.g., Brainerd & Reyna, 2005; Laney & Loftus, 2010; see chapter 3). Even individuals with unusually good memories (Patihis et al., 2013) and those with supposed photographic memories (a disputed phenomenon, as described in chapter 10) make errors and have limits to what they can remember. These errors occur for a number of reasons, such as individuals' expectations, schema and suggestibility effects, and self-presentation concerns (e.g., Bartlett, 1932; Neisser & Hyman, 2000). All of these processes show that rather than being simply a matter of hitting the "replay" button, memory retrieval is very much an active and reconstructive process.

BELIEFS ABOUT MEMORY ACCURACY

Depending on the survey, one-quarter of people or more believe that memory retains a perfect record of everything we experience (Lilienfeld et al., 2010), except in unusual, pathological cases like amnesia. Simons and Chabris (2011) found that 63 percent of a diverse adult sample agreed that "human memory works like a video camera, accurately recording the events we see and hear so that we can review and inspect them later," and 47.6 percent agreed that "once you have experienced an event and formed a memory of it, that memory does not change." Niedzwienska and colleagues (2007) found that all groups of participants they studied—psychologists, nonpsychologists, lawyers, and students—endorsed myths related to permanent storage more than those dealing with other aspects of memory (see also Loftus & Loftus, 1980).

The belief in memory's accuracy is especially strong for highly salient, emotionally charged memories. As Brown and Kulik (1977, p. 73) observed, for example, "'Hardly a man is now alive' who cannot recall the circumstances in which he first heard that John Kennedy had been shot in Dallas." One of the defining characteristics of such "flashbulb" memories is an unusually high degree of confidence that one's memory of the event is accurate. This shows up time and again in the various studies of flashbulb memories (reviewed below), as well as in memory belief surveys. For example, 70 percent of participants in the survey conducted by Magnussen and colleagues (2006) believed that memory for "dramatic events" is better than memory for everyday events. Similarly, only 17 percent of participants in the survey described in chapter 1 knew that flashbulb memories are *not* more accurate than memories for ordinary events.

However, research on flashbulb memories shows that compared to memories for everyday events, although individuals are more likely to remember that the precipitating event itself occurred, the properties of the memories, including their accuracy, are actually quite similar (e.g., Hirst et al., 2009; Weaver, 1993). Moreover, there is no correlation between the degree of emotional involvement in flashbulb memories and memory accuracy (Neisser & Harsch, 1992; Neisser et al., 1996). Such memories are also quite variable across individuals and events, with some people more accurate than others, and some events more likely than others to elicit a flashbulb memory (Brown & Kulik, 1977; Neisser et al., 1996). This chapter will summarize the findings on the surprising *in*accuracy, in many cases, of these flashbulb memories.

SOME GENERAL OBSERVATIONS ON MEMORY ACCURACY

Remembering, Forgetting, and Adaptiveness

A belief in the unerring accuracy of memory not only flies in the face of everyday experience but it also defies logic. Having a memory that functions like a video recorder would be advantageous in some circumstances (e.g., one would never forget a name, would ace every test, etc.), but the advantages would be outweighed by its gross inefficiency. Last night for dinner I had a salad with garbanzo beans, feta cheese, tomatoes, Kalamata olives, and anchovies. It was quite tasty, but odds are I will forget all about it—or at least the exact date on which I ate it (March 31, 2015)—within a couple of weeks, and almost certainly 6 months from now.[1] And that is as it should be. Although it is possible to imagine a situation where I would need to remember what I ate for dinner on a given date (suppose, for example, that there is a salmonella outbreak, I am afflicted, and the CDC is trying to trace the contaminated foods), it is extremely unlikely. Humans' cognitive resources are vast, but they are not—despite what the makers of the films *Lucy* and *Limitless* (also a short-lived television series), in which the title characters exponentially expand their mental powers, would have us believe—limitless. Investing a lot of effort into remembering what I eat for every meal would unavoidably draw cognitive resources away from more important tasks.

In other words, it would be inefficient and uneconomical to remember much of the trivial information that we process on a daily basis, and it would impede the retrieval of more important and useful information. Robert Bjork, one of the leading scholars of memory, concludes that "because we remember

so much, we do not *want* everything in our memories to be accessible"
(Bjork, 2011, p. 2; italics in original). Even if our brains could do it—and
they can undoubtedly do a great deal more than we usually ask of them, so it
is possible, but not a certainty—there is little reason for them to. Put another
way, much forgetting is adaptive, and it can even facilitate subsequent learning (Bjork, 2011). The catch is that at the time we do or do not store information in memory, we cannot anticipate with perfect accuracy whether we will
need the information later. Hence we sometimes wish we had retained some
of what we forget, and on occasion the forgetting can have negative consequences (e.g., failing a test, petting a dog that bit you last year, etc.). But most
of what we forget, we never miss.

This discussion of forgetting has focused on inaccuracy in terms of
failures to remember. Inaccuracy can also involve misremembering, that
is, remembering information erroneously. Another way of putting it is that
inaccuracy can involve errors of omission (failures to remember) or errors
of commission (misremembering). These sorts of commission errors can
range in degree from very slight confusion about details (e.g., remembering that the salad had kidney beans instead of garbanzo beans) to remembering entire events that did not actually occur (e.g., a false memory of
getting sick on garbanzo bean salad; cf. Laney & Loftus, 2010). It is a
little harder to make the case why mixing up details or falsely remembering an event, especially a traumatic event, would be adaptive. Nonetheless,
memory errors often are adaptive, in the sense of putting the rememberer
in a favorable light. For example, people have a tendency to remember
their grades in school as being better than they actually were (Bahrick,
Hall, & Berger, 1996).

Memory errors can also be adaptive in the evolutionary sense of increasing one's reproductive fitness, as in memory for pain. People generally rate
painful experiences as less painful in retrospect (i.e., when remembering
them) than they do at the time of the event. Although it might be adaptive
to remember some painful experiences accurately—if you remember how
much it hurt to place your hand on a hot stovetop burner, you will be less
likely to do it again in the future—there are other painful experiences that it
might be desirable to repeat. Childbirth and dental work are just two common examples. For example, women often remember childbirth as being less
painful than they reported it to be at the time (Niven & Murphy-Black, 2000),
which makes them more likely to go through it again. As the old saying goes,
if women accurately remembered how painful childbirth was, no one would
ever have more than just one child. With fewer children, they would be less
likely to pass on their genes to future generations.[2] Regardless of the reasons
for memory failures or memory errors, they conclusively show that memory
is *not* simply a video recorder.

Memory and Technology: Video Recorders and Beyond

An advantage of real, as opposed to metaphorical, video recorders is that they preserve a true record of what occurred. The study of memory, especially in real-world contexts, is challenging in many respects. First and foremost, outside the laboratory, it is often difficult, if not impossible, to document what actually occurred. Without such documentation, accuracy can be guessed at but not conclusively determined. Some studies work around this problem by having participants record their memories in diary form (e.g., Linton, 2000; Wagenaar, 1986) or immediately after some significant event (e.g., Neisser & Harsch, 1992). Then when they attempt to retrieve the information later on, their recollection can be compared to the original record.

As technologies improve for recording and storing information, this verification problem becomes less of an issue. If a store's security camera records a robbery, then the eyewitness's memory can be compared to what is on tape (of course, if there is a tape, then the eyewitness is to some extent superfluous). In Dave Eggers' novel *The Circle* (2013), the high-tech corporation known as The Circle develops miniature cameras that can be placed virtually anywhere to record and transmit information. Although *The Circle* is set in the (not-too-distant) future, similar technology already exists. Law enforcement agencies and private businesses (e.g., banks, retail stores) routinely use it to engage in video surveillance.

In *The Circle*, individuals, especially politicians, are also encouraged to "go clear," which involves wearing a camera that records and broadcasts everything they experience. The characters in the novel do not use the technology for purposes of memory testing, but they could, since all the information is in the archive. Again, the fictional technology is not as far-fetched as it might seem. Police increasingly use bodycams and dashcams to create a permanent repository of events rather than having to rely on participants' memories. And "lifelogging" (taken to extreme levels in *The Circle*), as with a Fitbit or similar tracker, primarily records personal activity related to health and fitness, but one can also use a wearable camera that literally creates a video log of one's life. Several companies make these tiny cameras, some of which cost less than $100 and take either still photos (multiple photos per minute) or digital video. With enough storage capacity, it is now theoretically possible to record everything that you experience. If you cannot remember it later, all you need to do is search your video archive. No more disputes about who said what, to whom, and when. Memory research may never be the same; nor may popular conceptualizations of memory itself (Garde-Hansen et al., 2009).

Most importantly, such technologies circumvent the common observation—well-known to both researchers and rememberers themselves—that our memory contains a great deal more information than we are able to retrieve at any given moment. In other words, information can be available—successfully stored in memory and potentially retrievable—but not necessarily accessible, or currently retrievable (Bjork, 2011; Neath & Surprenant, 2015; Schwartz, 2014). For example, in a recent conversation with my wife and daughter I was unable to remember one of the singular, gender-neutral, third-person pronouns that are currently being advocated by the transgender community. My daughter said "ze" (also spelled "zie"). I immediately recognized it as correct, showing that the information was indeed available, even though it had not been accessible a moment earlier.

A seemingly simple, but actually quite complex, question is: Did I accurately remember the information? The answer depends on whether we define remembering in terms of remembering on a given occasion or remembering *ever*; remembering in any manner or in a specific way (e.g., recall); the degree of correspondence between the memory produced if/when it is remembered and the information when it was encoded; and other even more subtle distinctions. There are numerous explanations of why information is often available but not accessible (e.g., interference, cue discrimination; see Neath & Surprenant, 2015; Schwartz, 2014), a detailed examination of which is beyond the scope of the present work. The main points are that (1) we cannot simply replay memories at will, and (2) when we do retrieve information in memory, it can contain errors ranging from omissions to minor discrepancies to gross misrepresentations of what actually occurred.

Also calling the videotape metaphor into question is the observation that if multiple cameramen film the same event—at least from the same vantage point—then the footage will be identical. Yet there are many instances where multiple observers who experience the same event have very different memories of it. These discrepancies include instances where one observer correctly remembers a detail that another one does not, as well as where one observer introduces an error that another one does not (Rush & Clark, 2014). If multiple observers remember the same event differently, then it goes without saying that at least some (and possibly all) of them must be remembering it wrong. In some sense, it might not really be the same event for all of them, as they might be encoding it differently depending on their degree of attention, expectations, prior experiences, current mood, and so on. Nonetheless, many features of the event are invariant, and disagreement about those features necessarily means either that someone's video recorder malfunctioned in the recording process, or that the recording degraded or was altered over time.

As Clifasefi and colleagues (2007) point out, the video camera model of memory has three important corollaries: first, we do not forget information so much as temporarily misplace it; second, the information is potentially recoverable, especially by using the right techniques; and third, once we find the missing information, it can simply be replayed in its original form. None of these corollary beliefs has a firm foundation. It is certainly true that we are often unable to retrieve information on one occasion, only to find it on another occasion; put another way, the information is "forgotten," only to be found subsequently. There is a temporary lapse in our ability to access discrete bits of information in memory (Capaldi & Neath, 1995). However, there is ample evidence that some of the information stored in memory simply decays over time, never to be regained, or is irrevocably altered, which amounts to much the same thing (Neath & Surprenant, 2015). More to the point, and relevant to Clifasefi et al.'s second and third corollaries, remembered information often bears only a loose resemblance to the originally encoded event and in some cases is a complete fabrication. Research on memory distortions and false memory (covered in more detail in chapter 3) provides particularly compelling evidence that memories are not simply stored in pristine form. However, it is not necessary to refer to false memories for evidence that memory is often inaccurate; we misremember information all the time, and for all different kinds of information.

These kinds of information are illustrated in the examples discussed above. Remembering what I ate for dinner last night is an *episodic* memory, as it pertains to a discrete event in my past situated in a particular time and place. Remembering the word "ze," in contrast, is impersonal, decontextualized knowledge. Such factual knowledge is commonly referred to as *semantic* memory. Finally, I have knowledge of how to perform certain skills, such as serving a tennis ball. Well-learned motor skills demonstrate *procedural* memory. These distinctions are useful, but they are not entirely clear-cut. I might (or more likely, might not) remember the occasion when I first learned "ze" or the conversation in which my daughter reminded me of it, showing the overlap between episodic and semantic memories. Similarly, I might remember the specific experience of learning to play tennis (the episodic component), and when I first learned how to serve, I thought about the steps, such as where to place my feet and racket and how high to toss the ball, in a very explicit manner (the semantic component). Despite the overlap, the distinctions provide a handy way of talking about different kinds of memory, and they are supported by evidence that brain damage affects them in different fashions (e.g., Rosenbaum et al., 2005; see chapters 5–7). More relevant to the present discussion, retrieval of any of them is imperfect—we misremember personal events, facts, and procedures. In other words, the video recorder metaphor is a myth regardless of what kind of memory we are talking about.

EMOTIONAL MEMORIES

A positive feature of *Inside Out* is its emphasis on the inextricable link between memory and emotion. In the film, each of Riley's discrete memories is associated with one of five emotions, which are personified as homunculi in her brain: Joy, Fear, Anger, Disgust, and Sadness (the bubbles are color coded to indicate the prevailing emotion). A memory's emotion can change, as when Sadness touches one of Joy's memories, but the emotions do not blend. Although this portrayal oversimplifies the relationship between memory and emotion, it accurately captures the emotional element that many memories have.

Like laypeople, researchers use a variety of words to refer to affective phenomena: emotions, moods, feelings, sentiments, temperaments, and so on. There is no universal agreement on how one differs from another, but common distinctions involve their respective antecedents and consequences, duration, relation to an identifiable external object or event, physiological or facial response, subjective experience, and function (e.g., Davidson, 1994; Frijda, 1994). For example, compared to specific emotions like anger, fear, or happiness, positive or negative moods last longer, are less likely to be reactions to discrete events, and bias cognition rather than action (Davidson, 1994). Because memory is largely (though not exclusively) a cognitive phenomenon, much of the research on memory and affect therefore focuses on the individual's mood—that is, a relatively long-lasting subjective state that varies in valence along a continuum ranging from extremely negative to extremely positive. Different moods trigger different information processing strategies (e.g., Forgas, 1995, 2010).

Other research on memory and emotion focuses on memory for stimuli that vary in their emotional content, such as remembering a traumatic experience or how one learned a piece of upsetting news. Thus, one potentially useful distinction is between the objects/events/stimuli that arouse some sort of emotional response in an observer (i.e., emotional stimuli) and affective response in terms of the subject/perceiver (i.e., mood). The distinction is not an entirely "clean" one, of course, because emotional stimuli often—and to some extent by definition—produce an affective response. Nonetheless, it is a useful framework for examining some of the ways in which memory and emotion interact.

MEMORY FOR EMOTIONAL STIMULI

Emotional stimuli are, simply, those that elicit an emotional response in someone who processes the information. Researchers have developed several methods for studying memory for emotional stimuli. The most common are memory for positive (or neutral) versus negative stimuli (i.e., stimulus valence); memory for an emotionally intense experience, especially the circumstances surrounding either the experience itself or how one learned about it (i.e., flashbulb memory); and memory for traumatic events. Memory for trauma is covered in the next chapter; the following two sections review research on memory for positive versus negative stimuli and flashbulb memory.

Stimulus Valence and Memory

Both semantic and episodic information can vary in their emotional valence, ranging from extremely negative to extremely positive. Certain words have emotional connotations (e.g., *death, orgasm*), as do many events (e.g., attending a funeral, engaging in consensual sex). Memory for emotional semantic information has most often been studied by testing participants' memory for words that vary in their emotional valence. For example, Kensinger (2008) presented participants with word lists containing neutral (e.g., *figment*), negative (e.g., *lonely, slaughter*), and positive words (e.g., *lake, casino*). Although there were slight differences depending on participants' age and whether the words were emotionally arousing (e.g., *lonely* vs. *slaughter*), in general, participants remembered emotional words, whether positive or negative, better than neutral words. Memory accuracy for emotionally arousing semantic stimuli is preserved or even enhanced as the delay between encoding and retrieval increases (Kleinsmith & Kaplan, 1963).

More research has been conducted on emotionally salient episodic information than semantic information, perhaps because personally experienced events are, on average, more capable of eliciting a strong emotional response than impersonal information like a list of words. Much of the research on memory for negative emotional events focuses on eyewitnesses' memory for crimes. Crimes, especially violent ones, presumably elicit negative emotions like fear (and possibly anger), are stressful and potentially even traumatic experiences, and are accompanied by a physiological arousal response. Importantly, responses vary widely depending on characteristics of the event and the individual, and the terms (e.g., emotion, stress, trauma, and arousal) have subtle shades of meaning that are used in different ways by different researchers (Bornstein & Robicheaux, 2009; Reisberg & Heuer, 2007). For present purposes, the concern is simply with the effects on memory of witnessing—as either a bystander or victim—an event that would elicit a negative emotional response in most people.

The literature on eyewitness memory and negative emotions is sizeable and not entirely uniform (e.g., Christianson, 1992; Deffenbacher, 2008; Deffenbacher, Bornstein, Penrod & McGorty, 2004; Reisberg & Heuer,

2007). Important considerations include: Is the witness a bystander or a victim? What is eliciting the emotional response—is it the thing to be remembered or some extraneous stimulus? Are we interested in the witness's recall of the event or ability to recognize the perpetrator? In looking at event recall, is the focus on central details like remembering that the event itself occurred or the type of weapon, or more peripheral details like the color of the perpetrator's shirt? The pattern of results varies depending on these distinctions, often substantially. For example, some research suggests that emotion enhances memory for central details of an event (e.g., Bornstein, Liebel, & Scarberry, 1998; Reisberg & Heuer, 2007). Eyewitnesses very rarely forget that they did, indeed, witness a crime, and they are more likely to remember the event than less emotionally laden events that took place at roughly the same time. This observation is strong evidence, in and of itself, against the argument that trauma victims often repress memory of the traumatic event (see chapter 3). Thus, the negative emotion associated with witnessing a crime can be beneficial to memory in some respects.

However, this benefit is countered, and arguably exceeded, by the detrimental effects of stress on eyewitness memory. Here it is necessary to consider what sorts of information will be most forensically useful. The highly variable circumstances of witnesses and crimes mean that the answer to this question could be almost anything, depending on the case. But for most crimes, the fact that the event occurred is not in dispute. Similarly, many of the central details (e.g., where and when it happened) can often be reasonably well determined. Rather, the information that is often most useful to the investigation and prosecution of the case are things like who did it (i.e., the eyewitness identification) and many of the smaller details (e.g., what was the perpetrator wearing, what did he say, what happened immediately after the crime, etc.). Experimental studies of the topic show that stress has negative effects on both eyewitness identification, especially when the perpetrator is in the lineup (i.e., a target-present as opposed to a target-absent lineup), and recall of details associated with the crime (Deffenbacher et al., 2004). For example, a meta-analysis conducted by Deffenbacher and colleagues found that overall, participants in high-stress conditions made correct identifications 42 percent of the time, compared to 54 percent in low-stress conditions. For target-present lineups, specifically, the comparable figures were 39 percent versus 59 percent. Much of the difference was in the form of false alarms: Heightened stress produced nearly twice as many false alarms in target-present lineups (34 % vs. 19 %). Although these false alarms are "harmless" in the sense that they mean someone known to be innocent (i.e., a "foil" rather than the target) was identified instead of the true perpetrator, they necessarily mean that the guilty party is less likely to be identified and hence more likely to go free—they are therefore not so harmless after all.

Many of these studies manipulate arousal by showing participants videos or slides that vary in their violent or graphic content, such as a film containing either a murder scene or a nonviolent replacement segment (e.g., Bornstein et al., 1998). Thus, they are open to criticism on the grounds that they are not really all that arousing, due to ethical constraints on conducting human subjects research—that is, they may be moderately upsetting or disturbing, but not as much as witnessing a real crime would be. In addition, participants are typically viewing stimuli that might be emotional in nature but that do not threaten them personally (Bornstein & Robicheaux, 2009). In other words, no matter how graphic or emotionally involving the material might be (and in many studies it is not all that graphic or involving), at some level the viewer knows he or she is in a safe research laboratory—similar to a moviegoer in a cinema—and is not in danger like someone would be who is witnessing a real crime. The Deffenbacher et al. (2004) meta-analysis addressed this concern by comparing studies that manipulated stress in the context of a staged crime to those that manipulated stress by some other means. The negative effect of stress on eyewitness identification was actually greater for the staged crime studies (although it was statistically significant for both).

Several field studies have circumvented this problem by investigating the memory of eyewitnesses to genuine events that are highly arousing. Because of their naturalistic context, not all of these studies included a (low-arousal) control group; nonetheless, they have generally found either negative effects of arousal or no heightened accuracy due to the events' emotional nature. The stressful real-life situations that have been studied include, among others, a haunted house (Valentine & Mesout, 2009), a POW interrogation (Morgan et al., 2004), and a concentration camp (Wagenaar & Groeneweg, 1990). For example, Valentine and Mesout studied visitors to the London Dungeon's "horror labyrinth." Among the frightening elements of the exhibit was a scarily made-up actor who stepped out suddenly in front of participants. About 45 minutes later, they rated how anxious they felt while they were in the labyrinth, completed a recall test of their memory for the "scary person's" appearance, and viewed a nine-person photographic lineup that contained the scary person. Participants who reported feeling more anxious during the experience recalled fewer correct details and more incorrect descriptors, and they were also less likely to make a correct identification in the lineup. Seventy-five percent of participants who scored below the median on state anxiety (i.e., their rating of how anxious they felt in the labyrinth) correctly identified the culprit, compared to only 18 percent of participants who scored above the median. Thus, the effects of emotional arousal on eyewitness memory are comparable for both laboratory research (Deffenbacher et al., 2004) and naturalistic studies. Although arousal can enhance memory for some central aspects of the event—such as remembering that one experienced the event at all—it generally impairs memory for details of the event and recognition of the perpetrator.

Flashbulb Memories

Large majorities of people believe that their memories of emotional events are more accurate than their memories of less emotional or everyday events (Conway et al., 2014; Magnussen et al., 2006). In large part, this is because emotional memories are often quite vivid and detailed, and most people also believe that the more detailed a memory is, the more accurate it is (Conway et al., 2014). Emotion, detail, and confidence are among the hallmark characteristics of a flashbulb memory, which can be defined as "a subjectively compelling recollection of an occasion when we heard an important piece of news" (Neisser, 2000a, p. 68). In addition to their emotional content, detail, and vividness, flashbulb memories are characterized by frequent covert and overt rehearsal (i.e., people both think and talk about them a lot) and a high degree of confidence in their accuracy. They can be for a public (e.g., a political leader's assassination) or personal event (e.g., a marriage proposal). Their emotional impact can be positive or negative, although they are more often negative, especially in the case of public events (perhaps because so few positive public events are deemed newsworthy). The events are usually, but not always, surprising or unexpected (i.e., one can have a flashbulb memory for an expected event like the birth of a child, or the death of a public figure or family member after a lengthy illness). Finally, they typically involve elements not only of memory for the event itself but also for the event's reception, or personal context—that is, one's circumstances on experiencing or learning about the event, such as what one was doing at the time, who the informant was, and how one felt on hearing the news (e.g., "Where were you when you heard about the terrorist attacks on September 11, 2001?").

Flashbulb memories have been studied for more than 100 years. For example, Colegrove (1899) documented Americans' flashbulb memories for learning of Abraham Lincoln's assassination. However, serious scholarly research on the topic dates to Brown and Kulik's (1977) study of flashbulb memory for a variety of events that took place in the 1960s and 1970s, such as the assassinations of John F. Kennedy, Robert Kennedy, Malcolm X, Martin Luther King, Jr., and Medgar Evers; failed assassination attempts on George Wallace and Gerald Ford; and the death of the Spanish dictator Francisco Franco. Brown and Kulik found that the prevalence of flashbulb memories for these events varied, but overall they were quite common; nearly 100 percent of participants remembered very clearly, and with great confidence, how they learned of the JFK assassination. Flashbulb memories were more common for events that participants rated as highly consequential and that they spent more time rehearsing, and there was some evidence of racial differences, with Black participants more likely than White participants to have flashbulb memories for events involving civil rights leaders.

Since Brown and Kulik's (1977) seminal study, flashbulb memories have been studied for myriad well-publicized events: space shuttle explosions (Bohannon, 1988; Coluccia, Bianco & Brandimonte, 2006; Neisser & Harsch, 1992), natural disasters and other hazard events (Er, 2003; Greenberg, Dyen & Elliott, 2013; Neisser et al., 1996), terrorist attacks like those of 9/11/2001 (Hirst et al., 2009; Talarico & Rubin, 2003; 2007; Tekcan, Ece, Gülgöz & Er, 2003), trial verdicts (Schmolck, Buffalo & Squire, 2000), deaths of public figures (Curci & Luminet, 2009; Hornstein, Brown & Mulligan, 2003; Lanciano & Curci, 2012), sporting events (Kensinger & Schacter, 2006), and the outbreak of war (Weaver, 1993). Although personal events have been studied as well, the literature focuses on large-scale, public events, as they permit the study of many individuals' memory for the same event (though the ways in which they learned of the events necessarily vary).

There are many unresolved questions associated with flashbulb memory, most of which have to do with whether, and in what way, they are special—that is, different from more mundane memories. Are they more accurate, longer lasting, and less subject to error or distortion than memories for ordinary events? Which characteristics of the event or rememberer make them more or less accurate? Are they formed by a different underlying cognitive and/or neurophysiological mechanism? The greatest challenge in answering these questions is that most of the time, people's flashbulb memories—just like their other memories—are unverifiable. I can confidently claim that I learned about the 9/11 attacks on the radio while driving to work, but there is absolutely no way to prove or disprove it.

A number of studies have addressed this limitation by having participants record their memories very shortly after a noteworthy, flashbulb memory-inducing event, when their memories were fresh and presumably highly accurate, and then comparing those memories to their recall much later (often years). These studies yield somewhat surprising conclusions (for review, see Conway, 1995; Luminet & Curci, 2009; Schwartz, 2014): First, despite the high confidence with which participants hold flashbulb memories, they are subject to a substantial number of errors and distortions (e.g., Lanciano & Curci, 2012; Neisser & Harsch, 1992; Phelps, 2012; Schmolck et al., 2000; Talarico & Rubin, 2007). Second, neither participants' degree of confidence nor the emotional intensity of the memory is a good predictor of accuracy (e.g., Neisser & Harsch, 1992; Neisser et al., 1996). And third, accuracy and the rate of decay are roughly the same for flashbulb and ordinary episodic memories (e.g., Talarico & Rubin, 2007; Weaver, 1993). These findings lead to the conclusion that "despite our beliefs that our flashbulb memories are potent and strong, evidence suggests that they are not more accurate than normal memories" (Schwartz, 2014, p. 207). Thus, flashbulb memories differ little from other memories on objective metrics like accuracy and consistency over time; rather, they differ fundamentally in their subjective characteristics: confidence, vividness, and emotion, all of which are maintained over time at high levels (Phelps, 2012).

Although the degree of neither confidence nor emotion strongly predicts flashbulb memory accuracy, some characteristics of the event, especially in relation to the person remembering the event, do appear to influence performance. Specifically, flashbulb memories are more accurate for individuals who experience an event directly than for those who merely learn about it secondhand (Neisser et al., 1996). Consistent with this idea, flashbulb memories are more accurate for individuals who perceive a given event as more meaningful or personally relevant (Conway et al., 1994; Lanciano & Curci, 2012), especially when the event is interpreted negatively (Kensinger & Schacter, 2006). For example, Conway and colleagues found that British participants were more likely than American and Danish participants to have a flashbulb memory of Prime Minister Margaret Thatcher's resignation, and their memories were also more accurate. Some studies also show that memory for the event reception—that is, remembering what one was doing at the time the event occurred or one learned about it—is better than memory for the event itself (e.g., Er, 2003; Tekcan et al., 2003).

Attempts to explain the mechanism by which we form flashbulb memories generally posit either that there is a special mechanism for encoding flashbulb-worthy events in memory, or that they are encoded in basically the same manner as any other episodic memory (Luminet & Curci, 2009; Schwartz, 2014). The former approach dates back to Brown and Kulik (1977), who proposed that a unique neurophysiological mechanism—which they referred to as the "Now Print!" hypothesis—was invoked for flashbulb memories. A key element of this hypothesis is that the memories should be unusually accurate, which, as discussed above, is not borne out by the research.

Although flashbulb memories are unique in a subjective sense—that is, they *feel* different, especially in terms of their vividness, emotional content, and amount of detail—little evidence exists that they are objectively unique, either cognitively or neurologically. Their subjective characteristics contribute to the high degree of confidence with which they are held (Phelps, 2012; Talarico & Rubin, 2003; 2007); yet as with other kinds of memory (e.g., eyewitness memory; see chapter 8), confidence is a poor predictor of flashbulb memory accuracy. It would be overstating the case to aver that flashbulb memories are any *less* accurate than ordinary episodic memories, but it is clear that their emotional content does not enhance their accuracy, and that they are much less accurate than is popularly believed.

In looking at the various events that are capable of producing flashbulb memories, it is clear that some events are more likely to produce them than others. A consideration of these events as a class suggests that the bar for flashbulb memories is possibly being raised. More participants had a flashbulb memory for the Kennedy assassination (99 %; Brown & Kulik, 1977) than for the Lincoln assassination (71 %; Colegrove, 1899). Flashbulb memories were more common for the 1986 Challenger space shuttle explosion than for the very similar Columbia explosion in 2003 (Coluccia et al., 2006; Neisser & Harsch, 1992). Years of informally polling students in my classes indicate that far more of them had flashbulb memories of the 1989 Bay Bridge collapse in San Francisco (Neisser et al., 1996) than the 2007 Mississippi River Bridge collapse in Minneapolis; a similar disparity exists for flashbulb memories of hearing about the 1999 Columbine school shooting compared to any subsequent mass school shooting, of which there have been lamentably many. To be sure, these superficially similar events differ in their particularities, as well as in the extent of news coverage they garner, and studies of the phenomena vary in terms of the participant sample, the delay between the event and testing, and other methodological details. Nonetheless, the pattern suggests that just as over time it takes a larger dose for a drug addict to get high and more graphic violence for a film to receive an R-rating, as a society we are developing tolerance to flashbulb memory-inducing events, at least public ones. Another assassination, another terrorist attack, another natural disaster? Been there, done that. As our society becomes more jaded and saturated with information, it is taking larger-scale events to produce flashbulb memories. The attacks of September 11, 2001 were one such "off-the-scale" event. What will the next one be?

MOOD AND MEMORY

Different Kinds of Mood Effects

One of the many things complicating the relationship between memory and mood is that it is very hard to treat them independently: Memories can influence one's mood, and vice versa. As an illustration of the former, consider someone who is in the process of remembering a prior traumatic experience. The act of remembering would almost certainly have a negative effect on her mood. Now consider someone who is having an (objectively) emotionally neutral or ambiguous experience, such as a friend declining an invitation to get together. Her mood at the time is likely to influence the way in which she encodes the event in memory—as a personal rebuff or an innocuous occurrence.

To conduct experimental research on mood and memory, it is necessary to have participants who vary in mood. Individuals' mood varies naturally as a function of numerous individual and situational factors, and some studies have capitalized on this variation by examining participants whose mood varies because of naturally occurring phenomena like the weather (e.g., Forgas, Goldenberg, & Unkelbach, 2009). However, for purposes of experimental control, studies typically induce a particular mood in participants prior to presenting them with some information. Techniques for this purpose include asking participants to think about (and sometimes write about) a positive or negative past experience; read a series of positive or negative statements (e.g., "I feel great today!"); experience success or failure in an ostensibly unrelated experiment; watch a funny or depressing film; and listen to upbeat or somber music. The mood can be induced prior to encoding the information and/or again at retrieval.

In a series of experiments, Forgas and colleagues have demonstrated that a mild negative mood can actually have beneficial effects on memory (for review, see Forgas, 2010). Compared to participants in a positive mood, those in a bad mood remember more details about a recently experienced event (Forgas et al., 2009) and are less likely to incorporate misleading postevent information (Forgas, Vargas & Laham, 2005). It is unclear why negative mood has these effects, but one possibility is that it improves attention to concrete, external information that is present in the situation (Forgas, 2010).

In addressing the relationship between mood and memory, it is important to distinguish between one's mood at the time of encoding and one's mood at the time of retrieval. After all, you might be trying to remember on a happy, sunny day something that happened on a sad, rainy day. Early research on mood and memory treated it as another instance of state-dependent memory, according to which one is better at remembering information if one's internal state at retrieval matches the state one was in when encoding the information, compared to a situation where the states differ (Neath & Surprenant, 2015; Schwartz, 2014). For example, a person is more likely to remember his drunken behavior when he is drunk again than when he is sober.[3] Treating mood in this fashion, if something happens when you are in a bad mood, then you would subsequently remember it better in a bad mood than a good mood. A number of experiments have demonstrated precisely this sort of mood-dependent memory effect (e.g., Eich & Metcalfe, 1989).

Subsequent research has shown, however, that the relationship between memory and mood is more complex. What matters in addition to the relationship between the mood at encoding and the mood at retrieval is the congruence between the mood at retrieval and the nature of the information (Eich, 2007). That is, when we are in a good mood, we tend to think of positive things; when we are in a bad mood, we tend to think of negative things.

In other words, a given mood cues memories that are consistent with that mood, partly because of the different brain regions involved in processing and storing emotional information (Eichenbaum, 2012). Mood dependence and mood congruence are not necessarily incompatible (Eich, 2007). Memory is best when the mood at encoding, the mood at retrieval, and the valence of the information all match—for example, a person in a bad mood attempting to recall details of a sad movie that she watched while in a bad mood. Fortunately, at least for successful remembering, these things very often do go together. But they do not always, and that is when retrieval failures are more likely to occur.

Depression and Memory

Because moods naturally fluctuate over time, everyone is susceptible to mood congruency effects. In some people, however, a given mood is relatively stable; depression is the best, and probably the most common, example. Considering that one of the DSM-V criteria for depression is "diminished ability to think or concentrate, or indecisiveness, nearly every day" (American Psychiatric Association, 2013), it is unsurprising that the disorder has diverse and profound effects on memory (see Table 2.1). Importantly, depressed persons do not simply experience more negative and fewer positive events (e.g., Lotterman & Bonanno, 2014); rather, they encode and remember events differently from nondepressed persons, attending selectively to negative information and interpreting ambiguous information in a negative light (e.g., Everaert, Duyck & Koster, 2014).

One way of thinking about the relationship between memory and depression is as an extreme instance of mood congruency. If negative moods favor the retrieval of negative information from memory, then a persistent and severe negative mood (i.e., depression) should strongly favor the retrieval of negative information. Indeed, depressed persons show precisely this memory bias: They have increased access to negative (i.e., sad) memories

Table 2.1   Memory Characteristics Associated with Depression

Selective attention to negative information
Interpreting ambiguous information in a negative light
Better memory for negative information (mood congruency)
Rumination (dwelling on negative mood and events)
Intrusive memories associated with negative events
Remembering the past as better than it really was
Overgeneral autobiographical memory
Working memory impairment

Source: Brian Bornstein.

and decreased access to positive (i.e., happy) memories (Mineka & Sutton, 1992). The bias extends to semantic (e.g., negative vs. positive words or sentences; Denny & Hunt, 1992; Everaert et al., 2014) as well as episodic information, and it is accompanied by a ruminative thinking style, according to which depressed individuals dwell on the causes and consequences of their negative mood (e.g., Nolen-Hoeksema, 2000; Sumner et al., 2014; Werner-Seidler & Moulds, 2014). Depressed persons, like those with posttraumatic stress disorder (PTSD), are also susceptible to intrusive memories associated with negative life events (Parry & O'Kearney, 2014). The tendency to remember negative things better and to ruminate has an adverse impact on mood, thereby perpetuating the depression and creating a vicious cycle. Instructing individuals in the midst of a current depressive episode to recall a positive memory fails to improve their mood, whereas it does have that effect on nondepressed persons, as well as those who previously had depression but recovered (Werner-Seidler & Moulds, 2014).

Despite this general tendency of depressed persons to overremember negative events, there is one situation in which they actually tend to overremember positive events. Lotterman and Bonanno (2014) conducted a prospective study in which a cohort of college students rated their mood and various life events repeatedly over a 4-year period. Participants with more depressive symptoms showed a greater tendency to overestimate the frequency of positive events, especially for memories of the self and for participants who also scored low on a measure of self-enhancement (i.e., exaggerated self-confidence and opinion of the self). Lotterman and Bonanno explain this finding in terms of self-comparison—that is, depression is associated with (mis)remembering more good things going on in one's life previously than are happening right now.

The memories of depressed persons differ from nondepressed controls in other ways as well. For example, they tend to perform worse on tests of both episodic (personally experienced events) and semantic memory (impersonal, factual information), in terms of remembering less information and information with less detail, although the episodic deficit is more pronounced (Semkovska, Noone, Carton, & McLoughlin, 2012). The relative lack of detail in episodic memories, which is referred to as "overgeneral autobiographical memory" or "reduced autobiographical memory specificity," is characterized by more repetitive, generalized, and summary-type memories than discrete, circumscribed memories with individuating detail. It has been found to correlate with depressive symptoms in both clinical (Williams et al., 2007) and nonclinical samples (e.g., Ros et al., 2014; Van Daele, Griffith, Van den Bergh, & Hermans, 2014), and some evidence suggests that the relationship is stronger for women than for men (Ros et al., 2014).

The tendency toward overgeneral memory, which is often accompanied by rumination (Sumner et al., 2014), could contribute to the depression itself, as very often "God is in the details." Longitudinal studies show that a predisposition toward rumination and overgeneral autobiographical memories can make one more vulnerable to depression (Van Daele et al., 2014), especially following stressful life events (Hamlat et al., 2015). Thus, interventions designed to train individuals in memory specificity and how to avoid rumination have the potential both to reduce the risk of developing depression and to be part of an effective treatment plan if depression does develop (e.g., Hamlat et al., 2015; Williams, Teasdale, Segal & Soulsby, 2000). When depressed patients are in remission, their memory functioning returns to normal (Semkovska et al., 2012).

As with any memory failure, the memory deficits associated with depression could be due to either (or both) of two broad classes of explanation: Depressed persons might encode information in memory less well, or they might do a poorer job of retrieving it. Evidence supports both explanations, but the primary deficit appears to be at encoding (Dietsche et al., 2014). For example, the effect of depression on memory is greater for harder-to-encode information, such as unstructured material (e.g., random word lists), than it is for more structured material (e.g., organized word lists; see Baddeley, 2013). Neuroimaging studies show that compared to nondepressed controls, depressed patients show decreased activation in certain brain regions during memory encoding (Dietsche et al., 2014). The encoding deficit makes sense in light of some of depression's other hallmark symptoms, such as lethargy, low motivation, and sleep disturbance (American Psychiatric Association, 2013). Encoding information effectively in memory takes energy, effort, and alertness; just as depressed persons lack energy to perform demanding and even some routine physical tasks, they lack energy for demanding mental tasks as well.

Depressed patients also suffer from impairments in some aspects of working memory (i.e., information in current conscious awareness), especially during an acute episode (Gruber et al., 2011; Joormann, Levens & Gotlib, 2011). Depression can affect not only the capacity of working memory but also the way in which individuals allocate attentional resources and the emotional valence they assign information as they are processing it (Baddeley, 2013; Everaert et al., 2014).

In addition to having a direct association with memory impairment, depression is a frequent accompaniment to certain memory disorders. Individuals suffering from pathological memory impairment, such as Alzheimer's disease and other forms of dementia, have elevated rates of depression (e.g., Karam & Itani, 2014; Knapskog, Barca & Engedal, 2014). Knapskog et al. found that 37.5 percent of patients referred to a memory clinic or an outpatient clinic for possible dementia diagnosis had mild depression, and 14.1 percent suffered from severe depression. As dementia patients, at least in the early stages of the disease, are often acutely aware of their memory lapses and other symptoms, the depression might simply be an understandable reaction to their cognitive decline; on the other hand, the mood disorder and the memory disorder might both result from the same underlying neuropathology.

In summary, mood has a pronounced effect on memory; to a large extent, memory affects mood as well. A mild negative mood can lead to better memory, and information in memory that is congruent with one's mood while trying to remember has a mnemonic advantage. Although a mild negative mood can enhance accuracy, it clearly has its limits. Mood congruency explains much of the memory bias in depressed persons, who are especially likely to remember and dwell on negative memories. Memory suffers during depression in other ways as well, such as a lack of detail. This is not to say, of course, that memory biases are one of the major causes or consequences of depression; a host of other cognitive factors are involved, as well as social, physiological, and neurochemical ones. Nonetheless, memory biases serve to perpetuate the mood disorder and are likely one of the reasons why depression can be so difficult to treat.

CONCLUSIONS

The ability to remember information that we have previously encountered is a remarkable and adaptive ability. It is one that humans share with many other species, yet our memory capabilities are more highly developed than most (although the memories of other primates, dolphins, and whales, among other species, are impressive). Indisputably, our memories are accurate much of the time. Yet just as indisputably, our memories are far from perfect records of what we experience. Each time we retrieve information in memory, we reconstruct the memories, incorporating the information we originally experienced with other information that came before and after. As Frederic Bartlett (1932, p. 213) observed 85 years ago, "Remembering is not the re-excitation of innumerable fixed, lifeless and fragmentary traces. It is an imaginative reconstruction, or construction, built out of the relation of our attitude towards a whole active mass of organized past reactions or experience."

Emotion has a complex relationship with memory. Memory is affected by the rememberer's affective state at the time of encoding, the affective state at the time of retrieval, and the emotional content of the information itself. There is a common perception that emotion makes things more memorable. People believe this as a general precept and also subjectively, as in the very high confidence with which they believe in the accuracy of their flashbulb memories. However, research shows that with some exceptions (e.g., mild negative mood can enhance memory compared to a positive mood, and stress can improve memory for central details of an event), emotion—especially negative emotions like stress or depression—does not benefit memory. In some cases, it can have a negative effect; but by and large, emotional memories function much like any other memories, in that they are sometimes correct, but they are also subject to error and distortion.

Thus, despite its widespread acceptance, the metaphor of memory as some sort of technological device that stores information with perfect veridicality (e.g., a wax tablet, tape recorder, video recorder, hard drive, etc.) is simply wrong. If I close the file on my computer that contains this chapter and reopen it an hour, 2 days, or 30 years later, it will look exactly the same. But if 30 years, 20 days, or even an hour from now, I attempt to remember the occasion of first writing this very sentence (March 17, 2015, in Coronado, California, and subsequently revised on multiple occasions), my memory will be incomplete and quite possibly erroneous in significant respects. Of course, external repositories like videotapes and computer files are subject to degradation over long periods—a digital memory can even be infected by a virus, causing a form of "digital amnesia" (Garde-Hansen et al., p. 13)—but any degradation is exponentially slower and less likely than what our internal repositories experience. Thus, "[r]ather than viewing our memory as a tape recorder or DVD, we can more aptly describe our memory as an ever-changing medium" (Lilienfeld et al., 2010, p. 69). It is impossible to predict in advance how it will change, but it must change. And perhaps that is one of the reasons why humans are more interesting than tape recorders, video recorders, and hard drives.

NOTES

1. I revised this chapter on multiple occasions in the nearly two years since writing this specific example, which gave me an opportunity to test the hypothesis in an informal way. Each time I worked on the chapter, I tested myself on my memory of the salad; despite the frequent rehearsal, on every occasion I forgot at least one of the ingredients.

2. I am grateful to Jeff Neuschatz for calling my attention to this connection.

3. For a realistic depiction of alcohol-induced blackouts, see the recent film *The Girl on the Train* (2016).

Chapter 3

An Unholy Tetrad

Repression, Recovered Memory, False Memory, and Hypnosis

Myth: Repression is a Real Phenomenon, Especially in Response to Traumatic Events

Related Myths: Recovered Memories Are Accurate; Hypnosis Is a Reliable Means of Eliciting Repressed Memories

The title character in The Who's rock opera *Tommy* is a classic example of how repression supposedly works: as a young boy, he sees his father (believed killed in World War I) kill his mother's lover; they tell him he did not see or hear anything, and they threaten him not to tell anyone; the trauma causes him to withdraw into himself, leaving him deaf, dumb and blind, and without any conscious recollection of the crime.[1] In other words, Tommy has repressed his memory of the traumatic event, and the repression produces symptoms—his deafness, mutism, and blindness—that symbolize the underlying conflict. Repression figures prominently in many other popular films (e.g., Alfred Hitchcock's *Spellbound*, *Shutter Island*), novels (e.g., D.M. Thomas's *The White Hotel*, in which Freud himself is a character; *The Double Bind* by Chris Bohjalian; *In the Woods* by Tana French), plays (e.g., Tennessee Williams's *A Streetcar Named Desire*), and television shows (e.g., those dealing with military combat, such as *M*A*S*H*). In these portrayals, where the individual with repressed memories receives psychotherapy, it frequently involves hypnosis as a tool to break through the repression (e.g., *Spellbound*). Indeed, cinematic representations of hypnosis—not always used for therapeutic purposes—have been around as long as cinema itself, dating back to the silent film era (Packer, 2012).

According to Freud, repression can occur even for seemingly innocuous, everyday material (1901/1960), but it is especially likely for trauma and other material associated with strong negative emotions (Erdelyi, 1985). There is, sadly, no limit to the number and type of traumatic events that this might encompass: committing, witnessing, or being a victim of a crime; surviving an accident or natural disaster; serving in the military during deployment; and many other negative occurrences that can range from mildly to extremely upsetting. Much of the current commentary on repression situates it within the context of the "recovered memory debate," which concerns the reliability of memories that have been forgotten for a significant period of time—arguably due to repression—only to be subsequently "recovered" (e.g., Belli, 2012). Just as many kinds of events can be traumatic, many kinds of events are candidates for recovered memories, including such outlandish ones as alien abduction (Clancy, 2005), past lives (Peters, Horselenberg, Jelicic & Merckelbach, 2007), and ritual Satanic abuse (Young, Sachs, Braun & Watkins, 1991).

A surprising number of laypeople claim to have recovered a repressed memory: 13 percent of college undergraduates (Golding, Sanchez & Sego, 1996) and even higher proportions in clinical samples (e.g., Polusny & Follette, 1996; Poole, Lindsay, Memon & Bull, 1995). The events most commonly reported as repressed are traumatic ones, especially sexual assault (Golding et al., 1996; Lindsay & Read, 1995). The prototypical case involves child sexual abuse (CSA), where an adult (or older child/adolescent) claims to have recovered a memory of being abused as a child. The incident in question (or incidents, in cases of alleged repeated abuse) was not previously remembered due to repression. In these cases, individuals allege that they witnessed a traumatic event—typically as victims, but occasionally as bystanders—but repressed the memory for many years, only to recover it later. Once recovered, the claimant's memory can lead to a police investigation and criminal charges and/or civil lawsuits. There is usually little, if any, corroborating evidence, leaving the case to turn on the reliability of the claimant's memory. Legal cases involving claims of repression and recovered memory pose some thorny legal issues, such as the scientific validity of repression, the timing of the statute of limitations, and the admissibility of expert testimony on the issue (Faigman et al., 2014; Gothard & Ivker, 2000; Piper, Lillevik & Kritzer, 2008; Piper, Pope & Borowiecki, 2000). Despite these complications and many courts' concerns about the science underlying repression and recovered memory, recovered memory cases have become increasingly common in both civil and criminal courts (Gothard & Ivker, 2000; Underwager & Wakefield, 1998).

For example, Melissa Phillips was a young New Jersey woman (19 at the time of the lawsuit) who sued her uncle, John Gelpke, for injuries due to his alleged repeated sexual abuse of her when she was three to eight years old. Due to the traumatic nature of the abuse, she claimed to have repressed her memories of the incidents until recovering them at age 11, after having a dream of a sexual encounter between herself and the defendant. Thus, according to the plaintiff, she repressed memories of the abuse for three years, at which point they came back. Ms. Phillips won $750,000 in compensatory damages, which was reversed on appeal; the New Jersey Supreme Court then reversed and remanded the appellate court's decision (*Phillips v. Gelpke*, 2007). The appeals centered on the necessity of expert testimony on the issue of repression and recovered memory. Although the Phillips case did not involve hypnosis as a means of recovering the memory, it likely included other suggestive techniques in eliciting her repressed memories, and many similar cases have involved hypnosis (Faigman et al., 2014).

Without disputing the reality of child sexual abuse and other forms of victimization—crimes that may not be reported for years after the event (e.g., Connolly & Read, 2006; 2007)—cases that involve claims of recovered memory are problematic. Some of the claims have proven to be false, even though the victims themselves firmly believe the events occurred (e.g., Loftus & Ketcham, 1994; Pendergrast, 1996). Psychological research, inspired largely by these cases, has now demonstrated that false memories are surprisingly common and result from a number of factors, such as fundamental cognitive processes, suggestive memory retrieval techniques (sometimes in the context of psychotherapy), and individual differences that make some people more susceptible to false memories than others. Repression, recovered memory, false memory, and hypnosis are distinct yet overlapping constructs; they combine to produce an "unholy tetrad" of processes that can increase the risk of memory errors and about which many laypeople have erroneous expectations.

The present chapter begins with a review of popular beliefs about repression as a response to traumatic memories and the use of hypnosis as a means of uncovering those memories. This section includes a discussion of psychotherapy, as many therapists share those beliefs. The chapter then summarizes research showing that despite the widespread belief in repression, there is little empirical support for the notion that individuals repress traumatic memories, at least in the classic Freudian sense. This is not to say that we do not fail, on occasion, to remember traumatic memories—merely that the failure is not due to repression. Much of the contemporary literature on repression focuses on recovered memories, where there are two central questions: When individuals recover memories of a previously forgotten event, how accurate are they? And is it possible to have a false memory of a traumatic event—that is, to recover a memory of an event that never actually occurred? The chapter's third section considers these and related questions, such as whether some individuals are more likely to have recovered false memories than others. Finally, the chapter discusses the use of hypnosis as a mnemonic technique, from both a legal and a psychological perspective.

BELIEFS ABOUT REPRESSION, MEMORY
FOR TRAUMA, AND HYPNOSIS

Laypeople's and Professionals' Beliefs

Like other Freudian concepts (e.g., free association, projection, Oedipal complex), notions of repression and recovered memory are widely understood and accepted. The survey described in chapter 1 contained four questions about repression, hypnosis, and recovered memory. Participants were somewhat knowledgeable about the possibility of error in recovered childhood memories (66.5 % correct) and hypnosis's potential to heighten suggestibility effects (50.3 % correct); however, only a minority of participants knew that it is generally not possible to tell the difference between true and false memories (45.4 % correct) or that hypnosis does not increase memory accuracy (35.7 % correct). Most strikingly, only 7.6 percent disagreed (correctly) with the question about repression: "Traumatic experiences can be repressed for many years and then recovered."

A number of other studies have likewise demonstrated erroneous beliefs associated with the constellation of repression, recovered memory, and hypnosis (e.g., Faimon, O'Neil & Bornstein, 2005; Garry et al., 1994; Garry, Loftus, Brown & DuBreuil, 1997; Golding et al., 1996; Patihis et al., 2014; Simons & Chabris, 2011). In the earliest systematic study of laypeople's beliefs about repression, Golding and colleagues (1996) administered a survey to over 600 undergraduate students (all surveys contained the same 30 items, and some participants answered four additional questions). The survey asked about participants' beliefs about repressed memories, whether they should be allowed in court, and the role of therapy in recovering repressed memories. It also asked about their experiences concerning media coverage of repressed memories and their actual experiences with repressed memories. Nearly all participants (89 %) reported having heard of someone recovering a repressed memory. The most common source of exposure was television (75 %), although other media (e.g., newspapers, magazines, radio) were frequent sources, as were friends and relatives.[2] Nearly one-quarter (22 %) of participants reported knowing someone who had recovered a repressed memory. Clearly, then, repression is a concept with which most people, at least in the United States, are familiar. On average, participants reported that repressed memories were moderately believable and accurate and should be allowed in court (M = 6.31, 5.57, and 5.53, respectively, on a 10-point scale). A more recent survey found that large majorities of undergraduate students agreed that traumatic memories are often repressed (81 %) and that repressed memories can be retrieved in therapy accurately (70 %; Patihis et al., 2014, Study 1). Adults drawn from the community are just as accepting of repression as student samples (Patihis et al., 2014, Study 2). These findings suggest that the proliferation and acceptance of recovered memories are simply part of the cultural landscape (Laurence, Day, & Gaston, 1998; Lindsay & Read, 1995).

Laypeople view some things as more "repressible" than others. For example, Bornstein, Kaplan, and Perry (2007) presented participants with a series of vignettes depicting possible CSA. The vignettes varied the victim's gender, the perpetrator's gender, the victim-perpetrator relationship (parent or babysitter), and the type of abuse (relatively mild sexual abuse [fondling], relatively severe sexual abuse [oral copulation], or physical abuse [beating with a belt]). Participants rated the probability that the victim would repress the abuse as highest for the severe sexual abuse, followed by the mild sexual abuse, and lowest for the physical abuse. Same-sex abuse was perceived as more repressible than heterosexual abuse, with a woman's abuse of a boy being seen as least likely to be repressed. The repressibility ratings tracked participants' ratings of how traumatic the event was for the child, indicating that laypeople are familiar with the Freudian notion that more traumatic events are more likely to be repressed.

Many laypeople believe that hypnosis enhances memory accuracy (e.g., Daglish & Wright, 1991; Patihis et al., 2014), and they are joined in this belief by members of the professional community (e.g., Yapko, 1994). Much of the controversy surrounding recovered memories revolves around mental health professionals' efforts to elicit them during therapy, often using hypnosis and other techniques with little demonstrated efficacy but high potential for suggestion (e.g., Lindsay & Read, 1994; Loftus & Ketcham, 1994). These techniques include age regression (often used in conjunction with hypnosis), guided imagery, journaling, interpreting physical symptoms as "body memories" of forgotten events, and dream interpretation (Lindsay & Read, 1994). Many psychologists and other therapists rely on such techniques (Feldman-Summers & Pope, 1994; Ost et al., 2013; Polusny & Follette, 1996; Poole et al., 1995), suggesting that the practices are not limited to a fringe group of poorly trained practitioners (Lindsay & Read, 1995). As critics of the techniques point out (e.g., Lindsay & Read, 1994, 1995), the claim is not that all or even most memories recovered in therapy are false, but merely that some may be, that certain therapeutic practices increase the risk, and that it is very hard to tell the difference. Consequently, recovered memory therapy is potentially harmful, in the sense that it demonstrates harmful psychological or physical effects in clients or others; the harmful effects are enduring; and the effects have been replicated by independent investigators (Lilienfeld, 2007).

Mental health professionals' belief in repression and use of therapeutic techniques to elicit recovered memories doubtless varies depending on the professionals' training and theoretical orientation. Practitioners of alternative therapies (e.g., neurolinguistic programming, hypnotherapy) are even more likely than psychoanalysts to believe that traumatic memories are often repressed and can be retrieved accurately in therapy (Patihis et al., 2014). Over the past half-century, the number of clinical psychologists who identify primarily with a psychodynamic orientation (including psychoanalytic and related approaches) has dropped steadily (Norcross & Karpiak, 2012), as has mainstream clinicians' belief in repressed memory (Patihis et al., 2014). Nonetheless, in the most recent survey of members of the Society of Clinical Psychology (Division 12 of the American Psychological Association; data were collected in 2010), "psychodynamic" was the second most popular specific orientation (18 %), behind only "cognitive" (31 %; an additional 22 % of respondents categorized themselves as "eclectic/integrative"; Norcross & Karpiak, 2012). These figures illustrate that notwithstanding the scientific backlash against repression and recovered memory therapy in the psychological research community (e.g., Lilienfeld, 2007; Lindsay & Read, 1994; Patihis et al., 2014; Piper et al., 2008), they are far from eradicated from professional psychological practice. Despite laypeople's general acceptance of repression in general, they are somewhat skeptical of therapists' role in bringing repressed memories to light. They are aware that therapists' role can be suggestive as well as therapeutic (Faimon et al., 2005) and that they are capable of implanting false memories (Golding et al., 1996; Patihis et al., 2014).

Indirect Measures of Repression/Recovered Memory Beliefs

Simply asking people what they believe about repression is a valuable means of assessing those beliefs, but as described in the introduction, the research on metacognition shows that we often do not have very good insight into our own mental processes. Another way of assessing attitudes and beliefs is indirectly, by measuring one's decisions or behavior. If Johnny consistently chooses other foods over broccoli, then we can infer that he does not much care for broccoli; he might also report that he does not like it, but then again, he might not; he might say he likes it just fine (and simply prefers the other food more), but his behavior belies his stated preference. Similarly, we can draw inferences about individuals' beliefs about repression by measuring their judgments and behaviors in reaction to instances of repression and/or recovered memory.

In response to the high visibility of legal cases involving claims of recovered memory, especially in CSA cases, several research studies have taken this approach by investigating perceptions of the alleged victim and perpetrator in such cases, often within a jury decision-making context. Typically, they compare laypersons' judgments (which may or may not include mock verdicts) for cases in which the alleged victim claimed to have repressed memory of the crime to those where the victim remembered the crime all along. Because claims of repression/recovered memory necessarily involve a delay between the incident and when it is reported, some studies also include a condition in which the victim reported the incident immediately. These studies have examined juror decision making in both civil and criminal cases involving recovered memory, and they have also examined a number of additional variables, such as age of the victim (Golding, Sanchez & Sego, 1999; Key, Warren & Ross, 1996), characteristics of the incident (e.g., type and number of CSA incidents; Faimon, O'Neil & Bornstein, 2005; Golding, Sego & Sanchez, 1999), manner of recovery (e.g., spontaneously vs. in therapy; Faimon et al., 2005), expert testimony (Nachson et al., 2007), and gender of the alleged victim and perpetrator (Bornstein & Muller, 2001; Clark & Nightingale, 1997; ForsterLee et al., 1999).

Alleged victims who report the incident immediately are perceived more favorably, and are more likely to win their case, than victims who report it after a delay (Golding, Sanchez, & Sego, 1999; Golding, Sego, Sanchez, & Hasemann, 1995). Most research shows that victims are less credible when the delayed reporting involves repression than when it does not (Bornstein & Muller, 2001; ForsterLee et al., 1999; Key et al., 1996; Loftus, Weingardt, & Hoffman, 1993), although some studies have failed to find a difference (Faimon et al., 2005; Golding, Sanchez, & Sego, 1999; Golding, Sego, & Sanchez, 1999; Golding et al., 1995). Case characteristics can also moderate the effect of testimony type. For example, alleged victims of heterosexual abuse (i.e., male perpetrator-female victim or female perpetrator-male victim) are perceived as more credible—and defendants in those cases as correspondingly more culpable—when the abuse was remembered all along than when it was purportedly repressed and then recovered. However, alleged victims of same-sex abuse are perceived as equally credible regardless of whether the abuse was remembered or repressed (Bornstein & Muller, 2001). This might reflect the tendency, as noted above, for same-sex abuse to be viewed as more traumatic and, hence, more repressible (Bornstein et al., 2007).

Individual Differences

Beliefs about repression are widespread, having been documented in numerous locales, including the United States (e.g., Golding et al., 1996; Patihis et al., 2014), Canada (Nachson et al., 2007), the United Kingdom (Conway et al., 2014; Nachson et al., 2007; Patihis et al., 2014), Israel (Nachson et al., 2007), New Zealand (Nachson et al., 2007), Norway (Magnussen et al., 2006), and South America (Alvarez & Brown, 2002). There are, however, some cross-national differences. Although the existence of differences varies somewhat depending on the specific belief, overall, citizens of the United States and

Canada are less likely to endorse myths about recovered memory and memory for trauma than citizens of New Zealand, the United Kingdom, and Israel (Nachson et al., 2007).

This pattern corresponds roughly to cross-national differences in self-reported exposure to and awareness of the recovered memory debate (Nachson et al., 2007). On the one hand, the correspondence suggests that public discourse about the recovered memory debate may be having a salutary educational effect; on the other hand, the benefit would seem to be rather minimal, as large numbers of citizens even in countries where the issue is prominent in the news media, such as the United States and Canada, persist in holding erroneous beliefs about repression and hypnosis. The nature of the exposure also seems to play a critical role. Those with personal exposure (i.e., having recovered a repressed memory themselves or knowing someone who had) believe in repressed memories more than individuals whose exposure is entirely through the media, who in turn are more believing than people with no exposure to repressed memories (Golding et al., 1996). Exposure to positive media coverage of repression is also associated with greater believability (Golding et al., 1996). Although these data are correlational, they strongly suggest that media coverage of repression, in terms of both amount and quality, is capable of shaping popular opinions about the topic.

Individuals who have a prior history of abuse are more likely to side with the victim in recovered memory cases (Faimon et al., 2005), and some surveys of laypeople's beliefs find that women believe in repression more than men (Golding et al., 1996; Patihis et al., 2014), although other studies have failed to find a gender difference (Nachson et al., 2007). If women are more accepting of repression, then they should be more influenced than men by whether an alleged victim at trial claims to have repressed his or her memory of the experience. Mock juror studies show that women are more likely to favor the alleged victim in recovered memory cases (i.e., to find for the plaintiff or convict a criminal defendant; Faimon et al., 2005; Golding, Sanchez & Sego, 1999; Golding, Sego & Sanchez, 1999; Loftus et al., 1993). The majority of studies also find, however, that neither men nor women are more likely to be affected by whether the victim claims repression (Golding, Sanchez & Sego, 1999; Golding, Sego & Sanchez, 1999; Golding et al., 1995; Loftus et al., 1993).

Intellectual and personality characteristics also appear to predict individuals' beliefs about repression. Patihis et al. (2014) found that individuals who were smarter (according to their SAT score) or scored higher on a measure of critical thinking ability were more skeptical about repression. Highly empathetic individuals were more likely to believe in repression, presumably because they would find it easier to identify with a victim claiming to have a repressed/recovered memory.

REPRESSION: A GENUINE RESPONSE TO TRAUMA?

The concept of repression is, of course, most closely associated with Sigmund Freud. Although Freud did not originate the idea, he quickly became its most well-known spokesperson and expounder.[3] Both the theoretical foundation and the clinical application of psychoanalysis have evolved since Freud's day; there is not a single, unified approach to psychoanalysis, and related psychodynamic approaches exist (Luyten et al., 2015). However, the notion of unconscious processes like repression is still central to both Freudian and more contemporary perspectives (Luyten et al., 2015). Freud's theory of repression is intricate, and it developed over the course of his long career and voluminous writings; it is beyond the scope of the present volume to dissect it in detail (see, e.g., Erdelyi, 1985, 1990, 2006), but it is worth noting that Freud's approach to repression as a reaction to trauma was somewhat narrower than the more expansive treatment repression receives in contemporary recovered memory cases (Piper et al., 2008).

The basic idea of repression is well known: An individual's unconscious blocks access to some information, such as memory of trauma, because consciously thinking about the information would create anxiety or conflict. Because repression is an imperfect defense mechanism, the material can surface in various ways: dreams, slips of the tongue, and most notably, symptoms of mental illness. Treatment requires recovering the buried memories, which are presumed to be highly accurate.

In some respects, memory for trauma can be thought of as an extension of the cognitive processes involving in remembering any kind of negative emotional information or experience (covered in chapter 2). One can think of trauma as being at the extreme end of the negative emotional experience continuum. Freud and his followers do conceptualize trauma, and its effects on memory, in this way; but memory for trauma has come to be viewed as qualitatively different from memory for other negative material (Erdelyi, 1985, 2006), and not merely quantitatively different (Piper et al., 2008). In particular, highly upsetting, traumatic events are seen as susceptible to complete forgetting of the experience.

A key question in these cases is: Does trauma lead to repression? This is a controversial subject within the psychological community, but the weight of scholarship in this area suggests that the answer is "No." Most scientific authorities, including several leading professional societies (e.g., the American Medical Association and American Psychiatric Association), do not generally accept repressed memory and related concepts (Piper et al., 2008). There are several reasons for this position. First, the theory of repression is notoriously difficult, if not impossible, to test. According to Freud, recovering a memory of trauma would be evidence for repression (i.e., the memory was repressed but has now been recovered); but failing to recover a memory of trauma would likewise be evidence for repression (i.e., the memory was repressed and is still repressed). So Freud wins either way, which is hardly the hallmark of a good scientific theory, which should be disprovable.

Second, although there is some disagreement in the field and empirical support for aspects of psychodynamic approaches to psychopathology exists (Luyten et al., 2015), experimental research that has sought to test the theory of repression has, on the whole, garnered only meager support (e.g., Holmes, 1990; McNally, 2012). Because of the lack of a firm scientific foundation for the theory of repression, many recovered memory cases are barred by statutes of limitations or rigorous evidentiary standards (Faigman et al., 2014; Piper et al., 2008). Nonetheless, other cases have been allowed to go forward, as in the New Jersey case described above. As many of these cases involve claims of CSA by family members—with few, if any, witnesses besides the alleged victim—they are usually hard to prove, hard to defend against, and difficult for everyone involved.

Third, although it is relatively straightforward (but not without its complications) to document that a trauma victim remembers the experience, it is notoriously difficult to document that a victim has completely forgotten the experience (Geraerts, Raymaekers & Merckelbach, 2008; Schooler, Bendiksen & Ambadar, 1997). The experience might simply be deliberately avoided or remembered but not reported (Goodman et al., 2003); partially remembered but lacking in details (Piper et al., 2008); remembered on some occasions but not others, accompanied by a failure to remember the prior remembering (known as the "forgot-it-all-along" effect; see Brewin, 2012; Geraerts, 2012; Geraerts et al., 2008; Merckelbach et al., 2006; Schooler et al., 1997); or genuinely forgotten, but for reasons having nothing at all to do with repression (Brewin, 2012). For example, traumatic memories—just like any other memories—might be forgotten because the cues at the time of encoding are a poor match for the cues available at retrieval (Capaldi & Neath, 1995; McNally, 2003; 2012; see chapter 2 on memory for emotional events).

Fourth, and most compellingly, the vast majority of trauma victims do not forget their experiences at all (e.g., Brewin, 2007; Goodman et al., 2003; Kendall-Tackett, Williams & Finkelhor, 1993; McNally, 2005; Seamon, 2015). Rather, they tend to remember the experiences in painful detail, and to an extent that the memories become quite intrusive and interfere with everyday functioning. Indeed, according to the latest *Diagnostic and Statistical Manual of Mental Disorders* (DSM-5), one of the hallmark criteria for PTSD is "recurrent, involuntary, and intrusive distressing memories of the event(s)" (American Psychiatric Association, 2013, p. 271, Criterion B.1.). Negative emotional events, including victimization, tend to be recalled quite well (Brewin, 2012; Lindsay & Read, 1995; Palombo et al., 2016; Porter & Peace, 2007). In some respects (e.g., vividness of recall, amount of detail, consistency over time), traumatic memories are remembered better than positive memories (Peace & Porter, 2004; Porter & Peace, 2007). This is particularly true for memories of sexual victimization, even compared to other kinds of trauma (Peace, Porter & ten Brinke, 2008). In their review of over 2,000 cases of historic child sexual abuse (defined as two years or more between the end of the alleged offense and trial), Connolly and Read (2006) found that claims of repression were rare, occurring in only 6 percent of cases. Female complainants were much more likely than males to claim repression (7.3 vs. 1.6 %), but even among women, fewer than 1 in 10 cases involved a claim of repression. Nonetheless, legal cases involving claims of repression and recovered memory arise not infrequently and have captured the popular imagination.

RECOVERED MEMORY ACCURACY AND FALSE MEMORY

Recovered memories are not necessarily inaccurate. Here it is important to distinguish between two important questions: first, whether traumatic experiences can be forgotten and then recovered and second, whether repression is the mechanism of any such forgetting. As discussed in the previous section, it is hard to show conclusively that repression has (or, for that matter, has not) occurred, but there is relatively little empirical evidence for it. Nonetheless, it is still possible that one can forget a traumatic event—in the sense of being unable to retrieve the information from memory for a significant period of time—only to remember, or "recover," it later. Like repression, the phenomenon of recovered memory is notoriously difficult to document. To be reasonably confident that a traumatic experience was genuinely forgotten and then subsequently remembered, one needs to show, at a minimum, that the event genuinely occurred; that the person failed to remember (or at least report) it, despite opportunities and willingness to do so; and that the recovery of the memory was sudden, authentic, and not motivated by other considerations (e.g., legal or personal benefit; see Schooler et al., 1997). As noted above, it is essentially impossible to prove conclusively that someone has genuinely forgotten something—whether that "something" is a traumatic event, a more mundane occurrence, or factual information—even though the person has never talked about it to others and may not be aware of any prior instances of remembering it (Geraerts, 2012; Geraerts et al., 2008).

Rigorous attempts to document actual cases of recovered memory have found that although such cases are rare, cases do exist where there is reasonably persuasive evidence that the event did occur, was forgotten for a substantial period of time, and then recovered (e.g., Bull, 1999; Schooler et al., 1997). For example, Schooler et al. describe the case of a woman (DN) who recovered a memory of being raped 13 years previously. The rapist was prosecuted and convicted at the time, so there was very strong evidence that the traumatic experience occurred. Yet although DN showed a clear willingness to talk about the event shortly after the crime (e.g., by testifying at trial) and subsequently spoke to others (e.g., her therapist) about other instances of victimization (CSA), in the intervening period she failed to mention the rape. When she eventually did remember it, prompted by her therapist's mentioning that CSA victims often continue to be victimized as adults, she was shocked and told her therapist about it.

Other research indicates that the manner of memory recovery is related to the memory's accuracy. Spontaneous memory recovery is not unusual; however, recovery more often happens in the course of psychotherapy (Connolly & Read, 2007; Lindsay & Read, 1994, 1995; Loftus & Ketcham, 1994; Pendergrast, 1996). Memories that are recovered spontaneously outside therapy are more likely to correspond to genuine events than memories that arise in the context of therapy (Geraerts, 2012; Geraerts et al., 2008). For example, Geraerts and colleagues (2007) compared adult participants who reported continuous versus discontinuous memories of CSA. The classification was based on participants' response to the question, "Do you believe there was a time when you were completely unaware that you had ever been a victim of abuse, and that you later came to remember that you were abused?" The discontinuous-memory group also specified the context of memory recovery (i.e., during vs. outside therapy). The researchers corroborated 45 percent of the CSA memories in the continuous-memory group and 37 percent of discontinuous memories that were recovered outside of therapy, but not a single event (i.e., 0 %) for memories that were recovered during therapy. Case studies like DN and other instances of spontaneously recovered memory provide evidence that, in rare cases, one can forget a traumatic event on one occasion and then remember it on another. However, a much larger body of research shows that recovered memories can be false.

False Memory Research

Not all recovered memories are false, and not all false memories are recovered. Nonetheless, recovered memory claims that have been shown to be false are legion. These cases run the gamut from allegations that are true in some respects but inaccurate in others, to alleged events that are plausible (e.g., CSA) but in some cases have conclusively been shown not to have occurred, to events like alien abduction, past lives, and other paranormal experiences that could not possibly have occurred (e.g., Clancy, 2005; French

& Wilson, 2007; McNally, 2012; Pendergrast, 1996; Peters et al., 2007). Because individual cases of recovered memory are highly variable and hard to study systematically, much of the research on false memory has focused on whether false memories can be created experimentally. The logic underlying experimental false memory research is that if research participants can be led to believe that they experienced false events, then people in more naturally occurring situations—especially if they are psychologically vulnerable (e.g., in therapy for some type of mental illness) or subjected to powerful suggestive techniques—are capable of having false memories as well.

Multiple research paradigms have been used to study the phenomenon of false memory (for review, see Brainerd & Reyna, 2005; Davis & Loftus, 2007; Gerrie, Garry & Loftus, 2005; Laney & Loftus, 2010; Schwartz, 2014). Among the more common ones are the *misinformation effect* paradigm, wherein participants experience or witness some event, then receive misleading information about the event before having their memory for the event tested (e.g., Loftus, Miller & Burns, 1978); the *Deese-Roediger-McDermott (DRM)* paradigm, in which participants learn lists of words before being tested for memory of the words, as well as a semantically associated word that was not on the list (e.g., Gallo, 2010; Roediger & McDermott, 1995); and the *rich false memory* paradigm, in which researchers implant entirely false memories into participants' minds (e.g., Hyman & Loftus, 2002; Loftus & Bernstein, 2005). Regardless of the research method, the results are clear: People remember aspects of their experiences, and in some cases whole experiences, that demonstrably did not occur. As discussed later, some people are more susceptible to false memories than others, but no one is immune; even individuals with highly superior autobiographical memories have them, at rates roughly comparable to that of the ordinary population (Patihis et al., 2013).

Public figures, such as Hillary Clinton and George W. Bush, have been "outed" for false memories on several occasions. While I was writing the first draft of this chapter (February 2015), the most recent prominent false memory case was receiving extensive media coverage: Brian Williams, chief anchor and managing editor for *NBC Nightly News*, remembered (and retold) an experience when his helicopter came under fire and was forced down during the US invasion of Iraq 12 years previously. Fact-checkers determined that it was actually the helicopter flying ahead of him that was forced down. Once confronted with the facts, he acknowledged his mistake, saying "I don't know what screwed up in my mind that caused me to conflate one aircraft with another" (Steel & Somaiya, 2015). In other statements he attributed it to his viewing the video of him inspecting the impact area and "the fog of memory over 12 years" (Somaiya, 2015). It is possible, of course, that Williams deliberately changed the facts for purposes of self-aggrandizement; but it is also quite possible that like many memories, his memory of the incident changed over time, and he simply misremembered it (McWilliams, 2015). In other words, he might have had a false memory. Williams' punishment for his memory error was six months suspension without pay. Fortunately, most of us do not have our memories scrutinized so closely; otherwise we would all be without jobs.[4]

Research on false memories shows that the kind of memory error committed by Brian Williams is exceedingly commonplace. For over two decades now, numerous experiments have demonstrated the feasibility of creating memories for things that never took place (e.g., Gerrie et al., 2005; Laney & Loftus, 2010). The standard paradigm in such studies involves leading adult research participants to believe that they had had certain experiences during childhood, typically using the participants' own parents as ostensible sources of the information. Thus, participants have "recovered" memories of being lost in a shopping mall (Loftus & Pickrell, 1995), spending the night at the hospital (Hyman, Husband & Billings, 1995), witnessing demonic possession (Mazzoni, Loftus & Kirsch, 2001), being attacked by an animal (Porter, Yuille & Lehman, 1999), being saved from drowning (Heaps & Nash, 2001), and meeting Bugs Bunny at Disneyland (Braun, Ellis & Loftus, 2002). Typically, only a minority of participants acquire these false memories, but three points are worth noting: first, false memories do occur, at least for some individuals; second (as described in the following section), some people are more susceptible to false memories than others; and third, the false memory often persists even after participants learn that it was "implanted" by the researchers (Hyman et al., 1995; Loftus & Pickrell, 1995). The proportion of individuals who develop false memories varies across studies, but it typically ranges from 10 to 40 percent (e.g., Laney & Loftus, 2010). Moreover, the false memories can have behavioral consequences, such as shopping and food preferences (Laney & Loftus, 2010). For example, Geraerts, Bernstein and colleagues (2008) gave participants false feedback about getting sick from eating egg salad during childhood. Those who believed the feedback subsequently ate fewer egg salad sandwiches when given the opportunity to do so, even four months later.

A process that is commonly invoked to explain false memories is source monitoring judgments (Gerrie et al., 2005; Hyman & Loftus, 2002; Johnson, Raye, Mitchell & Ankudowich, 2012). Source monitoring involves identifying the source of information in memory (Johnson et al., 2012; Mitchell & Johnson, 2009). For example, did I learn about Brian Williams' false memory by reading the newspaper or in a conversation with my mother-in-law? Did I actually tell my wife that her mother called, or did I only imagine telling her? And most relevant to the recovered memory debate, did someone who recovers a memory of CSA actually experience it, or did she misattribute a suggestion from her therapist to an actual experience? People are generally poorer at remembering the source of information in memory than they are at remembering the information itself (Johnson et al., 2012; Johnson, Hashtroudi & Lindsay, 1993); of course, if they do not remember the information, then its source is basically moot. Consequently, source monitoring errors are common, and they have been used to explain false memories ranging from misinformation effects to rich false memories (Hyman & Loftus, 2002).

A second process that contributes to false memories is event typicality or plausibility (Hyman & Loftus, 2002; Lampinen, Faries, Neuschatz & Toglia, 2000; Neuschatz et al., 2002). The more plausible an event, and the more consistent it is with one's prior knowledge and expectations, the more likely one is to form a false memory of it. For example, Pezdek, Finger, and Hodge (1997) used the false feedback paradigm to see if the likelihood of successfully implanting false memories depended on the event's plausibility. The researchers asked Catholic and Jewish high school students about two false events said to have occurred when they were around eight years old. One event described a Catholic religious ritual (receiving Communion), whereas one described a Jewish religious ritual (saying Sabbath prayers). Although the majority of all participants recalled neither false event, there was a clear effect of event plausibility. Of those who remembered only one false event, Catholics were much more likely to remember the false Catholic event than the false Jewish event (7 vs. 1), whereas Jews were more likely to remember the false Jewish event than the false Catholic event (3 vs. 0). Thus, complicating Brian Williams' situation was the fact that, given the nature of his job, flying in a helicopter that came under fire was perfectly plausible, and he had clearly had similar experiences—at least in terms of flying in a helicopter in a dangerous region.

These findings suggest that it should be very difficult to convince people that they were victims of a crime, such as sexual abuse, when they were not, assuming that for most people this would be a highly implausible event. Indeed, more extreme false memories are harder to implant. Although one could not ethically lead people to have false memories of sexual victimization, Pezdek and colleagues (1997) conducted a follow-up study in which they suggested to (adult and older adolescent) participants that they had had a very unpleasant experience involving an enema as a child, due to overeating junk food. This is a particularly nice choice of event because of its similarity, in some respects, to sexual abuse: It is uncomfortable, potentially painful, embarrassing, and involves bodily invasion (it is, of course, dissimilar in other key respects). For comparison purposes, they also asked about a false event of having been lost in a mall while out shopping. Three of 20 participants remembered the false event about being lost, but none remembered the false enema, suggesting that it should be very difficult to implant false memories of a traumatic event, such as childhood sexual abuse. Nonetheless, plausibility is a malleable phenomenon (Mazzoni et al., 2001), and in today's society, CSA is, regrettably, far from implausible. What is, perhaps, less plausible is the combination of being abused *and* having no conscious recollection of the abuse; but most people find that to be plausible as well (Rubin & Berntsen, 2007). Moreover, recovered memories of abuse that never happened clearly occur, as the experiences of those who claim to recover memories of abuse and later retract those allegations attest (e.g., Lindsay & Read, 1994; Pendergrast, 1996; see also materials made available by the False Memory Syndrome Foundation, http://www.fmsfonline.org/).[5]

False memory cases and experimental research demonstrating the feasibility of implanting false memories raise a number of questions, most of which revolve around characteristics of the remembered event, the rememberer, and the circumstances of the memory retrieval. Two of these questions are particularly important: first, who is more or less likely to develop a false memory? And second, can people tell true and false memories apart?

Who Has False Memories?

Because we all experience false memory, at least in the sense of misremembering details of an event and even remembering relatively mundane events that did not occur, false memory can be thought of as a part of "normal" memory processes. Nonetheless, there are categories of "abnormal" false memory, which occurs due to a pathological condition (Kopelman, 1999). For example, individuals with brain damage (especially to the frontal lobe) may confabulate (see chapter 6), and individuals with schizophrenia may experience delusions. In both of these instances, the person subjectively remembers something that demonstrably did not occur—a false memory. These pathological cases share certain characteristics with "normal" false memory, but they are best viewed as conceptually distinct (Kopelman, 1999). The focus here is on false memories that occur in the absence of underlying pathology.

Even in these cases, some individuals are more susceptible to false memories than others (Davis & Loftus, 2007). For example, misinformation leads to more memory errors among children (Ceci & Bruck, 1995; Ceci & Friedman, 2000) and elderly adults (Wylie et al., 2014) than among young adults. The tendency to experience false memories is also fairly stable over time; that is, someone who has a false memory on one occasion is more likely to have one on another occasion, compared to someone who did not have a false memory on the first occasion (Blair, Lenton & Hastie, 2002). Not surprisingly, then, susceptibility to false memories reflects certain stable personality and cognitive dispositions. Some research shows that the likelihood of forming false memories is related to overall memory ability or intelligence, with persons with poorer memory or lower intelligence being more susceptible to memory errors like misinformation effects (Davis & Loftus, 2007). In terms of personality variables, findings are somewhat mixed and effect sizes tend to be relatively modest, but some research shows that neuroticism, self-monitoring, empathy, a tendency toward dissociation, and absorption are all related to the tendency to form false memories (Davis & Loftus, 2007; Hyman & Billings, 1998).

Even relatively common and transitory experiences can affect the susceptibility to false memories, such as temporarily working under a heavy cognitive load or having one's attentional resources strained (Davis & Loftus, 2007). Specific experiences and beliefs also predict the likelihood of having a false memory. For example, children who believe more firmly in the Tooth Fairy are more prone to recount fantastical occurrences associated with losing a tooth (e.g., "She [the Tooth Fairy] flied in the window") and to recall actually hearing and seeing the Tooth Fairy, even when they are trying to be truthful in their retellings (Principe & Smith, 2008).

Of the myriad experiences that are, or might be, related to false memory formation, hypnosis (discussed in more detail in the next section) has probably been investigated more than any other. The scientific consensus is that hypnosis makes people more susceptible to false memories, such as those elicited in the misinformation effect paradigm (e.g., Scoboria, Mazzoni, Kirsch & Milling, 2002). And a large number of individuals who recover full-blown memories of past events that turn out to be false—such as memories of alien abduction—do so under hypnosis (Clancy, 2005; Newman & Baumeister, 1996). Although the precise mechanisms underlying the enhanced suggestibility of hypnotized persons have not yet been fully explained, despite extensive commentary (e.g., Faigman et al., 2014; Mazzoni & Lynn, 2007), the negative effects on memory of hypnosis are no longer in dispute (as described below, hypnosis can also have positive memory and therapeutic effects).

Because humans are a naturally imaginative species and imagery is used in a number of potentially suggestive therapeutic techniques (e.g., guided imagery, hypnosis, age regression, etc.; see Lindsey & Read, 1994), a number of studies have focused on the role of imagination in contributing to false memories. These studies have found that simply imagining a fictional event makes people more likely to believe that the event genuinely occurred (Garry, Manning, Loftus & Sherman, 1996; Mazzoni & Memon, 2003; Wade, Garry, Read & Lindsay, 2002). This "imagination inflation" phenomenon is consistent with research showing that people with a relatively high propensity for visual imagery are more susceptible to misinformation effects (e.g., Dobson & Markham, 1993; Hyman & Billings, 1998; Tomes & Katz, 1997). Although some research suggests that it is more likely for plausible than for implausible events (Pezdek, Blandón-Gitlin & Gabbay, 2006), imagination inflation occurs for both mundane and bizarre actions (Seamon, Philbin & Harrison, 2006; Thomas & Loftus, 2002). Encouraging innocent criminal suspects to imagine how they would have committed a crime can even make them come to believe that they actually committed the crime and falsely confess (Henkel & Coffman, 2004; Kassin & Gudjonsson, 2004; Kopelman, 1999; see chapter 9).

This is important because psychotherapists sometimes do ask clients to imagine an instance of victimization in an attempt to help them recover repressed memories of abuse (Lindsay & Read, 1994). Once imagined, however, the event can come to be remembered as real. Moreover, people who recover memories of abuse, especially if they recover those memories in therapy, are more likely to demonstrate false memories on other kinds of tasks, such as the DRM paradigm, suggesting a general predisposition to form false memories in some people (Clancy et al., 2002; Clancy, Schacter, McNally, & Pitman, 2000; Gallo, 2010; Geraerts, 2012; Geraerts, Raymaekers, & Merckelbach, 2008). Individuals who score higher on measures of depression or schizotypy are also more likely to have false memories (Clancy et al., 2002; Jelinek et al., 2009). Interestingly, merely having a history of being a trauma victim, even if the trauma led to PTSD, does not make false memories more likely (Jelinek et al., 2009). Thus, trauma, *per se*, does not increase the risk of false memories, but other things that might make one likely to seek psychotherapy, such as depression, do. Suggestive therapeutic practices can then make the risk even greater among these already vulnerable individuals.

Of course, imagining experiences that never occurred, even ones that are negative and potentially traumatic, does not occur only in therapy; it is a natural cognitive process that everyone engages in, although some do it more frequently and vividly than others. Another experience that everyone has, at one time or another, is sleep deprivation, whether due to work/school obligations, social activities, illness, or some other factor. Indeed, inadequate sleep is so prevalent that the Centers for Disease Control and Prevention (2015) have declared it a public health epidemic, with important consequences for health, safety, and cognitive functioning. Individuals who are sleep-deprived are more susceptible to false memories, whether the lack of sleep occurs naturally (i.e., they had restricted sleep the night before the study) or as part of the experimental procedure (e.g., Diekelmann et al., 2008; Frenda et al., 2014). Sleep deprivation seems to contribute to false memories by affecting both event encoding and retrieval processes (Frenda et al., 2014); that is, it impairs how well the event is stored in memory, making it more vulnerable to intrusions, and it also makes it harder to remember whether something genuinely occurred.

Can People Tell True and False Memories Apart?

If people remember something as true that did not, in fact, occur, then they are *ipso facto* unable to tell some false memories from true ones. Nonetheless, it is possible for true and false memories to differ in ways that could enable either the rememberers themselves or observers to tell the memories apart. As described in chapter 8, observers (e.g., mock jurors) are not very adept at distinguishing accurate from inaccurate eyewitnesses. An inaccurate eyewitness is essentially someone who has a false memory, and by and large, observers attempting to distinguish true from false memories perform relatively poorly, although any comparison is complicated by the fact that in most studies, the true and false memories are for different events (Laney & Loftus, 2010). Clinicians do not have a special talent for it (Lindsay & Read, 1995) nor, obviously, do those holding the false memories themselves. No doubt the reason it is so difficult for rememberers or observers to tell them apart is that the two types of memories simply do not differ all that much: They are largely comparable in their emotional content, in terms of the level of stressfulness (Porter, Yuille & Lehman, 1999), general emotionality (Laney & Loftus, 2008), and specific emotions (Laney & Loftus, 2008); their amount and type of detail (Lampinen et al., 2000; Loftus & Bernstein, 2005); the physiological responses that accompany them (e.g., heart rate; McNally et al., 2004); and how long they last (Geraerts, Bernstein, et al., 2008; Laney et al., 2008).

True and false memories do differ in some respects, enabling people to discriminate between them to an extent: True memories seem sharper and more detailed than false memories (Laney & Loftus, 2008), they are held with greater confidence (Laney & Loftus, 2008), they are rehearsed more (Heaps & Nash, 2001), and their phenomenological characteristics differ in some respects as the retention interval increases (Neuschatz et al., 2002). Some studies have found linguistic differences in the reporting of true versus false memories (e.g., hedges, number of words, use of the first person), but other studies have not (Laney & Loftus, 2010). Neuroimaging research has identified some differences in the brain activity that accompanies true versus false remembering, but this body of research is also somewhat variable (Johnson et al., 2012; Laney & Loftus, 2010; Mitchell & Johnson, 2009; Schacter, Chamberlain, Gaesser & Gerlach, 2012; Schacter & Slotnick, 2004; chapter 4 covers the neurophysiological processes involved in implanting false memories, as well as in erasing true memories).

Overall, then, despite a few modest predictors of true versus false memories, the evidence on people's ability to discriminate between them is less than compelling, leading to the conclusion that "No study has yet found a specific factor that will reliably signal a true or false memory. That is, just because a memory is confidently held, vivid, detailed, self-referent, and emotional, that does not mean that the memory is true. Likewise, a lack of any or all of these factors does not make a memory false" (Laney & Loftus, 2010, p. 180). As scientists develop better imaging tools, analytic techniques, and individual difference measures, our ability to discriminate true from false memories might improve (Bernstein & Loftus, 2009), but at present, it is not something we are very good at.

HYPNOSIS AND REPRESSION

Many fictional portrayals of repression, as well as real-life cases, also involve hypnosis, which is one of the leading treatments for repressed memory and popularly believed to be a reliable means of uncovering repressed material (e.g., Golding et al., 1996). Thus, although repression and hypnosis are distinct constructs—one is a proposed psychological defense mechanism for dealing with anxiety-producing thoughts and memories, whereas the other is a therapeutic technique—they are inextricably linked, perhaps because they both rose to prominence in the late nineteenth century and are associated with the work of Sigmund Freud.

Hypnosis has a long and fascinating history. As noted previously, researchers and clinicians besides Freud worked on repression, and the same is true of hypnosis. Hypnosis has been used therapeutically (e.g., as an anesthetic agent) since the mid-1800s, and the basic principles and phenomena go back at least as far as the treatment methods of Anton Mesmer in the 1770s, which he believed involved animal magnetism, but that we now refer to as mesmerism (Hunt, 2007). Starting in the 1860s, a number of medical practitioners, especially in France (e.g., Auguste Liébeault, Hippolyte Bernheim, Jean Martin Charcot, Alfred Binet, and Pierre Janet), popularized hypnosis for the treatment of hysteria and related neuroses (Lawson, Graham & Baker, 2007; Mazzoni & Lynn, 2007). Charcot taught hypnosis to Freud, as well as to other influential early psychologists like Binet and Janet. Freud used hypnosis in his early psychoanalytic work (e.g., Freud & Breuer, 1895/2000), yet ironically—in light of his close association with the practice in the popular imagination—he abandoned it relatively early on in favor of other techniques such as free association and dream interpretation (Gay, 1988; Hunt, 2007). There are many methods of inducing hypnosis (Gafner, 2010; Gibbons & Lynn, 2010). The classic technique has the participant fixate on an object, such as a pendulum, pocket watch, or pen. Other methods, such as progressive relaxation, are now just as common (Gibbons & Lynn, 2010).

The relationship between hypnosis and memory has, by now, been fairly well established. Many (though not all) well-controlled research studies show that hypnotized participants correctly recall more information than nonhypnotized participants (Mazzoni & Lynn, 2007). Thus, hypnosis produces a mnemonic benefit. This benefit comes, however, at significant cost. Hypnotized participants also make more errors, ranging from minor inaccuracies to rich false memories (Mazzoni & Lynn, 2007). At least in part, hypnotized participants adopt a lower response criterion, leading them to accept and report more information as genuine memories (Scoboria et al., 2002), and they are more likely to engage in repeated retrieval efforts (Erdelyi, 1994). These processes lead to an increase in both accurate and inaccurate reports, but the latter tend to outnumber the former (Mazzoni & Lynn, 2007). Hypnotized individuals also tend to be more confident about their recollections—false as well as true ones—than nonhypnotized persons. The tendency of hypnosis to elicit false memories is more pronounced in individuals who are moderately or highly suggestible than in low-suggestible persons (Mazzoni & Lynn, 2007).

The two most common situations for the mnemonic use of hypnosis are in forensic and clinical contexts. In forensic contexts, hypnosis is used to help an individual who witnessed a crime—as either a bystander or a victim—to remember details of the event. It may also be used, though less often, with criminal suspects. In clinical contexts, it is used to help mentally ill individuals remember autobiographical information that the therapist believes might be responsible for their current symptoms. In the case of recovered memory of trauma, the legal and the psychological often intersect, in the form of someone who recovers a memory, in the course of hypnotic therapy, of witnessing or being a victim of a crime.

Hypnosis in Psychotherapy

In addition to its mnemonic uses, hypnosis is used to treat a variety of medical and psychological conditions. According to the American Society of Clinical Hypnosis, hypnosis may be used for trauma, anxiety, depression, bed-wetting, athletic performance, smoking cessation, obesity and weight control, sexual dysfunctions, sleep disorders, and concentration difficulties.[6] For many of these conditions, hypnosis has proven to be effective. For example, it is one of the more effective smoking cessation methods (Viswesvaran & Schmidt, 1992).

Most of these uses of hypnosis do not employ it as a mnemonic device, but others do, especially in treating clients who have experienced some sort of trauma, as a means of helping them remember aspects of the trauma that they might have forgotten—particularly if the forgetting is presumably due to repression. In some cases, it is used to help them remember an entire event of which they have no recollection; that is, they have forgotten the trauma, but in the opinion of the therapist, a repressed trauma might be contributing to their current symptoms. Recovering the memory is then seen as an essential part of the healing process. Significant numbers of psychologists and other mental health professionals in the United States use hypnosis to help clients remember memories of trauma, such as CSA. For example, Poole et al. (1995) found that roughly one-third of American psychologists (across two samples) used hypnosis; significantly fewer British psychologists (5 %) used it, although a majority of both groups reported using some sort of memory recovery technique to help clients remember CSA.

Hypnosis and the Law

Estimates of the prevalence of hypnosis in the forensic context (i.e., for purposes of a police investigation) are hard to come by, but it has been at least somewhat widely used since the 1970s (Lynn, Neuschatz & Fite, 2002; Mazzoni & Lynn, 2007; McConkey & Sheehan, 1995). When used early in an investigation, as in developing leads, hypnosis is relatively unproblematic: false leads will presumably be rooted out, good leads will produce corroborating evidence, not all investigations lead to prosecution, and many prosecutions are resolved before going to trial. More problems arise when a case involving hypnosis winds up in court.

The most common way that hypnosis comes up in court is when the witness herself testifies about events that she remembered, in whole or in part, as a result of hypnosis (though the hypnotist might also testify). The courts vary widely in their approach to such hypnotically refreshed testimony, but on the whole, they are skeptical (Faigman et al., 2014). They are particularly concerned about the risk of heightened suggestibility, overconfidence on the part of the witness, and undue influence on the jury. These concerns are largely the same whether the hypnosis took place in a forensic or therapeutic context (e.g., *Borawick v. Shay*, 1995). Thus, the majority of jurisdictions either do not allow hypnotically refreshed testimony or admit it only if certain safeguards were in place during the hypnotic session (Faigman et al., 2014; see, e.g., *State v. Hurd*, 1981). To some extent, these safeguards mirror guidelines for forensic hypnosis that have been promulgated by professional organizations, which are designed to protect the welfare of the subject, establish standards and qualifications for the hypnotist, specify procedures (e.g., videotaping), and minimize suggestibility (e.g., McConkey & Sheehan, 1995). Adherence to such guidelines both improves the reliability of the hypnotically refreshed memories and increases their likelihood of being admitted as evidence in court.

INTERVENTIONS: FALSE MEMORY REDUCTION
AND REPRESSION EDUCATION

Most false memories are benign, but some, such as false memories of trauma, are malignant. Their consequences for the rememberer and for others, such as loved ones and alleged perpetrators (who are sometimes one and the same), can be catastrophic. It would be nice to reduce all sorts of false memories—who would not want to remember better?—but these are the ones in particular need of attention. One obvious means of reducing the incidence of false memories of trauma is to curtail the use of highly suggestive therapeutic techniques that lack efficacy and are likely to elicit false memories (Lilienfeld, 2007; Lindsay & Read, 1994; 1995). Because of the way in which professional psychology is (and in many respects is not) regulated, restricting potentially harmful therapies is challenging (Lilienfeld, 2007; Lindsay & Read, 1995). Nonetheless, it would offer protection to psychotherapy clients, a class of individuals who are, on average, relatively vulnerable psychologically.

Outside of the therapeutic context, certain mnemonic techniques might be effective. For example, instructing participants on the mnemonic features (e.g., sensory characteristics) that discriminate between true and false memories reduces false recognition on a DRM task (Lane et al., 2008). Many mnemonic techniques involve the use of imagery, which raises the possibility of imagination inflation; however, asking participants to mentally reinstate the context of a false event does not make false memory more likely (Sharman & Powell, 2013) and can even make people resistant to misinformation (Memon, Zaragoza, Clifford & Kidd, 2010). Thus, imagination is not invariably harmful; when used in the context of a structured mnemonic interview, it can improve memory for true events without necessarily leading to more memory errors (e.g., Fisher & Schreiber, 2007; Memon, Meissner & Fraser, 2010).

Although high-profile recovered memory cases are a relatively recent phenomenon, repression has been part of the popular consciousness for more than 100 years. That would seem to suggest that people are sufficiently well educated about how repression is supposed to work, and also that it is difficult to educate them about the lack of empirical support for repression. The plethora of fictional portrayals of repression in literature and film, as well as the large number of therapists who ascribe to a psychodynamic orientation and use techniques like hypnosis to uncover repressed memories, suggests that the construct has a certain intuitive and artistic appeal. To be sure, it makes a more compelling story than that of an abuse victim who remembered the abuse but simply never told anyone about the experience, or who forgot it for more mundane reasons. Popular depictions of repression are therefore unlikely to go away any time soon.

Unfortunately, longitudinal studies of repression beliefs do not exist, and the surveys that have been conducted do not span a long enough time period, or use comparable items, to determine whether beliefs about repression are changing over time. What comparisons have been done suggest little change (e.g., in undergraduate students' belief in the accuracy of repressed memories in 1995 vs. 2011; Patihis et al., 2014). Nonetheless, there are causes for optimism. Surveys of people's naïve beliefs about memory show that they tend to believe in repression, but when faced with a specific case of repression allegedly leading to a recovered memory, they are rather skeptical, finding an abuse victim who repressed memory of the abuse less credible than a victim who remembered it all along (e.g., Bornstein & Muller, 2001). Moreover, simply serving as mock jurors in a recovered memory case made people more skeptical about repression after trial than they were beforehand (Bornstein & Muller, 2001). Along similar lines, individuals in countries with relatively high exposure to the recovered memory debate endorse repression myths less than individuals in countries where there is less public awareness of the debate (Nachson et al., 2007). And more highly educated individuals are less likely to endorse false beliefs about repression than those with less education (Patihis et al., 2014).

These findings suggest that even though popular media continue to perpetuate myths about repression, many consumers of those products (books, movies, etc.) see them merely as entertainment and not as an accurate representation of the underlying science. To some extent, education is taking place naturally, albeit slowly, as the recovered memory debate enters the public sphere.

CONCLUSIONS

One leading scholar of recovered memory commented that "The concept of traumatic amnesia may be little more than psychiatric folklore" (McNally, 2004, p. 100). It is also a part of popular folklore. Repression is one of the most firmly entrenched beliefs about memory. According to Laurence and colleagues (1998, p. 323), "Freud achieved what no other person has been able to achieve since: he influenced the minds of therapists, clients, and the lay public for generations to come." Given this widespread acceptance, it is also unsurprising that repression has featured prominently in popular films and literature. It has been portrayed as a common response to trauma in numerous books and films, most of which unquestioningly accept the reliability of the subsequently recovered memories. Nevertheless, there is a dearth of reliable evidence that trauma victims respond by repressing their memory of the event. On the whole, then, there is little evidence that a trauma victim like Tommy in The Who's rock opera would respond to witnessing a murder committed by his father by repressing it.

Recovered memories are also somewhat suspect, albeit less so than repression. They are not a unitary phenomenon but a diverse category of memory experiences, and they are notoriously hard to corroborate, but genuine instances of recovered memory do appear to exist (e.g., Schooler et al., 1997). Genuine recovered memories are more likely for memories that return spontaneously, as opposed to during therapy (Geraerts, Raymaekers & Merckelbach., 2008). The occasional genuine recovered memory case notwithstanding, many apparent cases of recovered memory do not involve complete forgetting of the event during the intervening period; rather, people often forget the previous times when they remembered the event (Geraerts, Raymaekers, & Merckelbach, 2008). Whereas the majority of trauma victims remember it all along (e.g., Berwin, 2007; Connolly & Read, 2006), this subset "forgot it all along" (Schooler et al., 1997).

Although repression and recovered memory thus have relatively little empirical support, false memories are very real. They reflect normal reconstructive memory processes that are usually adaptive and rarely harmful. However, in some situations they can be quite damaging, and some people are more susceptible to them than others. One of the many perplexing things about recovered and false memories is why someone would "want" (in quotes because the role of volition is unclear) to remember a traumatic event that never occurred. Why would someone remember being shot down in a helicopter unless it actually happened? Who in his or her right mind would "invent" (again in quotes because of the questionable role of volition) a memory of being sexually abused as a child? It is possible that a minority of sincerely held false memories produce secondary gain, such as positive attention or retaliation against an alleged abuser. However, the vast majority are simply the result of naturally occurring cognitive operations and motivational factors, such as reconstructive memory, the mind's efforts to make sense of the world around us, and the search for a comprehensible explanation for ills one might be currently experiencing (Clancy, 2005; Ofshe & Watters, 1994). Discredited recovered memory claims and research on false memory show conclusively that not all memories can be trusted.

Despite the broad acceptance of hypnosis, by mental health professionals and the public alike, it is problematic from both a forensic and a therapeutic perspective. More often than not, hypnotically refreshed testimony is not admissible in court, in large part because of concerns about hypnotized persons' heightened suggestibility. Hypnosis has legitimate therapeutic uses, and there is some evidence that it can be a beneficial mnemonic tool; but as a part of recovered memory therapy, the risk of creating a false memory outweighs any potential benefit. In treating trauma victims, hypnosis and other memory recovery techniques should be used sparingly if at all (Lilienfeld, 2007; Lindsay & Read, 1995).

As many commentators have pointed out (e.g., Belli, 2012; Gerry et al., 2005), issues associated with the constellation of repression, recovered memory, false memory, and hypnosis have important theoretical and practical implications. With respect to theory, the issues speak to why we forget, how we forget, what we forget (e.g., trauma vs. more mundane events), the usefulness of various retrieval strategies (e.g., hypnosis), and the accuracy of what we remember. The practical components of the recovered/false memory debate are many and varied. Most prominently, many recovered memory claims involve victimization, and they consequently can initiate a sequence of events (e.g., investigation, prosecution, incarceration) that are costly to the individuals involved (the alleged victims and perpetrators, as well as other family members) and to society. These costs may be worthwhile if the claims are true, but not if they are false. And the psychological costs of erroneously believing that one has been traumatized—often at the hands of a trusted family member—are incalculable. Moreover, the very therapeutic techniques that elicit false memories of trauma can obscure the very real mental health concerns that brought the client to therapy in the first place.

When it comes to remembering different kinds of events, memories of trauma have no special pride of place, despite popular expectations that traumatic memories can be repressed and subsequently recovered with a high degree of veridicality. Memory is a reconstructive process. That reconstruction can lead to errors. And in extreme cases, it can lead to remembering entire events that did not occur, with damaging consequences for the rememberer as well as others implicated by the memory, such as alleged perpetrators. Repression, recovered memory, false memory, and hypnosis constitute an unholy tetrad that is perpetuated by popular portrayals of the phenomena, as well as, to some extent, common therapeutic practices. The tetrad's influence on society is difficult to mitigate because of how firmly entrenched Freud's ideas are and the role of fundamental cognitive processes in producing false memories. Nonetheless, it is incumbent on memory researchers and proponents of evidence-based therapy to try.

NOTES

1. To compensate for his sensory deficits, Tommy's other senses become keener. For example, "that deaf, dumb and blind kid, sure plays a mean pinball" ("Pinball Wizard"). The movie version of *Tommy*, released in 1975, starred Roger Daltrey, Ann-Margret, Elton John, and Tina Turner. The Who's album by the same name was

released in 1969 and performed live before that. Although it is not the first cinematic treatment of repression, it is the one with the best music.

2. Golding et al. (1996) apparently asked only about exposure to "real-world" cases; participants did not report on their exposure to fictional portrayals in film, literature, and so on.

3. A number of Freud's predecessors and contemporaries described repression and related phenomena in very similar terms, most notably Pierre Janet, Josef Breuer, and Carl Jung. Freud's work on the topic was original in many respects, but it was also a product of the zeitgeist.

4. After his suspension, Williams remained employed by NBC but was assigned a less visible and desirable position. For a thoughtful discussion of the Williams incident, see McWilliams (2015).

5. It is always possible, of course, that abuse did actually occur in cases where purported victims retract their allegations. There are doubtless as many reasons for retracting a recovered memory claim as there are for making one in the first place. Just as it is not my aim to argue that most (or even many) recovered memory claims are false, it is not my aim to argue that most (or even many) retractions are genuine. Nonetheless, at least some retractions have occurred in the face of overwhelming evidence that the originally alleged incident did not occur (e.g., Pendergrast, 1996).

6. See http://www.asch.net/Public/GeneralInfoonHypnosis/HypnosisInPsycho-therapyAndBehavioralMedicine.aspx.

Chapter 4

Memory and the Brain

Implants and Erasure

Myth: It Is Possible to Implant Memories in the Brain

Related Myths: Memories Can Be Transferred from a Donor to a Host Organism; It Is Possible Selectively to Erase Memories

Nepenthe is a potion used to induce forgetfulness. It comes from the Greek ne- (not) + penthos (grief or sorrow). Hence the narrator of Edgar Allan Poe's "The Raven" longs to "quaff, oh quaff this kind nepenthe and forget this lost Lenore! Quoth the Raven 'Nevermore.'" In the absence of nepenthe, many people turn to alcohol, like the protagonist of Paula Hawkins' (2015) novel *The Girl on the Train* (made into a 2016 movie starring Emily Blunt), who drinks to forget and suffers from alcoholic blackouts. The difference is that alcohol is usually only a short-term solution; the memories often come back when sober. Nepenthe, on the other hand, appears to be a means of permanently erasing painful memories, at least according to Poe.

As I have argued previously (see especially chapters 2 and 3), we forget discrete memories—painful, happy, or neutral—all the time. But that is very different from deliberately targeting certain memories for erasure. For example, the main characters in *Eternal Sunshine of the Spotless Mind* (2004), portrayed by Jim Carrey and Kate Winslet, undergo selective erasure of all memories involving one another after their relationship falls apart. Can forgetting really be that targeted and precise?

Until recently, selective erasure of memories was the stuff of science fiction—a myth. However, recent pharmacological advances are making it more of a reality. Although it does not work as cleanly as portrayed in films such as *Eternal Sunshine of the Spotless Mind*, research on memory suppression and directed forgetting suggests that it is indeed possible to lessen the chances of remembering unwanted material. Some drugs are also capable of essentially erasing memories of negative emotional events, while leaving other memories relatively intact (Eichenbaum, 2012).

Just as many people believe that specific memories in the brain can be targeted for elimination, they also believe that memories can be inserted into the brain. The issue here is not so much the creation of false memories as a result of suggestion—as discussed in chapter 3, false memories, even detailed memories of events that did not occur, are not uncommon. Some individuals are more susceptible to these false memories than others, but by and large they result from normal cognitive processes. The focus here is on the physiological rather than the cognitive—can something be done to the brain to implant a memory, or to transfer a memory from a donor to a host organism?

These assumptions have served as the premise for a number of science fiction films (e.g., *Total Recall*). Interestingly, contemporary neuroscience research suggests that the ideas are not quite as far off as they once seemed. Animal studies and a few clinical trials (e.g., with Parkinson's patients) show that brain tissue can be transplanted, with the effect of improving memory performance; however, discrete memories do not survive the transfer from donor to recipient. Nor can they be passed down genetically from one generation to the next, as in *Assassin's Creed* (the video game and 2016 film).

Other movies on the implantation theme, such as *Inception* (2010), raise legitimate psychological issues such as source monitoring (i.e., the ability to identify the source of one's memories). As with popular depictions of the erasure of unwanted memories, *Inception*'s portrayal of these phenomena grossly exceeds their reality, but there is nonetheless a kernel of truth, in that people routinely have difficulty determining whether they thought of something themselves, obtained it from an external source, or dreamt it (Mitchell & Johnson, 2009).

This chapter is divided into two parts. The first part describes popular beliefs about memory implantation, followed by a review of the scientific literature on the topic; the second part describes popular beliefs about memory erasure, followed by a discussion of the science on that topic. Both parts include examples from popular media portrayals that perpetuate the myths.

MEMORY IMPLANTATION

Beliefs about Memory Implantation

Can memories be implanted by chemical, surgical, or mechanical means? Several science fiction films are based on this premise. For example, in *Total Recall*, Douglas Quaid (portrayed by Arnold Schwarzenegger in the 1990 original, and by Colin Farrell in the 2012 remake; both films were adapted from a short story by Philip K. Dick) visits a company that uses a machine to implant fake memories of a fantasy life—except that it turns out the "fake" memories might actually be real. *Inception* (2010) does something similar, but within the context of dreaming—the characters' dreams are engineered, and the line between dream and reality blurs. And in the recent film *Self/less* (2015), Damian's (Ben Kingsley) entire mind, along with his store of memories, is transferred into another's body (Ryan Reynolds), which is supposedly nothing more than an "empty vessel." Trouble ensues when the host body's memories begin to intrude; the doctor who oversaw the procedure describes these as mere hallucinations, a common side effect, which can be controlled with medication (i.e., the erasure myth). Needless to say, it is not so simple, and the lives and memories of the two characters become entwined.[1] In an even more extreme version, in *Transcendence* (2014), Will Caster's (Johnny Depp) consciousness is transferred intact to a computer—again with predictably unpredictable consequences.

These depictions treat memory like a commodity: If one person can sell another person his car, thereby transferring full ownership, then it should also be possible to move memories around from one to another, or to create them *de novo*. The films reflect a belief that memories can be implanted or transferred. If, according to the popular view, one person's memories can be placed in another person's body, then the converse must also be true—transplanting part of another person's body presumably carries its memories with it. A number of films, novels, and even nonfiction works have relied on this premise of cellular memory—that is, the idea that memories reside in discrete, portable body cells (Della Salla & Beyerstein, 2007).[2] In the prototypical version, the organ recipient acquires knowledge and personality attributes from the donor (Della Salla & Beyerstein, 2007). These transplantation-acquired characteristics are sometimes innocuous (e.g., novel food preferences) but often more insidious (e.g., murderous impulses).

Two questions on the survey described in chapter 1 addressed different aspects of beliefs about memory implantation and transfer: "It is possible to 'implant' memories in a person's mind, for things that they did not actually experience, by brain surgery" and "People who receive organ transplants (e.g., heart, liver, cornea, etc.) can have memories for things that the organ donor experienced." Participants' knowledge regarding these phenomena was not especially good. Only 50 percent knew that it is impossible to implant memories in a person's mind by brain surgery, and only 69 percent were aware that people who receive organ transplants cannot have memories for things that the organ donor experienced.

These data, along with popular portrayals of memory implants, indicate a widespread misunderstanding about what is going on in the brain with respect to true, as opposed to false, memories, and how—not to mention where—memories are stored in the body. In particular, the implantation myth raises issues related to the neurophysiology of false memories, the possibility of transplanting brain tissue and its consequences for cognitive functioning, and the relationship between memory and dreaming. The remainder of this section covers each of these issues in turn.

The Neurophysiology of False Memories

Even if it is not possible to implant a memory by brain surgery or organ transplantation, the question remains—what do false memories implanted by psychological techniques (e.g., suggestion) look like in the brain? True and false memories might not differ much phenomenologically (i.e., they both feel real and have largely comparable subjective characteristics; see chapter 3), but do they differ at the physical level? Considerable research has used brain imaging to compare the neurophysiological characteristics of true and false memories. This body of research is not entirely consistent (e.g., Johnson et al., 2012; Laney & Loftus, 2010; Mitchell & Johnson, 2009; Schacter et al., 2012; Schacter & Slotnick, 2004); overall, it indicates that there are some physical differences between true and false memories, but those differences are relatively modest and not obtained in all studies.

For example, Schacter and Slotnick (2004; see also Schacter et al., 2012) reviewed neuroimaging (e.g., fMRI) and electrophysiology (e.g., event-related potential) studies of false recognition, many of which used the DRM paradigm to create false memories for words. Compared to false recognition, true recognition was often (but not always) associated with greater activity in brain regions associated with sensory processing. This observation is consistent with the *sensory reactivation* hypothesis, according to which true memories' greater sensory/perceptual detail reflects the reactivation of sensory/perceptual processes that were more heavily engaged during the establishment of true (versus false) memories (Schacter et al., 2012).

More broadly, the sensory reactivation hypothesis is compatible with the reality monitoring approach (discussed in more detail below), which concerns distinguishing between true memories of actually experienced events and imagination. Imagining something can mimic the brain activity of several structures (e.g., the hippocampus) associated with true memories (Gonsalves et al., 2004; Schacter et al., 2012), which explains how at least some reality monitoring errors occur—true memories and imagined ones can seem the same to the brain. Yet despite this overlap, there are also subtle differences in the neural activity associated with true versus imaginary or false memories (Schacter et al., 2012). Several brain regions, such as the hippocampus and medial temporal lobes, contribute to false recognition, whereas the prefrontal cortex is involved in the monitoring activity that ordinarily enables us to distinguish true from false memories (Schacter & Slotnick, 2004). Damage to the prefrontal cortex can impair the ability to tell truth from fiction (see chapter 6).

Recently, Ramirez et al. (2013) took a somewhat different approach to examining true versus false memories in the brain. Rather than measuring neural activity for the two different kinds of memory, they asked whether it is possible to create a false memory in the brain, in the absence of a corresponding experience. To do that, they first identified cells in the brains of mice (specifically, in the dentate gyrus of the hippocampus) that stored the animals' memory of a particular box. They then placed them in a different box, where they activated those same cells while simultaneously administering a foot shock. On subsequently returning to the first, previously safe box, the animals showed a conditioned fear response, whereas a control group (without the cell activation) did not. In other words, animals in the experimental group acquired a false memory of being shocked in a place where they had not previously had an aversive experience—yet the memory seemed perfectly real to the mice, and the brain activity was similar to that for naturally conditioned fear (for a nontechnical description of this research and related work, see Noonan, 2014).

These lines of research raise the question of whether a certain kind of brain activity reliably indicates a false memory—that is, "is there a neural signature of false memory retrieval" (Schacter et al., 2012, p. 243)? According to Daniel Schacter, who along with his colleagues is the leading investigator of this question, the answer is complicated. On the one hand, there are "striking similarities in the brain activity that accompanies true, false, and imaginary memories" (Schacter et al., 2012, p. 249). The research by Ramirez and colleagues (2013) on the creation of false memories via neural activation is powerful evidence of this similarity. On the other hand, a number of studies show different patterns of activity associated with each kind of memory— true, false, and imaginary. At present, there is no clearly legible signature denoting a false memory, but as research advances and technology improves (e.g., better imaging techniques), there might be in the future. When (or if) that day comes, a reliable test for identifying false memories would be incredibly valuable, in legal and other contexts (e.g., in investigating claims of victimization based on recovered memories, as discussed in chapter 3).

Memory and Brain Tissue Transplants

Transplantation science has advanced exponentially in the last few decades. Doctors can now transplant kidneys, hearts, lungs, livers, skins, hands, corneas, and faces; they cannot, however, transplant brains. Nonetheless, they can transplant modest amounts of brain tissue, and animal research on the topic dates back 125 years, with concerted research on the topic beginning around the 1970s (Oliveira & Hodges, 2005). These studies have yielded often surprising consequences for memory performance.

For ethical reasons—most prominently the risks to recipients and the common use of embryonic tissue as donors—most of this research has been conducted with nonhuman animals.[3] For example, Santucci, Kanof, and Haroutunian (1991) performed surgery on male rats to produce bilateral lesions in an area of the cortex known as the nucleus basalis of Meynert (NBM); a control group received sham surgery (i.e., they underwent a comparable procedure without incurring brain damage). Seven to ten days later, some of the animals received a transplant of cholinergic-rich, embryonic ventral forebrain tissue (as described in the following chapters on amnesia, acetylcholine is a neurotransmitter that is heavily involved in memory functioning). NBM damage impaired subsequent performance on several spatial memory tasks (e.g., learning which arm of a Y-maze contained water), but the deficit was reduced in animals that received the transplant. The location of the embryonic tissue appears to make a difference (Hodges et al., 1991; Patel, Clayton & Krebs, 1997); transplantation of cholinergic-poor embryonic tissue, even if taken from an area of the brain that is heavily involved in memory (e.g., the hippocampus), does not yield benefits, whereas cholinergic-rich tissue coming from different areas of the brain can produce improvements (Hodges et al., 1991).

Improved memory functioning following brain tissue transplants has been observed in multiple species of mammals (McDaniel, 1988) and birds (Patel et al., 1997). The precise mechanism(s) by which brain tissue transplants facilitate recovery from brain damage are unclear. The new tissue might replace lost cells, enable the reconstruction of damaged neural circuits, replace deficient neurotransmitters, or stimulate growth in surviving tissue to compensate for the loss (McDaniel, 1988; Oliveira & Hodges, 2005). There is also some evidence that transplants do more to enhance recipients' learning of new information than to restore memory for previously stored information (Gibbs, Yu, & Cotman, 1987), although recovery of predamage memories is possible, depending on the type of task (Patel et al., 1997).

The promise of brain tissue transplants for alleviating memory problems is perhaps greatest for the treatment of disorders like Alzheimer's disease (see chapter 7), and transplants have been tried in animals genetically engineered to develop Alzheimer's. Embryonic neural stem cells transplanted into the hippocampus of mice with an Alzheimer's gene differentiate into mature neurons, improve memory performance, and result in neural changes related to cognitive function (e.g., neuronal protein expression; Zhang et al., 2014). Comparable results have been obtained in animal models of other neurological disorders (Kanno, 2013; Oliveira & Hodges, 2005).

To the best of my knowledge, clinical trials of brain tissue transplants have not been attempted in Alzheimer's patients, although the procedure has been used in patients with Parkinson's disease (e.g., Dyson & Barker, 2011), another neurological disorder that is associated with aging and has marked behavioral symptoms (e.g., motor and speech impairments) with potential cognitive deficits as well. In one example of this approach, Brundin and colleagues (2000) transplanted embryonic mesencephalic tissue into the brains of five Parkinson's patients who had had the disease for an average of 12.6 years and were in an advanced stage of the disorder. Over the ensuing two years, the patients showed reduced symptoms and were able to cut their medication roughly in half. Research using longer-term follow-up shows that the improvements last as long as five years posttransplantation, with the greatest improvement in the first 1.5–3 years (López-Lozano et al., 1995). These findings, in conjunction with animal transplantation research on Alzheimer's, suggest that neural transplantation has the potential to be an effective clinical treatment for Alzheimer's disease as well as Parkinson's disease (Oliveira & Hodges, 2005).

Transplants restore memory functioning across a wide range of factors that cause the initial brain damage—surgical lesions (Patel et al., 1997; Santucci et al., 1991), alcohol (Hodges et al., 1991), and a genetic predisposition to Alzheimer's disease (Zhang et al., 2014). As covered in the next several chapters, these are all common causes of amnesia, especially alcohol abuse and Alzheimer's disease. Other leading causes of amnesia, such as traumatic brain injury, have not been investigated in this regard, but it stands to reason that tissue transplants would benefit cognitive functioning in those cases, too, unless the brain is so damaged that the grafted tissue could not survive. Although neural transplants may not be able to transfer discrete memories from one organism to another, they have enormous potential to improve transplant recipients' general memory functioning, in terms of both learning new information and retrieving previously stored information. There are, of course, caveats, with the most prominent ones being the ethical issues raised by transplanting embryonic tissue and the fact that virtually all of the research to date has been done on nonhuman animals. These concerns should not be taken lightly, but in view of the enormous psychological, social, and economic costs of memory disorders (see chapters 5–7), it is imperative to continue research on the efficacy of brain tissue transplants, in as thoughtful and humane a manner as possible.

Memory and Dreaming

There are, of course, other sources of brain activity for nonexperienced stimuli besides brain implants. Two of the more common ones are dreams and imagination. Dreams naturally draw on autobiographical memories. When I dream about my mother, or a high school classmate, or a familiar golf course, I am necessarily retrieving information from memory. Yet dreams, as is well known, also contain an element of the fantastic—I speak to my deceased mother on the phone; an old friend I have not spoken to in decades visits me in Lincoln, Nebraska; or I play a round of golf with my father, a nongolfer. On waking, we are usually adept at separating the dream's true elements (this is a real person from my past) from the false ones (this particular event never occurred). When the process breaks down, in the Hollywood version (e.g., in *Inception*), chaos ensues—one gets lost in the dream, and the dream becomes reality. In the more mundane version of the breakdown, false memories ensue. For example, I might now have a memory of golfing with my father. Rather than the product of external suggestion, the false memory results from the brain's own activity while dreaming.

Chapter 3 described the role of source monitoring in the creation of false memories. In many cases, the rememberer incorporates a suggestion (e.g., offered by a therapist or police interviewer) into memory and is subsequently unable to distinguish between real memories and suggested ones. These situations require one to tell apart multiple external sources of information, such as actual characteristics of an experienced event and a misleading suggestion about that same event. In other cases, as when the rememberer is encouraged to imagine an event that never occurred, the challenge is one of *reality monitoring*—that is, distinguishing between an external source (i.e., the actually experienced event) and an internal source (i.e., the imagined event; Johnson et al., 2012; Mitchell & Johnson, 2009). Dreaming is akin to imagining, with the same risk of memory error—one can come to believe that something one only dreamed about actually occurred (Johnson, Kahan & Raye, 1984). Thus, the challenge is in knowing that a particular memory *is* a dream and not an experienced event.

According to the leading reality monitoring framework, proposed by Marcia Johnson and colleagues (e.g., Johnson et al., 2012), externally derived and internally generated memories have a number of characteristic differences. For example, internally generated memories have more information about conscious, effortful cognitive operations (e.g., reasoning, search, imagining), whereas externally derived memories have more sensory and contextual detail. Dreams are anomalous in that, unlike most internally generated cognitions, they lack conscious cognitive operations and contain a high degree of vivid sensory detail (Johnson et al., 1984). These characteristics can make it hard to distinguish one's own dreams from similar information that one obtained from another source.

People naturally vary in their awareness that they are dreaming while the dream is happening—a phenomenon known as lucid dreaming

(Corlett et al., 2014). Because lucid dreaming entails an intrusion of reality into the dreaming state, it reflects a breakdown in reality monitoring (Johnson et al., 1984). Individuals with high dream awareness make more reality monitoring errors than those with low dream awareness, presumably due to an increased tendency for novel items to seem familiar (Corlett et al., 2014). This tendency might have an underlying neurological or physiological basis (Corlett et al., 2014), as persons with some sleep disorders—such as patients with narcolepsy, who have delusional memories as a result of confusing their vivid dreams with reality—likewise have reality monitoring deficits (Wamsley et al., 2014).

Similar problems can arise in the phenomenon of déjà vu, in which a person has the feeling that a novel situation has been experienced before. Déjà vu involves metamemory because the person knows objectively that the event has not previously been experienced, yet there is a sense of familiarity similar to that produced by an actual memory (Schwartz, 2014). The misplaced familiarity results from perceptual similarities between the new event and a memory, such as a past event that one genuinely experienced but cannot quite place (Cleary et al., 2012). Dreams can be a source of memories leading to misplaced familiarity (Gerrans, 2014). For example, suppose that I dream about going to Australia, a place I have never been. Years from now, when I go to Australia, I might have a sense of déjà vu where some of the sights seem familiar—because I already "saw" them in my dream. The false familiarity is compounded by my having previously seen pictures of some of the sights, such as Uluru (Ayers Rock) and the Sydney Opera House.

Summary

The research on the relationship among false memories, brain processes, and dreaming shows clearly that external suggestions are only one mechanism of creating false memories. The brain is perfectly capable of creating them on its own, as when dreams become confused with reality due to a source monitoring error. Of course, internally and externally generated false memories are not mutually exclusive. As we reflect on dreams and share them with others, we are exposed to possible misinformation, which can then be incorporated into the memory (Beaulieu-Prévost & Zadra, 2015), although some research suggests that, in the absence of suggestive information, distortion in dream memories is rare (Johnson et al., 1984). Because the underlying brain activity of true memories and dreamt, imagined, or implanted memories is quite similar, we have a hard time distinguishing among them.

Although the technology that is currently available for implanting memories in the brain is limited, the potential of brain tissue transplantation to alleviate memory impairment is enormous. And logically, why shouldn't it be? If skin grafts can be incorporated into a recipient's existing skin, and a kidney transplant can function like a missing kidney, then transplanted neural tissue should be able to restore lost cognitive function. Discrete memories cannot be transplanted, but every indication, based on animal models and clinical trials with other neurological disorders, is that general memory functioning can profit from transplantation. The future of such treatments is bright.

MEMORY ERASURE

Beliefs about Memory Erasure

The flip side of creating memories for nonexperienced events by implanting them is making the memory of events that one actually did experience go away. As described in chapter 2, many, if not most, memories eventually do go away—they are held only briefly, not elaborated, not strengthened by occasional remembering, and never needed. Viewed in this way, forgetting is normal and hardly pathological. More extreme cases of forgetting past information—retrograde amnesia—can also occur. Chapter 3 described the argument that repression can cause retrograde amnesia, as well as the general lack of empirical evidence for that argument. Much stronger evidence exists for retrograde amnesia due to brain damage, and these cases are covered in chapter 5. Just as one would not repress information on purpose (according to Freud, repression is an unconscious defense mechanism), one does not choose to experience brain damage. The remainder of the present chapter deals with the in-between cases: Can we purposefully erase certain information from memory, by either psychological or mechanical means?

Numerous popular portrayals of memory contain characters whose memories have been erased, in whole or in part, either voluntarily or against their will. Sometimes the erased memories are replaced by others, as in *Total Recall*; other times the "bad" memories are simply wished good riddance, as in *Eternal Sunshine of the Spotless Mind*. It can be undertaken voluntarily (e.g., *Eternal Sunshine*), or it can be done without one's consent, as when the government agents in the *Men in Black* movies use a "neuralyzer" to erase humans' memories of having witnessed an alien encounter. In rare instances, the protagonist's entire past is erased, as in *Blindspot*, a current television series about a woman who took so much of a memory-eradicating drug (apparently by choice, for reasons that are a little unclear) that she remembers nothing of her past life, not even her name. Most relevant to the plot, she does not remember getting the tattoos that cover her entire body or know what they mean. What all of these examples share are protagonists who either chose to erase selected information from memory or had the procedure done to them. They illustrate the popular belief that memory erasure is feasible and effective. Is it?

Feasible, yes; on effectiveness, the data are more equivocal. Relevant research comes from two lines of inquiry on intentional forgetting: psychological strategies, in which one deliberately tries to avoid remembering some information; and pharmacological methods, in which one takes a drug to eradicate specific information from memory. Both techniques are somewhat successful—if not at completely erasing an unwanted memory, then at least at making it less likely to be retrieved.

Intentional Forgetting

Just as we routinely try, and often struggle, to remember, we regularly attempt *not* to remember some things, with varying degrees of success; that is, although much forgetting is a natural byproduct of the way our minds work, at times we intentionally forget. "Thus, one of the most innocent assumptions one might make about memory—that remembering is good and forgetting is bad—is, in fact, often untrue. More often than we realize, forgetting is our goal, and remembering is the human frailty" (Anderson & Levy, 2011, p. 107). In other words, forgetting can be a good and sought-after thing. One aspect of metamemory involves invoking inhibitory control mechanisms to reduce the level of activation associated with unwanted memories (Anderson & Levy, 2009, 2011).

Sometimes we are explicitly instructed to forget, as when one member of a couple makes an ill-advised comment during a fight or blurts out a secret, followed by "Forget I said that, I didn't mean it"; or when a judge instructs the jury to disregard certain evidence. Other times, and probably more often, we do it on our own—essentially instructing ourselves to forget something—simply because the information is unnecessary or unpleasant, and remembering it would needlessly tax our finite cognitive resources or would be upsetting. We naturally do a better job of remembering pleasant than unpleasant events (a process that breaks down in depressed patients; see chapter 2), and one of the problems with repression as an explanation of why people sometimes forget traumatic experiences is that it is very difficult, if not impossible, to distinguish between an unconscious mechanism like repression and a more-or-less deliberate effort to avoid thinking about something. This deliberate avoidance or forgetting might have, at least according to Freudians, adverse mental health consequences, but in other respects it is clearly adaptive—remembering negative events can cause and perpetuate a negative mood (see chapter 2).

The question, then, is how effectively one can intentionally forget some information. Controlled research on this question typically employs the *directed forgetting* paradigm, according to which participants are told to remember some items on a list (or an entire list) but to forget others (Schwartz, 2014). For example, in one of the earlier demonstrations of the phenomenon, Bjork and Woodward (1973) presented participants with seven lists of words. Half of the words in each list were followed by a cue to remember the word (R words), and half by a cue to forget the word (F words). For three lists, participants were asked to recall only the R words, but for one "special" list, they had to recall both R words and F words (the remaining three lists were followed by a distractor task). For the normal lists, they received a monetary reward for each R word recalled, but they lost money for each F word recalled. Critically, for the special list, they were rewarded for recalling both R words and F words; they did not know which list was the special list until they attempted to recall it. At the end of the experiment, they were asked to recall all the words they could remember, regardless of list and R or F status; again, they were rewarded for any words they could recall. At both immediate and final recall, participants recalled significantly more R words than F words, regardless of whether they were punished or rewarded for remembering the F words (i.e., normal lists vs. the special list). For the normal lists, participants recalled at most 2 percent of the F words at immediate recall. Of course, they might have recalled the words but not reported them, since they lost money if they did. Importantly, when they were rewarded for recalling the F words (i.e., on the special list), their recall improved to only 5 percent, compared to 51 percent of the R words. The discrepancy between recall of R words and F words was less in final recall at the end of the experiment, but it was still substantial, and roughly the same for the special list and the normal lists. The results show that trying not to remember information is effective.

Multiple processes appear to underlie directed forgetting (Anderson & Levy, 2009; Lee, 2013). At the time of encoding, to-be-forgotten items are processed less thoroughly, such as by rehearsing them less and forming fewer associations among stimuli (Bjork & Woodward, 1973; Lee, 2013; Lin et al., 2013). Thus, they are stored less well in memory. Naturally, we do not always know while we are processing some new information that it will be desirable to forget it, just as we do not always know that it will be important to remember something later; that is, we rarely receive (or give ourselves) a "forget" instruction at the time of encoding. In situations where we want to forget something only after it has transpired, the retrieval mechanisms associated with directed forgetting become paramount. Even if the to-be-forgotten items are subsequently available, they are harder to retrieve, in part because fewer retrieval cues are available for them, but also because retrieving the to-be-remembered items interferes with retrieving the to-be-forgotten items (Lee, 2013). If additional retrieval cues are provided, as by including R words and F words that are semantically related, or context-specific retrieval cues are made salient, then directed forgetting is less likely to occur (Hupbach & Sahakyan, 2014; Woodward & Bjork, 1971).

Consistent with the involvement of both encoding and retrieval processes, directed forgetting produces enhanced memory for information that follows the instruction to forget (Pastötter, Kliegl & Bäuml, 2012). This enhancement suggests that part of the strategy to forget a piece of information is to devote more cognitive effort to encoding and then retrieving subsequent information. Directed forgetting effects are also fairly stable over time, persisting for at least 12 hours following exposure to the information (Abel & Bäuml, 2013).

Of course, forgetting words on a list is not the same as forgetting an event. Directed forgetting effectively impairs memory for episodic, as well as semantic, information (Anderson & Levy, 2009). For example, Fawcett, Taylor, and Nadel (2013) showed participants videos depicting events, such as baking cookies or getting ready for work. The videos, which were broken down into eight discrete segments (each lasting 35 seconds), were periodically interrupted, and participants were instructed either to remember or to forget the preceding segment. They remembered more R than F details, regardless of whether testing was done by cued-recall or true/false recognition, showing that directed forgetting works for continuous events—at least for aspects of the events, though not necessarily for entire events—as well as for word lists. Although the events studied by Fawcett et al. are relatively neutral in emotional valence and even slightly positive (e.g., baking cookies), retrieval of negative emotional events can also be intentionally suppressed (Anderson & Levy, 2009). Directed forgetting can also be used to reduce the accessibility of more procedural information, such as habits (Dreisbach & Bäuml, 2014). Thus, intentional forgetting works across a broad range of different types of information.

Some people are better at forgetting things on purpose than others. Specifically, those who are more mentally tough (Dewhurst et al., 2012) or conscientious (Delaney, Goldman, King & Nelson-Gray, 2015) show more directed forgetting. Mental toughness, for example, is defined as a tendency to see problems as opportunities (challenge), the ability to involve oneself in a task (commitment), having control over one's life and emotions (control), and having confidence in one's abilities and interactions with others (confidence; Clough, Earle & Sewell, 2002; Dewhurst et al., 2012). The higher people score on mental toughness, especially the commitment subscale, the better they do on to-be-remembered information relative to to-be-forgotten information. This is potentially because they are better at inhibiting unwanted cognitions (Dewhurst et al., 2012). Relatedly, people with better executive control (e.g., longer working-memory span) are better at controlling unwanted memories (Anderson & Levy, 2009).

Intentional forgetting is relatively stable as a function of aging, although there is a developmental trajectory (Anderson & Levy, 2009). Young children do not show directed forgetting, but the ability is present by middle childhood (Harnishfeger & Pope, 1996). This is likely due to the relatively late development of the prefrontal cortex, which is the main part of the brain involved in suppressing unwanted memories (Anderson & Levy 2009). Intentional forgetting remains intact up to about age 75, at which point it begins to decline (Aslan & Bäuml, 2013). It therefore belongs to the category of late-declining memory capabilities (see chapter 7). Sleep eliminates the directed forgetting effect (Abel & Bäuml, 2013), showing the benefits of sleep for memory consolidation (discussed in more detail in chapter 6). Sleep is so effective at consolidating information in memory that it can even lead to the consolidation of information one would rather forget.

Clinical populations are an especially intriguing group to examine with respect to intentional forgetting. People with depression are poorer at it than nondepressed controls (Anderson & Levy, 2009), which is consistent with depressed persons' heightened tendency to ruminate on negative events. The clinical population that has garnered the most scholarly interest is people with PTSD, as an inability to forget the trauma, characterized by intrusive memories, is one of the disorder's hallmark symptoms. Persons with a history of trauma might be more adept at using an avoidant encoding style, making them better at forgetting undesired information (Baumann et al., 2013). On the other hand, these same individuals, especially if they suffered lingering effects of the trauma, might be poorer at forgetting information intentionally. Given these competing hypotheses, it is perhaps unsurprising that research on directed forgetting with traumatized participants or PTSD patients yields inconsistent findings (Baumann et al., 2013; Geraerts & McNally, 2008). Whether PTSD is associated with a heightened or impaired ability to forget information on purpose likely depends on variables such as the nature of the trauma, the presence of any accompanying psychological disorders (e.g., anxiety) or a recovered memory, the emotional content of the stimuli, and individuals' processing style (Baumann et al., 2013; Geraerts & McNally, 2008). For example, persons with a predisposition to anxiety show greater directed forgetting, but only for threat-related words and if their general processing style inclines them to avoid (vs. attend to) threat-related stimuli (Noel, Taylor, Quinlan & Stewart, 2012).

People can, and do, forget things on purpose, and it is often beneficial to do so. However, forgetting as demonstrated in directed forgetting experiments is a relative term—participants are less likely to remember information that they are instructed to forget than information that they are instructed to remember. This is solid evidence of our ability to control the contents of memory, but it does not necessarily mean that every trace of an unwanted memory has been erased, once and for all. Are there means of erasing memories more thoroughly?

Pharmacologically-Induced Forgetting

Pharmacological interventions offer one possible means of erasing unwanted memories that cannot be forgotten via strategies like intentional forgetting. These methods raise a number of intriguing questions: Do they work? How does a drug target a specific memory? Is it ethical to use drugs to wipe out certain memories?

A number of drugs can enhance or retard memory retrieval; these drugs are discussed at greater length in the chapters on amnesia (chapters 5 and 6). For the most part, the drugs that suppress memory do so in a global fashion—that is, they suppress memory for all or most kinds of information, either material that was learned prior to the drug administration or material encountered after taking the drug. Drugs that reduce the activity of a number of neurotransmitters, especially acetylcholine, epinephrine, and norepinephrine, often have negative effects on memory (Eichenbaum, 2012). Except in experimental situations, these drugs are usually not used for amnestic purposes; rather, the memory impairment is a side effect, and given their lack of specificity, they would not be used in an attempt to erase specific memories—that would be akin to swatting a fly with a steamroller.

However, because some of these drugs selectively target brain regions involved in emotional memories, such as the amygdala, they raise the possibility of being used to eliminate upsetting memories. In a classic demonstration of this phenomenon, Cahill, Prins, Weber and McGaugh (1994) administered either a placebo or a β-adrenergic receptor antagonist (beta-blocker) to participants one hour before showing them slides with an accompanying narrative. The story was either neutral or emotionally arousing (a boy was involved in a serious accident); the two versions differed mainly in the middle portion of the story. On placebo, participants showed enhanced memory for the arousing story, especially the middle, most emotional portion. Taking a beta-blocker eliminated this recall advantage for the emotional material. Importantly, the drug had little, if any, negative effect on memory for the neutral story or for the nonarousing portions of the arousing story. Such drugs consistently impair the consolidation of negative emotional material (see, generally, Lonergan, Olivera-Figueroa, Pitman & Brunet, 2013; McGaugh, 2000).

Of course, people are seldom in a position to take an amnestic drug prior to an arousing or traumatic event. The greatest potential for such drugs would seem to be in the treatment of PTSD. Animal research suggests that even after a memory has been consolidated (see chapter 5), it can be blocked during the process of reconsolidation—that is, the strengthening/restorage process that occurs during memory retrieval, when the memory returns to an unstable state (Lonergan et al., 2013; Pitman, 2011)—although the research findings are somewhat inconsistent (Jaffe, 2013; Maren, 2011). Human studies with beta-blockers have successfully reduced memory for negative emotional information, such as by eliminating a conditioned fear response (Pitman, 2011). Sometimes the treatment eliminates only the negative emotional component (e.g., fear) without eradicating the memory itself, whereas other times it reduces subsequent retrieval of the emotional information (Lonergan et al., 2013; Pitman, 2011).

Scholars are somewhat skeptical about whether these findings can be applied to the clinical treatment of PTSD, given the greater magnitude in PTSD of both the fear-inducing stimulus and the emotional response, the frequent rehearsal (and hence strength) of the information in memory, and the age of the memories (Jaffe, 2013; Pitman, 2011). Indeed, the results of studies designed to block intrusive memories in individuals with PTSD are mixed (e.g., Brunet et al., 2008).

Although a drug to erase traumatic memories might seem like a silver bullet, it is important to consider the ethical implications of such treatment. Animal models of the process typically employ fear conditioning. In many situations, fear conditioning is adaptive—we learn to avoid stimuli that can harm us, as well as other stimuli that are associated with those harmful stimuli. Eliminating that association, or even just the fear response, might improve the organism's subjective wellbeing, but at the expense of not retaining the adaptive learning. Consider one extreme example: A woman is sexually assaulted by an acquaintance she previously trusted, and she develops PTSD. She takes a magic drug that eradicates memory of the trauma and along with it her PTSD. Would she be able to testify at the perpetrator's trial? Would she come to trust him again, thereby exposing herself to renewed risk?

In most cases, traumatic events are relatively straightforward—that is, one knows at the time of the event, as well as afterwards, that an event is really awful, and the appraisal persists over time. Crime victimization, especially when it involves violence, is a case in point—it is traumatic at the time, and the strong negative emotions associated with the memory likely persist. Often, however, the emotional valence associated with an event changes over time, as we acquire perspective and other events intervene. "In general, events that initially are perceived as important and highly emotional may be perceived as less emotional or important later as the result of changes in the real world. Events may similarly increase in importance or emotionality as our perspectives on them are modified" (Linton, 2000, p. 117).

A former graduate student, who survived cancer while in college, once made this clear to me. He said that the cancer was the best thing that ever happened to him, because of what he learned about himself and how it changed his outlook on life. Similarly, relationship breakups, though painful at the time, can prove to be educational growth experiences as new and more fulfilling relationships are formed, and as distance enables one to remember the good along with the bad. By erasing their memories, the unhappy couple Joel and Clementine in *Eternal Sunshine of the Spotless Mind* are depriving themselves of that opportunity. Thus, erasing a memory in haste might be shortsighted. It might be different if one could erase only the negative emotional element of the memory and preserve the memory itself, but these things cannot be so easily teased apart (Pitman, 2011)—without the emotion, the memory might have little meaning at all.

It is also possible that amnestic drug treatment would suppress retrieval of the information (i.e., its accessibility) but not the information itself (i.e., its availability), meaning that under the right circumstances the memory could be reactivated (note that this is *not* the same as arguing that the drug caused the memory to be repressed and subsequently recovered). Having ignored the memory in the interim, would delayed retrieval be better, worse, or just different? These questions have no easy answers. To be sure, PTSD symptoms like excessive rumination, intrusive memories, and the anxiety and negative emotions that characterize those symptoms are maladaptive, and lessening or eliminating the symptoms would be beneficial. But drugs to lessen or erase the memories are not a panacea.

Summary

As described in chapter 2, forgetting of some (and arguably most) information, under some circumstances, is adaptive. Yet it is clearly adaptive to remember certain information, too. Most of the time, we remember what it would be useful to remember and forget information that we do not need. But our cognitive triage system is not perfect, meaning that we often forget things we wish we could remember and occasionally remember things we would rather forget. Intentional forgetting can come to our aid in this latter situation, effectively enabling us to purge—or at least reduce the strength of— unwanted information in memory. Directed forgetting takes effort (Fawcett et al., 2013), but it can be effective.

When directed forgetting is not enough, or in extreme cases, such as suppressing memory for trauma, pharmacological options are becoming increasingly available. Medications such as beta-blockers can reduce both the consolidation and the reconsolidation of emotional material in healthy adults (Lonergan et al., 2013), although successful application in trauma victims has not yet been fully realized. Current findings with PTSD patients suggest that "translating reconsolidation blockade into clinical applications is unlikely to be simple or straightforward" (Wood et al., 2015, p. 38). We are a long way from being able to erase selected memories as cleanly and effectively as portrayed in *Eternal Sunshine of the Spotless Mind*, but hope is on the horizon.

CONCLUSIONS

There is a kernel of truth in the myths about memory implantation and erasure, but both are greatly exaggerated. The research summarized in the previous chapter demonstrates conclusively that false memories can be created by psychological means (i.e., suggestion), and recent research (e.g., Ramirez et al., 2013) shows that false memories can also be created by activating certain pathways in the brain. The brain can even create its own false memories, as when a dreamt event is confused with something experienced while awake. These pathways correspond to those used when encoding genuine memories, which is why there are few neurological differences among true, false, and imagined memories. At present, however, large-scale mechanical implantation of memories or transfer of memories from one body to another, similar to what happens in movies like *Total Recall* and *Selfless*, is not practical.

This is not to say that the implantation—more precisely, the *trans*plantation—of neural tissue yields no benefits for memory. It can and it does. Indeed, the transplantation of neural tissue improves memory functioning in nonhuman animals, and it is an effective (though still rarely used) treatment for neurological disorders like Parkinson's disease. However, none of this research indicates that the transplants transfer discrete abilities, knowledge, or memories; rather, they improve general memory functioning. The research bodes well for the potential of brain tissue transplants to alleviate neurological disorders affecting memory, such as Alzheimer's disease (Oliveira & Hodges, 2005).

There appears to be a disconnect between people's beliefs regarding false memory and repression, discussed in the previous chapter, and their beliefs regarding memory implants. Although many people believe that it is possible to implant a memory in the brain of something that never actually occurred—and an "implanted" memory is false by definition—they are reluctant to accept the notion that a recovered memory might be false. Essentially, they seem to be saying, "Sure, you can implant a (false) memory in someone's brain, but if the person remembers it, then it must be true." What explains this apparent contradiction? Three related possibilities come to mind. First, implantation procedures have the patina of medical science—they involve the brain, after all, an organ that is poorly understood by laypeople. And medicine and the natural sciences have long had an aura of trustworthiness (MacCoun, 2015). Perhaps people just have a natural tendency to accept an idea that sounds all "sciencey."

A related explanation is that scientific topics, such as brain mechanisms underlying cognitive performance, receive less media attention than "human interest" stories, especially from widely read print media like tabloids and local newspapers (Howard & Donnelly, 1999). Although the occasional story, such as Ramirez et al.'s (2013) work on implanting false memories in the brain, attracts mainstream media exposure (Noonan, 2014), its media footprint would pale in comparison to the extensive media coverage of the latest repression/recovered memory case. When the media do write about complex scientific topics, they do so fairly accurately, but they are much more likely to write about sensational topics (e.g., recovered memory) that have a less firm scientific foundation (Howard & Donnelly, 1999). Consumers are generally unable to distinguish reliable from unreliable science, leading them to believe both that memories can be mechanically implanted in the brain (sure, why not? medical science can do anything) and that recovered memories are accurate (sure, I can relate to that—I read about it all the time).

Third, implantation, at least as commonly portrayed, is performed by some outside agency, relying on sophisticated technology—you cannot just do it yourself. In contrast, although recovered memories very often result from another's suggestion, they require no fancy equipment (certain discredited therapeutic techniques notwithstanding—see chapter 3), and they can arise spontaneously. Consequently, they are within the realm of everyday experience—even if one has not personally had a recovered memory, it is easy enough to imagine. And as the research on reality monitoring and imagination inflation shows, the more readily we can imagine something, the realer it seems.

The kernel of truth in the erasure myth is that directed forgetting does inhibit the ability to retrieve unwanted memories, and pharmacological advances have produced drugs that not only impair memory functioning in general (see chapters 5 and 6) but that selectively target negative emotional stimuli. Directed forgetting operates both during encoding, if one knows at that time that the memory should be forgotten, and later on, at the time of retrieval. Drugs to induce forgetting typically operate during retrieval, when the memory is reconsolidated. However, the capability of either directed forgetting or drug treatments to eliminate memories that would be the best candidates for erasure—namely, memories of trauma—is as yet largely unproven. And as with strategies to implant memories, especially by biological means, strategies to erase memories raise a host of complicated ethical issues.

We are less fortunate than Lenore's forlorn lover in Poe's poem; there is no magical nepenthe, and some people are better at forgetting unwanted information than others. But making retrieval of an unpleasant memory less likely, or simply lessening the negative affect associated with it, is nonetheless a step in the right direction. Just as our metacognitive control of our memories allows us to implement strategies to help us remember better, it likewise allows us to implement strategies to help us remember less well when that is our goal.

NOTES

1. The plot of *Selfless* is very similar to that of *Criminal* (2016), except that in *Criminal*, Ryan Reynolds plays the memory donor rather than the memory recipient (played here by Kevin Costner).

2. Memories necessarily do involve cellular activity, specifically communication networks of neurons (nerve cells). But that is very different from the claim that moving those nerve cells from one organism to another would preserve the memories intact, let alone memories allegedly stored in other types of cells (e.g., nonneural organ tissue like a heart or liver).

3. Brain tissue transplant studies usually use embryos as the source of donor tissue, to minimize the risk of rejection. However, stem cells can be taken from other sources, such as the recipients' own bone marrow (Kanno, 2013) or even other species (Dyson & Barker, 2011), and stem cell lines can potentially be maintained indefinitely *in vitro* (Oliveira & Hodges, 2005). The use of fetal tissue raises a host of ethical concerns, even beyond those associated with other organ transplantation, which makes this area of research unusually controversial and limits the amount of research that can be done.

Chapter 5

Retrograde Amnesia

Myth: Retrograde Amnesia Can Be So Extensive as to Entail a Total Loss of Identity

Related Myth: Retrograde Amnesia Can Occur in the Absence of Other Cognitive Problems

Because myths about repression, as described in chapter 3, are so widespread, repression is viewed as a common cause of *retrograde amnesia*—forgetting of the past. However, retrograde amnesia much more often has an organic than a psychogenic basis. The difference is whether the memory loss has primarily a biological (organic) or a psychological (psychogenic) cause. (The distinction is not as simple as it sounds, as purportedly psychological conditions like mental illness often have neurophysiological correlates; but in some cases there is clearly identifiable organic damage, whereas in other cases there is not.) The organ in question in cases of organic amnesia is, naturally, the brain. A large number of things can produce brain damage resulting in amnesia—a traumatic brain injury (TBI), infection (e.g., a virus), drugs or alcohol, disease (e.g., Alzheimer's disease). In the context of TBI, "trauma" refers to a sudden injury to the brain, such as an automobile accident, blow to the head, gunshot, or concussive sound waves, as opposed to a more gradual injury like an infection or degenerative disease. This physical trauma is therefore distinct from the kinds of psychological trauma discussed in chapter 3, although a TBI can, of course, be traumatic in the psychological sense as well. Regardless of the cause, brain damage is associated with a wide variety of negative effects on mental (and in many cases physical) functioning, including retrograde amnesia.

It is impossible to estimate the prevalence of amnesia in general, or retrograde amnesia in particular. However, it is possible to glean some idea of the disorder's prevalence by considering a couple of the most common causes of retrograde amnesia, TBI and Alzheimer's disease. According to the Centers for Disease Control and Prevention, the rate of TBI-related emergency department visits increased over the first decade of the twenty-first century, reaching 715.7 per 100,000 in 2010. Roughly one in eight visits was severe enough to require hospitalization (Centers for Disease Control and Prevention, 2016). That translates to more than 1 million head injuries per year seen by American hospitals (Langlois, Rutland-Brown & Wald, 2006). Of course, not all persons who suffer a head injury go to the hospital; some, especially those injured playing sports, receive outpatient care or no treatment at all. By one estimate, there are 1.6 million to 3.8 million sports-related TBIs each year (the wide range reflects imprecision in measurement and reporting), and at least 5.3 million Americans currently live with a TBI-related disability (Langlois et al., 2006). According to the Alzheimer's Association, the estimated prevalence of Alzheimer's disease is, coincidentally, identical—5.3 million, a figure that is growing as the population ages[1]; chapter 7 covers Alzheimer's disease in depth). Between TBI and Alzheimer's disease, then, more than 10 million Americans suffer from a disorder that, in the vast majority of cases, entails retrograde amnesia as well as other cognitive difficulties.

Perhaps because retrograde amnesia is so widespread, it is probably the favorite memory topic of both Hollywood and daytime TV. However, these portrayals are unrealistic in many respects. Many of these depictions involve a protagonist who has no memory whatsoever of his/her former life, because of either a brain injury or psychogenic factors. This is especially true when the amnesiac's forgotten past contains secrets or other disturbing material, like maybe a career in espionage (e.g., the *Bourne Identity* novels/films, the TV series *Legends* and *Blindspot*), battlefield events (e.g., the film *Waltz with Bashir*, the novel/film *A Very Long Engagement*), or a crime (e.g., the movie *Trance*). Such extreme retrograde amnesia has been documented but is exceedingly rare (Simons & Chabris, 2011). For example, Kapur and Abbott (1996) describe the case of a 19-year-old man (named PP) who lost memory for most of his past life after apparently being mugged and hit over the head. He was found in a park, holding his head and confused. He told the person who found him and hospital personnel that he did not know who or where he was; he assumed he was in England because people were speaking English. When shown a photo ID, he asked, "Is this me?" He did not recognize his parents or friends when they visited him in the hospital. In addition to the amnesia for his own life, he had significant memory loss for public figures and events of the past few years.

PP's memory for events following the injury was good—he remembered being found in the park, taken to the hospital, and the visits from his family and friends. His memories began returning within a few days of the incident, with childhood memories returning before later memories. By 4 weeks after the incident, most of his memories had returned except for the 5 months preceding it, and he reported that the 3 weeks immediately before it was completely blank. Kapur and Abbott (1996) do not report any follow-up beyond 4 weeks postinjury. Other documented cases of pervasive retrograde amnesia, in some cases involving at least a temporary loss of identity, have been found to persist for years (e.g., James, 2011; Rosenbaum et al., 2005). Again, however, such extensive memory loss is the exception, not the rule.

A key feature of retrograde amnesia in the movies is that, like PP, the amnesic person typically suffers no cognitive deficits other than his or her profound memory loss, whereas such extensive retrograde amnesia would almost always be associated with additional memory problems, especially for learning new information, as well as impairment of other cognitive abilities (e.g., reasoning, language). One of the best examples is Jason Bourne. Bourne is the protagonist of several best-selling novels by Robert Ludlum, which were subsequently made into four popular films starring Matt Damon. In the beginning, Bourne has no memory of who he is, what he does for a living, or how he came to be in his current situation. He suffers from the most extreme form of retrograde amnesia, which is apparently due to a head injury, although there is some suggestion of psychological factors as well. Yet despite his pervasive amnesia for everything about his past, he speaks several languages, is mentally agile, and possesses an impressive array of lethal skills.[2]

The popular fascination with retrograde amnesia, especially in Hollywood, is hardly a new phenomenon. Lilienfeld et al. (2010) mention *Garden of Lies*, a 1915 film in which "a newly married bride forgets everything about herself, including who she is, following a car accident" (p. 78; see also Baxendale, 2004). *The Vow*, a 2012 movie starring Channing Tatum and Rachel McAdams, has almost the identical plot. Like Jason Bourne, the protagonists have no apparent cognitive deficits apart from the huge black voids of their pasts. In addition to misrepresenting the amnesia, many of these portrayals also mischaracterize the recovery process. Many novels and films, such as those featuring Jason Bourne, accurately show the memories returning gradually over time; however, others show them returning all at once, as in the novel *What Alice Forgot*, whose protagonist suddenly regains ten years of lost memories "as if a dam wall had burst in her brain, releasing a raging torrent of memories" (Moriarty, 2009, p. 418). In some of these fictional cases, the memories return following a second bump on the head (Baxendale, 2004).[3] These representations treat the amnesic brain like a faulty television set or jukebox—if it's not working properly, just whack it, and things will settle back into place. Brains, televisions, and jukeboxes might all be electrical devices, but the similarities end there. Hitting one's head a second time is likely to cause additional damage (the same could well be true of the television and jukebox, for that matter).

Although the extent and nature of the amnesia in *The Bourne Identity* and its ilk are unrealistic, these popular depictions are scientifically accurate in other respects, such as the gradual return of many of the forgotten memories and the retention of implicit memories for information that cannot be recalled explicitly. The present chapter begins with data on laypeople's beliefs about retrograde amnesia, followed by a brief overview of some of the key concepts and challenges about amnesia. The remainder of the chapter then reviews research on the causes and characteristics of retrograde amnesia.

BELIEFS ABOUT RETROGRADE AMNESIA

Erroneous beliefs about retrograde amnesia that are consistent with popular portrayals are widespread. Simons and Chabris (2011) found that 82.7 percent of lay respondents agreed that "people suffering from amnesia typically cannot recall their own name or identity." Strikingly, 0 expert respondents agreed with the statement. Several studies have focused specifically on laypeople's beliefs about characteristics of and recovery from brain injury. In addition to amnesia, these studies measure knowledge and expectations about TBI, coma, and unconsciousness.[4] Several of these studies have used identical or very similar items, making it possible to compare across studies (see Table 5.1). In one of the earliest surveys, Gouvier, Prestholdt, and Warner (1988) administered a structured interview to a reasonably diverse sample of Louisiana citizens (17 % non-White, 17 % rural residents, 48 % male, and representing a range of ages, occupations, and education levels). Participants indicated whether each of 25 statements about head injury and recovery was True, Probably True, Probably False, or False. Over 80 percent of participants believed that TBI can cause a complete loss of identity with no other ill effects, and only about half (49.3 %) correctly knew that trouble remembering new information (i.e., anterograde amnesia) is more common than trouble remembering things from before the injury (i.e., retrograde amnesia). These misperceptions have been demonstrated outside the Unites States (e.g., in Canada; Willer, Johnson, Rempel & Linn, 1993), and they have remained relatively stable over time (Guilmette & Paglia, 2004; Hux, Schram, & Goeken, 2006; O'Jile et al., 1997; Willer et al., 1993; see Table 5.1). Even in the mid-2000s, three-quarters or more of laypeople believed that "after head injury, people can forget who they are and not recognize others, but be

Table 5.1 **Endorsement of Retrograde Amnesia Myths**

Study	After head injury, people can forget who they are and not recognize others, but be normal in every other way (F)	Sometimes a second blow to the head can help a person remember things that were forgotten (F)	How quickly a person recovers from a head injury depends mainly on how hard they work at recovering (F)	Complete recovery from a severe head injury is not possible, no matter how badly the person wants to recover (T)
Gouvier et al. (1988)	82.4	45.7	70.1	57.9
Willer et al. (1993): NY	89.0	37.6	53.1	14.7
Willer et al. (1993): ONT	82.4	39.7	58.8	17.6
O'Jile et al. (1997)	5.5	46.5	53.9	67.7
Guilmette & Paglia (2004)	75.0	41.8	61.9	60.3
Hux et al. (2006)	93.4	28.6	52.5	72.0
Weighted mean	72.1	39.0	57.7	52.9

Note: Figures are percentages, reflecting the rate of incorrect responses (i.e., endorsement of the myth). Item wording differed slightly across studies. Response options were True, Mostly (or Probably) True, Mostly (or Probably) False, and False. The two true options and the two false options were each combined for analysis. Willett et al. (1993) included two separate samples: New York (NY) and Ontario (ONT). The correct response (True or False) is in parentheses. Sample sizes are as follow: Gouvier et al., 221; Willett et al. NY, 245; Willett et al. ONT, 68; O'Jile et al., 217; Guilmette and Paglia, 179; Hux et al., 318. The total sample used in calculated the weighted mean is 1,248.

normal in every other way" (Guilmette & Paglia, 2004; Hux et al., 2006). As shown in Table 5.1, across six different samples an average of 72.1 percent of participants endorsed this myth.

The mistaken beliefs extend to assumptions about recovery from amnesia (see Table 5.1). Across the six different samples (from five studies) summarized in Table 5.1, 39 percent of respondents believed a second blow to the head can bring back memories forgotten due to a first blow to the head, and more than half (57.7 %) believed that recovery depends mainly on how hard a person works at recovering and that complete recovery from a severe head injury is possible, if the person wants badly enough to recover (52.9 %). These findings show that laypeople simultaneously overestimate the extent of retrograde amnesia in some respects (i.e., believing a complete loss of identity is common) and underestimate the difficulty of recovering from it. Related to recovery, in the survey described in chapter 1, only 40 percent of participants knew that damaged brain tissue cannot repair itself the way other body tissues can.

Unlike some of the other memory myths, there are relatively few individual differences in people's susceptibility to false beliefs about brain injury
and amnesia. With the exception of isolated differences on a few items,
knowledge is fairly consistent across individuals differing in gender, age,
and education level (Gouvier et al., 1988; Guilmette & Paglia, 2004; Hux et
al., 2006). College students are somewhat more knowledgeable than community adults (O'Jile et al., 1997). Personal experience with head injury does
matter, but only to a modest degree. People who have survived brain injury
or are acquainted with a brain injury survivor are less likely than those who
do not know any survivors to endorse certain myths, such as a belief that
a second head injury can alleviate deficits caused by a prior injury (Hux et
al., 2006). For the majority of myths, however, experience with TBI is not
associated with a difference in knowledge (Gouvier et al., 1988; Guilmette
& Paglia, 2004; Hux et al., 2006; O'Jile et al., 1997). People cite media
sources, especially television, as a frequent source of information about head
injury (Gouvier et al., 1988). As the examples cited above illustrate, those
sources are more likely to provide misinformation than accurate information. With more soldiers returning with TBI from the recent conflicts in Iraq
and Afghanistan than from previous conflicts, media coverage has likely
increased in the past decade or so, but it is unclear whether that coverage has
become any more or less accurate.

Individuals with brain injuries and those who work with them agree that
the general public, as well as general healthcare providers (i.e., those without
expertise in brain injury), labor under these misconceptions, and that others' inaccurate knowledge about their condition complicates their recovery
and general social functioning (Swift & Wilson, 2001). The surveys of
laypeople described above bear out the low expectations that persons with
brain injury have of the general public. Unfortunately, additional research
bears out their low expectations of providers. For example, large numbers of
school psychologists endorse myths about amnesia and other aspects of brain
injury (Hooper, 2006). Because TBI is the leading cause of injury, death, and
long-term disability among children and adolescents (Hooper, 2006), school
psychologists are likely to interact with children suffering from cognitive
impairment due to TBI. Yet 60 percent of North Carolina school psychologists believed that a brain injury can cause a complete loss of identity with no
other cognitive effects, and substantial numbers endorsed other myths as well
(e.g., 19 % believed that a second blow to the head can improve memory, and
53 % believed that complete recovery from a severe head injury is possible;
Hooper, 2006). Although the school psychologists were more knowledgeable
about amnesia than the general population (i.e., 60 % endorsement of the lost
identity myth is lower than the comparable figures for laypeople, reported
above), the high rate with which they endorsed amnesia myths does not bode

well for their ability to work effectively with children suffering from memory or other cognitive impairments. Others' unrealistic expectations of a complete recovery can have negative consequences for brain injury survivors if they are made to feel—by providers, friends, or family members—that they are simply not trying hard enough (Hux et al., 2006).

AMNESIA BASICS AND CHALLENGES

Amnesia is challenging—for the person with amnesia, for those who care for the amnesic patient (e.g., healthcare providers and family members), and for those who conduct research on amnesia. From a research and treatment perspective, it is notoriously difficult to diagnose. If forgetting is normal and even adaptive, and the cardinal rule of memory is that we forget much more than we remember, then where does one draw the line between normal and abnormal forgetting? In some respects, amnesia is like obscenity—you know it when you see it. Physicians and neuropsychologists rely on tests for diagnosing it, but the tests lack precision (Parkin, 1997). Some diagnostic tools compare an individual's objective test performance to population norms, but the norms comprise a substantial range, and a person's performance at a single point in time cannot indicate a drop in performance compared to prior functioning. The diagnostic process also usually includes subjective data from the patient and those close to him or her (e.g., "Do you feel like your memory is getting worse, and if so, how?"), but such impressions are unreliable—especially for someone suspected of amnesia, who might not remember instances of prior forgetting (this is analogous to the "forgot-it-all-along" effect described in the previous chapter, in which people sometimes fail to remember instances of prior remembering). Indeed, many amnesia patients underestimate the extent of their memory problems (Squire & Zouzounis, 1988).

Imaging techniques to detect brain damage are continually improving, but they are still limited in what they can show. Moreover, prospective studies show that some people with significant brain pathology do not suffer from amnesia, whereas others who do have amnesia lack the anatomical changes that one would ordinarily expect (e.g., Snowdon, 2001). Ultimately, the best means of diagnosing amnesia is comparing a person's current memory functioning with her prior functioning, but on initial assessment patients typically lack appropriate baseline data. The picture is complicated further by the fact that although some causes of amnesia are dramatic and easily identifiable, producing a sudden decline in functioning (e.g., a TBI), others are much more gradual and less visible (e.g., Alzheimer's disease). Amnesia in the elderly is particularly hard to diagnose, inasmuch as some (though by no means all) deterioration in memory performance is a part of normal aging (see chapter 7). Thus, it is very difficult, and somewhat arbitrary, to say when someone has crossed the line from normal to abnormal, or pathological, forgetting. Nonetheless, many individuals with brain damage clearly do cross that line.

Similarly, as noted earlier, the distinction between organic and psychogenic amnesia is useful, but it is overly simplistic. Consider, for example, the case of Henry M, who is probably the most heavily studied and written about amnesic patient in the annals of the field (e.g., Bornstein, 1998; Carey, 2008; Corkin, 2013; Hilts, 1995).[5] Henry was born in 1926 and developed epilepsy, accompanied by severe seizures, at age 16. After many years of unsuccessful treatments, personal suffering, and family strife due in large part to his illness, Henry had surgery in 1953 to remove "a fist-sized piece of the center of the brain. In neuroanatomical terms, it was the area between the midlines of the two temporal lobes, and backward for eight to nine centimeters … most of the hippocampus, the parahippocampal gyrus, and the associated formations called the entorhinal and perirhinal cortexes, as well as the amygdala" (Hilts, 1995, p. 97).[6] After the procedure, Henry had profound amnesia, the most salient symptom of which was *anterograde* amnesia—the inability to store new information in memory (as Henry's most distinguishing feature was his anterograde amnesia, I return to his case in the following chapter).

However, he also had significant retrograde amnesia for personal and public events, remembering hardly anything at all from the 11 years prior to surgery. In one demonstration of this, researchers provided him with concrete nouns and asked him to relate each one to a personally experienced event from any period in his life. People with normal memory functioning provide memories from throughout their lives but that are concentrated in the most recent time period. All of Henry's memories dated to 1942, when he was 16, or earlier (Eichenbaum, 2012). He also had poor memory of public figures and events from the 11-year period prior to surgery (Hilts, 1995). This sort of semantic memory impairment is typical of patients with organic retrograde amnesia (Piolino et al., 2005).

In all likelihood, the brain damage from Henry's surgery caused his forgetting for those 11 years as well as for events that transpired after the surgery. Coincidentally, however, the retrograde amnesia dated back to the onset of his epilepsy at age 16. It is entirely possible that Henry's seizures, or the medications he took in unsuccessful attempts to treat them, interfered with his ability to store information in memory (see the section on "Consolidation," below). But it is also possible that psychological factors partially explain his inability to remember this dark period of his life, when everything basically fell apart. Henry's example shows that organic and psychogenic causes of amnesia cannot always be cleanly separated. Indeed, the majority of combat veterans with extreme amnesia did not experience a severe head injury (Witztum, Margalit, & van der Hart, 2002), suggesting that psychological factors may play a contributing role.

Retrograde amnesia in the absence of organic injury is often referred to in psychiatric parlance as "dissociative amnesia" or "dissociative fugue" (Hennig-Fast et al., 2008; Wiztum et al., 2002). Yet even without identifiable brain damage, persons with dissociative amnesia can have subtle abnormalities in neurological functioning (Hennig-Fast et al., 2008; Piolino et al., 2005). There are also functional differences between patients with organic and psychogenic amnesia. When there is brain damage, patients with retrograde amnesia usually can recall less information about the world around them (e.g., newsworthy events), as well as less autobiographical information, as in the cases of PP and HM. However, patients with psychogenic retrograde amnesia tend to do well at remembering public events; their memory loss is limited more to aspects of their own lives (Hennig-Fast et al., 2008). In other words, they lose episodic but not semantic knowledge, whereas patients with organic amnesia are more likely to lose both.

It can also be difficult to separate retrograde from anterograde amnesia. Retrograde amnesia refers to the loss of information in memory prior to onset of the amnesia, whereas anterograde amnesia refers to impairment in storing new information in memory after onset. In some cases it is easy to determine the onset of the disorder, such as a car accident with a head injury or Henry's surgery (setting aside, again, the possibility that his seizures might have caused brain damage). In many other cases it is much harder to say exactly when the brain damage occurred, such as a boxer or football player who endures repeated blows to the head, a soldier who experiences a number of forceful explosions, or an Alzheimer's patient whose brain damage progresses slowly over a period of months or years.

CAUSES OF RETROGRADE AMNESIA

Where in the Brain?

"The exact locus in the brain that causes retrograde amnesia is elusive" (Schwartz, 2014, p. 298). In large part, this is because memory is widely distributed throughout the brain (e.g., Eichenbaum, 2012). Brain regions that are substantially involved in memory processes include the cerebellum, the diencephalon (especially the mammillary bodies), the amygdala, the hippocampus, and the cortex. In the cortex, the temporal lobes are perhaps most heavily involved in retrograde amnesia, especially the medial temporal regions, although damage to other cortical regions can produce other kinds of memory impairment. For example, frontal lobe damage can produce confabulation (see chapter 6), and damage to the parietal or occipital lobe can result in prosopagnosia, or the inability to recognize faces.

Any number of things can damage one or more of these regions of the brain: traumatic injury, substance abuse (particularly alcohol), drugs (including recreational and medically approved drugs), environmental exposure to toxins (e.g., carbon monoxide poisoning), infection (i.e., encephalitis), electroconvulsive shock (ECS), hypoxia, brain tumor, vascular problems (e.g., stroke), and degenerative illness (e.g., Parkinson's or Alzheimer's disease). In short, although the skull does an excellent job of protecting the brain from injury under normal conditions, many things—most of them beyond our control, with the major controllable exceptions being the consumption of alcohol and other drugs, engaging in activities that increase the risk of TBI (e.g., contact sports, riding a motorcycle without a helmet), and exposure to some environmental toxins—can cause brain injury resulting in retrograde amnesia.

The large number of brain structures involved in memory is amnesia's curse, as well as its blessing. On the negative side, it means that damage to virtually any part of the brain can affect memory, or some related cognitive skill like reasoning or language. But on the positive side, it also means that virtually any brain damage that the organism survives—no matter how extensive or severe—leaves at least some aspects of memory intact. These dual aspects of the anatomy of memory doubtless reflect the evolution of this essential cognitive skill over many thousands of years.

Posttraumatic Amnesia

The most common cause of retrograde amnesia is TBI. The number of events responsible for TBI is limitless; the most common are falls, automobile accidents, striking against or being struck by an object, and assault (Langlois et al., 2006). The injuries may entail an external wound to the head (e.g., a gunshot), but more often the TBI results from a closed head injury. Traditionally, these injuries were thought to occur when a rapidly moving object (e.g., a fist or club) hit the head or when a moving head hit a stationary object (e.g., the car dashboard, the pavement); however, the brain can also be damaged by high-intensity shock waves hitting the brain, as occurs in military personnel or terrorism victims exposed to the concussive force of an explosion (Burgess et al., 2010). Such injuries, especially in the military, are increasingly common, largely because improved protective gear (i.e., body armor) and medical technology are enabling soldiers to survive more severe injuries than in previous conflicts. For example, blasts were the leading cause of TBI in the recent conflicts in Iraq and Afghanistan (Warden, 2006).

Because TBI is such a common cause of amnesia, posttraumatic amnesia is considered a special kind of amnesia with its own, relatively unique set of characteristics (Parkin, 1997). The injury often, but not always, induces a brief loss of consciousness. On regaining consciousness, the person is usually confused and disoriented. There is typically some degree of both retrograde and anterograde amnesia. The deficits are roughly symmetrical; that is, the longer the anterograde amnesia, the longer the retrograde amnesia. Both types of memory loss usually improve over time as the person recovers, but some degree of both often persists. With respect to the anterograde deficit, individuals typically have poor memory for events that occurred right afterwards. For example, someone who injures his head in a car accident might talk to other drivers and police shortly after the accident but have no recollection of the conversations. The duration of the anterograde amnesia is variable but usually ranges from a few seconds to a matter of months.

The same accident victim would likely experience a loss of memory for events leading up to the accident. The duration of the retrograde amnesia can range from a few minutes to a period of months or years, but short durations (minutes to hours) are much more common. This reflects the disruptive effect of the injury on memory consolidation (see below). With the exception of the period immediately before the injury, it is not uncommon for the past memories that have been lost to return (see the section on "Shrinkage," below); anterograde amnesia, on the other hand, is more likely to linger.

Posttraumatic amnesia is closely related to a couple of other syndromes: transient global amnesia and postconcussion syndrome. Transient global amnesia mimics the characteristics of posttraumatic amnesia—that is, profound anterograde amnesia and a variable degree of retrograde amnesia, which can extend up to several years—but in the absence of any discernible trauma. It occurs in roughly 3–8 per 100,000 people (Boovalingam & Shah, 2013). A distinguishing feature of the anterograde amnesia component of transient global amnesia is that patients repeat the same questions over and over—their amnesia means that they do not remember the answers. Despite the absence of obvious trauma, it is commonly believed to result from some sort of malfunction in the hippocampus, although the precise pathophysiological mechanism is unclear (Boovalingam & Shah, 2013; Noel et al., 2015), and emotional and psychological factors may also play a role (Quinette et al., 2006). Precipitating events differ for men and women, and some evidence suggests that a history of migraines is a risk factor (Quinette et al., 2006). It occurs almost exclusively in middle-aged or older people (i.e., age 40–80) and clears up in less than 24 hours (Boovalingam & Shah, 2013; Noel et al., 2015; Quinette et al., 2006). Most episodes last less than 10 hours (Quinette et al., 2006). Persons with transient global amnesia often recover completely, except for a permanent gap for the episode itself and the period immediately before it, and on average they do not differ from controls in long-term cognitive performance (Boovalingam & Shah, 2013; Jager et al., 2009); however, memory problems can persist, especially if persons have a high level of symptoms of anxiety and depression (Noel et al., 2015).

Postconcussion syndrome, as the name implies, refers to a constellation of effects following a concussion. It includes several physical and emotional/ behavioral symptoms in addition to memory and concentration problems: headache, dizziness, irritability, fatigue, noise sensitivity, judgment problems, depression, and anxiety. The memory problems are the same as those in posttraumatic amnesia, with both anterograde and retrograde deficits, although the anterograde problems are usually more prominent (Ryan & Warden, 2003). Like posttraumatic amnesia, postconcussion syndrome typically resolves relatively quickly, but in some cases symptoms persist for months or years and can even be permanent (Ryan & Warden, 2003).

As posttraumatic amnesia and its related disorders show, retrograde amnesia is almost always accompanied by other cognitive deficits. These deficits include, most prominently, anterograde amnesia, but they can also include impacts on cognitive processes like reasoning and judgment. There is some dispute about whether "pure" retrograde amnesia (i.e., without additional anterograde deficits) can ever occur, but it is clear that if it does occur, it is extremely rare (Kopelman, 2002; Piolino et al., 2005). The Hollywood variety of retrograde amnesia is a myth not only in terms of its extent, but also in its lack of other cognitive effects.

RETROGRADE AMNESIA CHARACTERISTICS

Although retrograde amnesia—like all forms of amnesia—is highly variable, several characteristics are fairly common. First, a temporal gradient exists with retrograde amnesia, such that the memories most likely to be affected are the most recent ones—that is, "last in, first out." This runs counter to the standard forgetting curve, whereby more distant memories are more likely to be forgotten, and it provides insight into the process of memory consolidation. Second, the forgotten memories often come back—a phenomenon sometimes referred to as "shrinkage" (i.e., the amnesia abates, albeit not in response to a subsequent blow to the head). When shrinkage occurs, it generally mirrors the temporal gradient, with more distant memories coming back first. Third, many memories are retained, even though the amnesic person cannot consciously access them. This *implicit memory* is another instance of the distinction between accessibility and availability discussed earlier. Finally, retrograde amnesia is associated with a host of negative psychological consequences (e.g., depression, anxiety, a diminished sense of self).

Consolidation

The reverse temporal relationship in retrograde amnesia, whereby more recent memories are more likely to be forgotten, is known as Ribot's law, after Theodore Ribot, the nineteenth-century French philosopher and psychologist who first described it (Eichenbaum, 2012; Wixted, 2004). It is commonly explained in terms of *consolidation* (e.g., McGaugh, 2000; Wixted, 2004). Memory consolidation is "the process by which initially labile memories become permanent and impervious to disruption" (Eichenbaum, 2012, p. 384). It is the physiological side of encoding information in memory—that is, the process of creating a permanent change in the brain to accompany the psychological and phenomenological experience of a memory. Consolidation can be separated into three partially overlapping phases: fixation, reorganization, and reconsolidation (Eichenbaum, 2012). Fixation occurs over a period of seconds or minutes (up to hours) following the processing of some information, during which molecular processes of protein synthesis, operating at the synaptic level, first "fix" the information in memory. Reorganization is a longer process (days or weeks, up to years) in which anatomical structures in the cortex and hippocampus interact to solidify the memories. Finally, reconsolidation occurs each time the original memory is retrieved—new information is encoded along with retrieval of the previously consolidated information, which involves additional protein synthesis. This fresh consolidation helps to explain why memories change over time, taking on a slightly different form on each subsequent retrieval. Every instance of retrieval is essentially another occasion for encoding (for additional neurological and physiological detail, see Eichenbaum, 2012).

The consolidation account of retrograde amnesia has been supported by both laboratory and naturalistic research, and any number of things can disrupt the neural activity underlying consolidation. Lynch and Yarnell (1973) conducted a unique study involving football players. They questioned players who had suffered a concussion within 30 seconds of their injury, asking them to state their name, where they were, who the opponents were, and what was happening in the game at the time of their injury. They interviewed them again after 3–5 minutes, and at regular intervals thereafter. They compared the concussed players' memory performance to that of noninjured players and players who had suffered a significant nonconcussion injury.

Lynch and Yarnell (1973) found that the players' memories were initially intact when questioned immediately after their concussion—that is, they remembered what the play was during which they were hit in the head. But within minutes, they had forgotten the play, even though they could usually remember the preceding portion of the game. For example, one player, in the initial interview, said he had been hit "from the front while I was blocking on the punt." Five minutes later, he said, "I don't remember what happened. I don't remember what play it was or what I was doing. It was something about a punt" (p. 644). This forgetting did not occur for the players who did not experience a concussion. For most of the concussed players, the retrograde amnesia for events just before the injury appeared to be permanent. Lynch and Yarnell's findings suggest that at the time of the injury, the information was still held temporarily in short-term memory, but that the blow to the head prevented it from being consolidated. The risk of brain damage from concussions is cumulative; on average, the same brain injury will produce more severe consequences for someone who has experienced previous concussions than for someone who has not (Schwartz, 2014). This is one of the main reasons why athletic organizations, including professional sports organizations like the National Football League, are paying greater attention to the risks of repeated concussions, and a number of retiring athletes have cited concussion risks as one of the main factors in their decision to retire.

It is possible to produce similar effects by means other than a blow to the head, such as the administration of an electrical shock or drugs. Thanks to popular portrayals like *One Flew over the Cuckoo's Nest*, electroconvulsive shock (ECS; or ECT, for electroconvulsive therapy) has the reputation of a barbaric and abusive treatment; but when used properly (e.g., unilaterally, with muscle relaxants, and with just enough intensity to induce a brief seizure), it can be quite effective in treating depression in some patients (Meeter et al., 2011; O'Connor et al., 2008). However, retrograde amnesia is a common side effect. The amnesia encompasses the ECT procedure itself, the period leading up to it, and up to a year or more before the treatment. The memory impairment shows up on both objective and subjective measures of memory; that is, patients do worse on measures of both episodic and semantic components of autobiographical memory after ECT than they did before (e.g., O'Connor et al., 2008; Sobin et al., 1995), and they also report having more memory problems post-ECT (Squire & Zouzounis, 1988). For example, Meeter and colleagues (2011) tested depressed patients the day before the start of ECT, within 3 days after treatment ended, and 3 months later. The retrograde memory test assessed participants' knowledge of news events from the past year. Their performance was significantly worse post-ECT than pre-ECT for events throughout the preceding year. However, the retrograde amnesia had mostly lifted by the 3-month follow-up.

The relatively long timeframe for ECT's amnesic effects suggests that it affects both the fixation and reorganization components of consolidation. This effect of ECT makes sense, when one considers that the brain is an electrical organ, and ECT involves passing a strong electrical current through the brain. It is a little bit like having a power surge in a computer, which overloads the circuits and causes the computer to reboot. Alas, unlike most computers, the brain has no surge protector.[7] The extent of amnesia is greater for patients with poorer cognitive functioning before treatment (Sobin et al., 1995) and for treatments involving more intense shock (Hughes, Barrett & Ray, 1970). There is also some, albeit mixed, evidence indicating that retrograde amnesia is greater for bilateral versus unilateral ECT (O'Connor et al., 2008; Sobin et al., 1995). It is unknown exactly how and why ECT has its therapeutic effects, but the amnesic effects can be well explained by consolidation theory—the shock is most likely to affect recent memories that are still in the process of being consolidated.

In much the same way, seizures in epilepsy patients often produce retrograde amnesia for the seizure and time leading up to it (Bergen et al., 2000); they also impair memory for events occurring right after the seizure (Parkin, 1997). Similar to victims of posttraumatic amnesia, epileptic patients sometimes carry out complex actions after having a seizure with no apparent volition and no subsequent memory of the events (a characteristic referred to as "automatism"; see Parkin, 1997). As mentioned earlier, the tendency of seizures to cause a degree of retrograde and anterograde amnesia could partially explain Henry's retrograde amnesia for the period prior to his surgery during which he had frequent epileptic seizures. An electrical surge, whether it is generated internally by epilepsy or administered externally via ECS, can disrupt consolidation in the same manner as a blow to the head.

Although ECT causes amnesia for recent events, recently learned skills can remain intact. Squire, Cohen, and Zouzounis (1984) demonstrated this by teaching depressed patients a new skill, specifically, reading mirror-reversed words—a skill that normally improves with practice. Some patients then received a course of ECT (either bilateral or unilateral), whereas others did not. Retention of the skill was the same for all three groups, even though patients who received ECT did not remember the previous testing sessions and did worse at recognizing the words on which they had practiced. Memory for posttreatment information also usually remains intact. After the disorientation produced by the seizures wears off, patients rarely experience anterograde amnesia (Meeter et al., 2011; O'Connor et al., 2008; Sobin et al., 1995).

Certain drugs and neurotransmitters can have comparable effects. Because neurotransmitters do not cross the blood-brain barrier easily, researchers typically infuse them directly into the brains of nonhuman animals or use drugs that are neurotransmitter agonists or antagonists in animal or human studies. Animal studies have shown that injecting potassium chloride into the hippocampus produces amnesia for information learned up to 24 hours beforehand (Avis & Carlton, 1968). The chances that a person will have potassium chloride injected into his or her brain are remote; however, widely prescribed drugs can also have an amnestic effect. For example, drugs that affect the activity of a variety of neurotransmitters (e.g., acetylcholine, epinephrine, and norepinephrine antagonists) can have a negative impact on memory (Eichenbaum, 2012). Certain drugs that reduce the activity of norepinephrine, such as beta-blockers, can even block certain memories, especially emotional ones, altogether or reduce their intensity (Eichenbaum, 2012). If the memory is an unpleasant one, then the drug-induced forgetting might be a desirable outcome (the possibility of using medication to erase unwanted memories is discussed in detail in chapter 4).

Conversely, some drugs can improve memory for previously learned material, an effect referred to as *retrograde facilitation*—that is, administration of the drug facilitates retrieval of information that was presented previously. Benzodiazepines (e.g., diazepam/Valium), which function mainly by increasing activity of the neurotransmitter GABA, are one of the most widely prescribed classes of drugs on the market. Several studies have shown that taking a benzodiazepine immediately after learning some information improves memory for the material, compared to a control group (e.g., Fillmore, Kelly, Rush, & Hays, 2001; Pomara et al., 2006). For example, Pomara et al. (2006) gave a sample of elderly, cognitively intact adults (*M* age = 66) either a placebo or one of two different doses of the short-acting benzodiazepine lorazepam (Ativan) immediately after presenting them with a list of words that they were instructed to remember for a later recall test. Participants recalled more words at the end of the session if they had been given the drug than if they took the placebo; there was also a dosage effect, whereby the high dose produced greater facilitation than the low dose. A surprising aspect of this finding is that it is inconsistent with the phenomenon of state-dependent learning (see chapter 2); that is, information encoded without a drug should be remembered better without the drug (i.e., on placebo) than under the influence of the drug. This suggests that retrograde facilitation is a very powerful effect.

The precise mechanism of the facilitative effect is unclear, although benzodiazepines appear to produce an increased reliance on automatic (vs. controlled) retrieval processes (Fillmore et al., 2001). It is also possible that they improve consolidation of previously encoded material partially by reducing interference from subsequent material (Reder et al., 2007). This effect on the encoding of subsequent material is associated with a curious secondary consequence of benzodiazepine use, namely, that it also impairs the learning of new information—that is, benzodiazepines produce an anterograde amnesia effect in addition to retrograde facilitation (e.g., Deckersbach, Moshier, Buschen-Caffier & Otto, 2011; Pomara et al., 2006; see chapter 6).

Similar effects can be obtained with other neurotransmitters or drugs that modulate their activity (McGaugh, 2000). Infusing norepinephrine directly into the amygdala improves memory, especially for emotional experiences (e.g., conditioned shock aversion), as does postlearning administration of related substances like epinephrine and adrenal glucocorticoids (a class of steroids; see

Eichenbaum, 2012). Depending on whether they pass the blood-brain barrier, some of these substances operate centrally, whereas others operate peripherally (Eichenbaum, 2012; McGaugh, 2000). And as discussed in chapter 2, drugs that alleviate depression—generally by increasing the activity of norepinephrine and/or serotonin—simultaneously improve memory functioning.

Thus a variety of interventions that occur after the initial encoding of information can modulate memory, making it better or worse, depending on the nature of their physiological effects (McGaugh, 2000). Some of these effects are relatively short-lived, such as drug-produced retrograde facilitation and many instances of TBI; other effects are longer lasting, such as ECS, and in a small subset of cases of brain injury, retrograde amnesia for temporally distant material can be permanent. In the majority of cases, amnesia shows a temporal gradient, with more remote memories more likely to be preserved, whereas events just before the injury are more likely to be affected—they simply are not consolidated in the first place. Even without some sort of brain injury, "[m]emories become less fragile to disruptive forces with the passage of time" (Wixted, 2004, p. 878). For example, the susceptibility to retroactive interference lessens over time (Wixted, 2004). The neurophysiological processes underlying consolidation are a large part of the reason why recently formed memories are easier to disrupt and therefore at greater risk of being lost in retrograde amnesia.

Shrinkage

The corollary to newer memories being affected more by retrograde amnesia is that older memories come back first—this is another part of Ribot's law (Wixted, 2004). Parkin (1997) describes the case of a 33-year-old man (originally reported by Benson & Geschwind, 1967) who was admitted to the hospital after a head injury:

> He was known to be separated from his wife and family (who lived in Washington), and had lived in Boston for the last two years. In Washington he worked as a bus driver, but in Boston he had held two different jobs, as a messenger and a labourer. During the first week after his accident, a number of mental impairments were apparent; but within a month, these had disappeared except for a severe amnesia. He was very disoriented, and thought he was still living in Washington. This continued for about three months, when suddenly he became concerned about his memory disorder, and his memory for new information showed signs of improvement. His RA [retrograde amnesia] also began to lessen; first he remembered the breakup of his marriage, followed by recollection of the first job he had had in Boston. A few days later memory of the second job returned, and by the time the patient was discharged, he had amnesia only for the 24-hour period preceding his injury. (Parkin, 1997, p. 151)

Retrograde amnesia due to ECT shows this same pattern, with most memories coming back, the more distant ones first; however, amnesia for a short period prior to treatment and the treatment itself typically persists.

Consolidation theory nicely explains the shrinkage phenomenon. Events immediately before the injury, which are still in the fixation phase, are not consolidated at all. Events from the preceding days and weeks, which are in the reorganization phase, have been initially consolidated but are still in a somewhat fragile state, accounting for their variable and often temporary loss of access. Finally, much older memories have been firmly consolidated; the brain injury might interfere with the reconsolidation process, but these memories, if affected at all, are likely to reemerge. Older memories, by virtue of the reconsolidation process—which involves retrieval and fresh consolidation—are also likely to be more broadly distributed in the brain than newer experiences (Parkin, 1997). Recovery would then restore the older memories, or at least some components of them, before the more narrowly distributed newer memories.

Shrinkage does not always occur. Pervasive retrograde amnesia can last for years (Piolino et al., 2005; Rosenbaum et al., 2005), and it can also get worse, as in degenerative conditions like Alzheimer's disease (see chapter 6). Thus, it is more apt to say that shrinkage describes the pattern of recovery when there *is* recovery.

Implicit Memory

In *The Bourne Identity*, Jason Bourne retains his skills as a highly trained assassin, even though he has no recollection that he *is* a highly trained assassin. Similarly, in *What Alice Forgot* Alice knows which key opens the door to her house, how to operate her unfamiliar car and cell phone, and type the right password to open her computer, without consciously remembering having done those things before (Moriarty, 2009). In other words, they have *implicit memory* of their prior experiences. Implicit memory is "the preserved ability to perform tasks that are influenced by a past event without the person being aware of the event experience" (Schwartz, 2014, p. 405). Explicit memory, in contrast, involves a conscious effort to search for specific information that one has previously experienced (Schacter, 1987). Thus, one displays implicit memory through indirect measures, such as changes in the performance of a task. Jason Bourne's unparalleled skills in hand-to-hand combat, despite not remembering that he ever studied martial arts, are proof that he retained the previously learned information in memory. Implicit memory applies most clearly to procedural skills, but it can also be demonstrated in semantic (e.g., priming for previously encountered words) and episodic memory (e.g., having a visceral reaction to a previously encountered person without remembering the encounter).

This preservation of procedural skills and other aspects of implicit memory is typical of patients with retrograde amnesia, even when it is quite extensive. For example, Piolino et al. (2005) describe the case of CL, whose amnesia was so extensive that he even forgot certain well-learned skills (e.g., driving a car, using a calculator) and vocabulary. He quickly relearned the skills and words, demonstrating that the original memories had been retained, at least to some degree, even though he was unaware of possessing the memories (see James, 2011, for a similar case). The experiment described above by Squire et al. (1984), in which patients receiving ECT demonstrated a skill they had learned prior to treatment but had no recollection of learning it, shows the same thing, as do priming effects after ECT (Dorfman, Kihlstrom, Cork & Misiaszek, 1995). In all of these examples, the amnesic person retrieves information from memory and uses it appropriately but has no conscious recollection of having acquired the information.

Implicit memory is also preserved in transient global amnesia (Noel et al., 2015) and psychogenic retrograde amnesia (Hennig-Fast et al., 2008). For example, Hennig-Fast and colleagues describe the case of a 39-year-old man who experienced a dissociative fugue in which he claimed to have no memories of his personal past (e.g., childhood, family, school, career). However, he could use a computer, play the guitar, and sign his name, despite having no explicit awareness of possessing those skills.

Psychological Consequences

As described in chapter 2, mood and memory are closely connected. Depressed patients have impaired memory, and persons with impaired memory are more likely to be depressed. It is hard to identify the direction of the causal relationship—most likely it is a two-way street. It is therefore unsurprising that patients with amnesia are unusually susceptible to depression (Knapskog et al., 2014). Patients with amnesia report numerous coping difficulties, problems that are compounded by others' misconceptions about their disorder (Swift & Wilson, 2001).

These problems are exacerbated in the small subset of persons whose retrograde amnesia is so severe that they lose their personal identity, their sense of self. Our memories help make us what, and who, we are; if I can remember nothing of my past, then who am I? As the neurologist Oliver Sacks (1998, p. 23) eloquently puts it, "what sort of a life (if any), what sort of a world, what sort of a self, can be preserved in a man who has lost the greater part of his memory and, with this, his past, and his moorings in time?" Suddenly realizing that you do not know who you are, have little if any memory for your past, and cannot recognize others would be distressing for anyone, and it helps to explain why patients with retrograde amnesia are so distressed by their condition, ranging from those with transient global amnesia to those with more lasting pervasive retrograde amnesia (Piolino et al., 2005). It also explains the apathy and detachment that can sometimes result, as the amnesic person loses a connection not only to his or her own self but to others as well (Piolino et al., 2005).

CONCLUSIONS

A large number of experiences and processes—some occurring naturally, others not—can result in the devastating condition of retrograde amnesia, in which the affected person loses memory for information encoded prior to the brain injury. Many of the forgotten memories often return, especially the more distant ones, and some kinds of information, such as implicit memory, are almost always preserved. However, the disrupted consolidation caused by the injury means that very recent events typically remain forgotten, and a consolidation deficit often persists moving forward, leading to anterograde amnesia as well (covered in the next chapter).

Of all the memory myths discussed in this book, false beliefs about amnesia, and retrograde amnesia in particular, are perhaps the most pervasive. Large majorities of laypeople believe, for example, that a head injury resulting in a complete loss of identity—but otherwise unimpaired cognitive functioning—is not uncommon. Although such cases have been documented, they are much rarer than the more routine cases of retrograde amnesia, which involve lost access to past memories for a brief or moderate period of time, with no loss of identity, and a degree of anterograde amnesia plus other cognitive effects.

In addition to false beliefs about memory loss, people are misinformed about the process of recovery from retrograde amnesia. Nearly four in ten people believe that a second blow to the head can jar forgotten memories back into place, and more than half believe that recovery from amnesia is largely a matter of hard work. The tendency to overestimate the extent of retrograde amnesia but underestimate the difficulty of recovering from it means that both amnesic patients and those who interact with them (e.g., family, friends, teachers, healthcare providers) might have unrealistic expectations that can hinder the patients' recovery and general wellbeing. Recovery from amnesia is hard enough without having to battle misinformation about the condition.

Cartoons, television series, movies, and novels all perpetuate these myths. A trained assassin with nearly total retrograde amnesia might make for a good novel or Hollywood blockbuster, but it is hardly representative of the population of amnesic cases. It is no exaggeration to conclude, as do

Lilienfeld et al. (2010, p. 81), that "[t]he true amnesia is Hollywood's profound loss of memory for scientific evidence."

NOTES

1. See http://www.alz.org/facts/.

2. Bourne's amnesia has resolved by the final film in the series, *Jason Bourne* (2016). Early on in the film, he states "I remember; I remember everything." A non-amnesia spinoff to the original series, *The Bourne Legacy* (2012), starred Jeremy Renner.

3. In David Baldacci's (2015) novel *Memory Man*, the blow to the head does even more than restore lost memories—it produces the ability to recall everything the protagonist experiences with perfect accuracy (for more on this sort of superior memory, see chapter 10).

4. The present discussion focuses on the survey items dealing with aspects of amnesia. The same studies show that laypeople also have misconceptions about other characteristics of brain injury (e.g., coma), although there is some evidence that general knowledge of TBI is improving over time (Hux et al., 2006).

5. The convention in conducting research on and writing about amnesia patients is to refer to them by their initials, to preserve their anonymity. For most of his career as a research participant, Henry was referred to as HM; since his death in 2008, he has been identified as Henry Molaison (Carey, 2008).

6. The surgery lessened but did not cure Henry's epilepsy. Most disturbingly, at the time there was only scant scientific evidence, at best, suggesting that the procedure would be successful. For an excellent summary of the medical, social, ethical, and psychological aspects of Henry's case, see Hilts (1995). A recent book by the surgeon's grandson also provides a unique perspective on Henry's case (Dittrich, 2016).

7. Like many analogies, this one is an oversimplification. The brain does not "reboot" after ECT in the same way that a computer does, but at a conceptual level, there are similarities. Moreover, it is now possible to implant a neurostimulator that essentially functions like a surge protector in the brain. The device, which received approval for treating epilepsy from the US Food and Drug Administration in 2013, detects abnormal electrical activity and normalizes it before it can produce a full-blown seizure (Gray & Mundell, 2013). If Henry M had had this technology available, perhaps he would not have had the surgery that robbed him of so much of his memory.

Chapter 6

Anterograde Amnesia

Myth: Anterograde Amnesia Is Rare

Related Myths: Anterograde Amnesia Is Funny; Sleeping Can Erase Memories

In Lewis Carroll's *Through the Looking-Glass*, the White Queen remarks that "It's a poor sort of memory that only works backwards" (Carroll, 1871/1960, p. 248). Like the Queen, most people think of memory as working only one way, namely backwards. And indeed, remembering previously encountered information, or retrospective memory, comprises the majority of what our memories do. Nonetheless, there are two respects in which memory works forward. First, we frequently need to remember to do things in the future, like take medication, attend an important meeting, or even brush our teeth. Such tasks, known as prospective memory, have recently begun to garner a fair amount of psychological attention (Einstein & McDaniel, 2014; McDaniel & Einstein, 2007).

Another respect in which memory works forward is in enabling us to store new information, as opposed to retrieving old information. Although we are very aware of occasions when we are unable to retrieve something we know we learned before, we are less aware of those times when we fail to learn some information in the first place. Yet in the case of brain damage, such anterograde memory deficits are more common than the retrograde amnesia covered in the previous chapter; and they can be every bit as devastating.

Consider, for example, the case of Henry M, introduced in the previous chapter (Carey, 2008; Corkin, 2013; Hilts, 1995). From the time of his surgery in 1953 until his death in 2008, he had virtually no memory of anything he experienced, at least on a conscious level (see the section on

"Implicit Memory," below, for a discussion of memory abilities he unknowingly retained). Consequently he was unable to live independently; could not remember people with whom he interacted regularly; remembered no personal happenings (e.g., the deaths of his parents) and almost no public events (stray facts did occasionally sneak through, such as John F. Kennedy's assassination); and read the same magazines, worked the same crossword puzzles, and watched the same television shows, always as if for the first time. It seems like such a condition would be incredibly depressing, but that would require him to be fully cognizant of his condition. Although Henry had some awareness of his memory disorder, and even its cause—occasionally referring to his surgery and resulting poor memory—he was consistently described as polite, amiable, and humorous—not depressed at all (Eichenbaum, 2012; Hilts, 1995). This suggests that either Henry had remarkable inner strength and resilience—certainly a possibility—or that he was sometimes aware of his profound memory loss "in the moment" but that those moments, like so many others, dissolved without leaving a lasting impact on his memory or affect.

In Yoko Ogawa's (2009) novel *The Housekeeper and the Professor*, the title characters must reintroduce themselves to each other every day, because the professor cannot remember anything he experiences for longer than 80 minutes. Despite this disability, he develops coping strategies as well as a meaningful relationship with the housekeeper and her son. Four widely seen films in the last several years (*Finding Nemo* and its sequel *Finding Dory*; *Fifty First Dates*; *Memento*) have similarly had a major character who suffers from anterograde amnesia, that is, difficulty storing new information in memory after a brain injury. These works are noteworthy for several reasons. First, despite the far greater number of fictionalized cases of retrograde amnesia, anterograde amnesia is actually a much more common consequence of brain damage. Second, the films appeal to diverse audiences, ranging from children and families to adults. In doing so, they have a tendency to play the memory loss for laughs; needless to say, amnesia is amusing neither for the amnesic person nor for those with whom he or she interacts. Third, popular portrayals of anterograde amnesia vary widely in terms of the accuracy with which they portray the phenomenon (Baxendale, 2004). For example, the main characters in the film *Fifty First Dates* and the novel *Before I Go to Sleep* (Watson, 2011) can remember events of the day just fine until they go to sleep, which runs counter to scientific research on memory consolidation during sleep; and the vast majority of individuals with anterograde amnesia forget information within just a few minutes, not 80 minutes like the professor in Ogawa's novel. In contrast, the protagonist of *Memento* can retain information for only a few minutes and is clearly struggling to function as a result—a fairly accurate depiction of someone with anterograde amnesia. Dory, the amnesic fish in *Finding Nemo* and *Finding Dory*, can similarly remember information for only a few minutes, but the impairment does not seem to have much effect on her overall level of functioning.

As discussed in the preceding chapter, retrograde amnesia has long been the memory darling of Hollywood and other purveyors of popular media. Perhaps it lends itself to better story lines. But anterograde amnesia has recently been catching up. However, the depictions of anterograde amnesia are no more accurate, in general, than those of retrograde amnesia. Much of the remainder of the present chapter parallels chapter 5: There is a brief description of laypeople's beliefs about anterograde amnesia, followed by a discussion of its causes and consequences. The remainder of the chapter considers some of the unique issues associated with anterograde amnesia, such as the relationship between memory and sleep and compensatory strategies for dealing with this form of memory impairment.

BELIEFS ABOUT ANTEROGRADE AMNESIA

Anterograde amnesia flies under the radar in the public imagination in the same way that it does not often figure in popular media. People do not know much about it. For example, Hux and colleagues (2006) found that barely half of their participants knew that "people with amnesia for events before the injury usually have trouble learning new things too" (51.9 %) and that "after head injury, it is usually harder to learn new things than it is to remember things from before the injury" (51.5 %). The public's performance was obviously not better than chance for these true-false questions.

Other studies have obtained comparable results, with only one-third to two-thirds of participants properly appreciating the encoding difficulties associated with TBI, based on their responses to these same two questions (Gouvier et al., 1988; Guilmette & Paglia, 2004; O'Jile et al., 1997; Willer et al., 1993). Professional school psychologists do somewhat better than laypeople, but Hooper (2006) found that more than one-third still failed to appreciate the high frequency of anterograde amnesia after a head injury. School psychologists' misconceptions about anterograde amnesia are likely to be even more problematic than their misconceptions about retrograde amnesia, as they are working with children in a learning environment that regularly requires them to store large amounts of new information in memory.

As anterograde amnesia can be construed as an encoding deficit, beliefs relevant to anterograde amnesia include not only beliefs about the effects of brain damage on memory, but also beliefs about how we learn information in general, such as the role of consciousness in learning. Can we remember information that we process subliminally—that is, information that we are unaware of at the time of encoding? Three of the survey items described in chapter 1 addressed this question, and participants' responses showed little appreciation of the limits of subliminal processing. Only 42.2 percent of participants knew that people generally cannot remember information presented to them while they are asleep (as discussed in the section on "Memory and Sleep," below, there are exceptions to this rule), and an even smaller proportion (approximately 10 %) knew that subliminal information does not affect either memory or behavior, advertisers' and marketers' expectations notwithstanding. In a way, these misconceptions are compatible with the false beliefs people have about encoding following brain damage. The expectation seems to be that encoding new information is no big deal: You can do it without even realizing it, and you can keep on doing it in the aftermath of a brain injury. For the most part, neither of those beliefs is true.

CAUSES OF ANTEROGRADE AMNESIA

There is considerable overlap between the brain regions involved in anterograde and retrograde amnesia, as well as the sorts of things that can damage them. As discussed in chapter 5, posttraumatic amnesia almost always involves some degree of anterograde amnesia. Tumors, drugs, stroke, degenerative disease (e.g., Alzheimer's disease), infection, and malnutrition, especially in conjunction with alcohol abuse, can also lead to anterograde amnesia. If any of these causes damage to the mammillary bodies or medial temporal regions (including the inner portion of the temporal lobes and hippocampus), anterograde amnesia results. Unlike retrograde amnesia, anterograde amnesia is almost always organic. Psychological forces might motivate the forgetting of the past, but there is little psychological impetus for losing the ability to encode new information.

The Amnesic Syndrome

Thus, anterograde amnesia can occur for many reasons, and depending on the type of brain injury, other cognitive and memory effects may also be present. But there is a relatively pure form of anterograde amnesia in which these other features are largely absent, known as the *amnesic syndrome*. Patients with the amnesic syndrome have severe and lasting anterograde amnesia but normal working memory and general cognitive functioning, as well as the ability to acquire new skills implicitly (see "Implicit Memory," below). There is usually some degree of retrograde amnesia, but it is highly variable, with some patients having intact past memory except for events immediately preceding the injury (Parkin, 1997). Two common causes of the amnesic syndrome are encephalitis and Korsakoff's syndrome.

Several documented cases of the amnesic syndrome have resulted from encephalitis—inflammation of the brain—caused by viruses, bacteria, parasites, or unknown etiology. There are approximately 20,000 cases of encephalitis in the United States each year (Shannon & Griffin, 2015). The most common source of viral encephalitis is the herpes simplex 1 virus. The damage, which occurs quickly—often before the infection is diagnosed and treatment initiated—tends to center on the hippocampus and temporal lobes. It has an 80 percent mortality rate if left untreated; the most frequent long-term consequence in surviving patients is memory impairment (Shannon & Griffin, 2015).

One of the better-known cases of herpes encephalitis-induced amnesic syndrome is Clive Wearing, a successful British musician, conductor, and producer (Wilson & Wearing, 1995).[1] Clive experienced recurrent headaches, along with feeling poorly and an intermittent fever, in March 1985, which the doctor thought was the flu. After several days he was hospitalized and treated with antiviral medication, but by that time the infection had damaged his hippocampus, temporal and frontal lobes. He initially forgot his wife's and daughter's names and his occupation, but these memories returned. He also initially had problems with semantic memory, with impaired comprehension, a tendency to refer to many different objects as "chicken," and a predilection for pronouncing words backwards (e.g., he called his wife "Harobed"). Years after his illness, his IQ was still normal to above average, but he continued to experience significant retrograde amnesia, not remembering much about his early life and occasionally forgetting that he knew how to play the piano.

Clive's most noticeable and lasting deficit is his anterograde amnesia (Wearing, 2006; Wilson & Wearing, 1995), which is similar in many respects to Henry's symptoms. He has no conscious recollection of anything that has happened since his illness. He does not recognize people he sees on a regular, even daily basis (e.g., caregivers, hospital personnel). If he talks to someone who leaves the room and then returns a few minutes later, he greets the person as though he or she has just arrived. Perhaps the most pronounced symptom of his anterograde amnesia is his constant sense, which he frequently expresses and writes down, that he has just become conscious and remembers nothing at all before the present moment.

The most common cause of the amnesic syndrome is prolonged alcohol abuse, which produces Korsakoff's syndrome (also known as Wernicke-Korsakoff syndrome; Parkin, 1997). Korsakoff's syndrome is closely linked to thiamine deficiency, which causes damage to the mammillary bodies. Alcoholism is frequently accompanied by malnutrition, and both naturalistic studies of malnourished humans (e.g., prisoners of war) and controlled animal experiments have shown that thiamine deficiency produces Korsakoff's-like symptoms; moreover, thiamine therapy can relieve some of the symptoms, especially when administered in the disorder's early stages (Parkin, 1997). It is unclear why only some alcoholics develop Korsakoff's syndrome, but it probably has to do with variations in diet and hereditary susceptibility. The central role of alcoholism in producing Korsakoff's syndrome means that, unlike nearly all other causes of amnesia, it is entirely preventable.

Not infrequently, Korsakoff's patients and others with the amnesic syndrome also show confabulation, in which they report, and genuinely believe, memories that are demonstrably false. For example, William, a Korsakoff's patient described by Sacks (1998, p. 110), regaled everyone he met with "amazing personal stories of fantastic adventures," sometimes incorporating the other people into his stories. Clive Wearing's most persistent confabulation was to say that he worked in the hospital where he resided and used to organize his fellow students to join him (Wilson & Wearing, 1995).

The sincerity of their belief in the memories distinguishes the fabricated events from deliberate lying; rather, they are unable to distinguish true memories from imagined ones, linking confabulation to the phenomena of false memories and source monitoring impairment (see chapters 3 and 4). As further evidence of this connection, confabulation and source monitoring deficits both result from frontal lobe damage (Parkin, 1997; Schacter, Harbluk, & McLachlan, 1984). Alcohol has well-known effects on frontal lobe functioning, and patients with Korsakoff's syndrome commonly have frontal lobe damage. Anterograde amnesia is not always accompanied by confabulation (Rosenbaum et al., 2005), particularly in the absence of damage to the frontal lobe.

Other Drug Effects

Many drugs besides alcohol can affect memory. Although benzodiazepines are effective at treating anxiety disorders and facilitate the retrieval of previously learned information (see chapter 5), their chronic use is also associated with cognitive impairment, including deficits in storing new episodic information in memory (Barker, Greenwood, Jackson, & Crowe, 2004; Deckersbach et al., 2011)—that is, they suppress consolidation. For example, in an experiment by Pomara et al. (2006), the researchers presented participants with new lists of words after they took the benzodiazepine lorazepam, in addition to a preadministration word list. As described in the previous chapter, participants demonstrated retrograde facilitation for the preadministration word list—they recalled more words on the drug than they did on placebo. However, they also recalled fewer words from the lists presented *after* administration of the drug (regardless of dosage) than from the list presented *before* administration. In other words, the drug had an anterograde amnesic effect. Interestingly, the effect was stronger for participants who showed greater retrograde facilitation than for participants who showed less retrograde facilitation. The more the drug helped memory in one respect, the more it also hurt memory in another respect.

Parkin (1997) records an unusually creative, albeit criminal, use of benzodiazepines' amnestic qualities. Several Parisian prostitutes allegedly laced their clients' drinks with Valium. They then persuaded the clients to write them checks for large amounts of money. When the clients sobered up, they could not remember the experience. An even more insidious use of benzodiazepines' amnestic property is date-rape drugs, such as Rohypnol (flunitrazepam), a fast-acting benzodiazepine. Perpetrators give the drug to an unknowing victim, who is then sexually assaulted but subsequently cannot remember the experience.

As Parkin points out, "there are more constructive uses for this induced amnesia" (p. 158), such as using benzodiazepines as an amnestic agent during medical or dental procedures. The drugs promote relaxation while removing the need for a general anesthetic. I can vouch for the practice personally: I have had multiple medical procedures performed while under the influence of midazolam (Versed) and gratefully remember nothing of the experience (nor their immediate aftermath, which led me to ask about the procedure repeatedly for some time afterwards, until the medication had fully worn off).

The memory impairment associated with chronic benzodiazepine use for treating anxiety is partly, but not entirely, a manifestation of the disorder itself (Deckersbach et al., 2011), and it persists even after cessation of the medication (Barker et al., 2004), suggesting that long-term use might change the brain's underlying neurophysiology. Patients who take benzodiazepines for the treatment of anxiety must therefore weigh the costs of their cognitive side effects against the benefits of symptom reduction.

CHARACTERISTICS OF ANTEROGRADE AMNESIA

Although half of survey respondents are unaware of the prevalence of antero-grade amnesia after brain injury, it is extremely common—considerably more common, in fact, than retrograde amnesia (Kopelman, 2002; Parkin, 1997). It is also more likely to occur alone; that is, anterograde amnesia with minimal or no retrograde amnesia is not unusual, but as discussed in the previous chapter, retrograde amnesia with minimal or no anterograde amnesia is quite rare.[2]

The hallmark feature of anterograde amnesia is the inability to store new information in long-term memory. Beyond that, though, a number of questions arise: How long does memory for new information last? Are all kinds of information affected equally, or are some aspects of memory retained? Are people with anterograde amnesia aware of their deficit? Is sleeping part of the problem or part of the solution? What can people suffering from anterograde amnesia do about their memory loss? The remainder of the chapter reviews research addressing each of these questions.

Duration

Without rehearsal, people with anterograde amnesia typically retain information for only 30–60 seconds. This is true for people without anterograde amnesia as well, with the critical difference that if memory is functioning normally, one can continue thinking about some information despite brief distractions and can relate it to other, previously stored information, thereby consolidating it in a more permanent form. Someone with severe anterograde amnesia lacks this ability. Numerous examples from patients with severe anterograde amnesia illustrate the phenomenon quite tellingly. For example, during one of his treatment sessions, EB became so agitated that he "punched the table with such force that his hand immediately began to swell. EB left the meeting with a member of the team and within 20 steps of leaving the meeting, EB turned towards the staff member and asked why his hand hurt" (Shannon & Griffin, 2015, p. 119).

Eichenbaum (2012) relates an interaction he had with HM while driving him from the nursing home to MIT for testing. Eichenbaum had a McDonald's coffee cup in the car.

> After just a few minutes HM noticed the cup and said, "Hey, I knew a fellow named John McDonald when I was a boy!" He proceeded to tell some of his adventures with the friend, and so I asked a few questions and was impressed with the elaborate memories he had of that childhood period. Eventually the story ended and HM turned to watch the scenery passing by. After just a few more minutes, he looked up at the dashboard and remarked, "Hey, I knew a fellow named John McDonald when I was a boy!" and proceeded to relate virtually the identical story. I asked probing questions in an effort to continue the interaction and to determine if the facts of the story would be the same. HM never noticed he had just told this elaborate tale and repeated the story more or less exactly as before. A few minutes later the conversation ended, and he turned to view the scenery again. Just minutes later, once more HM looked up to my dashboard and exclaimed, "Hey, I knew a fellow named John McDonald when I was a boy!" I helped him reproduce, as well as he could, the same conversation yet again, then quickly disposed of the cup under his seat . . . . (Eichenbaum, 2012, pp. 89–90)

These examples, which are drawn from numerous others involving Henry and other patients with anterograde amnesia (e.g., Hilts, 1995; Parkin, 1997), show that memory for new information in patients with this type of memory disorder is preciously short-lived. Yet popular portrayals of individuals with anterograde amnesia run the gamut, with the duration of memory ranging from a matter of seconds or a few minutes (e.g., Dory in *Finding Nemo* and *Finding Dory*, Leonard in *Memento*) to 80 minutes (e.g., the professor in *The Housekeeper and the Professor*) to an entire day (e.g., the main characters in *50 First Dates* and *Before I Go to Sleep*).

Implicit Memory

Just as patients with retrograde amnesia often demonstrate implicit memory, individuals with anterograde amnesia are often capable of learning new perceptual-motor skills, and drawing on previously processed information, without any conscious recollection of having done so. For example, Henry showed steady improvement in learning how to trace mirror-reversed images, despite not remembering that he had done the task before (Corkin, 1968; Eichenbaum, 2012), and densely amnesic patients not infrequently learn their way around the institution where they are living (e.g., Wilson & Wearing, 1995). These preserved abilities extend beyond mere motor skills. One of the earliest illustrations of this came from a study conducted by Cohen and Squire (1980), who taught a sample of severely amnesic patients to read mirror-reversed words. Over the course of three training sessions, their speed at reading novel reversed words improved at the same rate as control participants, and they retained the skill equally well 3 months later, even though they could not remember performing the task. The amnesic patients performed somewhat worse than controls when they were shown repeated words because they could not explicitly remember having seen the specific words, but they got faster at reading repeated words also.

These examples demonstrate that new procedural information can be encoded. Patients with anterograde amnesia also often show implicit retention of semantic and episodic information. With respect to semantic information, they show priming effects when recognizing previously encountered words and pictures (Eichenbaum, 2012; Parkin, 1997). Henry also showed some, albeit very limited, knowledge of newsworthy events (e.g., the John F. Kennedy assassination) and public figures (Eichenbaum, 2012; O'Kane, Kensinger, & Corkin, 2004).

With respect to episodic knowledge, Henry demonstrated implicit memory after meeting someone who gave him a slight shock with a hand buzzer when they shook hands. On reencountering him—as far as he knew, for the first time—Henry declined to shake his hand but could not explain why (Hilts, 1995). KC showed something similar, routinely guessing that he had not met one of the researchers who had visited him in his home approximately eight times per year over a several year period, yet demonstrating "a certain level of familiarity and comfort" (Rosenbaum et al., 2005, p. 993). Angie, a 50-year-old woman with profound anterograde amnesia due to TBI at age 29, could say which of her work colleagues she liked and trusted and which ones she did not, but she could not provide any evidence to support her feelings (Duff, Wszalek, Tranel & Cohen, 2008). And Clive Wearing, when prompted to put on his coat for a walk, knew that it meant they were going to feed the ducks that lived on the grounds (Wilson & Wearing, 1995). This same ability to learn information implicitly has been observed in patients in the acute phase of transient global amnesia (see chapter 5). For example, they show an enhanced preference for faces that they have seen before, even when they do not explicitly recognize the faces (Marin-Garcia, Ruiz-Vargas & Kapur, 2013).

To their credit, fictional portrayals of characters with anterograde amnesia often illustrate similar kinds of implicit memory. They develop kind of a gut feeling about people (or fish) with whom they have interacted previously, even though they cannot remember the previous encounters. For example, Dory in *Finding Nemo* seems to recognize Marlin at some level and remember that they are friends, although she cannot usually remember why they are together. And in one scene she cannot remember being instructed to swim through a certain trench, not over it, but she still has a sense that they should go through, not over. Although these examples are fairly plausible, toward the end of the movie she finally finds Nemo and sees the word "Sydney," and all of the things that she failed to encode previously come rushing back. The formerly implicit becomes explicit at last. Would that it worked that way for real people (or fish) with anterograde amnesia.

Subjective Memory and Awareness of the Deficit

A common technique for measuring subjective awareness in memory is the "remember/know" paradigm, in which rememberers evaluate the subjective nature of their retrieved memories (Tulving, 1985). "Remembered" information is associated with recollection of a specific instance of encoding, which includes some degree of re-experiencing the personal context in which one encountered the information (e.g., remembering the last movie I saw—*Self/less* (discussed in chapter 4), which I watched at home a few nights ago with my wife and daughter). In contrast, "known" information is associated with a feeling of familiarity, knowing that the information is in memory, but without the subjective sense of recollection (e.g., seeing a former student in a coffee shop and knowing I have encountered him before, but not remembering when or where). People can reliably make remember-know distinctions in judging both episodic and semantic memories (Neath & Surprenant, 2015), although episodic information is more likely to be remembered, and semantic information merely known (Tulving, 1985).

Patients with anterograde amnesia lose "remembering" more than "knowing" (Tulving, 1985) For example, Piolino et al. (2005) asked the amnesic patient CL, introduced in the previous chapter, to describe events from different periods of his life (e.g., a trip or family event). For each recalled event, he then indicated whether he remembered it or merely knew it (or was guessing). Compared to control participants, CL was less likely to judge events since the onset of his amnesia as remembered (vs. known), and he recalled them in less detail, except for those occurring in the last day or so. Consistent with his profound retrograde amnesia, he also could not give any "remember" responses for preonset events. For events both before and after his injury, he had a greatly reduced sense of having personally experienced the events, which is so much a part of what gives our memories their life, vibrancy, and color. As the renowned memory researcher Endel Tulving eloquently expressed it (1985, p. 1), this kind of self-knowing recollection "provides the characteristic phenomenal flavor of the experience of remembering."

Chapter 5 described how retrograde amnesia can be associated with a loss of one's sense of self; anterograde amnesia contributes to this phenomenon as well. The self is a fluid concept that requires continuity over time (Baumeister, 1998; James, 1890). In profound anterograde amnesia, time essentially stops; how can you have a sense of "yesterday" if you cannot remember it? Henry M, and patients like him, had no sense of time beyond 30 seconds; he was even unaware of how old he was. Losing track of time can contribute to unexpected problems. Angie could not remember whether she had completed everything she needed to do while showering. Consequently she repeated the tasks over and over and would spend more than an hour in the shower (Duff et al., 2008).

For amnesic patients who lose track of time, being confronted with evidence of the passage of time, such as their own aging, can be shocking. Sacks (1998, p. 25) describes the case of Jimmie, a 49-year-old patient with Korsakoff's syndrome. Evaluated in 1975, he thought the year was 1945 and he was 19 years old. Sacks handed the gray-haired, middle-aged man a mirror, telling him, "'Look in the mirror and tell me what you see. Is that a nineteen-year-old looking out from the mirror?' He suddenly turned ashen and gripped the sides of the chair. 'Jesus Christ,' he whispered. 'Christ, what's going on? What's happened to me? Is this a nightmare? Am I crazy? Is this a joke?'—and he became frantic, panicked." Jimmie calmed down and forgot the episode once Sacks distracted him.[3]

Some patients with anterograde amnesia have a similar reaction on continually rediscovering their disability, if they are unable to remember that they have an impaired memory (Andrewes & Gielewski, 1999). Without the ability to track time and form new memories, the sense of self can diminish in persons with anterograde amnesia, and being confronted with evidence contrary to one's sense of self—which for most of us includes having the ability to form new memories—can be very upsetting. Yet despite the challenges presented to one's self-concept by anterograde amnesia, in some cases the sense of self can evolve, just as it does in persons without amnesia. For example, Angie adapted unusually well to her disorder, returning to work and forming and maintaining satisfying interpersonal relationships (Duff et al., 2008).

Some patients with anterograde amnesia are more aware of their loss than others. As noted above, Henry had sporadic awareness of his amnesia, but he was not aware of it continuously enough that it caused him much concern. If memory is sufficiently impaired, then one fails to encode fresh instances of forgetting. Other persons with anterograde amnesia, in contrast, have a more stable awareness of their disorder. The great Russian neuropsychologist Alexander Luria describes the case of Sublieutenant Zazetsky, a Russian soldier who was shot in the head during World War II (Luria, 1987a; see also Hilts, 1995). In addition to his difficulties storing new information, he had problems with sensory and spatial memory and language. He knew he had been injured, was very distressed by his cognitive difficulties, and said that he felt he had really been killed on the day of his injury. Zazetsky described himself as being in a constant fog and feeling like he was living out a nightmare. Clive Wearing knows there is a large gap in his memory because he continually feels like he has just woken up; he seeks an explanation for it in news of the day that he reads about in magazines and newspapers (Wilson & Wearing, 1995). However, he is not aware of the previous days on which he felt the same way.

Other persons with anterograde amnesia due to herpes encephalitis have a more ongoing awareness of their impairment, for which they develop compensatory strategies (Berry et al., 2007; Shannon & Griffin, 2015; see "Compensatory Strategies," below). Patients with TBI and Korsakoff's syndrome likewise span the continuum from being completely oblivious to their disorder to being painfully aware of it (e.g., Duff et al., 2008; Parkin, 1997). Not surprisingly, for the majority of cases, the more one is aware of the memory loss, the greater the psychological distress. It is hard to say whether it is better to know or not to know what one has lost.

MEMORY AND SLEEP

The common view of sleep is as a period when the brain essentially shuts down—that is, even if it does not power off completely, it goes into screen saver mode with no discernible activity. In the animated film *Inside Out*, the main character's "train of thought" (naturally represented in the movie as an actual train) simply stops running when she goes to sleep. Somewhat paradoxically, she does dream despite the cessation of thought, but the dreams are amalgams of fantasy and past memories that can take place even while her brain is shut down. In this film, sleep plays a relatively benign role with respect to memory. In other fictional portrayals, however, sleep has a deleterious effect, completely erasing memories that were retained just fine while the person was awake (e.g., the film *50 First Dates* and the novel *Before I Go to Sleep*).

In *50 First Dates*, for example, Lucy, played by Drew Barrymore, suffered a severe brain injury in a car accident. Since the accident, her ability to form new memories is largely intact, but only while she is awake; once she wakes up from a night's sleep, she remembers nothing from the day before. As a result, she does not remember meeting and hitting it off with Henry (played by Adam Sandler) from one day to the next, forcing him to woo her afresh on each date. The movie's premise is clever and their developing relationship, in the face of her amnesia, is humorous—but is it realistic?

In a word, "No." Representations of sleep as having an amnestic effect are the exact opposite of sleep's actual effect on memory. Sleep *helps* memory, primarily by leading to better consolidation. A related question is whether we can remember information that is presented *during* sleep. The answer to this question is somewhat equivocal, but in some limited respects, information that is processed without conscious awareness can be retained in memory.

Sleep and Consolidation

Sleep's beneficial effect on memory has been known since the earliest research on memory 130 years ago (Ebbinghaus, 1885/1964; see Neath & Surprenant, 2015). Controlled studies show that information—whether procedural, semantic, or episodic—is retained better following a period of sleep than following an equally long period of wakefulness (e.g., Jenkins & Dallenbach, 1924; for review, see Gais & Born, 2004; Payne et al., 2012; Stickgold & Walker, 2007). Memory is better following sleep than waking whether awake participants are tested after a night of sleep deprivation or during the day (Gais, Lucas & Born, 2006). Sleep is beneficial, at least in part, presumably because being awake and active exposes one to a greater amount of potentially interfering information. It follows, then, that being awake and inactive would likewise facilitate consolidation, and some research supports this hypothesis (Neath & Surprenant, 2015). However, there is more to it than that; neural activity unique to the sleeping brain facilitates consolidation. Specifically, sleep fosters the interactions between the hippocampus and cortex that are central to the reorganization component of the consolidation process (Drosopoulos, Schulze, Fischer & Born, 2007; MacLeod & Hulbert, 2011).

Support for this view of sleep comes from research showing that in addition to facilitating the consolidation of recently acquired memories by reducing the amount of extraneous information, sleep can actually enhance memory for motor skills learned beforehand, independent of further practice (Stickgold & Walker, 2007). Moreover, certain properties of sleep appear to play an active role in the consolidation process. The sleeping brain engages in unique physiological processes during different sleep stages, and sleep's effectiveness at consolidating information depends on a number of factors, such as the stage of sleep, the type of information, the type of memory test (e.g., recall or recognition), the individual's motivation, and the amount of sleep (Diekelmann, Wilhelm & Born, 2009; Gais & Born, 2004; Stickgold & Walker, 2007). For example, REM (for "rapid eye movement") sleep aids in the consolidation of new procedural and emotional memories, whereas slow-wave sleep enhances the consolidation of semantic memories (Diekelmann et al., 2009; Gais & Born, 2004). Sleep benefits recall for semantic information more than recognition (Diekelmann et al., 2009), and it enhances consolidation more when the rememberer is motivated to remember (e.g., by a promise of financial reward; Fischer & Born, 2010). Only a relatively brief period of sleep (1–2 hours) is needed to achieve optimal consolidation of semantic memories (Diekelmann et al., 2009), and even an ultrashort nap of just a few minutes can yield significant benefits (Lahl, Wispel, Willigens & Pietrowsky, 2008). The consolidation of procedural memories, in contrast, is more dose-dependent (Diekelmann et al., 2009). The interplay among these many variables shows that the relationship between sleep and memory is complex; however, it shows conclusively that the nature of that relationship is for sleep to have a generally facilitative effect on memory consolidation.

In addition to aiding the consolidation of new memories, sleep also dampens the inhibition of weakened, previously forgotten memories, allowing them to become once again accessible (Drosopoulos et al., 2007; MacLeod & Hulbert, 2011). As with consolidation in general, REM appears to play an especially important role in this process. The more time spent in REM, the less retrieval of some information (e.g., part of a list of word pairs) inhibits the retrieval of other information (e.g., other word pairs from the list)—a phenomenon known as "retrieval-induced forgetting" (see Baran, Wilson & Spencer, 2010). This combination of enhanced consolidation and reduced inhibition enables sleep to help regulate and stabilize competing levels of excitation and inhibition in memory (MacLeod & Hulbert, 2011). Finally, sleep can also facilitate reconsolidation—that is, a subsequent consolidation of a previously consolidated memory once it has been reactivated (Stickgold & Walker, 2007).

It is possible to exploit this reactivation process by presenting cues during sleep that were also present during the initial (waking) consolidation. Rihm,

Diekelmann, Born, and Rasch (2014) had participants learn a visuospatial memory task, resembling the game "concentration," in the presence of a pleasant or unpleasant odor. They then presented the same odor, the other odor, or no odor during the slow-wave sleep stage of the first 3 hours of participants' sleep. The type of odor that was present during sleeping produced different patterns of brain activity associated with slow-wave sleep. Moreover, when participants were tested on waking, those who were exposed to the same odor while sleeping performed significantly better than the other two groups. Participants in the congruent odor condition even performed better, on average, after sleeping than they did at the end of the learning phase (i.e., before sleep; $M = 110.2$ %).[4]

Thus, there are a number of different ways in which sleep has beneficial effects on memory. The critical question is how sleep exerts these effects. Clearly, memory consolidation during sleep does not affect all recently encoded memories in a uniform fashion. A comprehensive theory of sleep and memory therefore needs to explain this selectivity. Stickgold and Walker (2013) propose a "triage" process, whereby the brain tags memories during or shortly after encoding in terms of their relevance, based on the organism's own autobiographical history. Relevance cues might come, for example, from high motivation or emotional elements of an experience. Selective consolidation during sleep then results in optimal retention and forgetting by producing enhanced memory for relevant but not irrelevant information. Beyond the enhanced consolidation of discrete memories, it can also contribute to the creation of new knowledge, by integrating item memories into already existing memory networks or enabling the extraction of generalized rules or schemas. Thus, sleep is a key component in the "long and complex process of memory evolution" over an individual's life history (Stickgold & Walker, 2013, p. 144).

Consistent with this triage process, research suggests that the brain is more "plastic"—that is, susceptible to structural and/or functional neural changes—during sleep than while awake (Stickgold & Walker, 2007). For example, imaging studies show that sleep-dependent motor learning is associated with neural reorganization, and plasticity has been demonstrated at the cellular and even the molecular level (Stickgold & Walker, 2007)—further evidence that the brain is hardly sleeping while the rest of the body is. As Stickgold and Walker point out, this plasticity stands to reason. Learning and memory necessarily depend on brain plasticity, so if sleep facilitates consolidation, then the facilitative effect must be mediated by processes indicative of plasticity.

Given sleep's role not only in strengthening consolidation for distinct memories but also in restructuring and reorganizing memories, there might be a tradeoff between sleep's benefits and its costs. That is, it might produce better memory for some information, while also leading to more errors, especially errors associated with reconstructive memory processes, such as the formation of false memories. Diekelmann et al. (2008) explored this possibility in several studies in which they manipulated sleep deprivation in participants undergoing the DRM false memory paradigm (see chapter 3). For example, their first experiment compared three groups of participants who (a) studied the DRM word lists in the evening and were tested the next morning after normal sleep; (b) studied the lists in the evening and were tested the next morning after being kept awake; or (c) studied the lists in the morning and were tested that evening after normal daytime wakefulness. The sleep-deprived group exhibited more false memories than participants in the other two conditions. The "day wake" group did not differ from the "night sleep" group, suggesting that sleep after learning does not increase (or decrease) false memories; rather, sleep deprivation at the time of retrieval appears to increase false memories. Diekelmann et al. confirmed this interpretation in subsequent experiments that varied whether participants were sleep-deprived at testing or immediately following encoding, but not both (the "night wake" group in Experiment 1 was both prevented from sleeping after encoding and sleep-deprived at retrieval). Participants who were sleep-deprived at retrieval produced more false memories, whereas participants who were sleep-deprived after learning the lists did not.[5] Overall, these findings indicate that the beneficial effects of sleep on memory consolidation are not offset by an increase in memory errors (at least not this kind of error).

The positive relationship between sleep and memory has many important implications. Two of the more important ones are for individuals whose memories are being taxed more than normal—namely students—and for individuals with impaired memories, such as those with Alzheimer's disease. It is well known that students, especially during adolescence, undergo changes in their circadian rhythms that result in a lack of sleep, primarily because they tend to stay up late but still have to wake up early for school. According to the National Sleep Foundation (2017), teens need 8–10 hours of sleep per night, but only 15 percent report sleeping that much on school nights.

Gais et al. (2006) conducted an experiment that demonstrated the effects of sleep on students' learning. In a within-subject design, American high school students studied English-German vocabulary lists in either the morning or evening. All participants then slept normally (depending on condition, for one or two nights) before being tested on their recall of the lists. The retrieval session was in the morning or the evening. Neither the length of the retention interval nor the timing of the retrieval session affected performance, but the timing of the learning session did. Specifically, participants who learned in the evening and slept after learning the vocabulary remembered more words than participants who learned in the morning and then stayed awake. The timing of learning is less important than whether sleep follows learning—sleep shortly after learning yields the greatest benefits (Payne et al., 2012).

In a follow-up experiment, Gais et al. (2006) found that participants who were sleep-deprived for one night following vocabulary learning remembered fewer words 2 days later (i.e., after being allowed to catch up on sleep) than participants who slept normally after learning. Thus, sleeping after studying enhances retention of the material; students who stay up late studying and do not get enough sleep are likely to remember the material less well than those who obtain adequate sleep. In addition to the benefits of sleep *after* learning, sleep *before* learning would also aid students, as tired students learn less well than rested students. The combination has led to a movement to push back high-school starting times so that teens can get more sleep (Carpenter, 2001).

At the opposite end of the developmental continuum, recent research has found a connection between sleep and Alzheimer's disease, in which one of the defining symptoms is anterograde amnesia (see chapter 7). Specifically, persons with Alzheimer's disease experience poor sleep quality and insufficient amounts of sleep, and these indicators predict mild cognitive impairment, a frequent precursor to Alzheimer's disease (e.g., Ju, Lucey & Holtzman, 2014; Roh et al., 2012; Yaffe, Falvey & Hoang, 2014), as well as the disorder itself (Lim et al., 2013). A variety of sleep disorders commonly affect Alzheimer's patients. They include "sleep fragmentation," which quantifies the number of "arousals" (i.e., episodes of waking) during the sleep period; diminished sleep duration, particularly the stages of slow-wave sleep and REM; napping during the day; sleep apnea; and inversion of the sleep-wake cycle (e.g., Peter-Derex, Yammine, Bastuji & Croisile, 2015; Yaffe et al., 2014). The connection between poor sleep and Alzheimer's disease has been demonstrated in humans with the disorder and in animal models of the disease, cross-sectionally and longitudinally, and based on both self-report and physiological sleep measures (Peter-Derex et al., 2015). Given the connection between sleep and consolidation, this suggests that poor sleep contributes to the memory deficits that are characteristic of the disease, although the causal relationship could be bidirectional. Chapter 7 provides additional detail on the relationship between sleep and Alzheimer's disease.

The sleep disturbances in Alzheimer's patients, in conjunction with animal and human research demonstrating the mnemonic benefits of sleep, provide conclusive evidence that fictional portrayals of characters whose memories are wiped clean while they sleep have no basis in fact.[6] The research shows, rather, that sleep is enormously beneficial to memory consolidation. As Diekelmann et al. (2009) observe, this might even explain why our bodies need to lose consciousness and sleep regularly—acute conscious processing of information and the subsequent storage of that same information "might be mutually exclusive processes that cannot take place in the same networks at the same time" (Diekelmann et al., 2009, p. 309). Without sleep, our memories could not function nearly as well as they do.

Memory for Information Presented during Sleep

Thus, information is remembered better following a period of sleep than following an equal period of awake time. Some research looks at memory for information presented *during* sleep, as opposed to *before* sleep. Certain popular portrayals, especially in the science fiction realm (e.g., Aldous Huxley's *Brave New World*), raise the possibility of inculcating specific knowledge, beliefs, and preferences in people by presenting information to them while they are asleep (Simon & Emmons, 1955). Against these futuristic representations of sleep learning, the conventional wisdom, as in *Inside Out*, is that the brain essentially shuts down during sleep and would therefore be impervious to external stimuli, except for an occasional noise (e.g., an alarm) that might be incorporated into a dream. Do we remember things that happen while we are asleep?

A number of entrepreneurs appear to think so. There is no shortage of products that purport to help people learn while they sleep; a Google search for "learn while you sleep" yielded 116,000,000 results, including several sleep-learning apps; and it has been depicted in popular media (e.g., a *Simpsons* episode in which Homer tried to reduce his appetite by listening to a tape while sleeping; Robson, 2014). Early research indicated that people did not remember information presented to them while they were genuinely asleep (e.g., Simon & Emmons, 1955, 1956); they were, however, able to remember information that they heard during brief periods when they were either awake or in a transitional state between sleeping and waking (Simon & Emmons, 1956). Importantly, in these states they could also recall hearing the information (Simon & Emmons, 1956), which raises the question of what constitutes "sleep" for purposes of learning during sleep. If sleep simply refers to the long period between going to bed and waking up the next day, then some learning occurs. But if sleep refers to the intervals wherein one is in deep sleep, then Simon and Emmons' (1956) research indicates that it does not. More recent research has been more promising, although the results overall are somewhat equivocal (Logie & Della Salla, 1999; Robson, 2014).

Much of the research on learning during sleep examines people who have been anesthetized for medical reasons, rather than sleeping naturally. Like the natural sleep studies, this research shows little in the way of explicit recall, but participants do show implicit memory, such as semantic priming effects, for information presented while they are anesthetized (Andrade, 1995; Logie & Della Salla, 1999; Parkin, 1997). Some research also shows that they are able to remember factual information. For example, Jelicic, Bonke, Wolters, and Phaf (1992) played a tape, via headphones, to 50 surgical patients while they were under general anesthesia. The tape contained either 20 minutes of seaside sounds or 5 minutes of seaside sounds plus 15 minutes in which four target words (pear, banana, yellow, and green) were presented 30 times apiece. The patients were interviewed shortly after surgery (*M* delay = 80.6 minutes). In the interview, they were asked to recall anything that happened during surgery, and then to name the first three exemplars of the categories "vegetables," "fruits," and "colors" that came to mind. Participants in the experimental group were significantly more likely to report the target words for the fruit and color categories (*M* = 2.4/4) than participants in the control group (*M* = 1.84/4). They did equally well at generating exemplars for the vegetable category. No one reported hearing any words during the operation.

The experiment by Jelicic et al. (1992) is an excellent demonstration of implicit memory because participants had elevated access to certain information, but they had no recollection of how or when they acquired it. Similar studies show that anesthetized patients lack explicit recall for intraoperative events (Schwender et al., 1994; there are, regrettably, numerous instances of patients recalling intraoperative events because the anesthetic did not work properly). Other studies have replicated the finding of implicit memory during anesthesia (e.g., Schwender et al., 1994), but still others have failed to find implicit memory for information presented during anesthesia or natural sleep (e.g., Wood, Bootzin, Kihlstrom & Schacter, 1992; for review, see Andrade, 1995; Bonebakker, Jelicic, Passchier & Bonke, 1996; Merikle & Daneman, 1996). It is also unclear how long any positive effect lasts; implicit memory for information presented during sleep is more likely when testing occurs after a relatively brief retention interval (Merikle & Daneman, 1996).

These inconsistent results could simply reflect the small magnitude of the effect. They may also be due to the particular neurological effects of different kinds of general anesthesia, variations in the depth of anesthesia, individual differences in suggestibility (see chapter 3), or methodological differences across studies (Andrade, 1995; Bonebakker et al., 1996; Schwender et al., 1994). For example, depth of anesthesia is notoriously difficult to measure (Andrade, 1995), and successful learning could occur during undetected moments of awareness.

The possibility of learning during sleep is interesting not only because of its contribution to our understanding of different kinds of memory (e.g., explicit vs. implicit memory) and the role of consciousness in learning and memory but also because of its practical applications. We spend approximately one-third of our lives asleep, so why not put the time to good use and learn something? The medical applications are potentially even more valuable. If information presented during anesthesia can have implicit effects, then it raises the possibility of providing information during surgery that would have a positive effect on postoperative behavior (e.g., length of hospital stay, amount of painkillers used), such as a suggestion that the patient will feel well or want to get up soon after surgery. Several studies have examined this possibility; some find a beneficial effect, whereas others do not (Andrade, 1995; Merikle & Daneman, 1996).

Overall, retention is substantially better for information processed while awake than when asleep. Nonetheless, information that is presented while one is asleep can, in some cases, have small effects at the implicit level, although there is no evidence to support large-scale benefits of sleep learning. The modest evidence of implicit memory for material that one "hears" while asleep is consistent with research on memory consolidation during sleep; both lines of research provide further evidence that even when we are unconscious, our brains are still quite active. They are processing new information, consolidating recent information, and reorganizing information in memory.

COMPENSATORY STRATEGIES

Rehabilitation of patients with anterograde amnesia is unusually challenging. Whenever someone has a medical problem in need of self-administered treatment—whether it be medication, injections, exercise, dietary changes, or something else—the person first needs to remember to implement the treatment. This can be challenging for any disorder; I forget to take my allergy pill, on average, a couple of times a month, despite using a weekly pill box with separate containers for each day. When memory loss *is* the disorder, it is that much harder for patients to remember to implement any compensatory strategies that they may have been taught. Nonetheless, there are a variety of techniques that can be used, some of which have been shown to have a degree of success.

A short-term solution to anterograde amnesia, which many patients adopt, is simply to mentally rehearse information to keep it active in short-term memory. For example, Henry M was able to retain information for at least 15 minutes by repeating it over and over and applying mnemonic schemes to it (Hilts, 1996; Milner, 1971). In *Finding Nemo*, Dory uses a similar strategy, repeating variations on the information crucial to the search for Nemo—P. Sherman, 42 Wallaby Way, Sydney—as a way to remember it. The problem with this strategy is that the capacity of short-term memory is severely limited, and once the person is distracted, the information disappears. Dory actually manages to remember it long-term despite being distracted, which could happen with enough repetition, but is unlikely.

A more effective approach is to take advantage of the intact implicit memory in amnesia patients. Andrewes and Gielewski (1999) describe the rehabilitation of JR, a 28-year-old woman with anterograde amnesia due to herpes simplex encephalitis. A law graduate, JR was trained after her brain damage to work as a law librarian. The specific tasks that were part of JR's treatment plan were filing updates to legal regulations, checking in library books, and shelving of journals and books. Each task was broken down into subcomponents; she had a folder with instructions for each procedure; and the initial training included social reinforcement, prompts, and cues (e.g., completing the checking-in task served as a cue for commencing the shelving task). With practice she reached a point where she could perform the tasks accurately and independently. JR also initially needed assistance to go to a different part of the library (e.g., to the restroom), but with the assistance of instructions written on small cue cards, she eventually learned her way around and no longer needed the cards. JR's improvements in her work performance occurred despite her having no memory of the training sessions.

Many treatment approaches incorporate some sort of external memory aid. The most popular aid is probably note-taking, which is cheap, easy, and familiar. A number of fictional and genuine amnesic patients engage in note-taking. Both Christine, the protagonist in the novel *Before I Go to Sleep*, and Clive Wearing keep diaries. Because Christine's memory functions just fine until she goes to sleep, her diary entries are rich narratives describing what she has learned anew each day. As a way of dealing with his seemingly constantly changing environment—because he continually rediscovers it from one moment to the next—Clive began writing down his impressions, along with the date and time (Wilson & Wearing, 1995). Many of his entries stated that he had just awakened and was conscious for the very first time. He did not remember making the entries and could become angry when asked to explain them. Angie addressed her problem of losing track of time in the shower by laminating a list of everything she needed to do in the shower each morning, bringing it into the shower, and moving a clothespin down the list as she completed each task (Duff et al., 2008). Like JR, Angie eventually reached the point where she preserved implicit memory of the showering procedures and no longer needed the list.

A written record can be used as a reference source as needed, and in some patients, reviewing the document can also aid in longer-term retention (Andrewes & Gielewski, 1999; Berry et al., 2007). However, without assistance in accessing the notes, locating the desired information can be difficult. The patient EB kept copious notes in an effort to organize his life, including information about his daily activities, future appointments, and people with whom he interacted, but the amount of information became so large that he was unable to manage it (Shannon & Griffin, 2015). Leonard, in *Memento*, solved this problem by using a rather unorthodox note-taking method—to avoid struggling to remember where he put his notes, he tattoos them on his body; a painful strategy and one with limited storage space, but effective.

Given the increasing availability and affordability of electronic devices with memory functions (e.g., smartphones, tablet computers), many rehabilitation efforts use such devices to help patients compensate for their memory loss. These devices function much like written notes but with vastly expanded capabilities. They can help with prospective memory tasks (e.g., storing appointments and issuing reminders), provide an external storage repository (i.e., a memory prosthesis), and facilitate the acquisition of new information by presenting patients with mnemonic exercises (Kapur, Glisky & Wilson, 2004). They are fairly successful at helping patients remember to perform tasks and as storage devices; perhaps even more impressively, patients implicitly learn how to use them and, on average, show improvement with practice (Kapur et al., 2004; Svoboda & Richards, 2009).

Once stored, the information in an electronic device is available for review. As described in chapter 2, there are now small, wearable cameras that can record one's daily activities by taking pictures at regular intervals (e.g., every 30 seconds). Patients with anterograde amnesia could use such a camera to record their experiences, which they would otherwise have difficulty remembering, and review the images as a means of strengthening encoding. Research has shown that this kind of procedure improves long-term retention in both adults (Berry et al., 2007) and children (Pauly-Takacs, Moulin & Estlin, 2011) with anterograde amnesia. Reviewing visual images is significantly more effective than reviewing a written diary (Berry et al., 2007).

Electronic devices are less effective at training patients on specific memory encoding strategies than they are at improving prospective memory and providing a memory prosthesis for storing and retrieving memories (Kapur et al., 2004). Patients can, however, be trained to perform job-related tasks on the computer, capitalizing on their preserved capacity for implicit learning (Andrewes & Gielewski, 1999; Kapur et al., 2004). Training with electronic memory aids is most likely to be successful for patients with mild-to-moderate anterograde amnesia, but it can be beneficial even for patients with relatively severe impairment (Svoboda & Richards, 2009).

A number of factors predict the likelihood of treatment success. Severity of the deficit is naturally one factor—the less that new learning is affected by the brain damage, the better the chance of learning new strategies for dealing with the memory loss. Having high premorbid cognitive functioning and educational level, an absence of physical disability (e.g., sensory or motor impairment), relatively intact memory for events prior to onset (i.e., less retrograde amnesia), an absence of other cognitive or motivational problems (e.g., an attention deficit), living or working in a familiar environment, having good family and medical/rehabilitation support, and certain personality characteristics can also predict a more successful outcome (Andrewes & Gielewski, 1999; Kapur et al., 2004). For example, Andrewes and Gielewski attribute some of JR's success to her courage, determination, and history of high achievement. Her example, and others like it, demonstrate that although recovery from anterograde amnesia is incredibly difficult, some improvement is possible.

CONCLUSIONS

It is always dangerous to say that some fictional portrayal of amnesia "would never happen that way in real life." Amnesia is such a diverse disorder (really, an assortment of discrete yet often overlapping disorders) that many such statements could lead to a successful search for a counterexample: "Look, here's someone whose memory functions just fine during the day but who forgets everything while asleep!" While following the dictum never to say never, it is possible to reach some general conclusions. Most people do not know much about anterograde amnesia or the recovery process. Their ignorance is unfortunate for many reasons, not least of which are the facts that anterograde amnesia is more prevalent than retrograde amnesia, it can occur largely in the absence of retrograde amnesia or other cognitive deficits (i.e., the amnesic syndrome), its consequences can be every bit as devastating as retrograde amnesia, and sufferers cannot simply work their way through it. Patients with anterograde amnesia can compensate for their memory loss to some extent, but the rehabilitation process is typically frustrating, labor-intensive, repetitive, and only modestly successful.

Misconceptions about and misleading portrayals of anterograde amnesia encompass many of its central characteristics, such as its duration and the role of sleep. For persons with the disorder, memories fade within a matter of minutes, not after 80 minutes and certainly not after a full day. And contrary to the widespread belief in subliminal perception, the brain's ability to encode new information during sleep is limited. Sleep does, however, contribute greatly to the consolidation of information learned beforehand. Movies and novels that portray sleep as having a deleterious effect on memory might be entertaining, but they are scientifically inaccurate. On the other hand, fictional characters with anterograde amnesia are often realistic in other respects, such as their capacity for implicit memory.

For the most part, the popular media have tended to avoid anterograde amnesia. Yet even when fictional characters do suffer from the disorder, it is often played for laughs (e.g., *Finding Nemo*, *Fifty First Dates*) and depicted in a scientifically erroneous manner (e.g., losing memories while asleep). This is not to say that there is anything wrong with finding humor in even the bleakest situations—it can provide a useful coping mechanism for the sufferers and can humanize the afflicted parties for others. But perpetuating myths about amnesia does no one any good.

NOTES

1. In addition to coauthoring a case study about Clive Wearing, his wife, Deborah, has published a book about their life together since his brain injury (Wearing, 2006). At this writing, Clive (born in 1938) is still living.

2. Retrograde amnesia without any anterograde impairment is rare at least in the case of organic amnesia. As discussed in chapter 5, psychogenic amnesia is commonly limited to a retrograde impairment.

3. Sacks (1998) is sensitive to the questionable ethics of his little experiment with Jimmie and the mirror, describing it as "an impulse for which I have never forgiven myself—it was, or would have been, the height of cruelty had there been any possibility of Jimmie's remembering it" (p. 25). Because Jimmie's distress was short-lived, it may not have been the "height of cruelty," but it was hardly an entirely benign procedure. Moreover, as discussed above, it might have had ensuing implicit effects.

4. The phenomenon documented by Rihm et al. (2014) shows that a stimulus presented during sleep (the odor) can affect memory even though participants were unaware of its presence. Thus, it has some similarities to research examining whether participants can remember information presented while they are asleep, which is covered in the next section. However, because the principal result is enhancement of memory for information learned before sleep, it is most directly relevant to the effect of sleep on memory consolidation.

5. In a fourth experiment, Diekelmann et al. (2008) demonstrated that taking caffeine prior to retrieval eliminated the tendency for sleep-deprived participants to have more false memories.

6. Amnesic symptoms are so varied, the brain is so complex, and the field of amnesia research is so voluminous that I am hesitant to say that a case of normal daytime memory paired with the erasure of all of the day's memories during sleep has never been documented or could never occur. But in light of what we currently know about how sleep and memory work—independently and in conjunction—it seems so implausible as not to be worth entertaining as a serious scientific possibility.

Chapter 7

Memory, Aging, Alzheimer's Disease, and Dementia

Myth: Anyone Who Lives Long Enough Will Develop Alzheimer's Disease

Related Myths: All Aspects of Memory Deteriorate with Age; Once a Person Has Alzheimer's, Not Much Can Be Done

In Billy Collins' poem "Forgetfulness," he describes how "The name of the author is the first to go followed obediently by the title, the plot, the heartbreaking conclusion, the entire novel which suddenly becomes one you have never read, never even heard of, as if, one by one, the memories you used to harbor decided to retire to the southern hemisphere of the brain, to a little fishing village where there are no phones." The poem eloquently captures what has long been known: Memory gets worse as we grow older. However, the situation is not as simple as it at first appears. Aging is continuous—at what point does one become "old"? Do all aspects of memory deteriorate as we age, or only some? Moreover, some people experience an abnormal degree of age-related memory loss, due to Alzheimer's disease or another form of dementia. And even "normal" age-related memory loss does not affect everyone; some people remain as sharp cognitively into their 80s and even 90s as when they were younger. These issues make memory and aging a complex topic of study, yet one that, given the large number of elderly in the population and the staggering personal and financial costs associated with their care if they do develop Alzheimer's disease (an estimated $1 trillion by 2019; Park, 2016), has enormous practical and theoretical implications. Research on memory and aging, and work with Alzheimer's patients, can be facilitated or impeded by popular beliefs about the issues.

Alzheimer's disease is the leading cause of pathological memory loss, afflicting millions of people; and the incidence is growing as the average life expectancy increases. There is now a sizeable nonfiction literature on Alzheimer's, including books on etiology, treatment, and memoirs (e.g., John Bayley's [1999] book *Elegy for Iris*, about his wife Iris Murdoch's struggle with Alzheimer's). Bayley's book was made into the movie *Iris*, and many other films and novels depict both the memory loss (and other symptoms) of Alzheimer's disease and the effects of the illness on family members and caregivers (e.g., *The Notebook* [Nicholas Sparks novel and film], *Away from Her* [film, based on an Alice Munro short story], *Still Alice* [Lisa Genova novel and film]). Popular TV shows, such as *Grey's Anatomy*, have had recurrent characters with Alzheimer's disease, and Alzheimer's characters are no strangers to the stage (e.g., "The Memory Show" by Sara Cooper, "Visitors" by Barney Norris). Thus, Alzheimer's disease is all around us: in popular media, in our loved ones, and in ourselves.

Many of these works are reasonably accurate in depicting Alzheimer's toll on others, and the attention—as well as public figures' disclosure that they suffer from Alzheimer's disease (e.g., President Ronald Reagan, University of Tennessee basketball coach Pat Summitt, Rita Hayworth, Glen Campbell, and Charlton Heston)—has demystified Alzheimer's and removed some of the stigma associated with the disease.[1] However, they generally do little to show either the abilities that many patients maintain until the disease is quite advanced, or the cognitive abilities that elderly individuals without Alzheimer's retain at a fairly high level. Many elderly adults suffer from mild cognitive problems without the problems advancing to Alzheimer's disease, and other elderly adults do not develop any problems whatsoever.

Unlike many of the other topics covered in this book, such as eyewitness memory, false confessions, amnesia, or superior memory, aging affects us all. Even individuals who do not live long enough themselves to experience age-related cognitive changes are likely to witness those changes in friends and family members. It should come as no surprise, then, that the literature on memory and aging is enormous (for a comprehensive summary, see the Institute of Medicine's recent report on cognitive aging; Blazer, Yaffe & Liverman, 2015). Alzheimer's disease is only one part of that. In light of the complex interplay of cognitive, social, behavioral, and biological forces at work in memory and aging, it would be impossible to provide a comprehensive overview of the topic in a single chapter. Nevertheless, as the examples of books and movies given above illustrate, these issues—the relationships among memory, aging, and Alzheimer's disease—are very much in the public eye. This chapter will summarize research on the relationship among Alzheimer's disease and related causes of dementia, "normal" aging, and memory impairment. Following a brief discussion of popular beliefs about memory and aging, the chapter reviews research on their relationship, focusing on memory abilities that usually are and are not impaired by advancing age. The remainder of the chapter addresses several of the more salient aspects of Alzheimer's disease: its symptoms and prevalence, the question of its inevitability, and treatments for it.

BELIEFS ABOUT MEMORY AND AGING

Several of the questions from the survey described in chapter 1 addressed beliefs about memory, aging, and Alzheimer's disease. Participants were fairly knowledgeable about general patterns of memory functioning as people age. For example, 78.9 percent knew that Alzheimer's disease is not an inevitable consequence of longevity, 71.4 percent were aware that remembering past events gets worse in elderly adults, and 52.4 percent knew that age-related memory decline usually starts around age 65. Even though performance on these items was relatively good, the data still show that one-quarter to one-half of participants responded incorrectly. Moreover, participants did less well on questions that asked about more specific aspects of memory functioning. As described in the following section, some components of memory, such as explicit remembering of episodic information (e.g., eyewitness memory), are usually affected by aging, whereas other kinds of memory (e.g., implicit memory, prospective memory) often are not. Yet only 41.1 percent of participants knew that elderly eyewitnesses are less accurate than young adult witnesses, and a mere 9.2 percent knew that prospective memory generally stays intact in elderly adults. Other research on laypeople's beliefs about the effects of aging on different aspects of memory has yielded somewhat more promising results, although the general perception is that aging affects pretty much all memory tasks (Ryan, 1992). Even when participants are somewhat sensitive to aging's differential effects as a function of task type (e.g., memory for recent versus more remote events), there is still substantial variability in the expected pattern of age-related decline on different tasks (e.g., Lineweaver & Hertzog, 1998).

The perception that memory declines with age is quite robust and has been found in the United States (e.g., Horhota et al., 2012; Lineweaver, Berger & Hertzog, 2009; Lineweaver & Hertzog, 1998), Canada (Ryan, 1992; Ryan & Kwong See, 1993), Norway (Magnussen et al., 2006), and South Korea (Jin, Ryan & Anas, 2001; Ryan, Jin, & Anas, 2009). For example, Magnussen et al. (2006) asked a single question about participants' beliefs about memory and aging: "It is generally believed that memory gets worse with age. When do you think the decline starts?" Response options were age 20, 30, 40, 50, 60, 70, 80, or never. Few participants (who ranged in age from 18 to 85 years) believed memory never declines or that it begins as young as age 20, but nearly 40 percent of participants believed that it starts at age 40 or earlier. The modal response was 50 or 60, each of which garnered approximately 20 percent of responses. Other research likewise shows substantial variability in laypeople's beliefs about when memory begins to decline, but with the greatest decline believed to occur starting at age 50 or later (e.g., Lineweaver & Hertzog, 1998). Although the relationship between aging and memory is almost certainly linear, most people believe it to be curvilinear (Lineweaver & Hertzog, 1998) or discontinuous (Ryan, 1992). For example, Ryan (1992, Experiment 2) found that participants perceived the "typical 45-year-old" and "typical 65-year-old" as performing roughly the same on a variety of memory tasks, while expecting both hypothetical targets to do worse than the "typical 25-year-old" and better than the "typical 85-year-old." In a follow-up study, Ryan and Kwong See (1993) again found an overall perception of age-related memory decline, but no perceived change between ages 65 and 85 years. This period—from 45 to 65 to 85 years—is when many memory problems begin to manifest themselves and gradually worsen (see the section on "Facts about Memory and Aging," below). Thus, as in the chapter 1 survey, participants knew that the effect of age on memory was generally negative; however, their knowledge of the precise contours of the age-memory function was limited.

In addition, people's beliefs about memory and aging vary depending on a number of factors, such as their own age. Although adults of all ages believe that memory declines during adulthood, middle-aged and elderly adults believe that the decline begins somewhat later than young adults (Lineweaver & Hertzog, 1998; see also Hertzog & Pearman, 2014). As Lineweaver and Hertzog observe, this pattern could reflect older persons' self-enhancement bias, denial of their own memory decline, or greater reliance on personal experience as opposed to stereotypes about aging. In subsequent research, they found that age-related stereotypes influenced participants' expectations about how memory changes in later life (Lineweaver, Berger & Hertzog, 2009). They expected less age-related memory decline for individuals who fit positive stereotypes of aging (e.g., self-accepting, sociable, independent) than for those who fit negative stereotypes (e.g., afraid, miserly, wary), whether or not the positive/negative memory characteristics had anything to do with memory performance.

Men perceive a later onset of decline than women (Lineweaver & Hertzog, 1998). People also have different expectations about how age affects memory in general and how it will, or does, affect their own memory functioning. General and personal beliefs about memory are correlated yet distinct (Lineweaver & Hertzog, 1998; Ryan, 1992). For example, Lineweaver and Hertzog questioned participants about their beliefs about their own memory (e.g., "my ability to remember in general"—rated on a scale ranging from very poor to very good) and also about their beliefs about memory in the general adult population (e.g., the ability of an average adult who is relatively healthy for his or her age to remember in general—rated on a scale ranging from very poor to very good). The correlations between personal and general beliefs were mostly significant but not very large.

These studies of people's beliefs about aging and memory offer both encouraging and discouraging findings. On the positive side, they show that most people appreciate the negative effects that aging can have on memory and do not view the relationship between aging and memory as a unidimensional construct (Lineweaver et al., 2009). They generally understand that memory decline can affect some persons more than others (e.g., not necessarily becoming severe enough for an Alzheimer's diagnosis), and they show some appreciation for age's affecting certain types of memory functioning more than others. On the negative side, the studies show considerable variability in beliefs about when age-related memory deterioration begins, different expectations depending on both participant (e.g., age, gender) and target characteristics (e.g., stereotypes), and only limited knowledge of the differential effects of aging on various memory tasks, suggesting that many lay beliefs are misinformed. Compared to lay knowledge about other memory phenomena (e.g., amnesia, eyewitness memory), knowledge of memory and aging is relatively good; nonetheless, it is less accurate than it could be, and arguably should be.

FACTS ABOUT MEMORY AND AGING

The popular belief that memory, and cognition in general, deteriorates with age is true in some respects, but it is a crude overgeneralization. The relationship between cognition and aging is best characterized by "differential decline" (Salthouse, 1991, p. 52), whereby performance on some kinds of cognitive tasks does decline on average (there are, of course, substantial individual differences), but performance on other kinds of tasks does not (Blazer et al., 2015). Memory functioning adheres to this same general pattern: Age-related decline typically occurs for some aspects of memory but not others.

The remainder of this section summarizes research documenting what usually does and does not get worse in memory performance as people age. This general pattern applies to "normal" aging, that is, aging in the absence of pathology like Alzheimer's disease, which is covered later in the chapter. Most studies of memory and aging are cross-sectional—that is, they compare participants who are different ages—although some studies are longitudinal, comparing the same participants' functioning as they age. For both kinds of studies, there is no universally agreed upon definition of what constitutes "old" or "older." In many studies the cutoff is age 65, although it is occasionally higher or lower.

What Usually Gets Worse

Explicit episodic memory is the form of memory that is most affected by aging, dropping off earlier and more rapidly than semantic and procedural memory (Balota, Dolan & Duchek, 2000; Blazer et al., 2015; Nilsson et al., 1997; Rönnlund, Nyberg, Bäckman & Nilsson, 2005; Salthouse, 1991). In some studies, nonepisodic memory did not deteriorate at all when controlling for level of education (e.g., Nilsson et al., 1997), and semantic memory actually improved until about age 60 (Rönnlund et al., 2005). Even though episodic memory is affected most by aging, it remains fairly stable until around age 60, at which point it typically deteriorates in a more-or-less gradual fashion (Rönnlund et al., 2005). The decline in episodic memory is exacerbated when encoding or retrieval conditions are more difficult than usual (Price, Mueller, Wetmore & Neuschatz, 2014). Eyewitness situations exemplify these challenging conditions: The events are often brief and encoded under suboptimal conditions (e.g., poor opportunity to view, stress, divided attention), and memory is often tested after a long retention interval and in demanding retrieval formats (e.g., free recall tests like "Tell me everything you remember"). Thus, research on elderly eyewitnesses can illustrate the ways in which older adults' episodic memory is impaired.

Older adults are poorer than young adults at face identification. This has been demonstrated in both face recognition studies, where participants are shown a series of unfamiliar faces and then given a recognition test, and more naturalistic eyewitness studies that include a lineup identification task (Bartlett, 2014a, b; Bartlett & Memon, 2007; Sporer & Martschuk, 2014). The difference lies mainly in older adults' greater tendency to make false recognitions of new faces, innocent suspects, or lineup foils; they are more comparable to young adults in terms of their hit rate, or correctly recognizing previously seen faces (Bartlett, 2014a, b; Bartlett & Memon, 2007). For example, in their meta-analysis of age effects in lineup identification, Sporer and Martschuk found that elderly witnesses (*M* age = 69.9 years) were 2.5 times more likely than young adult witnesses (*M* age = 21.9 years) to choose a foil from a target-present lineup and 3.1 times more likely to identify an innocent suspect in a target-absent lineup, but younger witnesses were only 1.6 times more likely than elderly witnesses to make a correct identification in a target-present lineup. The size of the effects increased with the age of the elderly sample (the "young" group was almost always college students, but the age of the elderly group varied across studies).

Notably, most eyewitness studies use young adult targets/perpetrators. This makes sense, as young adults are more likely to commit crimes than elderly adults. However, it raises the possibility that the poorer performance of elderly witnesses reflects an own-age effect; and indeed, the difference between young and older adult participants is less—though still present, especially in terms of false recognition—when they attempt to recognize elderly faces than young faces (Bartlett, 2014a, b; Rhodes & Anastasi, 2012; Sporer & Martschuk, 2014). Thus, an own-age effect cannot explain all of the age difference in face identification. Overall, elderly witnesses are simply more likely to choose someone from the lineup, whether or not the lineup actually contains the perpetrator. In the forensic context, false recognitions are particularly problematic, as they can lead to the prosecution and false conviction of innocent suspects (see chapter 8).

With respect to remembering details of the event, elderly witnesses remember fewer details than young adult witnesses—that is, they provide less information on average—and they are less accurate for the information that they do remember (Bartlett, 2014a; Gomes et al., 2014; Price et al., 2014). The magnitude of the age difference in event memory depends on the testing format. It is greater on recall than on recognition tests (Gomes et al., 2014) and on recognition tests with more (as opposed to fewer) response options (e.g., multiple-choice vs. yes-no tests; Bornstein, 1995).

Elderly witnesses are also more suggestible. A meta-analysis conducted by Wylie and colleagues (2014) showed that the misinformation effect is stronger in older than in younger adults, with the magnitude of the effect increasing with the age of the elderly witness sample. There are multiple explanations for elderly witnesses' greater suggestibility. They might simply be more compliant, making them more likely to accede to suggestive questioning, or they might apply a more lax response criterion in making their responses. But much of the effect appears to be due to a source monitoring deficit (Wylie et al., 2014). Older adults are worse than younger adults at identifying the source of information in memory (e.g., Boywitt, Kuhlmann & Meiser, 2012; Kuhlmann & Touron, 2012); in an eyewitness context, this could lead them to confuse information that they acquired from a post-event source (e.g., something implied during questioning or stated by a fellow witness) with information that they actually saw. Consistent with older adults' increased suggestibility, they are also more likely to experience false memories, as in studies using the DRM paradigm (Gomes et al., 2014; see chapter 3).

These effects of aging on episodic memory deal with both the encoding of new information and the retrieval of information in long-term memory. Older adults also show deficits in terms of short-term and working memory (i.e., information that is actively maintained in consciousness; Blazer et al., 2015; Fournet et al., 2012). For example, Fournet and colleagues administered five short-term and working memory tasks (e.g., word span) to a sample of 445 healthy adults aged 55–85 years (i.e., participants with mild cognitive impairment [MCI] or dementia were excluded). For purposes of analysis, they were divided into three age subgroups: 55–65, 66–75, and 76–85 years.

Participants' age predicted outcomes on each of the tasks, with performance decreasing as a function of age.

What Usually Doesn't Get Worse

To some extent, older adults are sensitive to these changes in their memory functioning. For example, older adults report having more memory problems than young adults (Hertzog & Pearman, 2014; Price et al., 2014), and they are more likely than young and middle-aged adults to report that their memory has become worse during the last several years (e.g., Horhota et al., 2012; Lineweaver & Hertzog, 1998; Magnussen et al., 2006; Ryan, 1992). They know that their memory is declining, and this knowledge accompanies a change in their memory self-efficacy—that is, their evaluation of their own memory functioning (Beaudoin & Desrichard, 2011; Hertzog & Dixon, 1994; Hertzog & Pearman, 2014). In some respects, then, elderly adults maintain reasonably accurate metamemory, at least in terms of monitoring their own memory performance (Hertzog & Dixon, 1994).

However, despite this awareness—and possibly because of it—they are not all that adept at implementing compensatory strategies; compared to young adults, they expend less persistence on memory tasks, use fewer mnemonic strategies, and are generally less likely to engage in control processes that would help them optimize their performance, especially internal memory strategies like forming mental associations (Beaudoin & Desrichard, 2011; Hertzog & Dixon, 1994; Horhota et al., 2012; Kuhlmann & Touron, 2012). However, older adults are more likely than young adults to use strategies related to overall cognitive and physical health (e.g., playing games, maintaining a healthy diet), which can also benefit memory (Horhota et al., 2012). Thus, both young and older adults believe they can do things to improve their memory functioning (Horhota et al., 2012); the extent to which they actually implement those strategies is, of course, another matter.

In other words, older adults' metacognitive monitoring is good, but their metacognitive control is more mixed. Knowing that one's memory performance is declining with age is well and good, but that knowledge is of limited value if it is not accompanied by efforts to do anything about it. The combination of intact metacognitive monitoring and impaired metacognitive control can lead to increased memory errors and overconfidence, as when an elderly person witnesses a crime. Consistent with this possibility, some evidence suggests that confidence is a poorer predictor of lineup identification accuracy for elderly than for young adult witnesses (Henkel, 2014; Sporer & Martschuk, 2014).

As mentioned above, certain kinds of memory, in addition to metacognitive monitoring, are also affected less by aging than others. Two types of tasks in particular that research has shown hold up relatively well are implicit memory and prospective memory (Einstein & McDaniel, 2014; Neath & Surprenant, 2015). Several studies have compared older and younger adults' memory performance on both implicit and explicit tasks (e.g., Balota et al., 2000; Nilsson et al., 1997). For example, Light and Singh (1987, Experiment 2) presented a group of young (*M* age = 23.1) and old (*M* age = 68.3) participants with a list of five- and six-letter words, which they were asked to rate for pleasantness. Subsequently, half completed a word-stem completion test, in which they were given the first three letters of a word and asked to complete it with the first word that came to mind. Participants had studied half of the words previously, and half were new. This is a common type of test used to demonstrate implicit memory, as participants are more likely to complete words that they encountered previously than words that they did not, even without connecting them to the initial encoding episode. The other half completed a cued recall test, in which they were told to use the stems as clues for recalling words from the previous list. Participants in both groups then completed a recognition test. Young adults did better than older adults on the cued recall and recognition tests—measures of explicit memory—but there was no age difference in terms of priming on the implicit word completion test.

This finding is consistent with other research showing that older adults are less likely than young adults to experience a subjective sense of recollection when remembering events (e.g., when tested with the remember-know paradigm described in chapter 6; see Kelley & Jacoby, 2000; Neath & Surprenant, 2015). In contrast, they rely more on their sense of familiarity, which could also explain their heightened suggestibility and tendency to make more source monitoring errors and false identifications (Bartlett, 2014a, b; Boywitt et al., 2012; Price et al., 2014). This pattern of relatively intact familiarity but impaired recollection is exaggerated in elderly patients with mild cognitive impairment (Hudon, Belleville, & Gauthier, 2009). Like patients with anterograde amnesia—though to less of an extent—older adults can encode and retrieve information in memory, but they lose their ability to refer back to the original encoding experience. This does not necessarily mean that their underlying functioning is as good as it ever was—as discussed above, in many instances it is not. What it does mean is that just as in most people, older adults' memory competence is greater than their performance would suggest (Salthouse, 1991). Their relatively intact implicit memory demonstrates this preserved, and at times overlooked, competence.

Prospective memory in older adults is often studied by embedding a prospective memory task (i.e., remembering to do something in the future) within a retrospective memory task (i.e., remembering previously encountered information). For example, participants might be shown a list of words and asked to press a certain key whenever a word satisfying some preestablished criteria (e.g., a particular part of speech, containing a particular phoneme, or even a particular target word itself) appears (McDaniel & Einstein, 2007). Afterwards, they are asked to recall or recognize words from the list. Thus, they engage simultaneously in a prospective (remember to press the key) and retrospective (recall/recognition) memory task. Several studies show that in this sort of paradigm, elderly participants do worse than young adult participants on the retrospective task, especially when it requires free recall, but they do just as well on the prospective memory task (for review, see McDaniel & Einstein, 2007; Neath & Surprenant, 2015). Thus, aging appears not to affect prospective memory, or at least to affect it less, than it does other kinds of memory tasks.

Other research has found that older adults might actually show some decrement in performance on prospective memory tasks, depending on the precise nature of the task and the availability of environmental cues (Anderson & Craik, 2000; Neath & Surprenant, 2015). For example, some prospective memory tasks are time-based, where one has to remember to do something at a certain time (e.g., "call Mom tomorrow to wish her a happy birthday"), whereas others are event-based, where one has to remember to do something when some event occurs, like "press the space bar whenever the word on the screen is a noun." Older adults do comparatively well when events or other environmental cues trigger the memory or when they can rely on spontaneous retrieval processes, but they do less well when they have to rely on internal, self-initiated retrieval processes (Anderson & Craik, 2000; Mullet et al., 2013). Even when older adults do worse than young adults on a prospective memory task, instructing them on the importance of the task can improve their performance (Smith & Hunt, 2014). Thus, despite some evidence of age differences, this body of research overall indicates that aging has less of an effect on prospective memory than on many other kinds of memory, and in some cases it appears to have no negative effect on prospective memory at all.

Unquestionably, aging adversely affects memory. Importantly, however, not all aspects of memory functioning are affected equally, and some even remain relatively intact in most people as they age. Aging does, of course, affect some individuals' memory more than others. This is especially true for those who experience an illness that aggravates any preexisting memory deterioration, such as Alzheimer's disease or another form of dementia.

SYMPTOMS AND PREVALENCE OF ALZHEIMER'S DISEASE AND RELATED DISORDERS

There is a saying among practitioners who work with Alzheimer's patients: When you've met one Alzheimer's patient, you've met one Alzheimer's patient. As this aphorism suggests, it is virtually meaningless to talk about what constitutes the "typical" Alzheimer's patient or the "normal" progression of Alzheimer's disease. Nonetheless, it is possible to identify a constellation of symptoms that occur in the majority of patients with the disease. The lion's share of these symptoms deal with memory and other aspects of cognition.

Alzheimer's disease is the most common cause of dementia, a loose diagnosis that encompasses an array of memory, other cognitive, and behavioral problems. The current psychiatric classification for dementia, according to the DSM-5, is Major Neurocognitive Disorder (the term "dementia" is still widely used in both medical and everyday parlance). The criteria for Major Neurocognitive Disorder are an acquired significant decline in one or more cognitive domains: attention, executive function, memory, language, perceptual-motor skills, etc. (American Psychiatric Association, 2013). The decline must be severe enough to interfere with independence in everyday activities, not occur exclusively in the context of delirium, and not be better explained by another mental disorder.

Alzheimer's disease is not the only cause of dementia. Related disorders include Lewy body dementia, vascular or multi-infarct dementia, and frontotemporal dementia. Dementia can also be caused by other advanced illnesses affecting the brain, such as Parkinson's, Huntington's, Pick's, Creutzfeldt-Jakob, or Prion disease; severe depression; and sexually transmitted infections such as HIV and syphilis. TBI and substance abuse can also produce dementia in some cases. Non-Alzheimer's dementias share many characteristics with Alzheimer's disease, and misdiagnoses are common; however, the presentation of symptoms differs in some respects, and treatments that are effective for one form of dementia are not necessarily effective for another. Because Alzheimer's disease dwarfs all other dementias in prevalence (Plassman et al., 2011), it is typically the default diagnosis. The remainder of the chapter therefore focuses on Alzheimer's disease, but it is important to keep in mind that not all dementia is due to Alzheimer's.

For a diagnosis of Alzheimer's disease, the memory deficit must be paramount. It can include a retrograde impairment, an anterograde impairment, or very often, both. The earliest signs usually reflect problems with episodic memory encoding—confusion, disorientation, forgetfulness, and repetitive comments. As the disorder progresses, semantic and procedural memory can also be impaired (e.g., Alice in the novel *Still Alice* forgets her material while giving a class lecture). Patients vary in the extent to which they are aware of their memory loss, but a significant proportion lack some degree of awareness of their impairment—that is, Alzheimer's often affects metamemory as well as memory (Cosentino, 2014). There is no clear-cut relationship in Alzheimer's patients between metamemory (i.e., awareness of the memory loss) and the level of memory impairment (Cosentino, 2014), and some components of metamemory are affected more than others (Souchay, 2007). As with amnesia patients in general, an awareness of the memory loss in Alzheimer's patients can be very upsetting. Thus, one way of characterizing the memory deficits associated with Alzheimer's disease is that it both accelerates deterioration in the abilities that aging usually affects and negatively affects the things that aging usually leaves intact.

The onset and deterioration in Alzheimer's patients must show a progressive, gradual pattern, although the rate of deterioration is highly variable. A definitive diagnosis also requires specific neuropathological changes, particularly amyloid plaques and neurofibrillary tangles. Until recently, the presence of these changes could not be determined conclusively until autopsy, which led to misdiagnoses (e.g., in patients with clinical symptoms but without Alzheimer's pathology). However, advances in medical technology (e.g., improved imaging, biomarkers in cerebrospinal fluid, etc.) are now making it easier to demonstrate evidence of the disease in live patients, leading to more accurate diagnosis (Dubois et al., 2010).

The prevalence of Alzheimer's disease is difficult to estimate with much precision, in large part because of the difficulty in making a diagnosis. Diagnosing Alzheimer's is challenging for a variety of reasons—the number of syndromes with similar symptoms, comorbidity issues in the mostly elderly patient population, the imprecision of neurocognitive assessment, and the unreliability of patients' self-reported memory functioning, to mention just a few. By far the biggest obstacle is the difficulty of determining the presence of the neuropathological markers of the disease. Even disregarding these difficulties, Alzheimer's disease and related dementias are indisputably widespread and becoming more so as the population ages. Although social norms for what constitutes "old" are changing as life expectancy increases and healthcare improvements allow more people to stay active and work longer, a common cutoff is age 65 years. According to the 2010 US Census, more than 40 million Americans were aged 65 or older, more than in any previous census—13 percent of the total population (Werner, 2011). This segment of the population increased 15.1 percent from 2000 to 2010, a growth rate faster than that for the US population as a whole (9.7 %; Werner, 2011). The percentage of Americans 85–94 years old increased 29.9 percent from 2000 to 2010, and the percentage aged 95 years and older increased 25.9 percent (Werner, 2011).

Recent attempts to estimate the prevalence of Alzheimer's disease, or dementia more generally, have distinguished between dementia and cognitive impairment without dementia, commonly referred to as mild cognitive impairment (MCI). MCI is a broad and somewhat loosely defined term. The definition used by Gauthier et al. (2006, p. 1262) is typical: "Mild cognitive impairment is a syndrome defined as cognitive decline greater than that expected for an individual's age and education level but that does not inter-fere notably with activities of daily life" (see also Feldman & Jacova, 2005). Thus, it differs from dementia more in degree—in terms of symptom severity and effect on daily functioning—than in kind.

Many elderly adults suffer from MCI ("mild neurocognitive disorder" in the DSM-5) without its advancing to Alzheimer's disease or another form of dementia. MCI causes significant problems even in the absence of demen-tia, with decreased quality of life and increased disability and healthcare costs. However, more than half of those with MCI progress to dementia within 5 years (Gauthier et al., 2006). MCI increases the risk of developing Alzheimer's disease roughly tenfold, from 1–2.5 percent per year among cog-nitively healthy older adults to 10–15 percent per year among those with MCI (Plassman et al., 2008, 2011). Patients with MCI who initially perform poorly on an array of cognitive tests are more likely to progress to Alzheimer's disease than MCI patients whose baseline level of performance is relatively good (Belleville et al., 2014).

The clear linkage between MCI and Alzheimer's disease raises the pos-sibility that a subtype of MCI is essentially prodromal Alzheimer's (Gauthier et al., 2006). Estimates of the prevalence of MCI are every bit as variable as Alzheimer's disease or dementia estimates, and for the same reasons—differ-ent samples (e.g., varying in age and overall health) and imprecise diagnosis. These estimates for elderly American samples range from 3 to 29 percent, but most estimates for American samples, as well as those in Canada and Europe, cluster in the 17–27 percent range (Plassman et al., 2008).

For example, based on a national study of 856 elderly adults that involved individual neuropsychological assessment, Plassman and colleagues (2008) estimated that 22 percent of adults aged 71 years or over had cognitive impairment without dementia (i.e., MCI). The largest number of these cases were prodromal Alzheimer's disease. The strongest predictive factor was age: the prevalence rate was 16 percent for persons aged 71–79 years, 29 percent for persons aged 80–89 years, and 39 percent for those aged 90 years and over (see Figure 7.1). Men and those with less education were more likely to experience MCI. Although race/ethnicity was not significantly associated with MCI, African Americans constituted 10.4 percent of participants with MCI but only 5.7 percent of participants with normal cognition (the propor-tion of Hispanics in the two groups was equal—5.4 %). These values make it clear that MCI is a major public health concern.[2]

The figures for dementia are equally scary and depressing. Using the same national sample as that described above, Plassman and colleagues (2007) estimated that 14 percent of Americans aged 71 years and over suffer from dementia, approximately three-quarters of which are due to Alzheimer's dis-ease. As with MCI, the strongest predictor of both dementia in general, and

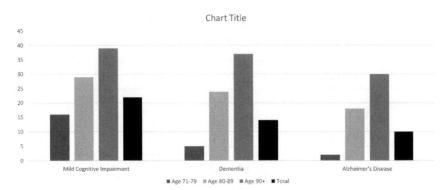

Figure 7.1 **Prevalence (Percentage) of Mild Cognitive Impairment, Dementia, and Alzheimer's Disease as a Function of Age.** *Source*: Values taken from Plassman et al. (2007) and Plassman et al. (2008).

Alzheimer's disease in particular, is age (see Figure 7.1). In the oldest age group (90 years and over), 37 percent had some form of dementia, and 30 percent had Alzheimer's. Given the robust relationship between Alzheimer's and age and the fact that only 2 percent of people in their 70s have Alzheimer's, patients like 50-year-old Alice Howland in *Still Alice* (Genova, 2007) are clearly an anomaly. The Alzheimer's Association (2017) estimates that only about 4 percent of Alzheimer's patients are under age 65. Still, cases like Alice's are not unheard of. Alzheimer's can strike individuals in their 50s and even in their 40s or late 30s, especially if they have Down's syndrome or possess one of several rare genetic mutations (e.g., Chartier-Harlin et al., 1991).

The risk of developing either dementia or Alzheimer's disease varies across race/ethnicity and level of education; African Americans, Hispanics, and those with less education are at greater risk (Alzheimer's Association, 2017; Plassman et al., 2007). Plassman et al. (2007) found no difference between men and women in terms of risk, although more women have Alzheimer's, by virtue of their longer life expectancy. Researchers have also investigated a number of behaviors for their potential to increase or decrease Alzheimer's risk; these factors are reviewed in the following section.

The prevalence estimates translate to as many as 4.7 million individuals aged 60 or older in the United States who suffer from dementia, more than 3 million of whom have Alzheimer's disease (Plassman et al., 2008). And that might be a conservative estimate—according to the Alzheimer's Association (2017), 5.3 million Americans have Alzheimer's disease; the Association projects that the number will exceed 7 million by 2025 and could reach 13.8 million by 2050. Global estimates range as high as nearly 50 million people with some form of dementia (Park, 2016). These staggering numbers—currently 5 million or so Alzheimer's sufferers in a nation of approximately

320 million, and several times that number worldwide—almost seem to suggest that Alzheimer's disease is inevitable if one lives long enough. As reported above, a nontrivial minority of people appear to believe that is the case. This raises the question of whether Alzheimer's disease is, in fact, an inevitable part of aging, and what, if anything, one can do to reduce the chance of its occurring.

IS ALZHEIMER'S DISEASE AN INEVITABLE PART OF AGING?

The figures on the prevalence of MCI and Alzheimer's disease are sobering, to be sure, but they obscure the fact that many elderly adults do not develop either one. Consider, for instance, the results of the studies by Plassman and colleagues (2007; 2008), described above (see Figure 7.1). Despite showing the high prevalence of MCI, dementia, and Alzheimer's disease, the studies also show that many older participants, even some in their 90s, do not meet the criteria for any of the disorders. After all, if 39 percent of people aged 90 years and above develop MCI, and an additional 37 percent of people in this age group suffer from some form of dementia, then approximately one-quarter (24 %)—do not. Would they develop one of these disorders or other cognitive problems, apart from MCI or dementia, if they lived long enough? Are the diagnostic procedures missing some cases of cognitive impairment?

These questions are impossible to answer, but studies of very aged people suggest not. As the population in the United States and other western countries ages, several studies have focused on the "oldest old," such as centenarians. Consistent with the findings of research on the prevalence of dementia more broadly, a substantial proportion of centenarians have dementia, but not all do. Estimates vary across studies, but the mean prevalence of dementia among centenarians is around 60 percent (Poon et al., 2012). For example, in a study of 244 centenarians in Georgia, Poon and colleagues found that about half (52.3 %) had some form of dementia, one-quarter (25.3 %) showed less severe symptoms of forgetting consistent with MCI (e.g., transient confusion), and nearly one-quarter (22.5 %) had no discernible cognitive impairment or memory deficits. This finding is striking. It means that if you live to be 100, you have nearly a one in four chance of maintaining normal cognitive functioning. Of course, you also have a three in four chance of experiencing some degree of impairment. The glass may not be half-full; but it is one-quarter full, and that is an encouraging sign.

The critical question, whether one is 100, 65, or 40 years of age, is why some people experience age-related cognitive decline while others do not. The identification of risk and protective factors offers the potential of delaying, or even eliminating altogether, the onset of problems.[3] Research has examined a wide array of such factors, and there are various ways of categorizing them (Blazer et al., 2015; Plassman et al., 2010). The present discussion distinguishes among cognitive factors, lifestyle (social and behavioral) factors, and sleep.

Cognitive Reserve

A constellation of factors relating to mental acuity and engagement fall under the general rubric of *cognitive reserve*, which "has been proposed as an explanation for why some people are able to tolerate the brain alterations associated with dementia (and other illnesses) without exhibiting the associated symptoms" (Blazer et al., 2015, p. 54).[4] Cognitive reserve is perhaps best exemplified by the popular notion that working crossword puzzles can stave off dementia. There is some empirical support for this idea. For example, Pillai et al. (2011) found that crossword puzzle participation at baseline delayed the onset of accelerated memory decline in older adults (*M* age = 79.5 years at baseline) by 2.5 years; the benefit of crossword puzzles held even when controlling for participants' level of education. Other studies have found, in contrast, that experience working crossword puzzles does not moderate the relationship between age and cognitive functioning (e.g., Hambrick, Salthouse & Meinz, 1999). Thus, research on a specific "crossword puzzle" effect is inconclusive. Nonetheless, as an exemplar of a broad category of activities contributing to cognitive reserve, crossword puzzles have the potential to yield cognitive benefits.

Anyone who enjoys crossword puzzles knows that they are mentally stimulating, but so are many other activities. Longitudinal and cross-sectional studies indicate that participating in cognitively stimulating activities such as reading books, writing letters, engaging in craft activities (e.g., knitting, quilting), and participating in lifelong learning—both in the past and in old age—is associated with better cognitive performance and a lower incidence of MCI and Alzheimer's disease (e.g., Bennett et al., 2012; Geda et al., 2011; Wilson et al., 2013). Staying cognitively active reduces Alzheimer's risk even after controlling for past activities (Bennett et al., 2012).

As mentioned above, MCI and Alzheimer's are both more common in people with less education, indicating that education is a protective factor. The relationship between education and age-related cognitive decline holds up into very old age, as demonstrated in studies of octogenerians and centenarians (e.g., Mitchell et al., 2013; Poon et al., 2012). Education early in life presumably builds up cognitive reserve. However, cognitive activities in late life play an even larger role than education (Bennett et al., 2012). This is an important finding because formal educational opportunities might be somewhat limited (though by no means entirely absent) in late life, but one can always engage in mentally stimulating cognitive activities.

Because a number of things are correlated with educational attainment—socioeconomic status, intelligence, literacy, and so on—it is hard to isolate which one(s) contribute most to cognitive reserve. It seems likely that all of them play a role. In one of the most comprehensive prospective studies of Alzheimer's disease, researchers administered a series of mental tests annually to retired nuns, who donated their brains to science after their death (the study is, aptly, known as the Nun Study; see Snowdon, 2001). Participants who had received more years of formal education experienced less cognitive decline and were less likely to be diagnosed with Alzheimer's disease than those with less education. In addition, the nuns' order had saved the autobiographical essays that each nun wrote prior to taking her vows as a young woman. The more linguistic complexity in the writing samples—for nearly all of them, written decades earlier—the better a participant's cognitive functioning. Apart from education, complex language use contributed to cognitive reserve. The related construct of literacy confers similar benefits (Blazer et al., 2015). Although these studies are correlational, making it impossible to establish causality, they strongly suggest that intellectual engagement can build up cognitive reserve and protect against Alzheimer's disease.

Lifestyle: Social and Behavioral Factors

A variety of social and behavioral factors relating to older adults' lifestyle are associated with their memory functioning in general and likelihood of developing a memory disorder (e.g., MCI or dementia) in particular. At the most basic level, simply engaging in social activity helps. Social engagement, which is measured in various ways (e.g., frequency of various activities involving others), is associated with a slower rate of cognitive decline; conversely, loneliness and social isolation increase the risk of cognitive impairment (Bennett et al., 2012; Blazer et al., 2015).

Several studies have also measured older adults' "purpose in life" (Bennett et al., 2012; Boyle et al., 2012). Purpose in life is "a complex and multifaceted traitlike construct" that taps into individuals' ability to find meaning in life and develop a sense of direction (Boyle et al., 2012, p. 503). It is an aspect of psychological wellbeing that is modifiable and an indicator of human thriving. Among elderly adults, having a stronger purpose in life is associated with a higher level of cognitive performance and a reduced risk of MCI and Alzheimer's disease (Bennett et al., 2012), and it also helps to protect against the damaging effects on cognition of Alzheimer's brain pathology (Boyle et al., 2012). Merely holding negative stereotypes about aging also predicts neurological markers of Alzheimer's disease (e.g., reduced hippocampus size, plaques and tangles; Levy et al., 2016). Thus, one's approach to life, especially with regard to aging, can serve as an important risk/protective factor.

The adage "healthy body, healthy mind" appears to be true when it comes to aging and memory. Older adults who are more physically active are less likely to develop Alzheimer's disease, even when controlling for social and cognitive activities and chronic health conditions (Bennett et al., 2012; Blazer et al., 2015; Buchman et al., 2012). Consistent with the beneficial effects of physical activity, older adults who have better muscle strength or are less frail are less likely to develop MCI or Alzheimer's disease (Bennett et al., 2012). The relationship between physical activity and cognitive health has been demonstrated cross-sectionally, longitudinally, and in studies with an intervention component (e.g., where some participants are randomly assigned to an exercise condition while others are not; Blazer et al., 2015). The cognitive benefits of exercise are greater for women than for men, for combined aerobic and strength programs than for aerobic exercise alone, for adults over aged 65 than for those aged 55–65, and for relatively long exercise sessions (Blazer et al., 2015).

In addition to being a protective factor, exercise and staying physically active can help patients cope with their illness, and some of the popular portrayals of Alzheimer's disease illustrate the use of physical activity as a coping mechanism. Alice (in *Still Alice*) runs; the aged Sherlock Holmes (in *Mr. Holmes*) walks and tends to his bee colony. The routine nature of these activities provides comfort, although depending on the activity, there may also be risks (e.g., Alice gets lost, and elderly exercisers might be at greater risk of injury should they fall). As the research on physical activity and Alzheimer's disease indicates, the mental and physical benefits of physical activity appear to outweigh the costs.

One of the advantages of physical activity is that it can provide the opportunity for positive social interactions, which are a protective factor in themselves, whereas negative social interactions increase risk. A recent study by Wilson and colleagues (2015) demonstrated this by prospectively following 529 older adults without cognitive impairment at the outset of the study. For roughly the next 5 years ($M = 4.8$ years of follow-up), participants completed annual evaluations that included an assessment of negative social interactions (e.g., rejection, failure by others to provide help) as well as cognitive testing. A higher frequency of negative social interactions was associated with a greater risk of developing MCI and a faster rate of cognitive decline, even after controlling for a number of social and behavioral variables (e.g., depressive symptoms, social activity).

Related to physical activity, a number of general health factors can raise or lower the risk of developing MCI or dementia. For example, hypertension and depression are both risk factors, and controlling them can reduce the risk (e.g., Gauthier et al., 2006). Avoiding risky, potentially harmful behaviors likewise reduces risk (Bennett et al., 2012). Nutrition is also important. Certain vitamin deficiencies (e.g., B_{12}) can cause dementia, and a healthy diet works as a preventive factor (perhaps not coincidentally, some older adults have difficulty absorbing vitamin B_{12}; Snowdon, 2001). The advantages of a balanced, healthy diet in staving off dementia are clearer than the advantages of specific nutrients. There is some—albeit inconclusive—evidence of the latter in naturally occurring diets (e.g., high levels of folic acid decrease the risk of Alzheimer's, and some studies show a benefit from antioxidants; Snowdon, 2001), but there is little evidence that vitamin supplements prevent cognitive decline (Blazer et al., 2015). As with most other risk/protective factors, the data on nutrition are largely correlational—it is unclear to what extent dietary interventions would have a prophylactic effect on cognitive performance (Blazer et al., 2015). But given the general health benefits of a balanced, vitamin-rich diet, it is hard to imagine how it could be bad for memory in older (or even younger) adults, and it might provide advantages in terms of slowing age-related decline.

The relationship between social/behavioral factors and memory performance holds even into advanced aging. Hansson and Hagberg (2005) examined a sample of 100 centenarians. Participants completed measures of personality, quality of life (e.g., activity level, contentment, loneliness), health, life-habits (e.g., education, social network, consumption of cigarettes, alcohol, coffee, and tea), and autonomy (e.g., living at home or in an institution), as well as a variety of memory tests (e.g., forward and backward digit span, vocabulary, memory for objects). Taking the memory tests as a whole, life habits and autonomy had the most consistent relationship to memory performance. For example, education and drinking of wine, liquor, and tea all had positive relationships with at least one measure of memory. The benefits of social engagement do not appear to end once one reaches a certain age.

Sleep

Sleep is a behavior that is especially strongly related to cognitive performance in older adults. Sleep normally changes as part of the aging process, with an overall decrease in sleep quantity and quality due to shorter duration, increasing sleep fragmentation (e.g., frequent waking), difficulty falling asleep, a reduction in slow wave sleep, an increase in restless leg syndrome, and more daytime sleep (Peter-Derex et al., 2015; Yaffe et al., 2014). More than half of older adults experience sleep difficulties (Zimmerman et al., 2012). The negative effects of sleep disturbance on cognitive performance are most pronounced in older adults with lower educational attainment, which is consistent with the hypothesis that cognitive reserve operates as a protective factor against age-related cognitive decline (Zimmerman et al., 2012). As discussed in the previous chapter, these changes are exacerbated in patients with Alzheimer's disease, who may also experience reduced REM sleep and circadian rhythm disturbances such as sleep-wake cycle reversal.

Not only do Alzheimer's patients suffer from more sleep problems, but sleep disturbances increase the risk of developing the disease (Blazer et al., 2015). For example, Lim and colleagues (2013) conducted a prospective study of 737 older adults who, at the beginning of the study, did not have dementia. Their sleep was evaluated by having them wear an Actical wrist monitor (similar to a FitBit) to measure sleep fragmentation; they then underwent annual neuropsychological evaluation over a 6-year period. Lim et al. found a positive association between sleep fragmentation and the likelihood of receiving an Alzheimer's diagnosis. Participants with the greatest degree of sleep fragmentation (i.e., at the 90th percentile) were 1.5 times more likely to be diagnosed with Alzheimer's disease than participants with the least sleep fragmentation (i.e., at the 10th percentile). The relationship held even after controlling for factors such as gender, total daily rest time, total physical activity, and medical history (not all studies have found an association between sleep disturbances and dementia or age-related cognitive decline; see Yaffe et al., 2014).

The precise mechanism for the relationship between sleep and Alzheimer's disease is unclear, but leading candidates include the neurotransmitter acetylcholine (ACh) and beta-amyloid (also referred to as amyloid-β), a sticky protein that is one of the hallmark features in the brains of Alzheimer's patients.[5] ACh, which is deficient in Alzheimer's patients, is also involved in regulation of the REM/non-REM sleep cycle, although the relationship between ACh and consolidation is complex and differs between waking and sleeping states and among different sleep stages (Gais & Born, 2004; Hasselmo, 1999). For instance, ACh levels increase during wakefulness and REM sleep but decrease during slow wave sleep (Peter-Derex et al., 2015). The central role of ACh in both sleep and Alzheimer's disease suggests that it could be responsible for both the sleep disturbances and memory impairment commonly observed in Alzheimer's patients. Animal models of Alzheimer's disease have shown that sleep deprivation increases the amount of beta-amyloid (Kang et al., 2009; Roh et al., 2014), and accumulation of beta-amyloid as animals age causes deterioration in the sleep-wake cycle (Roh et al., 2012). Conversely, increasing sleep time decreases the amount of beta-amyloid pathology in the brains of mice (Roh et al., 2014).

Improving sleep, by increasing the amount of sleep or improving its quality, is therefore a potential therapeutic strategy in treating Alzheimer's patients, and several such approaches have been tried (Peter-Derex et al.,

2015; Yaffe et al., 2014). The use of melatonin with Alzheimer's patients has shown only mixed effects. Benzodiazepines facilitate sleeping in general, but as described in the previous chapter, they also have an amnestic effect, which would clearly be undesirable in someone with Alzheimer's disease —they are therefore potentially inappropriate in older patients. Cholinergic agonists that are used to treat Alzheimer's disease (described in more detail in section "Treatments for Alzheimer's disease," below) have modest positive effects on the duration and onset of REM sleep, although nightmares are a possible side effect. For example, Petiau, Onen, Delgado, and Touchon (2013) conducted a study of 950 outpatients with mild to moderate Alzheimer's disease who were starting treatment with medication to increase ACh. Before treatment, 45 percent had insomnia, and 32 percent were already receiving medication to help them sleep. After 3–6 months of drug treatment, participants had fewer symptoms of sleep disturbances on average. Sleep improved for 32 percent of participants, remained unchanged for 52 percent, and deteriorated for 16 percent.

Nonpharmacological measures, such as increased daytime physical activity, a sleep hygiene program (e.g., limiting time in bed during the day, avoiding long or late-in-the-day naps), continuous positive airway pressure (CPAP) treatment, and bright light therapy are the most promising treatments for improving sleep in Alzheimer's patients. Even modest improvement in patients' sleep, along with any concomitant improvement in cognitive functioning, would enhance the quality of life of patients, as well as caregivers, and potentially delay institutionalization (Peter-Derex et al., 2015).

Summary

The presence (or absence) of these protective factors likely explains why some individuals with significant neuropathological signs of dementia (e.g., the plaques and tangles characteristic of Alzheimer's disease) fail to meet clinical criteria for the disorder, as well as why some persons show clinical symptoms without underlying neuropathology (e.g., Bennett et al., 2012; Poon et al., 2012; Snowdon, 2001). The risk of Alzheimer's disease does increase as people age, but it is not inevitable. A variety of cognitive, lifestyle, and sleep-related factors can help protect against the disorder, especially insofar as they increase individuals' cognitive reserve.

TREATMENTS FOR ALZHEIMER'S DISEASE

Treatments for medical disorders evolve, often quite rapidly, and Alzheimer's disease is no exception (Park, 2016). Vast amounts of effort and funding go into research on the causes and most effective therapies for the illness, and new treatments are investigated regularly—though only one new drug (not counting new combinations of existing drugs) has been approved since 2000 (Park, 2016). Despite these intensive efforts, Alzheimer's disease is presently incurable. Nonetheless, there are a number of treatments that can slow the progression of the disease and improve patients' functioning. Even in the absence of a cure, these outcomes are enormously beneficial because of their potential to prolong the period in which patients can live and function independently and to enhance the wellbeing of both patients and their caregivers. The two main classes of therapeutic techniques are pharmacological and psychological; the two approaches are not, of course, exclusive, and many patients would be good candidates for both. Any treatment is complicated by Alzheimer's high rate of comorbidity with a slew of other medical (e.g., age-related disorders such as diabetes, cardiovascular disorders, sensory impairments, etc.) and psychological ailments (e.g., depression, personality changes).

Drug Treatments

Alzheimer's disease is associated with a deficiency of the neurotransmitter acetylcholine (ACh). ACh is important for both the consolidation of new information in memory and the retrieval of previously learned information, but it is especially important for consolidation (Bermúdez-Rattoni, Miranda & González, 2001). During consolidation, it regulates the transfer of information within the hippocampus and also between the hippocampus and cortex (Hasselmo, 1999). Cholinergic antagonists have long been known to impair memory consolidation (Gais & Born, 2004). Conversely, cholinergic agonists have the potential to improve consolidation, and the majority of drugs currently available to treat Alzheimer's increase the activity of acetylcholine by inhibiting acetylcholinesterase, the enzyme that breaks it down. The most widely prescribed Alzheimer's drugs, such as Aricept (donepezil), Exelon (rivastigmine), and Razadyne (galantamine, formerly known as Reminyl), are cholinesterase inhibitors (CIs). They are used primarily in the treatment of mild to moderate Alzheimer's disease.

The clinical effectiveness of CIs varies widely: Some patients show no improvement at all, some show modest improvement, and still others (a minority) improve dramatically (Casey, Antimisiaris & O'Brien, 2010). On average, CIs are modestly more effective than placebo, with the greatest benefit in the first few months of therapy (Casey et al., 2010). The diminishing benefit might occur because as the disease progresses, the brain produces less and less ACh.

Namenda (memantine) is a drug used to treat moderate to severe Alzheimer's disease that works by a different physiological mechanism—it is postulated to lessen the toxic effects associated with an excess of the neurotransmitter glutamate by blocking a particular kind of glutamate receptor (the N-methyl-D-aspartate, or NMDA receptor). Excessive glutamate leads to overexposure to calcium, which can accelerate cell damage. Like with CIs, Namenda's effects are highly variable, but some clinical trials show that it is modestly effective at delaying the progression of symptoms in moderate to severe dementia (Casey et al., 2010), especially when used in conjunction with a CI (Tariot et al., 2004). Namzaric, the drug most recently approved by the Food and Drug Administration for the treatment of Alzheimer's disease (in 2014), combines memantine and donepezil.

The medications used to treat Alzheimer's disease are palliative, not curative—they slow the progress of the disease to an extent, but they do not cure it. Still, these palliative effects are far from trivial. Lessening and delaying symptoms can significantly enhance patients' ability to function independently, which improves their wellbeing and lessens the burden on caregivers. All of the Alzheimer's medications also have significant and common side effects. CIs frequently cause nausea, vomiting, diarrhea, and decreased appetite; side effects of Namenda include dizziness, headache, diarrhea, and constipation. Given these side effects, as well as the drugs' modest clinical effectiveness and substantial expense, patients and their healthcare providers should carefully weigh the costs and benefits in deciding whether to treat Alzheimer's disease pharmacologically.

Psychological Treatments

The limited success of medical treatments for Alzheimer's disease has led to an extensive search for psychological treatments. There is a broad array of psychological approaches available for treating Alzheimer's patients, and the present review is not meant to be exhaustive. A useful classification is to distinguish between treatments that target memory functioning directly and those that address patients' overall wellbeing. By improving patients' general functioning and quality of life, these latter approaches might indirectly yield benefits in terms of cognitive performance.

Strategies for improving the memory of patients with MCI or Alzheimer's disease are essentially the same as those used for rehabilitation in patients with any form of amnesia, regardless of the cause. Mnemonic strategies can be beneficial, especially in patients with relatively mild impairment. For example, Belleville and colleagues (2006) taught a sample of elderly participants with (M age = 62) and without (M age = 66) MCI to use a variety of mnemonic techniques (e.g., imagery, hierarchical organization, method of loci). The training took place in eight weekly group sessions, each lasting approximately 2 hours. MCI participants' performance improved from pretraining to posttraining on one of three episodic memory tasks, whereas nonimpaired elderly participants' performance improved on two of the three tasks. There was some, albeit weak, evidence that the training improved MCI patients' subjective sense of their memory functioning. Patients can also benefit from training with external memory aids like diaries and electronic memory prostheses, especially for relatively mild impairment.

However, just as with anterograde amnesia more broadly, the learning of new memory strategies is hamstrung by the encoding deficit itself. The challenges are compounded further by collateral issues that arise frequently in Alzheimer's and other dementia patients, such as attention deficits, emotional volatility, and sensorimotor deficits (e.g., visual impairment or lack of manual dexterity can impede the use of electronic devices). Moreover, unlike anterograde amnesia due to TBI, encephalitis, or Korsakoff's syndrome (assuming the patient has stopped drinking), the deficit in Alzheimer's patients typically worsens over time. Thus, training in mnemonic strategies is unlikely to yield dramatic improvement in cognitive functioning, especially for patients in more advanced stages of the disorder.

Alternative psychological treatments focus more on social/behavioral than on cognitive aspects of the disease. Innovative treatment approaches employ a variety of activities, such as music, art, or dance therapy. For example, Brotons and Marti (2003) had a group of Alzheimer's patients (*M* age = 76) and their caregivers participate in daily music therapy for 12 days. The therapy sessions involved listening to music, singing, instrument playing, and movement/dance. Some sessions included patients and caregivers together, and others included the patients or caregivers alone. At the end of the intervention, the patients showed less severe symptoms of dementia. They also reported less agitation and fewer psychopathological symptoms. Caregivers confirmed patients' social and emotional improvement and reported observing fewer memory and behavior problems; moreover, the caregivers benefited from the therapy themselves in terms of their wellbeing. The gains had diminished at a 2-month follow-up assessment, but performance on most measures was still better than it was at baseline. Music therapy can also improve the functioning of other cognitive faculties, such as language (Brotons & Koger, 2000; Suzuki et al., 2004).

Other alternative therapies, such as dance therapy and art therapy, yield comparable results—that is, improved or unchanged cognitive functioning (because of its progressive nature, "no change" in Alzheimer's over time is essentially a positive outcome) and enhanced wellbeing (e.g., Cowl & Gaugler, 2014; Ehresman, 2014; Hokkanen et al., 2003). Dance therapy typically involves light exercise and sensory stimulation, as well as music, whereas art therapy is quite varied and can involve either creating art using a variety of media (e.g., painting, coloring, sculpting) or viewing art made by others (e.g., museum visits).[6] The behavioral and emotional benefits of such approaches are typically greater than the cognitive benefits (e.g., Cowl & Gaugler, 2014). Equally importantly, unlike drug therapy, alternative and mnemonic treatments for Alzheimer's disease have no negative side effects.

CONCLUSIONS

In Alzheimer's disease, as the poet Billy Collins expresses it, "the memories you used to harbor decided to retire to the southern hemisphere of the brain, to a little fishing village where there are no phones." It might be a perfectly lovely little fishing village, and the absence of phones might be peaceful, but the memories' inaccessibility can be incredibly frustrating. Most, but not all, elderly people experience some degree of forgetfulness, even in the absence of significant pathology like Alzheimer's disease, other dementias, or MCI. Aging has negative effects on memory in some, though not all, respects; dementias like Alzheimer's disease make it worse—in many cases, much worse.

Compared to other memory myths, laypeople are relatively well informed about aging's effects on memory. Most people know that memory gets worse with age, especially episodic memory, and that Alzheimer's disease is not an inevitable consequence of aging. Consistent with these mostly accurate perceptions—and perhaps, in part, contributing to them—popular depictions of Alzheimer's disease are numerous, and many of them are reasonably accurate, at least in comparison with popular depictions of other forms of amnesia. Films and literature (both fiction and nonfiction) featuring Alzheimer's patients realistically portray the hallmark characteristics of the disorder and the effects it has on patients and their families. For the most part, however, they do not show the various factors, like cognitive reserve, than can increase or decrease the risk of developing Alzheimer's disease, and they also pay little attention to treatment options for the disorder.

In addition, despite holding beliefs that are accurate in some respects, people harbor certain misconceptions about memory and aging. There is considerable variability in laypeople's beliefs about when age-related decrements in memory begin to appear, and their awareness of differential age effects on specific kinds of memory (e.g., eyewitness memory, prospective memory) is limited. Their beliefs also vary depending on respondents' (e.g., age) and targets' characteristics (e.g., aging stereotypes). Thus, people know about the overall relationship between memory and aging, but they have an incomplete understanding of the particulars, which are a good deal more nuanced.

We all age. Many of us will develop age-related memory problems. And a substantial subset will develop MCI, in many cases leading to dementia.

An estimated five million Americans suffer from Alzheimer's disease. Nonetheless, Alzheimer's disease is not an inevitable consequence of aging, and certain activities (e.g., physical activity, education, cognitive, and social engagement) can reduce one's risk of developing the disorder. Unfortunately, once Alzheimer's strikes, treatments are only modestly successful, and many of them do more for patients' social and emotional wellbeing than for their cognitive functioning. These noncognitive benefits are far from trivial, but they do not offset the progressive deterioration in the primary symptoms of the disorder—decline in memory and other cognitive functions.

Alzheimer's disease is all around us, in popular media and in real life, presenting society with enormous social, emotional, and financial costs. The familiarity that many people have with Alzheimer's disease likely contributes to the relatively high degree of knowledge that they have about the disease, aging, and memory. As the population ages and Alzheimer's becomes even more prevalent, that knowledge might continue to improve. A better popular understanding of Alzheimer's disease has the potential to help those who have the disorder and those who care for them—not much of a silver lining for the growing ubiquity of such a devastating disease, but better than nothing.

NOTES

1. President Reagan designated November as National Alzheimer's Disease Awareness Month in 1983. The 2014 documentary *Glen Campbell: I'll Be Me* tells the story of Glen Campbell's struggle with Alzheimer's Disease.

2. MCI and Alzheimer's Disease are also a significant economic and human capital concern. According to the Alzheimer's Association, Alzheimer's and other dementias will cost the U.S. $226 billion in 2015. By 2050, the annual costs could exceed $1 trillion (http://www.alz.org/facts/overview.asp).

3. Risk and protective factors have a reciprocal relationship to one another (Plassman et al., 2010). Generally speaking, if a factor (e.g., disrupted sleep) increases risk, than removing or reducing that factor (improving sleep quality and quantity) reduces risk and can therefore be construed as a protective or preventive factor. Thus, it makes sense to treat risk and prevention together.

4. Researchers also refer to "brain reserve" when the emphasis is on the neurological characteristics that prevent Alzheimer's pathology from developing in some people (e.g., Bennett et al., 2012). Some relationship presumably exists between cognitive reserve and brain reserve, possibly mediated by neural plasticity, but the precise mechanisms largely remain to be explicated (Blazer et al., 2015).

5. Other possible mechanisms underlying the link between poor sleep and dementia include increased amounts of tau, inflammation, impaired synaptic plasticity,

degeneration of neural tissue, hypoxia, vascular changes, and depression (Yaffe et al., 2014). Genetics might also play a direct or indirect role (Yaffe et al., 2014).

6. Perhaps the best-known example of art therapy is the MoMA (Museum of Modern Art in New York City) Alzheimer's Project, a special initiative that took place from 2007 to 2014. Although the project has ended, MoMA continues outreach efforts to make art accessible to people living with dementia and their caregivers (see https://www.moma.org/meetme/).

Chapter 8

Memory and the Legal System

Eyewitnesses

Myth: Eyewitnesses Are Highly Accurate

Related Myths: People Can Tell If an Eyewitness Is Reliable; Child Witnesses Are Trustworthy; False Convictions Based on Eyewitness Testimony (Almost) Never Occur

Not all crimes involve eyewitnesses. In some cases, no one was present to observe the crime; in others, the nature of the crime (e.g., possession of stolen goods, insurance or credit card fraud) often precludes eyewitness observation or makes it superfluous. In still other cases, the eyewitness is familiar with the perpetrator, making recognition significantly more accurate (albeit not perfect, and recall of details of the event can still be erroneous; see Steblay et al., 2011). This familiarity can range from simply having seen the perpetrator previously, in which case familiarity judgments are not terribly accurate (Pezdek & Stolzenberg, 2013), to having an intimate relationship with the perpetrator (e.g., acquaintance rape, domestic violence), where we would expect recognition and familiarity judgments to be nearly perfect. As recognition is less of an issue in cases with a familiar perpetrator, the eyewitness research literature focuses on events where the target individual is unknown to the witness. Such cases are also what most people think of when they think about eyewitnesses to real crimes.

It is difficult to estimate the number of cases in which eyewitnesses attempt to make an identification of a suspect or go on to testify at trial, but it is indisputably substantial. One study placed the frequency of eyewitness identifications at over 80,000 per year (Goldstein, Chance & Sneller, 1989), which is probably a low-end estimate. Eyewitnesses have enormous impact, whether those weighing the witnesses' memories are police, jurors, judges, laypeople, or the witnesses themselves. In addition, eyewitness memory is malleable, changing in light of post-event information and feedback (e.g., Davis & Loftus, 2007; Steblay, Wells & Douglass, 2014).

Eyewitness errors are the leading cause of false convictions, at least as gauged by DNA exonerations. As of February 8, 2017, 349 individuals have been exonerated by DNA testing (for a current figure, see the Innocence Project website, www.innocenceproject.org); roughly three-quarters of those cases involve a misidentification by one or more eyewitnesses (Garrett, 2011; Gross et al., 2005; Lampinen, Neuschatz & Cling, 2012; Wells, Memon & Penrod, 2006). In many cases eyewitness testimony is the only evidence against a defendant, as in the case of Uriah Courtney. Courtney was charged in 2005 with kidnapping, rape, assault, robbery, and false imprisonment in the November 2004 sexual assault of a 16-year-old student in Lemon Grove, California.[1] The victim made only a tentative identification of Courtney from a photo lineup, but a second eyewitness positively identified him. Alibi witnesses and payroll records placed Courtney at work at the time of the attack, and forensic evidence (e.g., fingernail scrapings) was inconclusive. Yet the victim, whose certainty had increased since the initial lineup, and the second eyewitness both confidently identified him at trial; he was convicted and sentenced to life in prison, serving 7 years until DNA testing exonerated him in 2013.

DNA testing is only feasible if the perpetrator leaves a part of himself behind, such as tissue or bodily fluids. For that reason crimes such as rape and assault, as in Uriah Courtney's case, are overrepresented in the Innocence Project database. Because DNA is not available in many, if not most cases, the number of false identifications and false convictions is undoubtedly much higher, perhaps in the thousands (Gross et al., 2005).

BELIEFS ABOUT EYEWITNESSES

Courts commonly assume that the fallibility of memory is a matter of "common sense" and use this assumption to exclude expert testimony on eyewitness issues (Benton et al., 2007). Jurors do, in fact, have specific beliefs about eyewitness memory. Although some of those beliefs are accurate, many are erroneous. Moreover, others involved in the trial process, such as judges and attorneys, suffer from some of the same biases. This section reviews research on the eyewitness beliefs of laypeople, as well as those of legal professionals.

A great many variables can affect, or be correlated with, eyewitness performance: characteristics of the witness (e.g., age), characteristics of the perpetrator (e.g., disguise), the situation itself (e.g., opportunity to observe the perpetrator), the time between the event and when the witness attempts to remember (i.e., the retention interval), and the methods the authorities use to elicit an eyewitness's memory (e.g., interviewing techniques, lineup administration procedures). In addition to the operation of so many variables in isolation, many of them exert an effect only in combination, such as the cross-race (i.e., witness race × perpetrator race) and cross-gender (i.e., witness gender × perpetrator gender) effects (see, e.g., Brigham, 2008; Wright & Sladden, 2003). To help make sense of this plethora of variables, eyewitness researchers typically distinguish between *system variables*, which are under the legal system's control (e.g., how to conduct lineups), and *estimator variables*, which are not (e.g., characteristics of the witness, perpetrator, or event; see, e.g., Lindsay et al., 2007; National Research Council, 2014; Wells et al., 2006). For both classes of variables, laypeople are aware of some of the factors that predict eyewitness behavior but not others. Conversely, laypeople are aware that certain variables that are not associated with better/worse eyewitness performance are not, in fact, predictive; whereas they erroneously believe that others are (Boyce et al., 2007).

The three major techniques for assessing laypeople's beliefs about eyewitnesses are questionnaires, in which laypeople (or others) are surveyed about their beliefs regarding the various factors that do and do not affect eyewitness performance; prediction studies, in which participants observe eyewitness testimony, or read about an eyewitness situation, and evaluate the eyewitness's accuracy or credibility; and jury simulation studies, where mock jurors make judgments in a case involving eyewitness testimony (Bornstein & Greene, 2017; Boyce et al., 2007). Each technique has its pros and cons, which makes it important to compare across methodologies. The focus here is on questionnaires, which measure laypeople's beliefs directly, drawing to less of an extent on the other methodologies.

Eyewitness Belief Questionnaires

Eyewitness questionnaires have been used with a variety of populations: laypeople, experts, judges, attorneys, and law enforcement officers. Experts are a valuable population to study for two reasons: first, they are sometimes called to testify as expert witnesses in cases involving eyewitness testimony. Second, experts have a wealth of knowledge relevant to determining what the truth is regarding the various factors that do and do not affect eyewitness performance. A consensus has developed among eyewitness researchers on the impact of a number of variables (Kassin, Ellsworth & Smith, 1989; Kassin et al., 2001), and many studies compare the beliefs of experts to those of other populations, to assess how much the other groups know about eyewitness reliability.

Direct comparisons of experts and laypeople have found considerable disagreement between the two groups. For example, Kassin and Barndollar (1992)

asked samples of college students and community adults whether various statements about eyewitness memory were "generally true" or "generally false," such
as "Very high levels of stress impair the accuracy of eyewitness testimony," and
"The presence of a weapon impairs an eyewitness's ability to accurately identify the perpetrator's face." The beliefs of students and nonstudents were quite
similar; however, lay participants' opinions differed from the experts' opinions
on 13 of 21 topics. In some instances laypeople were less aware than experts
that some factor affected performance (e.g., lineup instructions, exposure time,
cross-race bias), whereas in other instances laypeople overestimated the impact
of a factor (e.g., the confidence-accuracy relationship, gender differences, hypnosis). Additional studies comparing experts and laypeople have likewise found
an unimpressive level of layperson knowledge (e.g., Benton et al., 2006).

Other eyewitness belief surveys have used somewhat different methods,
but with largely comparable results (Boyce et al., 2007; Desmarais & Read,
2011). For example, participants in the survey described in chapter 1 were
correct on 65 percent of the eyewitness memory questions overall. Performance on the individual items ranged from 24 to 92 percent correct, showing
quite a range of knowledge across various system and estimator variables.
Prior jury experience fails to improve laypeople's knowledge of eyewitness
issues (Deffenbacher & Loftus, 1982; Magnussen, Safer, Sartori & Wise,
2013), as does prior experience as a witness (Noon & Hollin, 1987). Overall,
then, laypeople—both students and adult community members—do not display an impressive level of knowledge about eyewitness memory. The major
caveat to this conclusion is that methodological issues in the questionnaires'
construction can influence respondents' performance. Rewording the questions for greater comprehension, or using multiple-choice rather than free
response questions, yields better performance (Houston, Hope, Memon &
Read, 2013; Read & Desmarais, 2009).

There is some evidence that laypeople's knowledge of eyewitness memory
is improving. A recent meta-analysis of eyewitness knowledge surveys found
that laypeople are becoming more knowledgeable over time, at least for some
topics (Desmarais & Read, 2011). Desmarais and Read categorized surveys
into three temporal groups: those administered in the late 1970s/early 1980s,
late 1980s/early 1990s, and late 1990s/early 2000s. Performance, as measured by the overall percentage correct, increased from 46.3 to 53.3 percent to
68.6 percent over the three time periods. Because the specific items included
in each survey varied, they were unable to measure improvement over time
for all topics covered in the surveys. Nonetheless, they found that laypeople's
knowledge improved significantly for three topics: mugshot-induced bias,
the accuracy-confidence relationship, and the cross-race effect. Overall, the
increase in knowledge was statistically significant for estimator variables but
not for system variables.

Desmarais and Read (2011) attribute the improvement to greater public awareness of wrongful convictions, false memories, and investigative procedures (see also Desmarais et al., 2008). This might reflect an instance where media coverage of eyewitness errors and false convictions has had a positive, rather than a myth-perpetuating effect. Nonetheless, even the most recent eyewitness knowledge surveys indicate that laypeople still labor under a number of misconceptions. Overall performance on the most recent surveys (late 1990s/early 2000s) was 68.6 percent correct (comparable to the 65 % correct in the chapter 1 survey), and performance on individual items ranged from 45.5 percent (presentation format, i.e., simultaneous vs. sequential line-ups) to 90.6 percent (alcohol intoxication; Desmarais & Read, 2011). Thus, the questionnaire studies suggest that laypeople's knowledge of eyewitness memory is limited.

Prediction Studies

The remaining two techniques for assessing laypeople's beliefs about eye-witness memory—prediction and jury simulation studies—differ from the knowledge surveys in that rather than asking about beliefs directly, they allow us to infer people's beliefs from their behavior. This indirect approach is useful because individuals' behavior does not always follow from their self-reported beliefs, either in the eyewitness domain (Alonzo & Lane, 2010; Lindsay, 1994) or more generally (McAuliff & Bornstein, 2012; Nisbett & Wilson, 1977). Both methods involve having third parties observe eyewitnesses and make judgments about them (Boyce et al., 2007). They differ in terms of what they observe and the kinds of judgments they make. In prediction studies, observers typically see an actual eyewitness—usually someone who has witnessed a staged crime—make an identification or provide a description of the event/perpetrator, and they then judge (i.e., predict) whether the eyewitness was accurate or not. In jury simulation studies, observers adopt the role of jurors and observe an eyewitness testifying in a mock trial that usually contains other witnesses, jury instructions, and additional features that simulate a real trial ("observe" does not necessarily imply visually, as mock jurors in many studies read a written summary or transcript of a trial). They then evaluate the eyewitness's credibility and typically render a verdict and/or make other trial-relevant judgments (e.g., defendant culpability, sentencing recommendation).

The results of prediction studies are mixed, but the majority show that people are not very good at distinguishing accurate from inaccurate witnesses—that is, witnesses' actual accuracy often has no effect whatsoever on observers' judgments of their accuracy (Wells & Lindsay, 1983) or affects their judgments only under very limited conditions (Beaudry et al., 2015; Reardon & Fisher, 2011). Rather, what most influences accuracy judgments is a witness's confidence level: Highly confident eyewitnesses are deemed more accurate than eyewitnesses low in confidence (e.g., Beaudry et al., 2015; Lindsay, Wells, & Rumpel, 1981). Telling observers to ignore eyewitness confidence eliminates the effect of confidence on their accuracy judgments, but it does not improve their ability to distinguish between accurate and inaccurate eyewitnesses (Wells, Lindsay & Tousignant, 1980).

Several prediction studies have asked observers to judge the accuracy of child eyewitnesses, as opposed to adult eyewitnesses. As with the adult prediction studies, the data on how well observers can do that are mixed, depending on things like the age of the adult observer and the type of assertion (e.g., an accurate or a false report) made by the child (Block et al., 2012). In one of the earliest child eyewitness prediction studies, Leichtman and Ceci (1995) exposed 176 preschoolers to a classroom encounter involving an individual named Sam Stone. He interacted with the teacher in the children's presence, walked around the classroom, and left after approximately 2 minutes. The children were interviewed about Sam Stone's visit four times over the ensuing 4 weeks and a fifth time 10 weeks after the visit (the researchers also manipulated the information that participants were provided about Sam Stone before or after the classroom encounter and measured the effects on recall accuracy, but those aspects of the study are not relevant for present purposes).

Leichtman and Ceci (1995) presented videotapes of three children, from the final interview, to adult observers. Importantly, the observers were not merely ordinary laypeople but researchers and clinicians who worked in the area of children's testimony and were attending a professional conference— that is, they were essentially experts. The observers were unable to tell reliably whether specific events reported by the children (some of which were true, and others false) had genuinely occurred or not. In addition, their ratings of the children's credibility did not correspond well to the children's actual accuracy; the child who was most accurate was judged as the least credible. Although a child's age does not have a consistent effect on whether adult observers can discriminate an accurate from an inaccurate witness, adults are generally more skeptical of younger than of older children (Golding, Dunlap & Hodell, 2009).

Overall, the prediction studies show that lay observers are relatively poor at distinguishing between accurate and inaccurate eyewitnesses; that is, they are insensitive to the cues that predict eyewitness accuracy. From this pattern of results we can infer that for the most part, people lack the knowledge of eyewitness memory that would enable them to perform the task of evaluating an eyewitness's credibility effectively.

Jury Simulation Studies

Not surprisingly, in light of the facts that eyewitnesses who testify tend to be highly confident, laypeople fail to appreciate many of the factors that are associated with eyewitness reliability, and they are not very adept at distinguishing accurate from inaccurate eyewitnesses, eyewitnesses are extremely influential at trial. Mock jury studies show that jurors are persuaded more by an eyewitness than virtually any other kind of evidence, and jurors are not very sensitive to factors that make eyewitness evidence more or less reliable (Bornstein & Greene, 2017). Specifically, they are largely insensitive to system variables that can influence eyewitness performance, such as foil bias, instruction bias, and lineup presentation format (i.e., simultaneous vs. sequential; Cutler, Penrod & Dexter, 1990; Devenport, Stinson, Cutler & Kravitz, 2002). Their verdicts also do not reflect differences in estimator variables such as disguise, the presence of violence or a weapon, or retention interval (Bradfield & Wells, 2000; Cutler et al., 1990); quality of the view or duration of exposure to the criminal (Bradfield & Wells, 2000; Lindsay, Lim, Marando & Cully, 1986); and the relationship between the race of the perpetrator and the race of the eyewitness (Abshire & Bornstein, 2003). Mock jurors are sensitive to the estimator variable of the degree of attention that the witness reports paying to the culprit (Bradfield & Wells, 2000); however, self-reported attention is not necessarily a reliable indicator of actual cognitive processing (Wells & Quinlivan, 2009). Overwhelmingly, however, mock jurors find an eyewitness more credible and are more likely to convict the defendant when the eyewitness's confidence in the identification is relatively high (Bornstein & Greene, 2017).

A number of jury simulation studies focus not on circumstances of the crime or the identification, but instead on characteristics of the eyewitness's testimony at trial, such as its consistency. There are multiple ways in which a given witness's trial testimony can be consistent: with the testimony of other witnesses, with the witness's own pretrial statements (e.g., police reports), with other evidence (e.g., the witness's description of the perpetrator vs. the defendant's actual appearance), or within the witness's trial testimony itself (Boyce et al., 2007). Mock jurors tend to take any kind of inconsistency as a sign of poorer reliability, and inconsistency thus leads to diminished perceptions of the defendant's guilt (Bornstein & Greene, 2017).

Inconsistency does not, however, invariably lead to a lower conviction rate. For example, an eyewitness whose testimony conflicts with that of another witness is evaluated more favorably (leading to a correspondingly higher conviction rate) when the eyewitness's confidence is relatively low than when it is relatively high (Tenney, MacCoun, Spellman, & Hastie, 2007). According to Tenney and colleagues, the low-confident, erroneous eyewitness is more credible than the high-confident, erroneous eyewitness because he or she is better calibrated—that is, the witness's confidence and accuracy are more in sync. A unique feature of the Tenney study is that the eyewitness's testimony was not only inconsistent but demonstrably erroneous, based on other evidence presented at trial. In many cases, inconsistency requires jurors to weigh competing versions of the same story—from the same witness or different witnesses—but the truth is unknown. In such cases, calibration is much harder to demonstrate, likely leaving jurors to fall back on the eyewitness's stated confidence level. Indeed, some research shows that confidence has a greater impact on mock juror decisions than this kind of inconsistency (Brewer & Burke, 2002).

As with the prediction studies, jury simulation research shows that laypeople's evaluations of eyewitnesses are relatively insensitive to both system and estimator variables that are associated with better or worse eyewitness performance, suggesting that they believe those variables do not matter. The exception is testimonial consistency—in most circumstances, inconsistent eyewitness testimony leads to a diminished perception of the eyewitness's credibility. On the other hand, mock jurors do respond to variations in eyewitness confidence, suggesting a belief that eyewitness confidence and accuracy are highly correlated. Although confidence can be a reliable indicator of accuracy under some conditions (see below), in general it is not a particularly strong predictor. Thus, the results of indirect measures of laypeople's beliefs—prediction and jury simulation studies—are largely consistent with those from the direct questionnaire assessments; that is, they show that their beliefs are not very accurate.

Beliefs of Legal Professionals

These erroneous beliefs could stem partly from the fact that apart from their everyday experiences with memory and its workings, most laypeople probably have little experience with eyewitnesses. However, there are groups of legal professionals who do interact regularly with eyewitnesses—namely, police, attorneys, and judges. It would therefore be reasonable to expect these groups to know more about eyewitness memory.

Several studies have measured the eyewitness beliefs of various legal professionals, in both the United States and elsewhere. As with the surveys of laypeople's eyewitness beliefs, the precise methodology of these studies varies, but they commonly test legal professionals' knowledge of the topics assessed by Kassin and colleagues (2001; Kassin & Barndollar, 1992) or some variation thereof. The results are not particularly encouraging. On the positive side, judges tend to know somewhat more than jurors and the general public, and defense attorneys know more than prosecutors; less positively, knowledge of eyewitness issues is relatively modest for all groups of legal professionals, who know considerably less than eyewitness experts. For example, Benton et al. (2006) compared the responses of adults summoned for jury duty, police officers, criminal and civil state court judges, and experts. Both judges and police officers agreed with experts on 12 of 30 items (40 %; see Table 8.1). This was considerably better than the 4 of 30 items (13.3 %) on which jurors agreed with the experts (effects of alcoholic intoxication, stress, and event violence, and whether trained observers are more accurate than the average person), but it is still an unimpressive level of performance overall. Moreover, the two groups of legal professionals agreed between themselves on only six topics (see Table 8.1), and all three groups agreed with the experts on only two topics: the effect of event violence and whether trained observers make better eyewitnesses.

Even the most learned jurists in the land, members of the US Supreme Court, labor under mistaken beliefs about eyewitness memory. The Court's current test of whether an eyewitness identification was reliable, even though the identification procedure was impermissibly suggestive, applies the so-called *Biggers*, or *Manson*, criteria (*Manson v. Braithwaite*, 1977; *Neil v. Biggers*, 1972): the witness's opportunity to view the culprit, attention to the culprit, descriptive detail, and certainty, as well as the retention interval between the event and the identification. Although the importance of these factors in determining eyewitness accuracy may seem like a matter of common sense, there exists only a "precarious … relation between the *Manson* factors and eyewitness identification accuracy" (Wells & Quinlivan, 2009, p. 9). Some factors (e.g., opportunity to view, retention interval) have a nonlinear relationship to accuracy; attention is a complex construct that is difficult to measure objectively; the amount of descriptive detail is a poor predictor of whether the description is actually correct, and even if it were a reliable predictor, the accuracy of descriptive recall and the accuracy of face recognition are not highly correlated (Meissner, Sporer, & Schooler, 2007); and as discussed below, a witness's level of certainty, especially after a delay, is not a terribly strong predictor of accuracy. Thus, "none of the five criteria are unequivocally related to the accuracy of identifications" (Wells & Quinlivan, 2009, p. 16). Moreover, a witness's assessment of three of the five criteria (certainty, view, and attention) can be influenced by suggestive procedures, leading to inflated self-reports in cases where such procedures have been used (Steblay et al., 2014; Wells & Quinlivan, 2009).

One could argue that Supreme Court justices, in deciding matters of law, are somewhat removed from routine evidentiary matters such as eyewitness testimony. However, greater professional experience does not lead to superior knowledge for police officers (Wise, Safer, & Maro, 2011), practicing attorneys (Wise, Pawlenko, Safer, & Meyer, 2009), or trial judges

Table 8.1   Beliefs of Police, Judges, and Jurors about Various Eyewitness Factors: Agreement with Experts

Eyewitness Factor		
1. Stress impairs accuracy[a,b]	2. Weapon presence impairs accuracy	3. One-person showups increase risk of misidentification[b,c]
4. Lineup fairness: resemblance of lineup members to suspect helps[c]	5. Lineup instructions can affect willingness to make an identification	6. Less exposure time leads to poorer memory[c]
7. Forgetting curve: rate of memory loss greatest right after event	8. Accuracy-confidence: confidence not a good predictor of accuracy	9. Postevent information affects eyewitness testimony
10. Color perception: Judgments of color are unreliale[b]	11. Wording of questions affects eyewitness testimony	12. Unconscious transference: witnesses may identify someone seen in another context
13. Trained observers are no more accurate than average person[a,b,c]	14. Hypnosis increases accuracy[b]	15. Hypnosis increases suggestibility
16. Attitudes & expectations can affect event perception and memory[b,c]	17. Event violence impairs memory[a,b,c]	18. Cross-race bias impairs accuracy[b,c]
19. Confidence malleability: confidence can be influenced by unrelated factors[c]	20. Alcoholic intoxication impairs memory[a,b]	21. Mugshot-induced bias increases likelihood of choosing suspect
22. Long-term repression can occur with later recovery of memory	23. False childhood memories can occur[c]	24. Discriminability between true and false memories is possible[b,c]
25. Child witness accuracy: young children less accurate than adults	26. Child suggestibility: young children more suggestible than adults[c]	27. Description-matched lineups facilitate accuracy[b]
28. Presentation format: simultaneous lineups lead to more misidentifications than sequential lineups	29. Elderly witnesses are less accurate than younger adults[b]	30. Identification speed: faster identifications are more accurate[c]

Note: Adapted from Benton et al. (2006). Item wording has been paraphrased for the sake of brevity. For actual wording, see the original source.
[a] Jurors agreed with experts on effect of this factor.
[b] Police agreed with experts on effect of this factor.
[c] Judges agreed with experts on effect of this factor.

(Wise & Safer, 2004). Thus, direct contact with eyewitnesses in the course of one's work does not appear to produce a better appreciation of the factors that do and do not affect eyewitness performance. The phenomenon is not peculiar to American legal professionals. Police, attorneys, and judges in other countries similarly have limited knowledge of eyewitness issues (Bornstein & Greene, 2017; Granhag, Strömwall, & Hartwig, 2005).

UNPACKING THE EYEWITNESS MYTHS

One of the more curious aspects of laypeople's high level of faith in eyewitness testimony is that they know that memory errors in general are common. What we might term the "eyewitness memory paradox" is that our metamemory awareness is generally good enough that everyone knows memory is fallible (see Introduction); yet in some circumstances, such as when an eyewitness testifies about what (or whom) she has seen, individuals judging the witness's memory report, such as jurors, find it to be very credible. Few, if any, kinds of evidence are as influential as an eyewitness pointing at the defense table and saying "that's the guy who did it." Why are we so inclined to believe some memories when we know that memory in general can be wrong? Both psychological factors and popular portrayals of eyewitnesses contribute to the persistence of laypeople's erroneous beliefs.

The Eyewitness Memory Paradox

There are a number of possible explanations for the paradox, which likely has multiple contributing factors. First of all, the mere existence of a victim, someone who has suffered harm—in many cases grievous physical and/or psychological injury—arouses sympathy in others. Sympathy at trial influences jury decisions, in large part because the principal (and sometimes the only) way to obtain redress for the victim is to hold the alleged harmdoer accountable (e.g., Greene & Bornstein, 2003). Second, jurors are inclined—not unreasonably—to assume that there is a decent chance someone being tried for a crime is guilty. Why else would the state, which has no interest in prosecuting the innocent, go to the trouble and expense of trial? Theoretically, the court's instruction on the presumption of innocence (i.e., that the defendant is presumed to be innocent until proven guilty beyond a reasonable doubt) should counteract any biased *a priori* assumptions about the defendant's guilt; but the instruction's ability to do so is limited at best (Simon, 2012).

Of course, sympathy for the victim and assumptions about the defendant's guilt are probably at work whether or not an eyewitness testifies; they therefore fail to explain the eyewitness paradox in its entirety. One important factor—not unique to eyewitness testimony but perhaps more salient than for other kinds of witness testimony—is the eyewitness's confidence. As in the case of Uriah Courtney, eyewitnesses—at least by the time of trial—are invariably highly confident. People naturally assume that individuals who are more confident are more knowledgeable, even when greater confidence does not mean greater accuracy (i.e., when the highly confident individuals are overconfident; Price & Stone, 2004); this "confidence heuristic" is a general metamemory strategy that applies to perceptions of eyewitnesses as well (Bornstein & Greene, 2017; Wells & Lindsay, 1983).

Just as people tend to be overconfident about their knowledge and abilities in many domains (e.g., Bornstein & Zickafoose, 1999; Dunlosky & Metcalfe, 2009), eyewitnesses are often overconfident (Leippe & Eisenstadt, 2007). The precise extent to which an eyewitness's confidence is a reliable index of his or her accuracy is a contentious topic within the eyewitness literature (e.g., Wixted & Wells, in press; Wixted et al., 2015; Wixted, Read, & Lindsay, in press). The general consensus is that when construed broadly, confidence is a relatively weak and highly variable indicator of accuracy (Kassin et al., 2001; Leippe & Eisenstadt, 2007; *New Jersey v. Henderson*, 2011). However, under some conditions, and depending on the measurement techniques used, confidence can actually be a reasonably good predictor of accuracy (National Research Council, 2014; Roediger, Wixted & DeSoto, 2012; Wixted & Wells, in press; Wixted et al., 2015). For example, confidence is a reliable indicator of accuracy when analyzed only for eyewitnesses who make a positive lineup identification (Sporer et al., 1995), identify the suspect (Wixted et al., in press), or are highly confident (Wixted et al., 2015; in press); provide a confidence statement from fair lineups and at the time of the initial identification (as opposed to unfair lineups or later in the course of the investigation or at trial; National Research Council, 2014; Wixted & Wells, in press; Wixted et al., 2015); or witness the crime under conditions that are conducive to good encoding of the event (Bothwell, Deffenbacher & Brigham, 1987). The magnitude of the confidence-accuracy relationship also depends on how the relationship is analyzed (e.g., using within- vs. between-subject correlations, calibration, receiver operating characteristic [ROC], or confidence-accuracy characteristic analysis; Mickes, 2015; National Research Council, 2014; Roediger et al., 2012; Wixted & Wells, in press). In light of all these qualifiers, "confidence and accuracy can be positively related, they can be unrelated, and they can even be negatively related" (Roediger et al., 2012, p. 85).

The ability of confidence to be a reliable predictor of eyewitness accuracy under some circumstances notwithstanding, the fact remains that those circumstances do not always prevail (Wixted & Wells, in press). Largely as a result, eyewitnesses who are highly confident at trial not infrequently make mistakes, as in the case of Uriah Courtney. In DNA exoneration cases involving eyewitness testimony, "almost without exception, the eyewitnesses who testified expressed complete confidence that they had chosen the perpetrator"

(National Research Council, 2014, p. 7). To a large extent the false convictions in these cases likely resulted from the confidence heuristic—jurors' overreliance on an eyewitness's confidence as a cue to the witness' accuracy. The irony is that witnesses who are low in confidence might, under some circumstances, be just as reliable as highly confident witnesses, but witnesses whose confidence is shaky rarely testify at trial.

Popular Portrayals of Eyewitness Memory and Procedures

A final contributor to the eyewitness memory paradox is misleading media portrayals of eyewitnesses. Virtually every police procedural on TV has prominently featured eyewitnesses in one or more episodes (e.g., *Hill Street Blues*, *Law & Order*, *Blue Bloods*, *CSI*, *NCIS*). In these dramas, viewers observe eyewitnesses being questioned about their recall of an event, attempting an identification at the police station or in the field, and testifying at trial. Estimates of the number of eyewitnesses the average viewer of such shows has seen—one might even say "witnessed"—being questioned, viewing a lineup, or testifying do not exist, but it is easily in the hundreds, if not thousands. Desmarais, Price, and Read (2008) provided some data relevant to this question by analyzing 263 episodes of 12 different television crime dramas from the 1980s, 1990s, and 2000s (one show, *Law and Order*, was represented in both the 1990s and the 2000s). They coded each episode for the presence or absence of 35 distinct eyewitness issues (e.g., the effect of eyewitness stress, the weapon focus effect). Eyewitness memory for details of normal events appeared in 96 percent of episodes, and memory for details of traumatic events appeared in 87 percent of episodes. Overall, there was an average of 13 eyewitness issues presented per episode; the rate was higher in the 1990s and 2000s than the 1980s, and some issues (e.g., memory for trauma) were presented more often than others (e.g., hypnotic accuracy). Most of the issues were presented implicitly, rather than being explicitly addressed. In most cases where an eyewitness factor was presented, there was no indication of how it affected eyewitness performance, leaving viewers to make inferences at odds with empirical data on eyewitness memory (e.g., assuming that some variables known to affect eyewitness accuracy, like witness intoxication, would have no effect). Desmarais and colleagues conclude that these fictional portrayals of eyewitnesses have considerable potential to mislead the public and foster erroneous beliefs about eyewitness memory.

Dramatic portrayals of eyewitness procedures are also misleading in a number of other respects. For example, TV identifications are almost always made from lineups of five or six individuals, whereas one-third to three-quarters of actual police identifications involve only a single individual (referred to as a "showup"; Dysart & Lindsay, 2007; Neuschatz et al., 2016). In a showup, the question posed to witnesses is along the lines of "Is this the person you saw commit the crime?" as opposed to "Which of these persons (if any) did you see commit the crime?" Showups are especially likely to occur in the field, with a live (as opposed to photographed) suspect (Dysart & Lindsay, 2007). The US Supreme Court has expressed concerns that showups are unduly suggestive and should be used sparingly (e.g., *Stovall v. Denno*, 1967). Indeed, showups generally lead to poorer performance than lineups (Neuschatz et al., 2016; Steblay, Dysart, Fulero & Lindsay, 2003; but see Valentine, Davis, Memon & Roberts, 2012), and roughly one-third of DNA exonerations involved showup misidentifications (Garrett, 2011).

TV lineups also tend to be conducted live (sometimes called "corporeal lineups"), usually at the station house, as opposed to showing witnesses a photoarray of either print or digital images. The reality, however, is that photoarrays, at least in the United States, are considerably more common (Behrman & Davey, 2001; Lampinen et al., 2012). Photoarrays have a number of advantages in terms of fairness: there are usually more photos available from which to choose fillers than there are live fillers loitering around the station house; the static images are more homogeneous than the mannerisms of live persons, which can introduce bias; and they avoid sending as strong a message that the police have a suspect in custody (which is potentially part of the reason that showups are biasing). Photographic lineups have the additional advantage—at least from the authorities' perspective—that a suspect's right to counsel does not attach to them, whereas it does attach to corporeal lineups (*United States v. Ash*, 1973). Eyewitnesses themselves would almost certainly prefer viewing a photoarray. It can be conducted anywhere (e.g., in their home) and would not have the feel of an in-person confrontation, both of which would likely make the identification experience less stressful (Bornstein, Hullman & Miller, 2013). The disadvantage of using photoarrays is that some research suggests they produce fewer hits and more false identifications than live or videotaped lineups (Cutler, Berman, Penrod & Fisher, 1994).

Regardless of whether a lineup is presented live or photographically, TV depictions almost never show how the police put it together. A number of factors make lineups more or less fair, such as the similarity of lineup members to one another (including the suspect), their similarity to eyewitness descriptions of the perpetrator, whether the suspect stands out in some way, and lineup size (Malpass, Tredoux & McQuiston-Surrett, 2007; National Research Council, 2014; Technical Working Group on Eyewitness Evidence, 1999). In the absence of such "behind-the-scenes" information, viewers are likely to assume that lineups are always fair and to be ignorant of factors that can make them less fair.

Finally, it seems that TV eyewitnesses almost always identify the suspect and do so quickly and with high confidence. The authorities accept the positive identification at face value and proceed to build a case against the suspect, neglecting to consider seriously that a confident witness might be mistaken. Again, the reality belies the fiction. Studies of actual eyewitnesses find that they fail to pick anyone from a lineup 25 percent of the time or more (e.g., Behrman & Davey, 2001), and variables like confidence, decision time, and decision strategy vary widely (Behrman & Richards, 2005). As the DNA exonerations poignantly demonstrate, eyewitnesses—even very confident ones—*do* make mistakes. And an unintended consequence of investigators being too quick to accept an eyewitness's positive identification is that it can lead them to zero in on a particular suspect and ignore alternative suspects and exonerating evidence (Simon, 2012).

As discussed in the introduction, popular portrayals of memory phenomena are not invariably misleading, and the same TV shows that present a skewed image of eyewitness identifications occasionally portray an erroneous eyewitness. Moreover, the news media have extensively covered cases of misidentifications and false convictions. No one seems to doubt the reality of these errors. Nonetheless, popular portrayals of eyewitnesses tend to emphasize their reliability. In conjunction with the psychological processes underlying the eyewitness memory paradox (e.g., the confidence heuristic), these portrayals contribute to the myth of the highly accurate eyewitness.

A SNAPSHOT OF EYEWITNESS RELIABILITY

The literature on eyewitness memory is much too large to attempt a comprehensive overview here, and some of the system and estimator variables affecting eyewitness accuracy have already been discussed (for relatively current reviews, see Lampinen et al., 2012; Lindsay, Ross, Read & Toglia, 2007; Toglia, Read, Ross & Lindsay, 2007). The focus of the present chapter is on what people, especially laypeople, believe about eyewitness memory; to help put those beliefs in context, the present section sketches briefly just how reliable eyewitness memory actually is. I first present some general findings involving adult witnesses, followed by a discussion of child witnesses

General Findings with Adult Witnesses

Most eyewitness research consists of laboratory studies, which are advantageous because they allow researchers to control extraneous factors, as well as to determine what really happened (Lampinen et al., 2012; Lindsay et al., 2007). In the "real world," by contrast, witnesses to the same event can have widely varying experiences; circumstances of the event are uncontrollable; and it is difficult, if not impossible, to ascertain what truly occurred. The trade-off is that experimental witnesses most often view a reenactment of a crime, such as a video, and have the perspective more of moviegoers than genuine eyewitnesses. Nonetheless, there are a number of experiments in which laboratory participants unwittingly view a staged crime (e.g., Wells & Lindsay, 1983) or researchers assess the performance of real adult eye-witnesses in the field, while maintaining a high degree of experimental control and isolating one or more variables of interest (e.g., Pigott, Brigham & Bothwell, 1990). Penrod and Bornstein (2007) aggregated the results of several field studies and found that, on average, 42 percent of real-world eyewitnesses made a correct identification from a target-present (TP) lineup, whereas 32 percent selected a lineup member known to be innocent (commonly referred to as a "foil" or "distractor"). In the two studies that also included target-absent (TA) lineups, roughly 35 percent of the eyewitnesses falsely identified an innocent suspect.

Archival studies of eyewitnesses, in which researchers analyze the iden-tification decisions of actual eyewitnesses from police records, show much the same thing (Lampinen et al., 2012; Penrod & Bornstein, 2007). Several British studies (Slater, 1994; Valentine, Pickering & Darling, 2003; Wright & McDaid, 1996) found that roughly one in three positive identifications were of innocent foils. For example, Valentine and colleagues examined the performance of 584 witnesses from the London area in 295 stranger identi-fication cases (i.e., where the witness did not know the suspect). Forty-one percent picked the suspect, 21 percent picked a known-innocent foil, and 39 percent failed to make an identification (the total of 101 % is due to rounding). Thus, a minimum of one-third of identifications were errors (21/ [41 + 21] = .34). Analogous American studies have found a virtually identical ratio, with roughly two suspect identifications for every one foil identifica-tion (Behrman & Davey, 2001; Wells, Steblay, & Dysart, 2014). The ratio varies somewhat depending on the lineup presentation procedure but is high regardless: Wells et al. found that 32 percent of positive identifications in sequential lineups were of a known-innocent foil, compared to 41 percent in simultaneous lineups. Although foil identifications are essentially harmless—that is, there are no consequences for someone known to be innocent—such a high error rate nonetheless casts serious doubt on the overall reliability of eyewitness memory.

Moreover, the true error rate is certainly higher, as some proportion of the suspects who were positively identified were undoubtedly innocent. In addition, some of the nonidentifications were almost certainly errors—that is, the guilty party was in the lineup, but the witness failed to identify him or her. Overall, then, the data show that a substantial number of positive identifications—at least one-third, and presumably a nontrivial number of nonidentifications as well—are errors. When considered in light of the fact that many eyewitnesses provide no information at all regarding the perpetrator's appearance (e.g., fully 71 % of fraud victims, compared to 9.5 % of robbery victims and 11 % of robbery bystander witnesses; see Tollestrup, Turtle, & Yuille, 1994), the high rate of identification errors should perhaps not be surprising.

Suspect identifications are more likely under some circumstances than others. Specifically, identification rates are higher when the witness is younger than 30 years old; the suspect is White or the same race as the witness; the witness gave a detailed description of the culprit, attempted an identification relatively soon after the crime, or viewed the culprit for over a minute; the witness views a one-person showup in the field, as opposed to a photographic lineup; and the witness makes a relatively fast, automatic lineup decision with high confidence (Behrman & Davey, 2001; Behrman & Richards, 2005; Tollestrup et al., 1994; Valentine et al., 2003). It is important to note that a greater tendency to identify the suspect does not necessarily mean witnesses are any more (or less) accurate in their identifications. Indeed, Behrman and Davey found that suspect identification rates across different levels of extrinsic incriminating evidence—a possible surrogate for the likelihood that a suspect was truly guilty—were fairly constant, although Tollestrup and colleagues found that positive identifications were more likely when there was stronger evidence implicating the suspect.

An additional means of investigating the performance of actual eyewitnesses is case studies, in which witnesses to one or a small number of crimes are interviewed. As with archival studies, it is difficult to determine whether witnesses in case studies are accurate, but based on the police investigation and extrinsic evidence (e.g., surveillance recordings), one can sometimes be reasonably confident of what actually occurred. Because case studies typically involve a small number of perpetrators (or only one), the emphasis is on witnesses' ability to recall details of the event, rather than to identify the perpetrator.

The results of case studies are somewhat at odds with those from the field and archival studies of eyewitness identification. For example, Yuille and Cutshall (1986) interviewed 13 adult witnesses to a shooting incident 4–5 months after the event. With the aid of police, witness, and medical reports, they were able to reconstruct the facts of the event with a high degree of reliability. Although the accuracy of eyewitnesses' recall varied depending on the type of information being assessed (e.g., they were more accurate in describing objects [85 %] and actions [82 %] than persons [73 %]), they were relatively accurate overall, as well as resistant to leading questions. Consistent with research showing little relationship between emotion and memory accuracy (see chapter 2), more emotionally involved eyewitnesses did not remember more information than less emotionally involved eyewitnesses (see also Christianson & Hübinette, 1993). A more recent case study of 14 Dutch witnesses to a supermarket armed robbery, interviewed 3 months after the event, found a similar level of overall accuracy (84 %), with roughly comparable performance across different types of information (Odinot, Wolters & van Koppen, 2009).

The case study results are noteworthy, but their positive message must be tempered somewhat by three observations. First, although they show that most of what real eyewitnesses recall is correct, they do not show how much they manage to recall. For example, the number of units of information (e.g., "one of the robbers had a black gun" contains two units of information: presence of a gun and the gun's color) provided by witnesses in the Odinot et al. (2009) study ranged from only 22 to 204. That is not a lot of information on which to build an investigation, especially in cases involving few witnesses. Second, as mentioned above, the nature of eyewitness case studies typically precludes an examination of identification decisions. Significantly, however, the type of information on which eyewitnesses do most poorly—person descriptions—is the information most relevant to making an accurate identification (Christianson & Hübinette, 1993; Yuille & Cutshall, 1986). And third, the results of eyewitness identification research are largely, though not entirely, comparable across different research methodologies, whether the research is conducted in the laboratory, in the field, or as part of an archival analysis (Behrman & Davey, 2001; Penrod & Bornstein, 2007). The overarching conclusion of most eyewitness research is that eyewitnesses are frequently inaccurate; moreover, as the previous discussion of laypeople's beliefs about eyewitness memory shows, they are less accurate than people generally think they are (e.g., Boyce et al., 2007; Memon & Thomson, 2007).

Child Witnesses

One of the most controversial topics concerning eyewitness memory is the reliability of child witnesses, primarily because of children's heightened vulnerability, psychological developmental factors, and legal issues related to their competency as witnesses. A child could witness any crime, either as a bystander or a victim, but the principal concern is with child victims, especially in cases of child sexual abuse (CSA), where there is often little evidence besides the victim's testimony. Children's memory processes and reliability are similar in some respects whether they are victims or bystanders (Lamb et al., 2003), but they necessarily differ in important ways, such as the witness's viewing perspective and subjective experience. Although

CSA has long been a significant societal problem, issues surrounding child eyewitnesses have become particularly prominent in the last few decades, due largely to extensive media coverage of some CSA trials, such as those of Peggy and Ray Buckey (in the McMartin Preschool case), Kelly Michaels, Catholic priests, Jerry Sandusky, and others.

In one such case, Kelly Michaels, a teacher's aide at Wee Care Day Nursery in Maplewood, New Jersey, was tried on 163 counts of alleged sexual abuse. The jury convicted her on 115 counts, including aggravated sexual assault, sexual assault, endangering the welfare of children, and terroristic threats, and the court sentenced her to 47 years in prison (Cheit, 2014; Rabinowitz, 1990; *State v. Michaels*, 1994). A striking feature of the Michaels case, as with several of the others, is the bizarre nature of some of the allegations. For example, a four-and-a-half-year-old child told investigators that he and another child put their penises into Kelly at the same time, which they accomplished by chopping off their penises. He stated further that the children urinated in her mouth (and vice versa) and she put a fork in his "hiney" (*State v. Michaels*, 1994). Significantly, transcripts of this and other interviews in the Michaels case are replete with instances of cajoling, reinforcing children for certain responses, and refusing to accept their denials. Bizarre allegations in other cases (e.g., McMartin Preschool) occasionally involved claims of Satanic ritual abuse. Although defendants in these cases may ultimately be exonerated—the McMartin case resulted in no convictions and Kelly Michaels' conviction was eventually reversed on appeal—the damage to reputations and time incarcerated before (and in Michaels' case, after) trial cannot be undone.

The major concerns about children as witnesses are that they are less competent—hence less likely to provide accurate memory reports and more likely to make errors—and more suggestible (Klemfuss & Ceci, 2012). A large body of research shows that these concerns are justified and, especially with regard to suggestibility, can be exacerbated by the manner in which children are questioned (e.g., Ceci & Bruck, 1995; Ceci & Friedman, 2000). Techniques such as reinforcing children for providing incriminating information, exerting pressure on children to conform (e.g., by telling them others provided certain information), expressing disapproval when they deny allegations, inviting them to speculate, and even merely repeating questions can all make children more likely to report events that did not genuinely happen than merely asking suggestive questions (Garven, Wood, Malpass & Shaw, 1998).

Garven and colleagues (1998; Garven, Wood, & Malpass, 2000; see also Billings et al., 2007) tested the effect on 5–7-year-old children's reports of a number of suggestive interview techniques. For example, Garven et al. (2000) questioned children about a young man's (Paco) visit to their grade school classroom, during which he read a story and distributed treats.

All of the children were asked suggestive questions about events that did not occur, as well as about true events. Some of the misleading questions concerned mundane items (e.g., whether Paco tore a book or tickled the child on the tummy), whereas others concerned highly implausible, fantastic events (e.g., whether Paco took the child on a helicopter ride or to a farm). The experimenters varied whether the children received reinforcement (i.e., praise when they answered "yes" and mild disappointment if they answered "no") and whether the interviewer told them how other kids had supposedly answered a question. Reinforcement increased the percentage of "yes" responses to misleading mundane questions from 12.5 to 34.7 percent, and to misleading fantastic questions from 4.9 to 51.6 percent. Cowitness information increased the likelihood of responding yes to misleading mundane questions, but not to misleading fantastic questions. The effect of reinforcement persisted in a second interview, whether or not the reinforcement continued. Reinforcement is so powerful that it can even induce children to incriminate themselves (Billings et al., 2007).

It is tempting to assume that children might falsely report a helicopter ride or farm trip but not something as severe, painful, and invasive as sexual abuse. Unfortunately, some of the highly sensationalized cases, such as the McMartin Preschool and Kelly Michaels cases, in which extremely suggestive techniques were particularly prominent (Schreiber et al., 2006), suggest otherwise. Current recommendations on how to interview child eyewitnesses explicitly advise against using these and related techniques, in order to decrease suggestibility and increase the amount of correct information elicited (e.g., Krackow & Lynn, 2010; Lamb, Hershkowitz, Orbach, & Esplin, 2008).

Laypeople's expectations about child witnesses are correct in some respects but incorrect in others (Bottoms et al., 2007). For example, the eyewitness belief survey conducted by Benton and colleagues (2006) included three questions on topics that dealt with children: child witness accuracy ("Young children are less accurate as witnesses than are adults"), child suggestibility ("Young children are more vulnerable than adults to interviewer suggestion, peer pressures and other social influences"), and false childhood memories ("Memories people recover from their own childhood are often false or distorted in some way"). The percentage of jurors who answered correctly ("true" for each question) was 32, 82, and 35 percent, respectively.[2] These figures seem inconsistent, as recovered memories (covered in greater depth in chapter 3) are in many respects an exemplar of suggestiveness (Belli, 2012; Lindsay & Read, 1994). Nonetheless, they indicate a disjunction, where most people know that children are more suggestible than adults, but not that their eyewitness memory tends to be less accurate overall; other research does show, at least, that relatively few people expect children to be *more* reliable eyewitnesses than adults (Neal, Christiansen, Bornstein &

Robicheaux, 2012). Most laypeople also tend to overestimate the extent to which alternatives to traditional, in-court testimony, such as closed circuit TV, will alter the behavior of child witnesses, which has implications for how child witnesses are perceived at trial (McAuliff & Kovera, 2012).

As discussed above, adults are not particularly good judges of whether child witnesses are accurate. The jury simulation literature shows that mock jurors often, but not always, respond to variations in eyewitness age, but the effects are complex. Some studies show that younger children are perceived as more credible than older children (e.g., Holcomb & Jacquin, 2007; Read, Connolly & Welsh, 2006), whereas others find little effect of child witness age (McCauley & Parker, 2001; Myers et al., 1999). Age effects vary depending on factors such as whether the eyewitness testimony emphasizes the witness's honesty or cognitive ability (Leippe & Romanczyk, 1987; Ross, Jurden, Lindsay & Keeney, 2003). Younger witnesses (i.e., younger vs. older children and children vs. adults) tend to be perceived as more honest than older witnesses but as less cognitively competent (at least until the point when elderly witnesses' cognitive abilities become suspect; see Ross, Dunning, Toglia & Ceci, 1990). Overall, then, laypeople are somewhat aware of child witnesses' limitations—especially with regard to suggestibility—but do not necessarily treat child witnesses as the empirical evidence suggests they should.

Public awareness of child witnesses' susceptibility to suggestive questioning could reflect attention to the issue in both movies (e.g., *Capturing the Friedmans*) and television shows (e.g., *Law & Order: SVU*). *Capturing the Friedmans*, which was nominated for an Academy Award for best documentary feature in 2003, dealt with the case of Arnold and Jesse Friedman, who were charged with—and pleaded guilty to—multiple counts of CSA. Despite their confessions, doubts about the veracity of the allegations remain, as do questions about the tactics used by the authorities in the course of the investigation, including the interviewing techniques. Television portrayals have likewise shown how easily child witnesses can be misled, often inadvertently, by suggestive questioning. Yet consistent with the research showing that many laypeople are unaware that child witnesses are less accurate than adults, and that child witnesses are fairly credible at trial, in these same dramatic treatments children make very powerful and persuasive witnesses. By the time they testify, few raise doubts about their testimony's veracity besides the legal defense team.

EYEWITNESS ERRORS: A PEBBLE IN THE OCEAN?

As of February 8, 2017, the Innocence Project has documented 349 false convictions. When considered against the backdrop of the thousands of criminal prosecutions each year, that number seems relatively small. It might be tempting to conclude, therefore, that the system is working reasonably well, and that existing safeguards are mostly effective. However, as described at the outset of the chapter, the number of DNA exonerations is necessarily a gross underestimate—by precisely how much it is impossible to say—of the true number of false convictions. And archival and field studies of actual eyewitnesses have repeatedly found that eyewitnesses' error rate is substantial. Although eyewitnesses are undoubtedly accurate much, and maybe even most, of the time, the evidence strongly suggests that eyewitness errors are much more than a pebble in the ocean. Or, if they are a pebble, then they are a pebble whose ripples make themselves felt on every shore.

The legal system employs a number of techniques, or "safeguards," to aid jurors in evaluating eyewitness testimony (Devenport, Kimbrough & Cutler, 2009; Simon, 2012; van Wallendael, Cutler, Devenport & Penrod, 2007). The most common strategies include (in the order in which they appear at trial) voir dire (i.e., jury selection), cross-examination, testimony from an expert in the field, closing arguments, and jury instructions provided by the judge. With the exception of expert testimony, these are inherent in every trial's structure itself and do not require any major procedural changes for dealing with eyewitness testimony, although they can involve substantive changes to address eyewitness issues specifically, such as extensive voir dire or more elaborate jury instructions (Bornstein & Greene, 2017).

In addressing the effectiveness of various legal safeguards, researchers often distinguish between skepticism and sensitivity (e.g., van Wallandael et al., 2007). Skepticism occurs when a particular technique makes jurors weigh eyewitness testimony less; that is, it makes the eyewitness seem less credible. Sensitization, on the other hand, occurs when a particular technique makes jurors better able to discriminate between good eyewitnesses (i.e., those relatively more likely to be accurate because of features of the witnessing situation, procedures used to elicit their memory of the event or perpetrator, etc.) and bad eyewitnesses. Considering that jurors tend to overvalue eyewitness testimony, skepticism in and of itself is not necessarily a bad thing. However, sensitization is preferable, because it means that jurors are responding appropriately to differences in the strength of the evidence. Overall, traditional legal safeguards have little effect (Devenport et al., 2009; van Wallandael et al., 2007). Expert testimony and jury instructions are the most promising safeguards, as studies have shown that they frequently induce skepticism and, in some cases, sensitization (e.g., Laub, Kimbrough & Bornstein, 2016; Papailiou, Yokum & Robertson, 2015; see, generally, Bornstein & Greene, 2017). Nonetheless, both techniques raise legal concerns, so neither one is an easy fix by any means (Benton et al., 2007).

CONCLUSIONS

Beliefs about eyewitnesses are not as simple as "eyewitnesses are always right" or "eyewitnesses are always wrong." Rather, laypeople's beliefs about eyewitnesses take account of various factors that can, and do, lead to better or worse eyewitness performance. Some of those beliefs are in accord with empirical research on eyewitness memory, whereas others are not. In particular, laypeople fail to appreciate many of the system and estimator variables that do affect eyewitness memory, whereas they are overly influenced by an eyewitness's confidence at trial. Media portrayals of eyewitnesses, such as those commonly presented in television crime dramas, do little to educate viewers and can even present or imply erroneous information about eyewitness behavior. In addition, observers are not very good judges of whether an eyewitness—adult or child—is accurate and should be believed. Despite laypeople's erroneous beliefs—or perhaps because of them—eyewitness testimony is an incredibly powerful determinant of trial outcomes. The DNA exoneration cases, such as the false conviction of Uriah Courtney, make that poignantly clear.

A frank discussion of the limitations of eyewitness memory, and the misconceptions that most people have about it, should not obscure the fact that eyewitnesses, even young children, are very often accurate. Dispelling one myth can sometimes create a countermyth, and just as it can be a problem to believe eyewitnesses too much, it can also be a problem to believe them too little (granted, the latter risk seems less likely to come to pass, and it is one that is more in keeping with the standard ethos that it is far better to let a guilty party go free than to convict an innocent person). That is the argument of Ross Cheit (2014), who argues that the narrative of innocent people, especially CSA defendants, being persecuted by runaway investigators and an overly credulous legal system is itself a myth. Although a flawed system means that suspects might be falsely accused, the mere existence of those flaws does not necessarily mean that suspects are innocent.

As Cheit (2014) observes, there is more to the story than the reliability of children's memories (e.g., political considerations), but ultimately, sensational CSA prosecutions come down to beliefs about the accuracy of what the alleged victims remember. In some of the cases where eyewitnesses make errors, the authorities are nonetheless prosecuting the right (i.e., guilty) person. But in many such cases, not only is an innocent person convicted, but the truly guilty party remains unpunished. Eyewitness memory myths held by everyone involved in the process, from police, attorneys, and judges to potential jurors, make a regrettable contribution to that state of affairs. One can only hope that recent gains in popular knowledge about eyewitness memory will continue.

NOTES

1. See https://www.innocenceproject.org/cases/uriah-courtney/.

2. These three questions were also included on the chapter 1 survey. The respective figures for percentage correct were fairly comparable: 40.5 percent (child witnesses less accurate than adults), 81.1 percent (children's greater vulnerability to suggestion), and 66.5 percent (recovering memories from childhood).

Chapter 9

Memory and the Legal System

False Confessions

Myth: People Cannot Come to Believe, and Confess to, Something They Did Not Actually Do

Related Myth: People can Tell If a Confession Is Genuine.

As discussed in the previous chapter, erroneous eyewitness identifications are the leading cause of false convictions, according to data compiled by the Innocence Project. The third leading cause is false confessions, which were involved in 28 percent of the first 349 DNA exonerations (the second leading cause, involved in 46 % of cases, is the misapplication of forensic science).[1] Figures from other wrongful conviction studies vary but consistently show that somewhere in the neighborhood of 15–50 percent of wrongful convictions involve a defendant who confessed to a crime he did not commit (see, generally, Acker & Redlich, 2011; Bornstein & Greene, 2017; Gross et al., 2005; Simon, 2012). These data make clear that false confessions are a significant problem for the criminal justice system.

One of the better-known false confession cases is that of 14-year-old Michael Crowe, charged along with two of his friends in the 1998 murder of his 12-year-old sister. As described by Kassin and Gudjonsson (2004, p. 50):

> At first, Michael vehemently denied that he had stabbed his sister Stephanie. Eventually, however, he conceded that he was a killer: "I'm not sure how I did it. All I know is I did it" (see Drizin & Colgan, 2004, p. 141). This admission followed three interrogation sessions during which Michael was told that his hair was found in Stephanie's grasp, that her blood was in his bedroom, that all means of entry to the house were locked, and that he had failed a lie test—all claims that were false. Failing to recall the stabbing, Michael was persuaded that he had a split personality, that "good Michael" had blocked out the incident, and that he should try to imagine how "bad Michael" had killed Stephanie.

One of the other two boys also confessed. Both subsequently recanted their confessions, claiming coercion. The charges were dropped after belated DNA testing revealed the victim's blood on a shirt belonging to a local vagrant, Richard Tuite, who had been seen in the neighborhood on the night of the murder. Tuite was convicted of voluntary manslaughter in 2004; his conviction was reversed on appeal, and he was acquitted in a 2013 retrial. Michael Crowe and his friends were declared factually innocent by a California court in 2012.[2] Why would Michael Crowe not only falsely confess to killing his sister, but apparently come to believe he had done it? This chapter reviews many of the individual, social, and cognitive factors that can make criminal suspects vulnerable to a false confession. To compound the problem, neither laypeople nor law enforcement fully appreciate the risk, in large part because "many people still cannot wrap their heads around the notion that innocent people sometimes admit to crimes they did not commit" (Lassiter, Meissner et al., 2010, p. 3).

Although the problem of false confessions has been widely disseminated, through fictional (e.g., John Grisham's [2010] novel *The Confession*, a #1 *New York Times* bestseller) and news media portrayals (e.g., coverage of cases like Michael Crowe and the Central Park jogger), the vast majority of popular depictions of confessions show them in the context of guilty criminals admitting their dastardly deeds to the authorities, usually as the result of investigators' skillful questioning. The same television series that show eyewitnesses giving a statement or making an identification (e.g., the *CSI*, *NCIS*, and *Law and Order* franchises) show countless scenes of police investigators interrogating suspects who ultimately crack and, after the final commercial break, confess. The authorities have their man (or woman); the crime has been solved.

Indeed, large numbers of suspects confess. In one study of more than 600 police investigators from 16 North American (14 American and 2 Canadian) police departments, participants estimated that an average of 67.6 percent of suspects made self-incriminating statements, with 38.4 percent providing partial admissions and 32.1 percent providing full confessions (Kassin et al., 2007). Analyses of actual custodial interrogations in the United States confirm that suspects confess in approximately 40–55 percent of cases (Kassin & Gudjonsson, 2004).[3] Several recent studies in England found a confession rate of 30–40 percent (Bull & Soukara, 2010), although other British studies have detected somewhat higher rates that are comparable to American figures (Gudjonsson, 2003; Kassin & Gudjonsson, 2004). The confession rate is substantially higher in other countries, such as Japan (Kassin & Gudjonsson, 2004).

Because many, if not most, confessions occur in the course of a custodial interrogation, the literature on confessions is closely linked to that on

interrogation practices. The permissibility and utilization of different interrogation practices vary considerably across countries (see, e.g., Bull & Soukara,
2010; Soukara et al., 2009) and to some extent across jurisdictions within the
United States; but American authorities in general have a variety of techniques at their disposal, which are on full display in TV crime dramas: implied
promises of leniency, displays of empathy, threats, deception, and so on. A
common taxonomy of interrogation tactics distinguishes between "maximization" and "minimization" techniques (e.g., Horgan, Russano, Meissner &
Evans, 2012; Houston, Meissner & Evans, 2014; Kassin & Gudjonsson,
2004). Maximization techniques are confrontational and designed to emphasize the seriousness of the situation. They seek to persuade suspects that they
should confess because the evidence against them is so overwhelming that
they would fare better by confessing than by going to trial. A common maximization tactic is the "false evidence ploy," in which the authorities falsely
tell a suspect that they have incriminating evidence, such as an eyewitness,
fingerprints, or DNA (the legality of this kind of deception has been upheld
by the courts; see, e.g., *Frazier v. Cupp*, 1969).

Minimization techniques are part of a gentler approach that seeks to gain
the suspect's trust and downplay the situation's seriousness. They invite
confession by showing sympathy, stressing the importance of cooperation,
justifying the suspect's actions, and implying lenient treatment. The two
sets of tactics are widespread and often used in tandem (Kassin et al., 2007;
Reppucci, Meyer & Kostelnik, 2010), but they are coercive and can make
false confessions more likely to occur (Kassin, 2015; Kassin et al., 2010;
Kassin & Gudjonsson, 2004; Lassiter & Meissner, 2010; Simon, 2012). They
do so in large part because they manipulate the perceived consequences of
confessing or not confessing—which may be stated by the authorities or
simply implied—such as a more versus less favorable disposition of the case
(Horgan et al., 2012).

In some cases, a false confession is instrumental, in the sense that it
serves to obtain some desired result. The motivating factors for such confessions can include the cessation of a harsh interrogation, protecting others
(i.e., confessing to spare the true culprit), and the expectation of lenient treatment (Bornstein & Greene, 2017). Instrumental confessions can be purely
voluntary, without pressure or prompting from law enforcement, or they
can be "coerced-compliant" false confessions (Kassin & Gudjonsson, 2004;
Kassin & Kiechel, 1996), where the confessor complies with the request
to confess in order to escape the situation, avoid negative consequences,
or obtain some reward. Neither voluntary nor compliant false confessions
involve a memory component; that is, the confessor knows that he is innocent
but says otherwise. In other cases, the suspect genuinely comes to believe
that he/she has committed the act in question—these are often referred to

as "coerced-internalized" false confessions (Kassin & Gudjonsson, 2004; Kassin & Kiechel, 1996). Thus, some of the research on false confessions has similarities to the research on false memory, covered in chapter 3.

Confessions are such compelling incriminating evidence that most suspects who confess likely plead guilty and avoid trial. However, suspects who retract their confession—which includes many false confessors, as well as truly guilty suspects who regret confessing and feel they would do better at trial than accepting a plea—often go to trial. The confession and its withdrawal are both presented as evidence, and the defendant testifies about why he initially confessed to a crime that he now claims he did not commit. Jurors' beliefs about whether, and under what circumstances, the average person would falsely confess necessarily color their evaluation of that evidence. Defendants who recant their confessions do not fare well at trial; roughly three-quarters of false confessors are convicted (Drizin & Leo, 2004; Leo & Ofshe, 1998). This occurs largely because of jurors' erroneous beliefs about confessions and their inability to tell true and false confessions apart. The present chapter reviews research on laypeople's beliefs about confessions, followed by a discussion of the prevalence of false confessions, with special attention to internalized false confessions.

BELIEFS ABOUT CONFESSIONS

As with the topic of eyewitness memory, the two principal research approaches to studying laypeople's beliefs about confessions are questionnaires that measure their beliefs directly and indirect methods that ask participants to act like jurors and make judgments about individuals who have confessed to a crime (several studies also analyze actual jury verdicts in wrongful conviction cases that involved confessions; see Bornstein & Greene, 2017). This section describes the findings from confession questionnaires and mock jury trials in cases where the principal evidence against the defendant is his confession.

Confession Questionnaires

Several studies have surveyed laypeople's beliefs about confession evidence (for review, see Bornstein & Greene, 2017). These studies consistently show that most people believe an innocent person might falsely confess to a crime, especially in response to coercive interrogation, but that *they personally* would not do so. For example, Henkel, Coffman, and Dailey (2008) conducted two different surveys of Connecticut adults. Some of the participants were students, and others were drawn from the community. The questions varied slightly between the two surveys, but both addressed participants' views of confessions as an indicator of guilt, awareness of the extent to which false confessions occur, beliefs about factors that might lead to false confessions, judgments about the necessity of coercion to elicit true confessions, the likelihood that participants would personally confess falsely, and predictions about jurors' false confession beliefs.

Henkel et al. (2008) found that 64.2 percent of participants agreed that "a confession is a strong indicator of a person's guilt." Compared to other kinds of evidence, a confession was perceived as less indicative of guilt than only physical evidence (e.g., DNA or fingerprints) and roughly as incriminating as an eyewitness identification. However, in this same study, nearly half of the respondents (48.7 %) agreed that "Criminal suspects sometimes confess to crimes they did not commit," and the mean response to "What percentage of people who are arrested for committing a crime falsely confess?" was 24.9 percent (the median was 20 %). Overall, then, confessions are compelling, yet people know that false confessions can occur. However, despite this awareness of false confessions as a general phenomenon, participants did not believe that they themselves would falsely confess. Eighty-seven percent agreed that "I personally would be very unlikely to confess to a crime I didn't commit" (75 % gave the highest possible rating of "strongly agree"). Only 8.4 percent of participants disagreed with this statement, indicating that they believed it was possible they would personally make a false confession. With the exception of physical torture, a majority of participants believed that considerations such as covering for another, a need for notoriety, stress from the interrogation, or a promise of leniency would be "very unlikely" or "never" to lead them to confess falsely.

Other confession questionnaires have obtained comparable results: Laypeople consistently believe that other people might confess falsely, but they would not. For example, Costanzo, Shaked-Schroer, and Vinson (2010) asked a diverse sample of jury-eligible citizens from seven American cities to estimate the percentage of confessions that are false in four different types of cases: theft, rape, murder, and child molestation. The mean estimated false confession rate ranged from 19.5 percent (child molestation) to 24.2 percent (theft). However, when asked "If interrogated by the police, I would falsely confess," only 3.9 percent agreed for a minor crime, and 5.0 percent agreed for a major crime (an additional 4.8 % and 1.9 %, respectively, were uncertain). Horgan and colleagues (2012) described a cheating procedure used in laboratory experiments on false confessions (see below) to a student sample and asked them to estimate the probability that if placed in that situation, (a) they would sign a confession statement and (b) other people would. Among participants told to assume further that they were factually innocent, the mean estimates were a 7.5 percent probability of confessing oneself, compared to a 55.5 percent probability that others would confess. Woody and Forrest (2009) asked participants whether another person or they themselves would falsely confess without physical coercion. Whereas 87.3 percent believed someone else would falsely confess, only 32 percent said they would confess themselves. And in their survey of more than 500 jury-eligible citizens from 38 different states, Chojnacki, Cicchini, and White (2008) found that 67 percent of participants believed an innocent suspect would confess after strenuous pressure; only 6 percent believed that an innocent person would never confess. Although the figures vary substantially across studies, probably due to the use of different question wording and response options, these studies as a whole illustrate a consistent pattern: Laypeople view themselves as far less likely to falsely confess than others.

Henkel et al. (2008) also asked participants to rate their degree of exposure to cases of wrongful conviction and false confession in the media. The greater their self-reported exposure, the less they agreed that a confession was a strong indicator of guilt, and they were more likely to believe that they personally would falsely confess or that people falsely confess to end stressful interrogations or achieve notoriety. These correlations suggest that as with news coverage of false convictions due to eyewitness misidentifications, the media can have a positive effect in getting the word out about false confessions.

Laypeople believe that a variety of interrogation techniques, such as lengthy questioning sessions, minimization and maximization, depriving the suspect of sleep, food, or water, and confronting a suspect with false evidence (e.g., deceptively telling a suspect "We have DNA evidence that places you at the scene of the crime"), are commonplace (e.g., Henkel et al., 2008). They also view many of these tactics as potentially coercive (Blandón-Gitlin, Sperry & Leo, 2011; Leo & Liu, 2009). For example, Blandón-Gitlin et al. (2011) asked participants to rate 18 different interrogation tactics (on 5-point scales, with 5 being high) in terms of their coerciveness and likelihood of eliciting a true or a false confession. The individual tactics were grouped into five different categories: actual or threat of violence, presentation of false evidence, promise of leniency, accusation and confrontation, and request and presentation of evidence. Except for requesting and presenting evidence (e.g., results of a polygraph), they were all viewed as at least moderately coercive, with mean ratings greater than three on the 5-point scale. Not surprisingly, actual or threatened violence was judged as most coercive; but presentation of false evidence was also seen as highly coercive, with mean ratings greater than four for all items (e.g., confronting the suspect with false DNA or fingerprint evidence). Importantly, although actual or threatened violence is illegal, false evidence ploys are not.

With the exception of actual or threatened violence, all the categories of tactics were perceived as more likely to elicit a true than a false confession

(Blandón-Gitlin et al., 2011). Moreover, the risk of a false confession was judged to be relatively low. Only two tactics, "threatening suspects with physical violence" and "physically beating or assaulting the suspect" received mean likelihood ratings greater than three on the 5-point scale (3.07 and 3.38, respectively). The authors conclude that there is a disconnect between people's beliefs about what constitutes coercion and whether coercive inter-rogation tactics could elicit a false confession, despite ample evidence (as discussed below) that such techniques do increase the chance of obtaining a confession from an innocent suspect.

Their understanding of the legality of various interrogation tactics is also quite variable. Large majorities (i.e., >75 %) know that it is generally impermissible for the police to harm a suspect physically; threaten violence; deprive a suspect of food, water, or sleep; make a direct promise of leni-ency; or ignore a suspect's Miranda rights (Chojnacki et al., 2008). Yet fewer than 60 percent know interrogators can lie, cut off a suspect's denial of guilt, downplay the significance of the crime (a common minimization tactic), or be rude and insulting (Chojnacki et al., 2008; as the authors point out, these were essentially true-false questions, so chance performance would be 50 %).

Most laypeople are unlikely to have direct experience with police inter-rogation and confessions (assuming they have not been interrogated them-selves) unless they serve as jurors in a case with confession evidence. In such a situation, they might reasonably assume that the confession has already been vetted by the police and prosecutors. Indeed, a majority of respondents believe that the police are better than ordinary people at telling true from false confessions (Costanzo et al., 2010). Kassin, Meissner, and Norwick (2005) investigated whether the police are actually better at evaluating confessions, by exposing laypeople (college undergraduates) and police investigators to either true confessions by prison inmates or "confessions" by inmates about crimes they did not commit. For the false confessions, the inmates were given a brief description of a true crime committed by another inmate and instructed to "make up a confession as if you did it. Try to imag-ine the crime and imagine yourself doing it. Then make up a story filled with details of what happened, what you did, when, where, who you were with, and so on" (p. 215). Participants heard or viewed the confessions on either audiotape or videotape and judged whether each confessor was guilty of the crime or innocent and telling a false story. Overall, students were actually *more* accurate than the investigators, correctly classifying 58.8 percent of the confessions, compared to 48.3 percent for the investigators. The only condi-tion in which performance was better than chance was when the students heard audiotaped confessions (64.1 %). In a follow-up experiment where participants were explicitly instructed that half of the videotaped confessions were true and half were false, student participants again did slightly better than police participants (53.8 % vs. 48.5 %; the comparison was not statistically significant), and neither group did better than chance performance. In both experiments, police investigators were significantly more confident in their judgments than students. These results show that neither laypeople nor police are very good at distinguishing true from false confessions, and that police do not have a special talent for it, although they (and others) might think that they do.

Related research points to the same conclusion. For example, police are not much, if any, better than laypeople at detecting lies (e.g., Granhag & Stromwall, 2004; Vrij, Granhag & Porter, 2010), although they might have an advantage at detecting certain categories of lies (e.g., "high-stakes" lies that result in significant consequences for the liar; O'Sullivan, Frank, Hurley & Tiwana, 2009). Distinguishing between a true statement and a lie is not exactly the same as distinguishing between a true confession and a false confession, for at least a couple of reasons. First, especially in forensic contexts, a lie is usually exculpatory (e.g., "I didn't do it"), whereas a confession, true or false, is an admission of guilt and therefore inculpatory. Second, a liar knows, by definition, that his or her statement is false. As discussed in more detail later in the chapter, some false confessors genuinely come to believe that they committed the acts in question. Nonetheless, it seems reasonable to assume that if police are not unusually adept at detecting lies, they also would not be unusually adept at detecting false confessions.

Previous chapters have described the existence of individual differences in certain beliefs about memory (e.g., cross-national and gender differences in beliefs about repression and recovered memory; see chapter 3). There are individual differences in beliefs about confessions as well. Specifically, female laypeople (Henkel et al., 2008) and police officers (Reppucci et al., 2010) are both more likely than their male counterparts to agree that criminal suspects sometimes falsely confess. The more educated laypeople are, the better informed they are about interrogation practices and confessions (Chojnacki et al., 2008). Non-White Americans are more likely than White Americans to believe that false confessions are possible, across a range of different kinds of cases (Costanzo et al., 2010); again, this difference holds for police officers as well as for laypeople (Reppucci et al., 2010). Minorities are also more likely than Whites to believe that they themselves might confess falsely under interrogation, for either a minor or a serious crime (Costanzo et al., 2010). In light of research suggesting that minorities are more susceptible than Whites to false confession (e.g., Villalobos & Davis, 2016; see also the section on *The Prevalence of False Confessions*, below), this belief appears to have some basis in fact.

Jury Simulation Studies

Confession evidence is incredibly powerful at trial. Not surprisingly, jurors are much more likely to convict when defendants confess than when they do not (e.g., Appleby, Hasel & Kassin, 2013; Kassin & Sukel, 1997; Kukucka & Kassin, 2014), and they are more likely to convict when there is a confession compared to other highly influential evidence like eyewitness testimony (Kassin & Neumann, 1997). The US Supreme Court has held that evidence of coerced confessions is harmless error, in part, because jurors can tell the difference between a voluntary (hence true) and a coerced (and potentially false) confession (*Arizona v. Fulminante*, 1991; see Acker & Redlich, 2011). This means that jurors are almost certainly exposed to both "good" (voluntary and true) and "bad" (coerced and false) confessions. Jury simulation research speaks directly to the question of whether jurors can, in fact, distinguish between the two. A number of studies have examined mock juror (or jury) decisions as a function of the presence of a retracted confession and the police interrogation tactics used to elicit the confession.

In one of the earliest such studies, Kassin and Sukel (1997) presented mock jurors with a murder trial transcript that included no confession, a confession made immediately upon the start of questioning (the low-pressure condition), or a confession made after the detective yelled aggressively and waved his gun around (the high-pressure condition). Participants were sensitive to the coercive nature of the high-pressure interrogation, judging the confession to be less voluntary than in the low-pressure condition. However, conviction rates did not differ between the two conditions, even when the judge instructed them to disregard a confession if it had been coerced. Mock jurors even perceive confessions made to third parties, such as jailhouse informants—so-called "secondary confessions"—as credible as those made to the police, despite the fact that the individual to whom the secondary confession was made has a clear incentive to lie (informants often receive a reward for their incriminating testimony; see Wetmore, Neuschatz, & Gronlund, 2014).

As discussed earlier, false evidence ploys are a widely used interrogation technique (Kassin et al., 2007) that has come under particular scrutiny, in large part because of concerns that they heighten the risk of a false confession (Kassin et al., 2010). Laypeople perceive false evidence ploys in general as deceptive and coercive (Forrest et al., 2012; Woody & Forrest, 2009; Woody, Forrest & Yendra, 2014) and the resulting confessions to be less voluntary (Pickel, Warner, Miller, & Barnes, 2013). Moreover, they do not evaluate all false evidence ploys equally. They perceive ploys that invoke false testimony (e.g., from an eyewitness) as more deceptive and coercive than those that focus on the suspect's demeanor (e.g., telling a suspect that his appearance or behavior indicates guilt; Forrest et al., 2012). False evidence ploys that purport to have scientific evidence (e.g., DNA, fingerprints) are roughly intermediate, but some evidence suggests that they are also perceived as relatively deceptive (Woody & Forrest, 2009). However, people do not distinguish between explicit (i.e., direct claims of nonexistent evidence, such as "We have your DNA") and implicit false evidence ploys (e.g., "What if I said we have your DNA") in terms of their deceptiveness or coerciveness (Woody et al., 2014).

The data are somewhat inconsistent on whether the perceived coerciveness of false evidence ploys translates into different verdicts when such ploys are part of the interrogation. Woody and Forrest (2009) found that mock jurors were marginally less likely to convict in a simulated murder case when the police used a false evidence ploy in interrogating the suspect/defendant than when they did not. They also recommended shorter sentences. The type of ploy (demeanor, testimonial, or scientific) did not affect participants' verdicts, but they recommended longer sentences for a defendant subjected to a demeanor ploy than for defendants subjected to a testimonial or scientific false evidence ploy. However, Woody et al. (2014) failed to obtain an effect of false evidence ploys on mock jurors' verdicts or recommended sentences, and Pickel and colleagues (2013) found that the presence of a false evidence ploy made a murder defendant seem less guilty but did not affect mock jurors' verdicts. Thus, despite seeing some interrogation tactics as more coercive than others, mock jurors' decisions, by and large, do not take those tactics into account.

Although mock jurors are not very sensitive to characteristics of the interrogation that might make a confession less reliable, they do respond to some aspects of the confession itself. Appleby et al. (2013) varied the amount of details about the crime in an abduction-rape-murder case. In the *details-present* condition, the defendant's confession included specific details about what the victim wore, said, and did, as well as what the alleged accomplices said and did. In the *details-absent* condition, the defendant admitted guilt but did not provide these details. Mock jurors perceived the defendant as guiltier when his confession contained specific details, especially when the confession also lacked a clear statement of motive.

The manner in which confession evidence is presented at trial can also have a substantial effect. Depending on law enforcement practice within a given jurisdiction, confessions may be written by the suspect, tape recorded (audio), or videotaped. When audiotaped or videotaped, some or all of the interrogation leading up to the confession may be recorded as well. Mock jurors who see the entire interrogation are better able to distinguish true from false confessions than those who watch only the final confession (Kassin, Leo, Crocker & Holland, 2003). Video recording is becoming increasingly common, but the other recording methods are still used in many jurisdictions

(Acker & Redlich, 2011; Kassin et al., 2010; Sullivan, 2012). Mock jurors respond similarly to written, audiotaped, and videotaped confessions, although it depends on characteristics of the filming (for review, see Lassiter, Ware, Lindberg & Ratcliff, 2010; Lassiter, Ware, Ratcliff & Irvin, 2009). If the confession is videotaped, the camera perspective makes a difference. When the camera focuses on the suspect, as compared to the interrogator or both participants equally, the confession seems more voluntary and mock jurors are more likely to convict (e.g., Lassiter, Beers, et al., 2002; Lassiter, Geers, et al., 2002; Lassiter & Irvine, 1986). Videotaped confessions are most comparable to audiotaped and written confessions when the video focuses equally on the suspect and the interrogator (Lassiter, Beers, et al., 2002).

The effect of camera perspective occurs even when mock jurors engage in deliberation, are warned not to let the camera perspective influence their judgments, pay greater attention to the content of the interrogation, or anticipate having to justify their judgments afterwards to a judge (Lassiter, Beers, et al., 2002; Lassiter et al., 2001). The effect is especially pronounced when the confession contains a high amount of detail about the crime, even when that detail is nonprobative with respect to the defendant's guilt (e.g., the suspect's stating that he arrived home "at exactly 7:56" rather than "a little before 8"; Warner & Pickel, 2010, p. 498). Video recording of interrogations and confessions is perhaps the leading proposed reform in this area (e.g., Garrett, 2010; Kassin, 2015; Kassin et al., 2010; Simon, 2012). The practice has many advantages, such as dispelling erroneous beliefs that jurors might harbor about the circumstances leading to a confession; but the research on the effects of how the confession is filmed, and which parts, suggests that policy makers need to be very thoughtful in implementing this reform (Lassiter, Ware et al., 2010).

A particularly insidious aspect of confession evidence is that it can taint jurors' perceptions of other evidence, such as eyewitness testimony or scientific evidence, even when that evidence is completely independent of the confession (Bornstein & Greene, 2017). The incriminating confession evidence makes other incriminating evidence seem more damning and exonerating evidence seem less persuasive. For example, Kukucka and Kassin (2014) demonstrated that mock jurors who heard that a defendant confessed were more likely to conclude that his handwriting sample matched one left by the perpetrator (a note given to a bank teller during a robbery) than mock jurors who did not know about the confession (26.7 % vs. 10.8 %). Unsurprisingly, they were also more likely to convict (24.4 % vs. 6.0 %). Learning that a suspect confessed can even lead eyewitnesses to change their lineup choice, making them more likely to identify the suspect despite previously identifying someone else or rejecting the lineup altogether (Hasel & Kassin, 2009). Conversely, just as confession evidence can influence jurors' perception of other evidence, other evidence can influence how they perceive a confession. Shaked-Schroer, Costanzo, and Berger (2015) found that mock jurors who learned that evidence had been found corroborating a confession (i.e., discovery of the murder weapon) rated the interrogation as less coercive than when the confession was uncorroborated, and they also perceived the defendant as relatively more guilty. These effects of corroborating evidence on the perceived coerciveness of the interrogation and guilt of the defendant occurred only when the interrogation used high-pressure (as opposed to low-pressure) tactics.

Thus, the jury simulation literature is largely consistent with findings from confession belief questionnaires. Mock jurors' judgments show some awareness that certain interrogation tactics (e.g., false evidence) are coercive, but they do not fully appreciate the risk that those tactics can lead to false confessions, and they are just as likely to convict when a defendant's confession is potentially or demonstrably false as when it is genuine. Laypeople's beliefs about confessions (e.g., "most people wouldn't confess to something they didn't do") doubtless contribute to this failure to appreciate the danger of false confessions, but there are other contributing factors as well (Bornstein & Greene, 2017). For example, people generally assume that others' behavior results from dispositional rather than situational factors (i.e., they commit the fundamental attribution error; see Ross, 1977). Within the interrogation context, this would produce a tendency to see a confession as the product of a suspect's free will and true nature—a guilty conscience—rather than the suspect's succumbing to external forces. As discussed above, the inclination to make certain kinds of attributions can be exacerbated by aspects of the interrogation and how it is filmed, such as the camera perspective (Lassiter & Irvine, 1986).

Knowledge of Risk Factors

To some extent, laypeople are aware that members of certain groups are more vulnerable than others to making a false confession. Henkel et al. (2008) asked participants to rate several risk factors for "how much each factor would contribute to a person falsely confessing to a crime he or she did not in fact commit," on a scale ranging from 1 (little/no contribution) to 7 (large contribution). Being mentally ill, under 10 years old, suggestible and overly trusting, a teenager, and having a low IQ all received mean ratings over 4, and the modal response for being mentally ill or under 10 years old was 6. They were least likely to believe that having a poor memory contributed to false confessions ($M = 3.5/7$). Chojnacki et al. (2008) likewise found that many people knew that minors and mentally impaired persons were relatively more likely to falsely confess (43 % and 54 %, respectively); nonetheless, large numbers of participants were either incorrect or uncertain about these risk factors. Thus, laypeople appear to know that age, mental illness or incapacity, and personality can all predispose a person to falsely confess, but they are somewhat more suspicious of the notion of internalized false confessions, where the suspect misremembers having committed the crime.

They are less knowledgeable about the role of race. For example, confessions made by minority group members, such as Blacks, Chinese, or Arab Americans, seem more voluntary and incriminating than those made by Whites (Pickel et al., 2013; Ratcliff & Lassiter, 2010). The pattern holds even when the suspect's actual physical appearance is held constant (i.e., when participants are simply led to believe that the person is a member of a certain social category) and extends to members of sexual as well as racial/ethnic minorities (Pickel et al., 2013). This suggests that observers at least implicitly see minorities as less likely to make a false confession, whereas there are compelling reasons to believe that the opposite is actually the case (Villalobos & Davis, 2016).

THE PREVALENCE OF FALSE CONFESSIONS

Attention to false confessions should not obscure the observation that in all probability, the vast majority of suspects who confess are presumably guilty. However, this observation in no way lessens the importance of minimizing the use of techniques that increase the likelihood of a false confession. Despite the documentation of false confessions, such as the case of Michael Crowe described at the beginning of the chapter, it is very difficult, if not impossible, to estimate how many of the confessions elicited by the interrogation process are false. It would hardly be unheard of for a genuinely guilty perpetrator to have second thoughts after confessing and make a false claim of a false confession; whereas some individuals who make "true" false confessions presumably plead guilty and simply serve out their sentence without recanting.

Among those who confess falsely and do recant, it is even more difficult to estimate how many of those false confessions are internalized false confessions, where the suspect comes to believe that he actually committed the crime, as opposed to instrumental ones. And to complicate matters still further, many confessions contain elements of both truth and falsehood (Reisberg, 2014). Nonetheless, the prevalence of false confessions is likely substantial. Studies conducted in Iceland have found that more than 10 percent of prisoners and suspects questioned at police stations reported giving false confessions to the police during interrogation (Gudjonsson, 2003; 2010; Gudjonsson et al., 2010). The self-reported false confession rate among community samples of older adolescents and young adults (e.g., college students) is somewhat lower but still generally in the neighborhood of 5–10 percent of those experiencing police interrogation (Gudjonsson, 2010). More than three-quarters of police officers recognize that false confessions occur (Reppucci et al., 2010), and even police interrogators themselves estimate that almost 5 percent of innocent suspects admit to part or all of the crime for which they are being questioned (Kassin et al., 2007).

Laboratory Research on Interrogations and Confessions

Because of the difficulties involved in ascertaining whether real-world confessions are genuine or false, psychologists have developed research paradigms that simulate the process of interrogating someone about a "bad act" that the person did not commit. The two most common experimental paradigms involve accusing participants of inadvertently crashing a computer they are using for the laboratory task (e.g., Kassin & Kiechel, 1996) or of deliberately cheating (e.g., Russano, Meissner, Narchet & Kassin, 2005). In the former approach, all participants are typically innocent—that is, no participants caused the computer to crash; it appeared to crash as part of the study. In the latter approach, the experimenter usually gives some participants but not others the opportunity to cheat, which allows a comparison of confession rates for factually guilty versus factually innocent participants.

In the computer-crash paradigm, the experimenter warns participants working on a computer study that pressing a certain key (e.g., the ALT key) would cause the computer to crash (e.g., Kassin & Kiechel, 1996). The experimenters then surreptitiously crash the computer and accuse the participant of having pressed the taboo key (which none actually did). Typically, participants deny the allegation initially, but substantial numbers of participants falsely confess to making the computer crash after coercive or suggestive questioning. For example, Kassin and Kiechel manipulated participants' vulnerability by varying the difficulty of the computer task (i.e., requiring them to perform a fast- or slow-paced task) and whether a confederate provided false incriminating evidence (i.e., claiming to have witnessed the participant hit the forbidden key). The researchers measured the rate of participants' willingness to sign a written confession ("compliance"); admission to an ostensibly unrelated third party after the experiment was over that they had crashed the computer ("internalization"); and "recall" of embellishing details to fit the allegation ("confabulation").

Thirty-five percent of participants signed the false confession in the baseline version of the task, where they performed the slow-paced task and there was no incriminating witness (Kassin & Kiechel, 1996). The false confession rate exceeded 50 percent when the task was relatively difficult (65 %) or a confederate claimed to have witnessed the bad act (89 %), and it was fully 100 percent when the task was difficult *and* a confederate provided false incriminating evidence (Kassin & Kiechel, 1996). Of those who confessed, a substantial number internalized—65 percent in the fast-paced, incriminating witness condition. That is, they genuinely seemed to believe that they had committed the act in question and said as much to another person without any prompting beyond being asked "What happened?" (Kassin & Kiechel, 1996). Confabulation rates were considerably lower; still, 35 percent of participants in the fast-paced, incriminating witness condition "recalled" details of the action that they had not actually performed.

These findings have been replicated numerous times, including in studies that have attempted to simulate real-world confession situations more closely by having explicit negative consequences for confessors (for review, see Houston et al., 2014; Meissner, Russano & Narchet, 2010). For example, Horselenberg, Merckelbach, and Josephs (2003) informed participants in the computer-crash paradigm that if they confessed, they would receive only $2, instead of $10, as compensation for their participation in the experiment. All participants were presented with false incriminating evidence from an eyewitness (in this study, the witness was the experimenter, rather than a confederate playing the role of another participant, as in the study by Kassin & Kiechel, 1996). Of 34 participants, 82 percent signed the confession, 42 percent showed internalization, and 58 percent confabulated. To be sure, a reduction in compensation is not the same as a financial penalty (i.e., having to pay money out of pocket), let alone the negative consequences associated with a false confession in a real criminal investigation. Nevertheless, this line of research demonstrates persuasively that innocent suspects can be induced to confess, that false evidence ploys are a powerful means of eliciting a false confession, and that a nontrivial number of false confessors form a memory of the alleged act.

The other main experimental method for studying false confessions is the "cheating" paradigm developed by Russano and colleagues (2005). In this paradigm, participants are instructed to complete a series of problems— some working with a partner (in reality a confederate), and some working individually. The confederate either asks the participant for help on one of the individual questions, providing an opportunity to cheat, or does not seek assistance. Most participants comply with the illicit request, thereby creating a "guilty" condition, as opposed to the "innocent" participants who are not asked to cheat. The experimenter subsequently accuses the participant of cheating by breaking the rules of the experiment and sharing answers. The experimenter then asks the participant to sign a statement admitting to the rule violation. The negative consequences, which are mostly implied, include having to face the annoyed professor in charge of the experiment and being formally accused of cheating.

In their initial demonstration, Russano and colleagues (2005) varied whether the interrogator employed minimization tactics (e.g., an expression of sympathy, an offer of face-saving excuses) and offered an explicit deal. In the "deal" condition, the interrogator offered to settle the matter in exchange for a signed confession and the participant's returning for another session without receiving additional research credit. Not surprisingly, guilty participants confessed more often than innocent participants. However, the false confession rate among innocent participants was far from trivial, ranging from 6 percent when no special tactics were used to 43 percent when the interrogator both used minimization and offered a deal. The basic finding has been replicated in a number of other studies (Houston et al., 2014).

Taken as a whole, the laboratory research provides a useful model for false confessions in the field. A variety of techniques, such as minimization and maximization, increase the false confession rate (e.g., Klaver, Lee & Rose, 2008; Russano et al., 2005), especially when they influence suspects' perceived consequences of confessing versus not confessing (Horgan et al., 2012). Moreover, coercive interrogation tactics diminish the diagnosticity of a confession; that is, they reduce the likelihood of eliciting a true, as opposed to a false, confession (Horgan et al., 2012; Houston et al., 2014). False evidence ploys are especially likely to elicit false confessions (Drizin & Leo, 2004; Perillo & Kassin, 2011). False evidence necessarily contributes to suspects' perception of the strength of the evidence against them. Perceived evidence strength is a key factor in the decision to confess, especially when the suspect is genuinely guilty (Houston et al., 2014). False evidence can contribute to false confessions as well; it is more likely to do so when the false evidence is plausible (Klaver et al., 2008).

Soukara and colleagues (2009) found little correlation between the likelihood of confessing and the use of various interrogation tactics, but their study analyzed real-world interrogations, meaning that they were unable to distinguish between true and false confessions. Experimental research comparing true and false confessions has found that they are associated with different motivations. True confessions tend to have internal motivations, such as the desire to resolve feelings of guilt, whereas false confessions more often have external motivations, especially the social pressures inherent in the interrogation context (Houston et al., 2014).

At-Risk Groups

Some individuals are especially vulnerable to interrogation tactics, making them more likely than others to confess falsely. This same vulnerability might also make them more likely to make a true confession when they are guilty. These risk factors include a number of stable characteristics, such as race/

ethnicity, age, personality, and mental status (i.e., disability or mental illness; for review, see Kassin & Gudjonsson, 2004).

Minorities are at heightened risk of false confession (Villalobos & Davis, 2016). A number of factors contribute to this increased risk, such as stereotypes associating racial minorities with crime, especially violent crime; language and cultural barriers; and the enhanced power differential between minorities and law enforcement (Villalobos & Davis, 2016). The stereotypes and power held by investigators might lead them to adopt more coercive interrogation tactics when questioning minorities; while stereotype threat, linguistic limitations, cultural differences, and the lack of power could all make minority suspects appear more deceptive than White suspects. It is, of course, misleading to lump all minorities into a single category. The most vulnerable minority groups might be those with a low level of trust in law enforcement to begin with, such as African Americans (e.g., Tyler & Huo, 2002), or those with a different cultural or linguistic background (e.g., Hispanic Americans).

In many countries, such as the United States, race and ethnicity can be confounded with language differences, especially among immigrant populations. For example, suspects with limited English proficiency face a number of additional obstacles during interrogation, for which an interpreter may or may not be provided (Berk-Seligson, 2009). Villalobos and Davis (2016) give the example of Eddie Torbio-Ruiz, who was questioned by police in Reno, Nevada in the course of a child sexual abuse investigation. The detective questioned him in English, even though Torbio-Ruiz's native language was Spanish and he spoke English poorly. He gave conflicting answers to the same questions about whether he had committed the sexually abusive acts, and at times he appeared not to understand what he was being asked. When confronted with his recorded confession, he denied that he had admitted to the allegations and even insisted that the tape must have been doctored.

People who do not understand what is being said have a tendency simply to agree, and this tendency is heightened when there is a clear power differential (Berk-Seligson, 2009; Liberman, 1995). The cognitive demands of trying to comprehend can make it hard to grasp conversational subtleties like indirect or implied requests, impairing understanding further (Villalobos & Davis, 2016). Thus, language problems can exert a direct effect on false confession, by making a suspect more likely to accede to an allegation; they can also have an indirect effect, by making the suspect appear more anxious, thereby increasing the interrogator's suspicion and efforts to induce a confession (Villalobos & Davis, 2016). An interpreter would seem to solve these problems, but interpreters introduce their own set of difficulties (Berk-Seligson, 2009; Villalobos & Davis, 2016). Interpreters can be inaccurate, and a suspect might (rightfully) perceive the interpreter as an additional authority figure, especially if the interpreter is another police officer.

Juveniles are also at an increased risk of false confession. One study of false confession cases found that nearly one-third involved juveniles (Drizin & Leo, 2004). Malloy, Shulman, and Cauffman (2014) found that roughly one-third of a sample of nearly 200 incarcerated male teenagers (aged 14–17 years) reported making an incriminating false statement (i.e., a confession or guilty plea) to law enforcement officials. Most reported experiencing high-pressure interrogations, and relatively lengthy interrogations (>2 hours) were especially likely to produce false confessions. Secondary school students report falsely confessing during police interrogation significantly more often than college students only a few years their senior (Gudjonsson, 2010). Age is also related to the rate of false confessions in the computer-crash paradigm. Redlich and Goodman (2003) found that the false confession rates in the procedure were 59 percent for 18- to 26-year-olds, 72 percent for 15- to 16-year-olds, and 78 percent for 12- to 13-year-olds.

Some individuals' personality predisposes them to falsely confess. People naturally vary in how compliant they are—that is, how much they wish to please others and avoid conflict (Kassin & Gudjonsson, 2004). The tendency is exacerbated when dealing with others who are authority figures; it would therefore logically come into play in an interrogation situation. Suspects who confess falsely score higher on measures of compliance (Kassin & Gudjonsson, 2004; Klaver et al., 2008; but see Horselenberg et al., 2003). As discussed in chapter 3, individuals also vary in terms of their suggestibility; some individuals are naturally more susceptible to misleading suggestions than others (Gudjonsson, 1984). More suggestible persons are more likely to confess to something that they did not do (Klaver et al., 2008; Redlich & Goodman, 2003; but see Horselenberg et al., 2003).

"Mental status" is a broad term that can mean different things in different contexts; with respect to false confessions, it most often comes up with respect to suspects who have abnormally low intelligence or who suffer from mental illness. In Drizin and Leo's (2004) sample of false confessors, approximately one-fifth could be classified as mentally retarded, and 10 percent were described as mentally ill. Garrett (2010) similarly found that among a sample of known false confessors (the confessions were known to be false because the individuals were exonerated by DNA testing), 43 percent were mentally ill, mentally retarded, or borderline mentally retarded. Persons who are mentally retarded display increased compliance, heightened suggestibility, and diminished capacity to foresee the consequences of their actions (Kassin & Gudjonsson, 2004). All of these characteristics would make them more likely to falsely confess in an interrogation context.

Distorted perception and memory, impaired judgment, anxiety, and lack of self-control typify many mental disorders. These symptoms of mental illness can make individuals more vulnerable to interrogation tactics or more suggestible and therefore at greater risk of falsely confessing (e.g., Gudjonsson, 2003; Redlich, 2004). Although little systematic research has been conducted on which specific disorders are most problematic in this regard (Redlich, 2004), certain disorders appear to increase interrogated suspects' vulnerability to false confession. For example, persons with symptoms of attention deficit/hyperactivity disorder (ADHD) or a history of substance abuse are more likely to report falsely confessing (Gudjonsson, 2010; Gudjonsson et al., 2010). It is unclear exactly why ADHD or substance abuse would increase a suspect's vulnerability to false confession. The disorder could make the interrogation more unpleasant (e.g., excessive fidgetiness, substance withdrawal symptoms), leading to greater acquiescence to escape the situation; those same symptoms of the disorder could increase interrogator suspicion, leading to the adoption of more coercive tactics; or the underlying disorder could make suspects more compliant or suggestible. Regardless of the precise mechanism, it is clear that mental illness, and likely some disorders more than others, places suspects at heightened risk of making a false confession.

False Confessions and Memory Errors

False confessions often contain an impressive amount of detail, with frequent references to the victim's appearance and behavior, other persons (e.g., coperpetrators, witnesses), and the suspect's own internal state (thoughts, feelings, motives, etc.; see Appleby et al., 2013; Garrett, 2010). In Garrett's analysis of 38 false confessors who were exonerated by DNA testing and for whom trial and pretrial records could be obtained, 97 percent of the confessions contained a series of specific details about the crime. This very detail—some of which had not been publicized and could allegedly be known only to the perpetrator—is a large part of what makes the confessions so credible. However, it overlooks the fact that many of the details are fed to suspects by police (Garrett, 2010; Simon, 2012). After all, if the confession is false and the suspect is truly innocent (and was presumably not at the crime scene), then the details were either a lucky guess or must have come from somewhere. These details can then be incorporated into a credible-sounding confession.

As mentioned above, in most false confessions, the suspect is complying with the request to confess for any number of reasons yet knows that the confession does not represent the truth. But in a minority of cases, the suspect internalizes the confession and comes to believe that he is actually guilty; that is, he forms a false memory of the event (Kassin, 2007; Kassin & Gudjonsson, 2004). It is just as hard to estimate the frequency of internalized false confessions as it is to estimate the prevalence of false confessions in general; but an examination of DNA exonerations, other false confession cases, and laboratory research on false confessions suggests that the phenomenon is not uncommon (Henkel & Coffman, 2004; Kassin, 2007).

A common reaction to this idea is "Who in his (or her) right mind would want to have a memory of committing a horrific crime?" The answer to this question has at least three parts. First, the suspect who internalizes a false confession is not necessarily *in* his right mind. As discussed in chapter 3 and in the preceding section on risk factors, some individuals are predisposed to form false memories, and certain individuals are also more vulnerable to falsely confessing than others. To some extent, these could be the same people (e.g., youth or people with certain personality attributes). Thus, whether by disposition or in reaction to the stress of the interrogation, they may not be in their right mind (whether someone who would falsely confess is arguably not in his right mind by definition is a separate issue, with valid arguments on both sides). Some suspects are simply more susceptible than others not only to confess falsely, but also to internalize their confession.

Second, "want" has nothing to do with it. As I have argued throughout this book (see especially chapter 2), the mind works the way the mind works. This is not to say that we are unable to control and improve our memory and other cognitive functions; we can and we do (see the introduction and chapter 10). Nonetheless, the basic processes involved in storing information in, and retrieving it from, memory require little deliberate oversight. And that is true of accurate as well as false memories.

Third, someone would presumably no more want a memory of committing a horrible act than one would want a memory of being a victim of a horrible act. Yet both occur. If one person can have a false memory of being sexually assaulted (see chapter 3), it stands to reason that another person can have a false memory of perpetrating the assault. The false memories may be equally implausible. But that does not mean they do not happen.

Consider, for example, the case of Paul Ingram, described by Kassin and Kiechel (1996).[4] Ingram, a deputy sheriff and Republican Party chairman in Thurston County, Washington, was accused in 1988 by his daughters of sexual abuse and satanic ritual abuse, including the slaughter of 25 babies. "During 6 months of interrogation, he was hypnotized, exposed to graphic crime details, informed by a police psychologist that sex offenders often repress their offenses, and urged by the minister of his church to confess. Eventually, Ingram 'recalled' crime scenes to specification, pleaded guilty, and was sentenced to prison" (Kassin & Kiechel, 1996, pp. 125–126). However, there was no physical evidence, and most experts now believe that Ingram was innocent. He apparently genuinely believed he was guilty at the time of his confession and guilty plea, although he subsequently maintained that he was innocent.

Ingram's confession incorporated details provided to him by the police. In many instances, this involves the interrogator providing some information, such as the location of the crime or the victim's appearance, and then asking the suspect—who has initially denied committing the crime—to imagine how it might have occurred. Because it might be too upsetting for the suspect to describe an imagined version of committing the crime himself, interrogators will often ask suspects to imagine a hypothetical third person doing it and to guess or speculate about details if they are unsure about something (Henkel & Coffman, 2004). As described in chapter 3, this sort of "imagination inflation" can lead individuals to incorporate suggested information in memory and create false memories (Garry et al., 1996), especially in highly suggestible individuals, such as Michael Crowe or Paul Ingram. The suggestive tactics essentially cause confusion about the source of the memory: Is it from something that actually occurred, that one merely imagined, or that an external source (the interrogator) claimed to have occurred? This source monitoring framework can be applied to internalized false confessions in the same manner as to other sorts of false memories (Henkel & Coffman, 2004).

False memories, especially those elicited during therapy, and internalized false confessions share many characteristics (Kassin & Gudjonsson, 2004; Ost, Costall, & Bull, 2001): An authority figure (therapist or police officer), who is certain of the individual's involvement in the act in question, claims to have insight into the individual's actions and motivations; the individual is in a malleable state; the interactions occur in a private and socially isolated setting; and the authority figure, who is there to help (especially in the case of the therapist), encourages the individual to accept a negative and painful admission that goes against his or her self-interest. One study of individuals who had retracted allegations of victimization based on false memory found that their experiences were highly similar to internalized confessions, although there were similarities to other kinds of confessions (voluntary and coerced-compliant) as well (Ost et al., 2001). Both kinds of experience can, and often do, involve lengthy questioning in an isolated social context and overt pressure to accept the authority figure's version of events.

Thus, a contributing factor to a subset of false confessions—those that suspects internalize as true—is the fundamental cognitive processes associated with false memory. Not all suspects are susceptible to internalized false confessions, just as not all patients receiving psychotherapy are susceptible to false memories of abuse. Nonetheless, the suggestive nature of the interrogation setting can lead suspects to misattribute imagined details or information provided by the interrogator to their own memory (Henkel & Coffman, 2004). The additional stress of the interrogation can exacerbate the natural tendency to make such source monitoring errors (Henkel & Coffman, 2004).

Avoiding the practice of asking suspects to imagine how a crime could have been committed would reduce the risk of these kinds of memory errors.

CONCLUSIONS

Although the problem of false confessions is slowly infiltrating the public consciousness, the overwhelming majority of popular portrayals on television and in movies show truly guilty suspects who initially deny their involvement but then admit to their crimes in the course of a professional, custodial interrogation. Most confessions are almost certainly true. Nonetheless, false confessions can and do occur, as demonstrated by analyses of actual cases and laboratory simulations. A number of social, cognitive, and individual factors increase the risk of a false confession. False evidence ploys are particularly problematic, and some individuals are more vulnerable than others. A significant minority of suspects develop false memories for the offenses of which they are accused.

Laypeople, including jurors, fail to appreciate the situational and dispositional factors that can lead innocent suspects to confess falsely. They understand that false confessions occur and that certain widely used interrogation tactics are coercive; but they believe that only "others" would falsely confess and not themselves. And despite recognizing that characteristics of an interrogation might be coercive, laypeople underestimate the chance that coercive interrogation tactics could elicit a false confession, and they are not very good at distinguishing true from false confessions. Within the context of a trial, mock jurors' verdicts take little account of the tactics used to elicit a confession. This might be due to their misguided assumptions that if they were in the defendant's shoes, they would not admit to something unless they had actually done it; and that others' behavior results from their stable disposition and free will. Aspects of the confession, such as the amount of detail it contains and how it was filmed, do influence mock juror judgments, even though they have no direct bearing on the confession's reliability.

Police officers are not significantly more knowledgeable than laypeople about the problem of false confessions. They acknowledge the existence of false confessions, but they continue to engage in practices, such as false evidence ploys, that make them more likely to occur. Moreover, even though they know about certain risk factors that make suspects more vulnerable, such as youth, their interrogation practices do not apply that knowledge.

The previous chapter raised the question of whether eyewitness errors are "a pebble in the ocean." Most eyewitnesses—at least those who are deemed reliable enough to testify at trial—are presumably accurate to a considerable extent, and the criminal justice system has procedural safeguards in place to lessen the impact of those who do testify but whose testimony is questionable. Similarly, most confessions are presumably true, and the criminal justice system has safeguards in place to lessen the impact of those that might not be. The principal safeguard is the jury, which has the job of determining whether an eyewitness or a confession is reliable. Both jury research and DNA exoneration data show that juries' ability to accomplish these tasks is limited. In part, the limitation results from jurors' erroneous beliefs about the phenomenon in question. Just as they fail to appreciate many of the factors that can make eyewitness memory more or less reliable, they lack an understanding of the prevalence of false confessions and the factors that can make them more or less likely to occur. Just as with trials of defendants who have been falsely identified by mistaken eyewitnesses, trials of defendants who have falsely confessed mean not only that an innocent defendant might be convicted, but also that the actual perpetrator remains at large.

On a more promising note, people with greater exposure to cases of wrongful conviction and false confession have a better appreciation of the problems and risks of false confession. Further increasing media attention to the problem of false confessions—and not merely showing police dramas where guilty suspects inevitably confess—will hopefully continue to ameliorate the situation.

NOTES

1. See https://www.innocenceproject.org; another good source of exoneration data is the National Registry of Exonerations, http://www.law.umich.edu/special/exoneration/Pages/about.aspx.

2. The case was made into a 2002 television movie, "The Interrogation of Michael Crowe." See, generally, http://en.wikipedia.org/wiki/Murder_of_Stephanie_Crowe; Tracy (2003).

3. The variability across studies is likely due to differences across jurisdictions, in the constellation of cases, and in how researchers operationalize a full confession as opposed to a partial admission.

4. For additional information on the Ingram case, see White (1995), as well as http://www.justicedenied.org/paul.htm and http://en.wikipedia.org/wiki/Thurston_County_ritual_abuse_case.

Chapter 10

Superior Memory

Myth: Photographic Memory Is a Real and Not Terribly Uncommon Phenomenon

Related Myths: A Superior Memory is Something You're Just Born with (or Not); Persons with Autism Have Unusually Good Memories

Just as there are misconceptions about basic memory processes and memory loss, so too are there misconceptions about superior memory. I was recently describing the premise of a novel I was reading, *Memory Man* by David Baldacci (2015), to my wife and daughter. The main character, Amos Decker, develops perfect recall of everything he experiences after a traumatic brain injury that he suffers while playing football (Baldacci describes the hit as so savage that Decker died and had to be revived, twice, on the field; the hit became a YouTube sensation). My daughter Melissa asked whether such a thing was possible, and my wife, a physician, responded "I wouldn't go banging your head against the wall to get a photographic memory." Is it possible? Probably not; in any event, it is so far-fetched as not to be worth banging your head against the wall. On the contrary, as covered in previous chapters, a TBI like the one Decker experienced (or from head-banging) is much more likely to cause memory loss and other cognitive impairments. The growing awareness of the cognitive effects, as well as other adverse psychological and physical consequences, of head injuries while playing football makes this painfully clear. A belief that a TBI can produce a phenomenal memory is akin to the belief that it can restore memories previously lost due to retrograde amnesia (see chapter 5)—it is a myth.

Whether it purportedly results from a TBI or some other cause (e.g., good old-fashioned genetics), many people expect that photographic memory is not that uncommon. The popular view is that some lucky few are just born with it, and hence that it is not the sort of thing that one can somehow acquire. There is also a popular view that this kind of memory invariably accompanies disorders such as autism (as portrayed, e.g., in the movie *Rain Man*).

BELIEFS ABOUT PHOTOGRAPHIC MEMORY
AND MEMORY IMPROVEMENT

Baldacci's Amos Decker is far from the first detective to rely on his phenomenal memory to help him solve crimes. Carrie Wells (played by Poppy Montgomery), the main character in the recent television show *Unforgettable* (on CBS from 2011–2014, then picked up by A&E), is a police detective who can remember everything she experiences, including verbatim conversations. As she says in one episode, "My memory is more than incredible—it's perfect." Most strikingly (at least to this memory scholar), when she plays events over in her mind, she can adopt a point of view different from the one she had during the event. For example, when she remembers investigating a crime scene, she can see herself moving through the scene, in the same way that a third party would see her.[1] Patrick Jane in the television series *The Mentalist* (2008–2015), though lacking a perfect memory, likewise has an unusually prodigious one, coupled with extraordinary powers of observation. The *sine qua non* in the genre is undoubtedly Arthur Conan Doyle's Sherlock Holmes, who seems to notice everything and retain it all.

An interesting twist on literary figures with perfect recall is the Fair Witness in Robert Heinlein's (1961) science fiction classic, *Stranger in a Strange Land*. These individuals are professional recorder-witnesses whose job is to store information in its exact, original form, so that if there is any dispute about it later (e.g., in legal matters), they can serve as an accurate record of what transpired, and their recollections are dispositive. They effectively serve as a combination court reporter-notary public. Although it is set in the future, Heinlein's novel was written in an era when electronic recording technology was neither widely available nor inexpensive; yet in an interesting twist, it turns the relationship between recording technologies and memory on its head. We typically write things down and record them to overcome the limitations and fallibility of normal memory, especially in legal contexts. In contrast, the Fair Witness relies on memory so as to avoid having to deal with recordings, which can presumably be lost, damaged, or altered.

Fair Witnesses are an interesting exemplar of superior memory in two respects: First, they undergo training to acquire their skill—they do not appear to be born with it (whether they have an innate aptitude that facilitates their acquisition of the skill is a separate issue, and one that Heinlein does not address).[2] As described below, some persons' superior memory does appear to be innate, often associated with unique perceptual-cognitive characteristics; but in many other cases, it results largely, if not entirely, through extensive training. Second, Fair Witnesses' precise and unusually veridical memory appears to be mostly verbal—that is, they can report conversations and written documents like wills verbatim—although they are also adept at remembering visual stimuli and events. Many of those with superior memory are likewise better at remembering some kinds of information than others.

These fictional characters show that the photographic memory trope is well represented in the popular media. Not surprisingly, then, most laypeople expect that such folks exist in real life. For example, in the survey described in chapter 1, only 12 percent of respondents knew that photographic memory is not a real phenomenon. Of course, the prevalence of photographic memory in TV shows, movies, and novels likely reflects more than just a popular misconception about how memory works. Real or not, photographic memory is cool, in the same way that X-ray vision, an enlargeable/shrinkable/indestructible body, super strength, invisibility, or the ability to fly is cool. Like these other superpowers, it is clearly adaptive, especially in academic and many occupational contexts, and characters like Sherlock Holmes have a certain heroic appeal (though like other superpowers, there are some respects in which it can be a curse, as discussed below).

Alas, like X-ray vision, the ability to fly, or innumerable other superhero powers, photographic memory belongs in the realm of fiction. Yet although nearly everyone (except, perhaps, for impressionable young children) knows that no one can really fly like Superman or Thor, they are generally accepting of the photographic memory superpower. This acceptance of the myth is perhaps due in part to the fact that, as a mental ability, it cannot be readily seen or measured. But it may also be partly due to an awareness that one's memory can be improved. Indeed, of all the beliefs about memory covered in the chapter 1 survey, people were most knowledgeable about mnemonic techniques. Large majorities knew, for instance, that chunking and imagery are effective ways of storing information in memory. Of course, there is a considerable gap between using a simple mnemonic device to make some piece of information more memorable and having perfect recall of everything one experiences. But in the case of many other superpowers, one cannot fly a little bit, or become a little bit invisible (one can certainly become stronger, but not to the level of Superman, the Incredible Hulk, or Thor). Moreover, there are documented, albeit rare, cases of people who, while not having perfect recall, do have astoundingly good memory. For these reasons, photographic memory just seems to make sense. Unfortunately, the myth far outstrips the reality; moreover, like other superpowers, it might have a downside.

DEFINING SUPERIOR MEMORY

Although photographic memory is a concept with which most people are familiar, it is worthwhile to consider what, exactly, it supposedly is. In technical terms, "a truly photographic memory would contain representations isomorphic to the world that could be retrieved essentially perfectly" (MacLeod, Jonker & James, 2014, p. 391). This definition begs the question: What kind of representations? The "photograph" metaphor implies that it is necessarily visual—that is, one essentially takes a photograph of a visual experience, and the image is preserved in memory indefinitely, precisely as the original event transpired. (Despite its intuitive appeal, the metaphor itself is imperfect. Prior to the digital age, print photographs did fade with age, as anyone knows who has old photographs of great-grandparents; whereas photographic memories presumably never fade). Any visual stimulus could be recorded this way: one person's face, another's actions, or words on a page. According to this definition, stimuli in other sensory modalities—sounds, smells, tastes, tactile sensations—would not be retained in the same fashion. How do you take a picture of something like Yo-Yo Ma playing a Bach cello suite, or the taste of gelato at Vivoli in Florence?

Thus, a narrow definition of photographic memory is the long-lasting, and arguably permanent, retention of images that are perfect representations of visual stimuli—and not just selected visual stimuli, but essentially all of those that someone with the alleged photographic memory encounters. People differ widely in their ability to form, retain, and manipulate visual images (MacLeod et al., 2014). The vast majority of people have at least some images of previously encountered visual stimuli (e.g., a loved one's face, the spatial layout of one's home), although the correspondence between the image and the object is highly variable and usually inexact to some degree (e.g., Kosslyn, Thompson, & Ganis, 2006). Up to five percent of people report having no mental images at all, and a comparably small proportion have abnormally detailed, accurate, and long-lasting visual images (MacLeod et al., 2014)—a phenomenon referred to as *eidetic imagery*. Eidetic imagery is more common in young children (i.e., children younger than 10 years old, approximately 5–8 % of whom have it) than in older children and adults (MacLeod et al., 2014; Schwartz, 2014). Cases of adult "eidetikers" exist (e.g., Stromeyer, 2000), but research shows that even they make errors when "reading" from their photographic images (Crowder, 1992). The narrow definition of photographic memory, then, is basically synonymous with eidetic imagery, but even this ability is quite rare and not as error-free as commonly portrayed.

Moreover, the popular view of photographic memory typically goes beyond the narrow definition. Some of the fictional cases described above, like Amos Decker, Carrie Wells, and Heinlein's Fair Witnesses, might have eidetic imagery, but their abilities transcend that. For example, they can remember conversations verbatim—perfect memory for auditory information. The works do not describe whether they can also remember every smell, taste, and touch, but it would not be surprising if they could. With effort, anyone can memorize a bunch of words—actors and singers do it all the time. The key difference is that these fictional characters do it automatically, *without* apparent effort. And unlike normal memorization, they might even continue to hear the sensory qualities of the speakers' voices in memory, a phenomenon often referred to as "auditory imagery" (Hubbard, 2010). This capacity for auditory imagery—an oxymoron if there ever was one (isn't an "image" necessarily visual?)—is, like the capacity to form and retrieve visual images, a normal, and normally distributed, ability (Hubbard, 2010). And just as with eidetic imagery, cases of persons who can automatically store a wealth of precise auditory information that preserves its original sensory qualities have been documented, but they are very rare (Sacks, 1998). Extreme cases of auditory imagery are often associated with musical ability and experience (Hubbard, 2010; Sacks, 2007) and, not infrequently, intellectual impairment (see "Savant Syndrome," below).

In *Memory Man* (and its sequel *The Last Mile*; Baldacci, 2016), Decker even has additional cognitive abilities connected to his unusual memory, such as being able to tell time down to the second without a watch, and synesthesia. Synesthesia, which literally means "senses together" (syn- plus -esthesia), is the spontaneous subjective experience of sensory qualities in a sensory modality other than (and usually in addition to) the one being directly stimulated. So, for example, different sounds, numbers, or words— whether spoken aloud or read—might elicit unique color and even olfactory or taste experiences. Synesthetic experiences are not far removed from what can sometimes occur under the influence of certain hallucinogenic drugs, such as LSD. Yet in synesthetes, it occurs normally (for them) and effortlessly. Synesthesia occurs in up to 4 percent of the population and has a neurological and presumably genetic basis (Ramachandran & Brang, 2008).

This more expansive view of photographic memory, then, encompasses memory for nonvisual stimuli. Thus, it seems clear that the colloquial notion of photographic memory is simply shorthand for unusually detailed, accurate, and essentially perfect memory, which (a) retains much of the sensory flavor of the original experience, regardless of how one processes the experience (i.e., which sensory modality) and (b) occurs more or less effortlessly and automatically. Yet as the remainder of this chapter will show, many individuals with unusually detailed and accurate memory do not necessarily retain a stimulus's original sensory qualities, and their recall involves considerable effort and practice. If the narrow definition of photographic memory fails to pass empirical scrutiny, then the broad definition necessarily does as well.

The consensus among researchers is that photographic memory, at least in the colloquial sense, does not exist (MacLeod et al., 2014; Wilding & Valentine, 1997). Nonetheless, it is indisputable that some people have better memories than others, and that a small subset of individuals with above-average memories have truly extraordinary abilities. Because of the narrow and potentially misleading connotations of the term "photographic memory," it therefore makes sense to think of the phenomenon more broadly, in terms of superior memory (e.g., Wilding & Valentine, 1997).

This term, however, is not without its own complications. What constitutes "superior"? The same problems arise here as in diagnosing amnesia (see chapters 5 and 6). If memory ability exists on a continuum, then it is just as hard to establish a cutoff for an abnormally good one as an abnormally bad one. Wilding and Valentine (1997, p. 4) use three criteria to define superior memory: "(1) rapid acquisition of material or (2) acquisition of an unusually large quantity of material in a measured time, and (3) long-term retention of an unusually large quantity of material acquired under controlled conditions." Importantly, this definition highlights both the relative ease of encoding and the long-lasting nature of memories that we commonly think about when we consider cases of superior memory. The definition's drawback is that terms like "rapid" and "unusually large" are themselves subjective and relative. They necessarily refer to the upper end of presumably normal distributions (i.e., bell-shaped curves), but without guidance as to where to set the cutoffs.

The definitional problem is especially true if, as in many cases, the individuals in question rely on normal memory processes and do not have some extraordinary perceptual power (as discussed below, a few do have some extraordinary ability). Like intelligence, memory ability is presumably normally distributed and a relatively fixed trait. (Memory is, of course, a large part of both what intelligence tests measure and what most people think of as intelligence—that is, people we deem smarter have better memories and vice versa.) It seems to follow, then, that superior memory is also stable and, presumably, largely innate—either you're born with it or you're not. But because of the diagnosis problem, there is no definitive test for identifying those with a superior memory. "Nothing like a normative study of memory abilities—a 'memory census'—has ever been undertaken" (Neisser, 2000b, p. 476). And because superior memory is rare—by definition, just as anything "superior" is relatively infrequent—case studies are much more prevalent in the literature than systematic comparisons (but see Bywaters, Andrade, & Turpin, 2004; LePort et al., 2012).

There is not even agreement on what term to use to refer to possessors of superior memory. Most commonly they are called "mnemonists" (derived from Mnemosyne, the Greek goddess of memory), but that term implies that they use mnemonic techniques to help them remember, which many do, but not all (Neisser, 2000b). Neisser and others (e.g., Thompson, Cowan, & Frieman, 1993) therefore prefer the term "memorist," and he also suggests that they may be more numerous than generally believed, as accomplished figures in many fields might benefit from superior memories without being known merely for their memory abilities (e.g., Bill Clinton is renowned for having an impressive memory for facts, figures, and faces, which doubtless contributed to his success as a politician). Whatever they are called, a description of their abilities makes it clear that they are outside the norm. Yet despite their "abnormal" abilities, they can teach us a great deal about "normal" memory functioning.

KEY QUESTIONS ABOUT SUPERIOR MEMORY

There are a number of cases in the literature of people with extraordinarily good memory (e.g., LePort et al., 2012; Neisser & Hyman, 2000; Sacks, 1998; Wilding & Valentine, 1997), and some of them are well-known, such as the Russian mnemonist S. (Luria, 1987b) and the conductor Arturo Toscanini (Marek, 2000). However, these individuals are quite rare (Neisser & Hyman, 2000; Wilding & Valentine, 1997). It is impossible to obtain an estimate of the number of people with superior memory, partly because of the definitional and measurement issues described above, but also because they might be unaware that their abilities are extraordinary. Although they would likely realize at some point, particularly in educational settings, that they are better at remembering information than most of their peers, they might not realize that their means of doing so are unusual. If your mind naturally preserved exact images of visual stimuli for a period of minutes or even longer (eidetic imagery) or conjured up colors or tastes to accompany certain visual or auditory stimuli (synesthesia), how would you know that others' minds did *not* also work that way? Because we can know only our own minds—and given metamemory limitations, imperfectly at that—we tend to assume that our own cognitive processes are normal. For example, people with synesthesia often do not realize that their capacity to perceive stimuli in a multisensory fashion is abnormal until they come to the attention of a professional memory researcher (e.g., Luria, 1987b), which explains why the prevalence of synesthesia is often underestimated (Ramachandran & Brang, 2008).

In addition to being fascinating in their own right, individuals with superior memory raise a number of important questions. Three overlapping questions are of particular interest: Are mnemonists born that way or bred? Are their memory abilities qualitatively or quantitatively different from those of "normal" people? Are their skills limited to certain kinds of material, or do they have superior memory for pretty much anything and everything? The remainder of this section explores each of these questions, while introducing some of the mnemonists that have been studied. A subset of those with superior memory possess extraordinary memory skills against a backdrop of overall intellectual impairment—these cases, which are generally referred to as *savant syndrome*, are considered in a separate section.

Born versus Bred

Many, if not most, questions about psychological characteristics raise the question of nature versus nurture; that is, is some characteristic innate or the result of the environment, broadly construed? The distinction is not as simple as commonly portrayed: Innate causes are presumably genetic, but they could also include other biological factors, especially during fetal development; "environment" is a vague term that encompasses things to which an organism is exposed at the micro (e.g., temperature, nutrition, exposure to toxins, family context) and macro (e.g., neighborhood, society, culture, educational opportunities) levels. It is generally agreed that virtually everything in psychology results from some combination of nature and nurture, though to varying degrees. The same combination occurs with respect to superior memory, where a mnemonist might have a special aptitude for retaining information in memory and then exploit that aptitude through a great deal of training and practice. Nonetheless, it is meaningful to ask whether these special abilities require an innate component, or if anyone can acquire them with sufficient effort.

Many adult mnemonists displayed prodigious memory abilities at a young age, suggesting that their talent was innate. For example, Rajan Mahadevan is best known as the record holder (according to the *Guinness Book of World Records*), from 1981 to 1987, for memorizing the mathematical constant pi. Rajan could correctly recite pi to the first 31,811 digits.[3] Rajan realized he was good at remembering numbers at age 5, when he memorized the license plate numbers of all of the approximately 50 guests at a family party (Thompson et al., 1993). A.J., studied by Parker, Cahill, and McGaugh (2006), could report for any date of her life (since age 8) what day of the week it was, what she did that day, and what (if any) newsworthy events transpired that day. A.J. reported that "she had always had a richly detailed memory for episodes" (Parker et al., 2006, p. 37), but that it became particularly acute at age 8, when her family moved—a disruptive and traumatic incident in her life. Other individuals with superior memory for their own personal history likewise report becoming aware of their ability during middle childhood (e.g., a sample studied by LePort et al., 2012, reported a mean "age of awareness" of 10.5).

A.J.'s remarkably detailed memories were verified from her diaries (which she did not review, and specific entries in which she was tested on without forewarning), family members, and public news and records. At the time of testing, A.J. was in her late 40s, meaning that she could remember what happened on every day of her life for approximately the past 40 years. She reported that her recall was automatic and involved neither mnemonics nor conscious control, suggesting that she was simply born with the ability. Parker et al. coined the term "hyperthymesia" (from the Greek "hyper-" for "more than normal" + "-thymesis" for "remembering") to describe cases like A.J. that have an extraordinary capacity to recall events from their past (David Baldacci adopted the term in his Amos Decker novels).

Other carefully documented mnemonists also report demonstrating their unusual ability at a young age (e.g., Hunt & Love, 2000; Hunter 1977; Luria, 1987b). What is also clear from many of these cases, however, is that these children are reinforced for their extraordinary memory performance, in the form of attention from parents and teachers, outstanding academic achievement, and the admiration of peers. A.J.'s superior autobiographical memory was a large part of her identity, and her friends and family relied on her as the repository of information about their shared activities (Parker et al., 2006). This reinforcement naturally leads them to put additional time and effort into refining their memory skills, making it hard, if not impossible, to disentangle biological and environmental influences.

Thus, although few of those with superior memory receive formal mnemonic training, *per se*, the large majority of them are highly motivated to hone their memory skills and spend a great amount of time practicing them, often devising their own mnemonic techniques in the process. Perhaps the best-known example of a trained mnemonist is S.F., who was studied by Ericsson, Chase, and Faloon (1980; see also Ericsson & Chase, 1982). At the beginning of the study, his digit span—the number of random digits that he could repeat back accurately, in the correct sequence—was seven, which is average. Ericsson and colleagues had him practice the digit span task for 1 hour per day, 3–5 days per week, for 20 months (more than 230 hours of total practice time). By the end of the study, S.F.'s digit span was 79 digits, and his long-term retention of the material improved as well, as did his performance on other numerical tasks (e.g., recalling a matrix of 50 digits). He accomplished this feat largely by dividing a long string of digits into manageable chunks and assigning them meaning. For example, he recoded the sequence 3492 as "3 minutes and 49.2 seconds, near world-record mile time" and 1944 as "near the end of World War II" (Ericsson et al., 1980, p. 1181). He also organized the chunks into larger groups; this hierarchical organization aided his retrieval.

Other mnemonists also rely on specific strategies to help them remember. For example, Rajan memorized pi in 10-digit (i.e., unusually large) chunks. Although the chunks were not meaningful in the sense that S.F.'s numerical chunks were meaningful, he nonetheless processed them as distinct perceptual entities, which enabled him quickly to retrieve the second five digits of a 10-digit block when given the first five digits. Hideaki Tomoyori, the memorist who supplanted Rajan at the top of the pi memorization rankings by reciting the first 40,000 digits (the world record from 1987 to 1995), used a digit-syllable mnemonic to form words for multidigit sequences, which he then associated with images (Takahashi, Shimizu, Saito & Tomoyori, 2006). "For example, when Tomoyori learned the number string of 1415926535 (the first 10 digits of pi following the decimal), he first divided the string into four parts (words): 141 *toshi-no* (in the city), 592 *koku-zin* (a Black man), 65 *muko* (the bridegroom), and 35 *sango* (a coral). After that, he could form a vivid image of the sentence, 'In the city, a black man gave the bridegroom a coral'" (Takahashi et al., 2006, p. 1195). Like Rajan, Tomoyori spent thousands of hours practicing.

"Mental athletes," who train for and participate in memory competitions, use mnemonic techniques extensively. In these tournaments, they compete in events like "speed cards" (memorizing a deck of cards as fast as possible), "speed numbers" (memorizing a 25 × 20 digit matrix), "names and faces" (memorizing the first and last names associated with a series of head shots), and poem memorization (Foer, 2011). Although many of the contestants might have an aptitude for memorization, they practice for hours a day and employ mnemonics like the method of loci, which incorporates imagery and spatial cues. As proof of the power of training, in *Moonwalking with Einstein*, Joshua Foer, a journalist with an average memory, describes the rigorous training that he undertook to be able to compete in the 2006 USA Memory Championship (*Spoiler Alert*: Do not look at the footnotes unless you want to know how he did.)[4]

Foer's (2011) experience improving his memory, and those of other trained mnemonists, show that with sufficient motivation and practice, anyone—at least anyone starting at a more or less normal level—can attain a superior memory. The titles of some of these case studies say it all: "Exceptional memorizers: Made, not born" (Ericsson, 2003); "One percent ability and ninety-nine percent perspiration: A study of a Japanese memorist" (Takahashi et al., 2006). The leading proponent of this view is K. Anders Ericsson. With his colleagues, Ericsson has produced a large body of work showing that exceptional memory represents practice effects more than anything else (e.g., Chase & Ericsson, 1981; Ericsson, 2003; 2006; Ericsson & Chase, 1982; Ericsson & Faivre, 1988; Ericsson & Moxley, 2014). Exceptional memory is therefore "developed within the basic abilities and limits of the normal cognitive system" (Ericsson & Chase, 1982, p. 615). According to Ericsson, the main thing that is "abnormal" is the amount of practice necessary to attain an exceptional memory. In nearly all cases, acquiring exceptional memory skills requires thousands of hours of deliberate practice (Ericsson, 2006). Just as professional athletes and musicians invest enormous amounts of time in honing their skills, most memory experts likewise spend countless hours practicing memorization. For many of those who compete in memory tournaments, it is basically a full-time job (Foer, 2011).

There are exceptions to most rules, and the "most mnemonists are bred, not born" rule has its share. A small number of cognitive-perceptual anomalies that promote superior memory are neurologically determined. They are usually present at a very young age—hence presumably genetic—but occasionally acquired as a result of brain damage, typically due to illness. The most common inborn exceptions are savant syndrome, eidetic imagery, and synesthesia. Savant syndrome is a complex condition, in terms of both its causes and characteristics, as well as its relationship to memory—it will be discussed in detail below. The remainder of the present section expands briefly on eidetic imagery and synesthesia.

As noted above, eidetic imagery is not terribly uncommon in children, but most of those who have the ability outgrow it; adult eidetikers are rare, but they are not unheard of. Stromeyer (2000) describes the case of Elizabeth (a pseudonym), an artist and teacher with a remarkable visual memory. For example, "[y]ears after having read a poem in a foreign language, she can fetch back an image of the printed page and copy the poem from the bottom line to the top line as fast as she can write" (Stromeyer, 2000, p. 503). Perhaps even more astounding, she was tested using a stereoscope, a device for presenting different stimuli to each eye. Each stimulus on its own shows nothing meaningful, but combining the two allows a three-dimensional figure (e.g., a letter or shape) to emerge in depth. Elizabeth viewed a 10,000-dot pattern for 1 minute using her right eye. Ten seconds later, she viewed another 10,000-dot pattern with her left eye. She then superimposed her mental image of the first pattern upon the actual second pattern and reported seeing the letter T coming toward her. She could do the same thing with a 24-hour delay between presentation of the two patterns. Unless she could memorize the precise position of all 10,000 dots in just a few minutes, she must have retained an exact image of the stimulus. It is unclear how long the images lasted, and Stromeyer (2000) does refer to their fading (by dimming and breaking apart). But even if they did not last indefinitely, Elizabeth's eidetic images clearly resulted from a neurological anomaly that no amount of training could replicate.

Similarly, synesthesia is a biologically determined, perceptual/neurological anomaly—either you have it or you don't, and most of us don't. One of the most thoroughly studied, and most impressive, mnemonists on record is S., studied by the Great Russian neuropsychologist Alexander Luria (1987b). Luria describes some of S.'s synesthetic experiences as follows:

> Presented with a tone pitched at 30 cycles per second and having an amplitude of 100 decibels, S. stated that at first he saw a strip 12–15 cm. in width the color of old, tarnished silver. … Presented with a tone pitched at 50 cycles per second and an amplitude of 100 decibels, S. saw a brown strip against a dark background that had red, tongue-like edges. The sense of taste he experienced was like that of sweet and sour borscht, a sensation that gripped his entire tongue. … Presented with a tone pitched at 250 cycles per second and having an amplitude of 64 decibels, S. saw a velvet cord with fibers jutting out on all sides. The cord was tinged with a delicate, pleasant pink-orange hue. Presented with a tone pitched at 500 cycles per second and having an amplitude of 100 decibels, he saw a streak of lightning splitting the heavens in two. When the intensity of the sound was lowered to 74 decibels, he saw a dense orange color which made him feel as though a needle had been thrust into his spine. … (pp. 22–23)

S.'s synesthesia undoubtedly facilitated his extraordinary memory, as it enabled him to form additional associations to material. A small number of other persons with superior memory also have synesthesia (Foer, 2011; Treffert, 2010).

S.'s feats of memory were nothing short of phenomenal: He could report large matrices of random numbers and lengthy verbal passages perfectly, years after being exposed to them. In a particularly telling example, he reproduced several stanzas of Dante's *The Divine Comedy*—in Italian, a language he did not understand—with perfect accuracy and pronunciation, 15 years after first hearing and memorizing it—and without being forewarned of the memory test. There is also some evidence that S. possessed eidetic imagery. His abilities were so impressive that he worked for a while as a professional mnemonist, performing on stage. He remembered so well that he actually had difficulty forgetting information he no longer needed or that interfered with his thinking to such an extent that "his mind was a virtual chaos" (Luria, 1987b, p. 67). S. devised several means of forgetting information, ranging from writing it down (which would mean he did not have to remember it), to burning the paper with the to-be-forgotten information, to visualizing erasing a blackboard containing the material and then covering the board with an opaque film. None of these techniques worked particularly well, and in the end, deliberately avoiding thinking about some material (i.e., directed forgetting; see chapter 4) worked as well as anything. S.'s phenomenal memory produced a problem opposite that encountered by most people: Most of us bemoan what we forget and wish we could remember more; S. at times bemoaned what he remembered and wished he could forget. The situation results at least in part from his innate perceptual abilities, such as synesthesia and eidetic imagery. Yet even in such an unusual case, with clear evidence of an innate component to his memory skills, S. also spent a great deal of time practicing and refining his memorization methods, and he used mnemonic techniques like the method of loci. His case shows that in very few cases is superior memory purely an inborn ability.

S.'s case also shows that superior memory might not be the unalloyed advantage that it appears to be. When people learn about him, it is often with a touch of envy. In some respects, his memory literally drove him crazy. In addition to being unable to forget the things that he wanted to forget, he was so adept at forming and using associations that he had a hard time maintaining his train of thought. One thing would cue another in his memory, whether he wanted it to or not. S. had a hard time keeping a job, lived more in his mind than in reality, and was institutionalized toward the end of his life. Some others with superior memory, especially those whose abilities are automatic and therefore uncontrollable, similarly describe their "gift" as "a burden" and "totally exhausting" (Parker et al., 2006, p. 35). In the words of Hugh, a character in Brian Friel's (1981, p. 88) play *Translations*, "To remember everything is a form of madness." Still others, however, view it as a positive attribute (LePort et al., 2012). Thus, having an unusually good memory might contribute to one's overall wellbeing, but it does not invariably do so.

Qualitatively versus Quantitatively Different

The "qualitative versus quantitative" distinction essentially asks whether superior memory is merely at the upper end of the normal distribution (i.e., quantitatively different) or something altogether different in kind. As Neisser (2000b, p. 476) asks, "Are these talents simply the upper extremes of continuous distributions of ability, or are the distributions bimodal?" The same question could be asked of those at the lower end of the memory distribution. Are they simply at the bottom of the bell curve, while having memory that functions the same as everyone else, albeit less effectively? Or do their minds function in a fundamentally different manner?

These questions are difficult to tease apart, but the research on training and practice suggests that the vast majority of differences in memory functioning can be attributed to quantitative differences. To be sure, some people naturally have better memories than others, just as some are naturally smarter than others. But the underlying basis of their memory performance is more or less the same, as is demonstrated by the dramatic cases of memory improvement (e.g., S.F.). There are, of course, exceptions. Abilities like eidetic imagery and synesthesia are not something that everyone has to a greater or lesser degree—they are unique qualities. Thus, the answers to the first two questions go hand-in-hand. Certain innate abilities underlying superior memory performance are qualitatively different. But there is considerable room for movement along the memory functioning continuum (i.e., quantitative shifts) merely as a function of practice and environmental influences. This is not to discount entirely the role of inherited individual differences—some individuals are likely born with a predisposition to high memory functioning, just as some are born with a greater facility for learning languages or spatial orientation. However, superior memory is within the reach of most of us, if we are willing to put in the work to attain it. The annals of memorists make it abundantly clear that one can develop a superior memory without possessing special abilities (e.g., Neisser & Hyman, 2000; Wilding & Valentine, 1997; Worthen & Hunt, 2011).

An issue that comes up with respect to the existence of any qualitative differences is what, exactly, might be the nature of the difference at the neurological level. For the most part, the answer to this question is unknown, mainly because of the small number of cases and their variability. As noted above, synesthesia appears to have a genetic component, and some research has detected physiological differences in the brain activity of those with and without synesthesia, such as differences in brain waves and the extent of cross-activation between brain regions (Ramachandran & Brang, 2008). Superior memory can also result from brain damage (see the section on savant syndrome, below), but the precise mechanisms by which the damage and resultant neural reorganization produce memory effects are poorly understood (Treffert, 1989).

Studies comparing the neuroanatomy of memory experts to that of controls have found a few differences (LePort et al., 2012; Maguire, Valentine, Wilding & Kapur, 2003; Maguire et al., 2000; Maguire, Woollett & Spiers, 2006; Woollett & Maguire 2009). For example, Maguire and colleagues (2000) performed brain imaging on the brains of 16 right-handed male London taxi drivers—an occupation that relies heavily on spatial memory—and compared them to 50 healthy right-handed male controls (the training for London drivers is particularly extensive, lasting 2 years on average; Maguire et al., 2000). The taxi drivers' posterior hippocampi, in both hemispheres, were significantly larger than those of control participants, whereas their anterior hippocampi were significantly smaller (see also Woollett & Maguire, 2009). These differences persisted even when the control group consisted of bus drivers, who follow a constrained set of routes and therefore have fewer demands on their spatial memory (Maguire et al., 2006). Moreover, the size of these regions was correlated (positively for the posterior hippocampus, and negatively for the anterior hippocampus) with the amount of time spent as a taxi driver, suggesting that the changes in hippocampal gray matter were acquired and not the result of those with a larger posterior hippocampus gravitating toward a profession relying heavily on navigational skills. There were no other neuroanatomical differences between the two groups. Comparisons between individuals with highly superior autobiographical memory and controls have also identified structural differences, especially in brain regions known to be involved in autobiographical memory, such as the hippocampus and medial temporal region (LePort et al., 2012).

Separate studies suggest that these brain differences are limited to expertise in very specific kinds of memory. In one study, Woollett, Glensman, and Maguire (2008) compared the brains of medical doctors and an IQ-matched control group without any university education. They chose doctors because, like taxi drivers, they acquire knowledge-based expertise in adulthood over a period of years of intensive training, and their work entails high demands on memory; unlike taxi drivers, however, their work is less spatial (except, of course, for certain specialties like radiology). Neither the groups' hippocampi nor other brain structures differed in their gray matter volume.

In a second study, Maguire and colleagues (2003) compared the brain anatomy and activity patterns of ten memory experts (most of whom were chosen based on their performance at the World Memory Championships) and ten control participants who were matched to the experts on spatial ability and intelligence. Structural MRIs showed no structural differences between the two groups in the hippocampus or elsewhere. However, there were functional differences while the participants attempted to memorize information, reflected in greater activation in the memory experts in brain regions linked to spatial memory and navigation (specifically, the medial parietal cortex, retrosplenial cortex, and right posterior hippocampus). Maguire et al. attribute this difference to the memory experts' greater use of spatial mnemonics like the method of loci. They conclude that the differences in memory performance result not from qualitative brain differences, but from the application of specific encoding strategies acquired through lengthy practice (see also Ericsson, 2003). Together, these studies suggest several things: first, that the hippocampus is preferentially engaged in spatial memory; second, that some, but not all kinds of, memory training can produce anatomical changes in the brain; and third, that most kinds of superior memory performance reflect differences more in how one uses the brain and any accompanying cognitive techniques than in any underlying differences in the brain's organization itself. In other words, memory expertise is more of a quantitative than a qualitative distinction.

Domain-Specific versus Domain-General Memory Expertise

Most mnemonic techniques lend themselves better to some kinds of material than others. For example, translating inherently meaningless stimuli like random digits into times, dates, or syllables works great for numbers, but it would work less well for other stimuli like pictures or stories. Consistent with this expectation, after greatly expanding his digit-span capacity, S.F.'s memory span was still average (about six) when he was tested with letters instead of numbers (Ericsson et al., 1980). This domain specificity of superior memory— that is, its applicability for some types of material but not others—is the norm.

Rajan's skills extended to essentially any memory task involving numbers (Ericsson, Delaney, Weaver & Mahadevan, 2004; Thompson et al., 1993). His initial digit span was 28 for visual and 43 for auditory presentation—well beyond the norm of roughly seven items regardless of presentation modality—and he subsequently increased his visual digit span to 60. He made hardly any errors when memorizing matrices composed of random digits that were up to 20×20 (i.e., 400 digits); his performance was considerably faster and more accurate than controls; and if he rehearsed them periodically, he could recall the matrices months later. In contrast, he did much less well with nonnumerical information, such as verbal material, complex figures, or random symbols. On these kinds of material, his performance was roughly comparable to controls—often slightly but not outstandingly better, and occasionally worse (e.g., with categorized word lists). His memory span for letters was 13—better than average, but not dramatically greater than a comparison group of control participants (6–9 letters). With practice, Rajan was able to improve his memory for nonnumerical information, showing his skilled application of general memory-enhancing mechanisms (e.g., forming meaningful associations). As partial as he was to numbers, this unsurprisingly involved recoding the symbols and letters as digits and then memorizing the stimuli as a sequence of digits (Ericsson et al., 2004). Nonetheless, the gap between his performance and that of control participants remained much less than for numerical stimuli.

Similarly, Tomoyori, who memorized pi to 40,000 digits, had a slightly above average digit span (though less impressive than Rajan's): 10 for auditory presentation and 8 for visual presentation (Takahashi et al., 2006; the authors note that the speed of presentation—1 digit per second—made it difficult for him to use his mnemonic on this task). He also performed better than control participants at memorizing a 5×5 number matrix, in terms of learning time, amount recalled, and long-term retention. However, his performance with verbal stimuli (word lists and a story) was roughly the same as controls.

Even professional memory competitors, whose mnemonics work for a variety of different kinds of stimuli, do not show superior performance on absolutely everything. Maguire et al. (2003) tested their memory for snowflake patterns, and they did no better than controls. And despite their superior ability on laboratory tasks, which tend to mimic those used in competition (e.g., memorizing long lists of digits or verbal material), they are generally just average at remembering autobiographical details from their past (Wilding & Valentine, 1997). Conversely, A.J.'s highly superior autobiographical memory allowed her to remember anything and everything from her personal history (i.e., episodic knowledge) and to score above average on some standard memory tasks (e.g., those involving episodic memory, digit span), but she was only average or even below average on others (e.g., executive functioning, memory for faces, organizationally demanding semantic memory tests; Parker et al., 2006; see also LePort et al., 2012). And even her incredible autobiographical memory was selective in some respects. For example, she did not record conversations verbatim, and she made numerous errors when tested on the content of previous testing sessions. Like a number of other mnemonists, she did much better at remembering material that was of personal interest to her (e.g., Hunter, 1977; Thompson et al. 1993). Moreover, persons with hyperthymesia are just as susceptible to false memory as anyone else (Patihis et al., 2013; see chapters 3 and 4). Thus, even superior memory appears to have its limits.

Indeed, one of the distinguishing features of expertise, in any domain, is its specificity—experts are really good at *something*, but not at *everything*. This point seems obvious, but it is worth mentioning because a crucial skill underlying expertise is memory: Experts have superior memory within their domain of expertise, whether the domain be a motor skill (e.g., musical or athletic performance), complex problem solving (e.g., computer programming, judicial decision making, medical diagnosis, mental calculation), or something in between (e.g., chess, acting, taxi driving) (Ericsson & Moxley, 2014; Chi, Glaser & Farr, 1988). Their superior memory is an incidental consequence of acquiring expertise in a particular domain; accordingly, their memory for material outside the domain is typically merely average (Ericsson & Kintsch, 1995; Ericsson & Moxley, 2014). Taxi drivers have better spatial memory, especially for local landmarks, than matched controls, but their memory for nonspatial relationships (e.g., for some verbal and visual information) is no better, and in some cases worse, than controls (Woollett & Maguire, 2009). This content-specific expertise distinguishes them from those whose area of expertise *is* memory. Yet even in those cases, as with Rajan, their exceptional performance is often limited to specific domains. The domain specificity of superior memory suggests that memory is modular and not all one thing (Wilding & Valentine, 1997).

SAVANT SYNDROME

One of the best-known instances of superior memory is Kim Peek. Readers who do not recognize his name will probably recognize the film *Rain*

Man, whose main character (Raymond Babbitt, played by Dustin Hoffman) was inspired by the real-life Peek.[5] His memory abilities rival, and arguably exceed, those of any mnemonist described in this chapter (for review, see Peek & Hanson, 2008; Treffert & Christensen, 2005). He memorized thousands of books (and not just short books—Tom Clancy and Shakespeare were on his list); knew all the area codes and zip codes in the United States; could identify hundreds of classical music pieces, including when and where each was composed and first performed, and could play many of them; and could provide the day of the week for any date. Yet he could not button his clothes or manage the chores of daily life. His overall IQ was 87, with scores on subtests ranging from mentally disabled to superior. Kim did not have autism; on the contrary, he was outgoing and personable (this is one of several respects in which Kim differed from the fictional *Rain Man*, who is more of a composite character; see Treffert, 1989, 2010).

Kim Peek is an outstanding example of a person with *savant syndrome*—someone with an extraordinary talent (or talents) in one area despite having an overall intellectual impairment. The narrow, but very deep, band of expertise is an "island of genius" amid a sea of disability (Treffert, 2010). The original term, coined by J. Langdon Down (after whom Down syndrome was named) in 1887, was "idiot savant," but the condition is now referred to as *savantism* or *savant syndrome* (the etymology of "savant" is from the French "savoir," to know). By whatever name, cases of mentally impaired individuals with skills in a particular domain that rival anyone of normal, or even above average, intelligence have been documented for hundreds of years. Although the domain of expertise exhibited by persons with savant syndrome varies, they all have superior memory. For example, many of the musical savants can hear a song once and play it back on the piano perfectly, despite being unable to read music—indeed, many of these musical savants are blind, illiterate, and mentally retarded.[6]

Beliefs about Savant Syndrome and Memory

The belief that people with autism often possess special talents along the lines of Kim Peek's is widespread (Lilienfeld et al., 2010). We do not have "pre-*Rain Man*" versus "post-*Rain Man*" data to determine how much of the myth can be attributed to the film, but there is evidence that the film did increase public awareness of autism (Lilienfeld et al., 2010). *Rain Man* was extremely successful when it came out in 1988 (it was the year's highest-grossing film and won Academy Awards for Best Picture, Best Actor [Dustin Hoffman], Best Director [Barry Levinson], and Best Original Screenplay [Barry Morrow and Ronald Bass]), and it continues to be popular.

Erroneous beliefs about savant syndrome are even prevalent in the autism community. Stone and Rosenbaum (1988) surveyed teachers of students with autism (*M* years teaching = 4.8) and parents of children with autism (70 % mothers; child's *M* age = 10.5; *M* age at diagnosis = 4.0) about their beliefs regarding various aspects of the disorder. Participants rated their (dis) agreement with a series of statements on a 6-point scale, where 1 indicated "fully agree" and 6 indicated "fully disagree." The mean rating for "most autistic children have special talents or abilities" was 2.76 for parents and 2.85 for teachers, placing the mean somewhere between "mostly agree" and "somewhat agree." In contrast, the mean rating by a group of specialists in the field of autism (researchers and clinicians) was 4.82 (between "somewhat disagree" and "mostly disagree")—significantly higher than the other two groups. A misguided belief that most people with autism possess savant-like skills can lead to unrealistic expectations among teachers and caregivers, and it can even contribute to treatments that lack a sound evidentiary basis and are potentially harmful (e.g., facilitated communication; see Lilienfeld et al., 2010).

The Reality about Savant Syndrome and Memory

Savant syndrome is incredibly rare. Males are roughly six times more likely to have savant syndrome than females. It occurs most often in individuals with autism, mental retardation, and other brain diseases and disorders. Savant syndrome is more common in autism than in any other condition, or in the general population; approximately 10 percent of persons with autism possess savant-like skills (Rimland, 1978; Treffert, 1989, 2010). But because mental retardation is much more common than autism, this means that roughly half of persons with savant syndrome have autism as their underlying disorder, and half have mental retardation or another brain disorder (Treffert, 2010). Importantly, then, not everyone with autism has savant syndrome, and not everyone with savant syndrome has autism. The vast majority—at least 90 percent—of those with autism do not have unusually good memories or any special skills. The IQ of persons with savant syndrome is usually between 40 and 70 (Treffert, 1989).

Special abilities in savant syndrome tend to cluster in a small number of areas, with music (most often piano), art, calendar calculating (e.g., quickly determining on which day of the week a given date fell, or will fall, for a period spanning hundreds and even thousands of years), mathematical skills (e.g., lightning calculation—the rapid solution of complex multiplication or division problems), and mechanical and spatial skills being the most common (Treffert, 2010). For example, there are cases dating back to the nineteenth century of persons with savant syndrome who memorized thousands of complex musical pieces without being able to read music (or in most cases, read at all) and could play a piece back perfectly on hearing it a single time. One of the better-known cases is commonly known as Blind Tom. Tom was a slave around the time of the Civil War "whose vocabulary was less than 100 words, but his musical repertoire was over 5,000 pieces," including Bach, Beethoven, Chopin, Rossini, Verdi, and many others (Treffert, 1989, p. 37; see also Sacks, 2007). Not only could he play any once-heard piece perfectly, but he could also sing in English, French, or German, despite not understanding the words. Like many other musical savants, Tom could improvise but not create original compositions. Despite his impressive musical ability, by today's standards he would be considered intellectually disabled. In addition to his very limited language skills, he required constant supervision and could not care for himself.

As the instances of Tom and Kim illustrate, what unites all of these instances is their memory: In all cases memory for material within the given domain is phenomenal, and in some cases, as with Kim, memory essentially *is* the condition's defining characteristic. Treffert (1989, p. 200, quoting the nineteenth century scholar Forbes Winslow) refers to it as "great vigor of memory." Within the domain of expertise, the heightened abilities would stand out in anyone, but they are even more striking in light of the individuals' general intellectual impairment. Memory for material outside the domain of expertise is typically below average, or normal at best.

Precise figures for the incidence of savant syndrome are hard to come by, but Darold Treffert, the leading contemporary scholar of savantism, distinguishes between "talented" and "prodigious" savants. Although there is no clear cutoff between the two conditions, talented savants' abilities would not be spectacular if found in a nonimpaired person; they are spectacular in an otherwise intellectually disabled person. In contrast, prodigious savants' abilities would be remarkable in anyone. For example, many professional musicians and artists can perform at the same level as a talented savant, but there are hardly any Mozarts or Picassos out there, in either the savant or the nonsavant population. In Treffert's (1989) review of the entire literature on savant syndrome, he identified approximately 100 known prodigious savants. This elite group includes Kim Peek. The number of talented savants is larger but still quite modest (Treffert, 1989; 2010).

Savant syndrome can be innate or acquired, especially when there is brain damage during infancy or early childhood (the existence of rare cases of acquired savant syndrome in adults makes Amos Decker's TBI-induced hyperthymesia theoretically, albeit only remotely, possible). There are numerous candidates for what causes savantism, but none has proven definitive (Treffert, 1989; 2010; Treffert & Christensen, 2005). Brain damage or abnormalities, especially in the left hemisphere and accompanied by right hemisphere overcompensation, are common, possibly in response to prenatal or perinatal exposure to toxins (e.g., excessive levels of testosterone, which would help to explain the higher incidence of savantism in males). Interestingly, Parker et al. (2006) propose that A.J.'s hyperthymesia might result from a variant of a neurodevelopmental disorder of the frontostriatal system in the brain. Other frontostriatal disorders include autism and schizophrenia, both of which can produce savant syndrome. Although some persons with savantism have eidetic imagery, it is no more common in persons with savantism than in similarly retarded persons without savantism. Moreover, a nontrivial number of those with savantism have been blind since infancy, making any sort of imagery impossible. Hereditary and psychological factors, especially motivation, extensive practice, and environmental reinforcement (e.g., encouragement and approval from family and others), also play a role in many, though not necessarily all, cases.

IMPLICATIONS OF SUPERIOR MEMORY CASES

If the abilities of savants and even some cases of superior memory in nonsavants reflect unique biological characteristics, then what are the implications of these cases for understanding memory functioning in the vast majority of people without those characteristics? The answer, as the previous discussion of nonsavant mnemonists makes clear, is that cases involving neurological anomalies are the exception. Overwhelmingly, the brains of most individuals who exhibit superior memory are indistinguishable from anyone else's brain, and they rely on normal cognitive strategies as well. Consequently, the bulk of the superior memory cases, though "abnormal" in some respects, are highly relevant to "normal" memory. Superior memory has implications both for our understanding of how memory normally functions (including its biological underpinnings) and for how to improve it.

At a conceptual level, the study of superior memory leads to several conclusions. First, memory abilities, like other cognitive abilities (e.g., reasoning, language, general intelligence), vary widely within the population. Yet with rare exceptions (e.g., savant syndrome, eidetic imagery), these differences are much more a matter of degree than a matter of quality or neurological differences. Second, although there is almost certainly a biological, and presumably genetic, component to overall memory functioning, one is not simply born and therefore stuck with a relatively good or poor memory. Rather, memory performance is enormously modifiable with training and practice. Third, memory performance varies substantially across types of tasks. Mnemonists are usually more adept at remembering some kinds of information than others. Experts within a particular domain frequently have exceptional memory for domain-specific stimuli but merely ordinary memory outside their area of expertise. Even more extreme, most savants have extraordinary memory for certain types of stimuli (e.g., music, dates) but below average memory for other kinds of information. Similarly, people with no special memory skill often feel that they are better at remembering some classes of stimuli (e.g., names, dates, numbers) than others. Thus, research on superior memory shows that memory functions largely the same way in everyone; is modifiable, to an even astonishing degree, with sufficient motivation and investment of effort; and is not a monolithic, unitary construct but an assemblage of related yet distinct capacities.

Finally, the small subset of memory abilities (concentrating on music and math) in nearly all savants has implications for the neurobiology of memory. The close linkage among memory, math ability, and music ability in savant syndrome suggests that these abilities are closely linked in the human brain (Treffert, 1989). The study of "abnormal" memory, in both savants and non-savants, can greatly expand our understanding of the biological and psychological processes in normal memory functioning.

Superior memory also demonstrates that memory improvement, often of a dramatic nature, is within the capabilities of most people. Although a comprehensive discussion of the topic is beyond the scope of the present chapter, a number of techniques can improve one's memory (for review, see Herrmann & Gruneberg, 2008; Worthen & Hunt, 2011). These methods have demonstrated effectiveness in a wide variety of educational, everyday, and clinical contexts (see, e.g., chapters 5 and 6 on the use of memory improvement strategies with amnesia patients). Importantly, like many other skills, mnemonic techniques are not cost-free. They take time and effort to learn and implement (although, to be sure, they take less time and effort the better they are learned; Foer, 2011; Worthen & Hunt, 2011). Most mnemonics also work better for some types of material than for others, and their effectiveness can vary depending on users' aptitude, personality, and learning style (Worthen & Hunt, 2011). Thus, "[m]nemonics are useful in almost any situation in which learning and memory are the goals, but one size does not fit all" (Worthen & Hunt, 2011, p. 19). The achievements of mnemonists, nearly all of whom use some sort of mnemonic strategy, convincingly demonstrate that one is not just "stuck with" a certain level of memory functioning, but that it can be improved.

CONCLUSIONS

"It is generally agreed that such an ability [photographic memory] does not exist" (MacLeod et al., 2014, p. 391). This statement is true whether one adopts a liberal or a conservative definition of photographic memory. Nonetheless, most people believe that photographic memory is a genuine phenomenon, and characters who are lucky enough to possess one are well-represented in fiction, film, and television. In the popular view, photographic memory is the defining cerebral superpower, on a par with the abilities displayed by various superheroes.

Although photographic memory might be a myth, it is indisputable that cases of truly superior memory do exist. As memory, like any other mental or behavioral characteristic, is normally distributed within the population, this almost goes without saying—a normal distribution presupposes that a small number of observations will occur at either end of the distribution. But the memory abilities of some people are so striking as to seem to belong on a separate distribution altogether. We can learn a number of things from these cases.

First, although some people with superior memory are born with some unique ability (e.g., eidetic imagery, synesthesia) or neurological anomaly (e.g., savant syndrome), the majority of mnemonists are bred rather than born. Most rely on mnemonics and practice their memory skills extensively. Even persons with savant syndrome invest a great deal of time in memorizing certain kinds of information, and they are socially reinforced for doing so. Deliberate practice can produce superior memory in the same way that it can produce other forms of expertise (Ericsson, 2006; Ericsson & Moxley, 2014). This is not to say, of course, that a preexisting aptitude has nothing at all to do with it. Many mnemonists are above average in intelligence (e.g., Hunt & Love, 2000; Thompson et al., 1993), but by no means all, as the savantism cases clearly show. Moreover, given the prominent role of memory on standard IQ tests, it would be surprising if persons with extraordinary memory—at least some kinds of it—did *not* tend to score well on such tests. Nonetheless, there is little overall correlation between IQ and superior memory, and many of the most impressive mnemonists are professionally undistinguished (even excluding those with savant syndrome, whose intellectual disabilities generally prevent them from traditional employment; see, e.g., Hunt & Love, 1972; Luria, 1987b; Parker et al., 2006; Wilding & Valentine, 1997).

Second, most persons with superior memory are not literally "off the charts" but simply at the upper end of the normal distribution. In other words, their memory skills are abnormal more in a quantitative (i.e., well above the norm) than in a qualitative sense. As with the nature-versus-nurture question, there are exceptions to this rule. Research strongly suggests that savantism is associated with unique neurological characteristics; rare abilities like eidetic imagery and synesthesia have a neurological basis; and research shows that some kinds of specialized superior memory (e.g., spatial memory, highly superior autobiographical memory) is associated with structural brain differences. However, the brains of many individuals with superior memory do not appear to differ from the brains of control participants. And even when they do differ, it is difficult, if not impossible, to tell whether a preexisting brain feature predisposes one to have superior memory, or if training one's memory produces neurological changes (cases of children with savant syndrome and the observation that many adult mnemonists had superior memory as children suggests that the former occurs in at least some instances). Overall, then, some qualitative differences exist, but in many, if not most cases, memory experts' memory functions the same as anyone else's memory—only better.

Third, having superior memory for certain kinds of material does not translate into having superior memory for all kinds of material. Some people are especially good at remembering numbers (e.g., Thompson et al., 1993); some are especially good at remembering events from their own life history (e.g., LePort et al., 2012); and some are especially good at remembering music (e.g., Treffert, 1989). In some mnemonists, their memory prowess does include multiple domains (e.g., Hunter, 1977; Treffert & Christensen, 2005), but even in these cases, they do not have absolutely perfect memory for everything they encounter; rather, they are more adept at remembering some kinds of stimuli than others. This domain specificity of superior memory confirms other research indicating that ordinary memory is not a unitary construct but a modular entity that is associated with multiple regions of the brain.

Ordinary memory is also a modifiable skill, and the study of superior memory makes that perfectly clear. Although there are no magic pills for enhancing memory performance, it can be improved through hard work and the strategic use of mnemonics. Numerous examples of those with superior memory illustrate these fundamental principles. Persons with extraordinary memory abilities might, and rightfully should, fill us with awe; but they should also reassure us with the knowledge that the same high level of performance—or something close to it—is open to us all. Photographic memory might not really exist, but unlike X-ray vision, instant healing, or indestructibility, superior memory is a superpower that is within mere mortals' grasp.

NOTES

1. This is, of course, utterly ludicrous. Even if you could remember everything you saw and heard, it would be impossible to remember something you did not see or hear, like how you yourself would appear to someone else.

2. In *Stranger in a Strange Land*, one of the places a Fair Witness may receive training is the Rhine Foundation. The name is quite likely Heinlein's subtle tribute to J.B. Rhine, a pioneering (and many would say misguided and overly credulous)

researcher on parapsychology (e.g., ESP). Rhine's work continues at the Rhine Research Center in Durham, North Carolina.

3. The current world record, set by Suresh Kumar Sharma on October 21, 2015, is 70,030 digits. Marc Umile's American record of 15,314 has held since 2007. The current record for reciting pi while juggling is 9,778 digits (set by Mats Bergsten of Sweden in 2005). For information on all things related to memorizing pi, see www. pi-world-ranking-list.com.

4. He won. In addition to being a fascinating account of his journey to becoming the United States' top mental athlete, Foer's (2011) account is chock-full of useful and interesting information about the field of memory research, mnemonics, people with superior memory, and the role of memory in education, intelligence, and creativity.

5. Kim Peek died in 2009 at the age of 58 years. Much has been written about Peek, including a first-person account by his father (Peek & Hanson, 2008).

6. Terms like "retarded" and "retardation" have, in recent years, taken on a pejorative connotation. I follow Treffert (1989, 2010) in using these terms because they are recognizable, easily understood, and descriptive (i.e., a slowing of normal development). In using the terms, I mean no disrespect. Relatedly, I have tried to avoid defining persons in terms of their disorder or condition and therefore usually refer to persons with autism or savant syndrome, rather than to "autistics" and "savants."

Conclusion

According to Della Salla and Beyerstein (2007, p. xxxvi), "We all carry around with us a plethora of false beliefs, especially if we cannot or will not subject them to careful scrutiny and demand for evidence." They made this statement in the context of reassuring readers not to feel bad if they endorsed psychological myths before learning about the evidence debunking those myths. In other words, there is no shame in holding false beliefs. The shame is in failing to analyze our beliefs carefully, rather than simply accepting them at face value, and in ignoring evidence that refutes the myths. The temptation to hold onto myths, and to ignore disconfirming evidence, is strong. Why do people subscribe to myths in the absence of scientific support, and in the face of disconfirming evidence? What are the consequences of memory myths? And finally, what can we do about them? These are the questions explored in this concluding chapter.

THE PERSISTENCE OF MEMORY MYTHS

Memory has fascinated laypeople and scholars for thousands of years. The ancients had specific gods whose purview was memory: the Greek goddess Mnemosyne (mother of the Muses, and therefore of all the arts), the Roman goddess Moneta (also goddess of prosperity), and the Egyptian god Thoth (or his feminine counterpart Seshat, who are also the god/goddess of writing and record-keeping). It is surely no coincidence that gods and goddesses of memory were also associated with the arts, writing, and prosperity. The arts both draw on memory and serve as a repository of a culture's collective memory; writing things down contributes to better memory encoding, retention, and retrieval; and not only can memory be compared to a storehouse of

233

riches, but a superior memory can help one prosper in many areas of life. In the twenty-first century, we have an array of memory-enriching devices like never before, thanks largely to digital media and the increasing availability and affordability of electronic memory prostheses. These devices, which facilitate the storage, retention, and retrieval of information, are powerful and effective, both for normal memory functioning (Garde-Hansen et al., 2009) and in cases of memory impairment (see, e.g., chapter 6). Nonetheless, they cannot overcome memory's inherent fallibility. We no longer pray to the gods for help with memory; but perhaps we should.

Like any myths, memory myths persist for a number of reasons, both psychological and sociological. Psychological explanations reflect the operation of fundamental cognitive processes, whereas sociological explanations look at the myths within the broader social and cultural context. In our media-saturated society, this necessarily involves the clash between media representations of memory phenomena and scientific research on memory.

Psychological Explanations

At a psychological level, the myths might persist because they are somehow adaptive—that is, they contribute to individuals' wellbeing. Some myths, such as an exaggerated belief in memory's overall accuracy, are comforting; they make us feel better about ourselves. For example, paralleling Freud's (1928/1961) argument in *The Future of an Illusion* about why people hold religious beliefs in the absence of objective evidence of their veridicality, Clifasefi et al. (2007, p. 61) maintain that "To believe in the permanence of memory protects us against loss of self-identify in the same way that believing in heaven protects us against loss of life after death." Since our memories are such a central component of who we are, acknowledging the fallibility of memory would potentially diminish our sense of self. Similarly, it might be comforting to believe that unpleasant memories can be repressed from consciousness or simply erased altogether, or reassuring to believe that innocent people would not confess to crimes that they did not commit.

Along the same lines, many myths have considerable intuitive appeal (Bornstein & Greene, 2017). It just makes sense that the mind would protect itself by repressing information that would be upsetting to remember, and that if and when we do remember such information, it is accurate; that the memory of someone who witnesses a crime can be trusted; or that a criminal suspect would not confess to something he did not do. Some memory myths, such as the belief that retrograde amnesia can be so extensive as to wipe out one's entire identity, that unwanted memories can be selectively erased, or that memory is like a videorecorder, make for good and straightforward stories, and there is a kernel of truth to some of them (e.g., very infrequent cases of pervasive retrograde amnesia do exist, and directed forgetting can effectively reduce the retrievability of unwanted information). This kernel of truth reflects the fact that "normal" memory is enormously variable. Short of transferring memories directly from one person's mind to another's (see chapter 4; and who knows, in 500 years maybe even that will be possible), it is hard to state with absolute certainty that some sort of memory anomaly could simply never happen. Persons with savant syndrome, discussed in the previous chapter, are just one example of the truly remarkable ways in which memory can manifest itself. The trouble with myths is that they can make it seem as if the few kernels of truth populate the entire cornfield.

In addition, outlier cases are often more normal under close scrutiny than they first appear. For example, false memory and forgetting are both part of normal processes, but both can fall in the abnormal range, due either to the breadth of individual differences or brain pathology (Kopelman, 1999). Some people are more susceptible to false memories than others, while some people—those with superior memory—forget less than others, especially for certain kinds of information (see chapters 3 and 10). Yet even those with superior memories do not remember everything with perfect accuracy, and they are just as susceptible as anyone else to some kinds of memory error and distortion (Frenda et al., 2014).

Unfortunately, commonsense notions of memory, like many other seemingly "obvious" psychological notions, turn out to be wrong (Banaji & Crowder, 2000; Della Salla, 1999, 2007; Lilienfeld et al., 2010). The truth behind the myths is a good deal more prosaic and nuanced. For example, we forget much more than we remember, and often what we do remember is incomplete, inaccurate, or even a complete fabrication. The vast majority of this forgetting is adaptive (see chapter 2)—it prevents us from expending our finite cognitive resources on retaining and retrieving unnecessary information, and the tendency to remember pleasant experiences better than unpleasant ones contributes to wellbeing (via mood congruency) in non-depressed persons. Directed forgetting (see chapter 4) and routine memory processes (e.g., the diminished rehearsal and elaboration of upsetting memories, absence of suitable retrieval cues) are common mechanisms of adaptive forgetting. Some of these mechanisms are deliberate (e.g., directed forgetting, diminished rehearsal), whereas others (e.g., lack of effective retrieval cues) typically occur without conscious awareness.

Cognitive biases are another psychological factor that contributes to the persistence of myths. People naturally tend to seek information that confirms their beliefs, interpret information in a way that supports their beliefs, and selectively remember information that is consistent with their beliefs while discounting or ignoring contradictory information (e.g., Baron, 2008). These confirmatory biases affect human reasoning regardless of the domain; beliefs about memory are no exception (Garry et al., 1994). So, for example, someone who believes that Alzheimer's disease is an inevitable consequence of aging would be inclined to probe for instances of forgetting in elderly acquaintances or family members, take instances of normal forgetting (in oneself or others) as a sign of incipient dementia, and remember those memory failures more readily than the times the older person's memory works just fine. To be sure, an alertness to memory or other cognitive dysfunction in others, especially aging family members, can be beneficial insofar as it contributes to the early detection of genuine impairment; but being overly alert to it can contribute to the perpetuation of myths related to memory and aging. It can also be a source of considerable stress and frustration (e.g., worrying that unremarkable instances of forgetting are possible signs of Alzheimer's disease can cause significant anxiety).

In presenting research findings, psychologists themselves are not immune to these biases. Textbook coverage of "classic" studies has, in many instances, become distorted over the years as theoretical orientations and methodological paradigms evolve (Friend, Rafferty & Bramel, 1990; Griggs, 2015). For example, many psychological textbooks emphasize research on brain stimulation as supporting the memory accuracy/permanence myth; yet a reappraisal of that research shows that the data provide much less evidence for the myth than commonly thought (Loftus & Loftus, 1980). Thus, although research can be, and frequently is, used to combat psychological myths, in some cases biased expositions of the research can inadvertently perpetuate the myths.[1]

Related to cognitive biases, our knowledge and awareness of our own memory processes, as well as how memory works in general—that is, our metamemory—are not always accurate (Beran et al., 2012; Dunlosky & Nelson, 1992). In part, this results from imperfect feedback—except in educational settings, we do not often receive explicit, verifiable feedback informing us that our memories were in error. For example, if years from now I were to misremember running my one marathon race (in 1995) in 3:45 rather than the much more pedestrian time of 5:15 that I presently believe it to be, no one is going to correct my memory unless I tell someone the wrong time instead of keeping it to myself. And even then, the only person who would know the faster time is wrong is my wife, who ran the race with me—and she might not say anything for the sake of our marriage.

We share our memories all of the time with others—both those who shared the original experience (e.g., "Remember that time we broke your mother's large ceramic dog and then tried to cover it up?") and those who were not there (e.g., telling our children about things we did before they were born). But much of the time, information that we retrieve in memory goes no further than our own consciousness. It is an entirely different matter if you are a public official. Current Speaker of the House of Representatives (and then Vice

Presidential candidate) Paul Ryan created a minor firestorm in 2012 when he said that he had run a marathon in "under three, high twos." A subsequent investigation determined that his time had been 4:01:25. Ryan claimed the mixup was a simple memory error, but as with the case of Brian Williams (see chapter 3), others looked for a more sinister explanation (Thompson, 2012).[2]

Sociological Explanations

These psychological explanations apply to the persistence of false beliefs about many phenomena, scientific and otherwise. What is unique about the incorrect hunches that people develop about memory, *per se*? The answer to this question requires us to look at memory myths from a broader, more sociological perspective. In this broader approach, memory myths persist because of the social function that memory serves, the social function that the myths themselves serve, and the widespread misrepresentation of how memory works.

Although memories are a personal, private, and ultimately subjective experience, they serve an important social function. Not only do people rely on their memories constantly in social interactions (e.g., remembering what we talked about the last time we had a conversation, remembering where you work and how many children you have, etc.), but they also share memories as a means of social bonding. When people share memories, they do not merely report the factual information; they exchange impressions, evaluations, and applications to their current situation (Hyman, 1994). This is especially true of flashbulb memories (see chapter 2); the sharing of flashbulb memories (e.g., "Where were you when you heard about the 9/11 attacks?") in narrative form brings people together as a way of making a private experience a communal one (Neisser et al., 1996). Unfortunately, it can also exacerbate the tendency to make memory errors (Neisser et al., 1996). Because of the importance of memory in social situations and everyday life, people are constantly confronted with evidence of memory and memory failures. This distinguishes memory from other psychological processes about which people might also have erroneous beliefs.

Just as memory serves a social purpose, so do memory myths. According to Bangerter and Heath (2004), scientific legends, or myths, serve a valuable function for the population that ascribes to them. They allow for the rapid diffusion of ideas within a society; this diffusion of myths can create and reinforce social bonds, in much the same way that the sharing of memories has this effect. Bangerter and Heath give the example of how the legend of the Mozart effect might allow people to share concerns about their children's intellectual development, thereby alleviating anxiety. Similarly, the myth of repressed memory might allow people to share concerns about how they or their loved ones will respond to trauma; myths about retrograde amnesia might allow them to share concerns about recovery from a TBI. Thus, the myths might not only make us feel better about ourselves, as discussed above; they could also enhance our relations to others.

Finally, as the previous chapters show, popular representations of memory phenomena—in movies, television shows, theater, fiction, and so on—frequently clash with the scientific evidence and perpetuate false information about memory. These media range widely in the accuracy with which they depict memory, just as they vary in how they depict other scientific phenomena (e.g., Griep & Mikasen, 2009; Kirby, 2011), mental illness (Packer, 2012; Walker et al., 2010), historical events, or anything else. It may be tempting to give these media a pass in the name of entertainment. After all, everyone knows that they are purveying works of the imagination that are not meant to be taken literally, right? Moreover, the media portrayals sometimes are accurate (Seamon, 2015), which makes it particularly hard for the lay viewer or reader to know what to accept as a realistic portrayal and what to dismiss as implausible.

It is impossible to say whether, on balance, the multifarious popular depictions of memory are relatively accurate or relatively inaccurate. The present work has emphasized the erroneous and misleading ones; other work (e.g., Seamon, 2015) has emphasized the ones that do a reasonably good job of portraying memory. The proliferation of memory myths suggests that the misleading representations predominate. Of course, a correlation between false representations of memory and the existence of memory myths does not necessarily mean that one causes the other, or a specific causal direction in the event that a causal relationship does exist. Widespread acceptance of the myths could result in their adoption by various entertainment media; conversely, the ready availability of false information in widely consumed media could create, or at least contribute to, false beliefs; some third variable might produce both the myths and the misleading portrayals of memory phenomena; or the two might be completely independent. It seems likely, however, that a reciprocal relationship exists, such that popular misunderstandings about how memory works lead to false depictions in the media, and those media portrayals further strengthen the myths (Lilienfeld et al., 2010). It is a vicious circle—and one with potentially serious consequences.

THE CONSEQUENCES OF MEMORY MYTHS

By definition, myths are beliefs that we accept without inspecting them too closely. Although they are often innocuous, they can have negative consequences. In the case of memory myths, little research has directly addressed the relationship between people's knowledge about memory and their behavior, but their beliefs can affect both how they subjectively interpret experiences and how they act, in a number of respects (Lane & Karam-Zanders, 2014). At an individual level, holding false beliefs about memory can affect one's thinking and behavior, as well as one's interactions with others. "The beliefs that we have about memory and how it works drive the way in which we remember, what we remember as well as the decisions that we make when judging other people's memories" (Clifasefi et al., 2007, p. 72). Insofar as the beliefs are fueled by media misrepresentations, then, reality can come to imitate art.

To take one example, believing in the concept of repression—whether that belief arises from exposure to the many novels and films featuring characters with repressed memories or some other means—could make one more susceptible to having false memories. Supporting this hypothesis, Niedzwienska et al. (2007) found that the less participants knew about how memory works (i.e., the more mistaken their intuitive beliefs), the more susceptible they were to misleading information in a memory experiment. Similar effects could occur with respect to other memory myths: believing that anterograde amnesia is rare and not very serious could lead to additional frustration following TBI and a failure to seek appropriate rehabilitation; believing that Alzheimer's disease is an inevitable consequence of aging could lead to a failure to engage in protective behaviors; and believing that eyewitnesses are rarely wrong could lead legal authorities to prosecute the innocent and juries to convict them. Thus, misunderstanding how memory works impairs people's ability to be productive citizens and function effectively in a variety of different contexts (Alvarez & Brown, 2002).

Each of these examples could, and frequently does, affect others: False memories might contribute to unfounded accusations of crime; caregivers might not provide appropriate support to individuals with anterograde amnesia or age-related symptoms of memory decline like mild cognitive impairment; and prosecuting innocent persons based on a false eyewitness identification allows the truly guilty perpetrators to remain at large and commit additional offenses. All of these interpersonal consequences, when multiplied over numerous cases, create substantial societal costs.

Additional consequences of accepting memory myths have to do with opportunity costs and spillover effects (Lilienfeld et al., 2010). Opportunity costs are when a particular choice precludes the opportunity to reap the benefits of a better alternative. Suppose, for instance, that you make a misinformed decision to buy an ill-fitting and unreturnable pair of pants. Not only are you stuck with the pants, but you no longer have as much time and money to use in buying a better pair. Many of the myths covered in earlier chapters involve persons with mental (e.g., trauma victims) and/or physical health issues (e.g., amnesia patients). If the individuals themselves have erroneous beliefs about memory, then they might seek a form of therapy that is less effective than others would be, or they might fail to seek potentially beneficial therapy altogether. Caregivers and healthcare providers who subscribe to the same myths might have unrealistic expectations and lack the knowledge to provide the most efficacious forms of treatment. Groups that one would expect to know better, such as school and clinical psychologists, parents and teachers of children with autism, and people who have experience with TBI (either themselves or in someone close to them), are somewhat more knowledgeable than laypeople, but they still hold a number of mistaken beliefs about how various disorders and experiences (e.g., TBI, autism, trauma) affect memory. Not only can the false beliefs reduce the efficacy of treatment or caregiver support, but they reduce and potentially preclude the opportunity of more effective treatment. The false expectations can also create difficulties for those suffering from the disorder, if the expectations lead to their feeling frustrated and misunderstood (Hux et al., 2006).

Finally, an uncritical acceptance of memory myths could be symptomatic of an uncritical mindset in general. Socrates is credited with saying that "the unexamined life is not worth living" (quoted in Plato's *Apology*). This is usually taken to mean: "Question everything." Critical thinking, along with a healthy dose of skepticism, contributes to success across a broad swath of interpersonal and professional domains. Lilienfeld et al. (2010) maintain that an unquestioning acceptance of some myths (e.g., those having to do with memory) could predispose a person to accept false information in other, completely unrelated domains (e.g., claims of advertisers, policy makers, etc.). In other words, it bespeaks a certain mental laziness that could lead to trouble in any number of ways. Hence, not only are the myths themselves potentially dangerous; believing in them is indicative of a more general pattern of gullibility and failure of critical thinking.

WHAT TO DO ABOUT IT: DEBUNKING THE MYTHS

Myths are tenacious. As described above, they persist for a variety of psychological and sociological reasons, most of which are part of fundamental cognitive or interpersonal processes and that operate without our being consciously aware of them. Thus, "demythologizing" is hard—but it is not impossible. Two means of debunking memory myths are education and, perhaps ironically, the judicious use of popular media.

Several surveys of laypeople's beliefs about memory have investigated the relationship between knowledge of how memory works and individual differences, such as respondents' educational history (see chapter 1). Although the pattern of findings is not entirely consistent across studies (e.g., Magnussen et al., 2006), some evidence suggests that education can be a protective factor against myth acceptance. Education and knowledge about memory are related in at least three respects. First, survey respondents with a higher level of education (e.g., postbaccalaureate education) have more accurate beliefs about memory than those with less formal education (e.g., some or no college experience; Patihis et al., 2014; Simons & Chabris, 2011). Second, those who score higher on a measure of critical thinking ability know more about how memory really works than those who score lower (Patihis et al., 2014). And third, training in psychology—operationalized, for example, as majoring in psychology or the number of psychology books read or classes taken—is associated with better knowledge about memory (Patihis et al., 2014; Simons & Chabris, 2011). Something as simple and straightforward as a single class on memory can even improve individuals' implicit knowledge of memory (Niedzwienska et al., 2007). Other research has also found that coursework in psychology reduces people's beliefs in myths about other psychological phenomena (e.g., the "people use only 10% of their brain power" myth; see, generally, Laub, Maeder & Bornstein, 2010; Lilienfeld et al., 2010; Standing & Huber, 2003).

The causal mechanisms (if any) underlying the negative correlation between education and myth acceptance is unclear (French & Wilson, 2007). Education in general, and in psychology in particular, could explicitly debunk myths about memory, as well as false assumptions about any number of other topics. At a more subtle level, greater education—again, either in general or on psychological topics—could inculcate the sorts of critical thinking skills that make people skeptical about popular assumptions.[3] Indeed, this is one of the principal goals of much education, especially at the postsecondary level. Alternatively, both obtaining more education and knowing more about memory could simply reflect some third variable, like higher socioeconomic status (Simons & Chabris, 2011) or being smarter (Patihis et al., 2014). To answer the question definitively, some aspect of education would have to be manipulated (e.g., in a longitudinal research design) while holding the other variables constant (for an example of this approach, see Laub et al., 2010; Niedzwienska et al., 2007).

Another approach is to use the same mechanisms that currently perpetuate the myths as a means of correcting them. In the twenty-first century, we have access to more information than ever before in history. Various media can be used—and already are used—to shape people's thinking and behavior (Okdie et al., 2014). For example, television dramas have been used to promote prosocial behavior (e.g., Bandura, 2006). In the same fashion, television and other entertainment media could promote a more accurate understanding of memory and other psychological phenomena. This would require writers to do the necessary research and, in some cases, to hire scientific experts as consultants (Kirby, 2012). A critical question here is whether scientifically accurate depictions would be as entertaining, and as profitable, as the more fantastic ones. Is a superspy/assassin whose head injury causes him some degree of retrograde amnesia, but only for the hours or days leading up to the injury, and lingering anterograde amnesia that makes it hard for him to retain new information, as exciting to watch or read about as Jason Bourne?

The question is difficult to answer. The success of the occasional realistic offering, such as *Memento* or several realistic movies and novels about Alzheimer's disease (see chapter 7 and the Appendix), provides evidence that it is feasible to create something that appeals to the masses while portraying memory fairly. And I would certainly not want to argue that works of the imagination must necessarily be true to life—that would defeat much of what makes them imaginative in the first place, fun to create, and fun to watch or read. Perhaps a disclaimer along the lines of "Warning: What you are about to read is completely fabricated and does not accurately portray the way memory [substitute other scientific phenomenon here] really works" would do the trick. A more realistic solution would be simply to increase the number of scientifically accurate works in the entertainment marketplace, to help redress the imbalance.

How much education and myth-busting are necessary? In both regards, more is better, but ultimately, "[w]hat do lay people need to know about memory, and in what depth?" (Lane & Karam-Zanders, 2014, p. 359). As Lane and Karam-Zanders explain, the answer to this question is tricky, as criteria for the sufficiency of knowledge can vary depending on the circumstances. For example, it is more important for those dealing with eyewitnesses (e.g., police officers, attorneys, judges, and jurors) to know about the factors that do and do not affect eyewitness reliability than for those who do not interact with eyewitnesses. Of course, anyone could be an eyewitness to a crime, and the principles of eyewitness memory generalize to memory for many other kinds of events—but for most of us, most of the time, knowing about eyewitness memory is not unduly critical. This suggests that general education efforts, especially with respect to critical thinking, might be broadly advantageous, but that a more tailored approach might yield even greater benefits (e.g., educating jurors about eyewitness memory; see Bornstein & Greene, 2017; Pawlenko, Safer, Wise, & Holfeld, 2013).

LOOKING AHEAD

Belief change is often difficult, but it is not impossible. If people can come to believe false information, then they can also rectify those false beliefs

(Baron, 2008). Erroneous beliefs about memory are a type of metamemory shortcoming—that is, a failure to observe one's own and others' memories well enough to form an accurate impression about how memory functions (this is not to say that it is wholly *in*accurate—just that people labor under some common misconceptions). The field of metamemory is well established, and metamemory research has made numerous contributions in terms of understanding the accuracy of metamemory judgments, the development of metamemory skills, individual differences in metamemory, and metamemory capabilities in nonhuman animals (e.g., Beran et al., 2012; Fleming & Frith, 2014). The majority of this research addresses the aspect of metamemory dealing with awareness of one's own memory abilities. This kind of metamemory has obvious implications in educational (e.g., "How do I learn best?") and clinical contexts (e.g., "Is my memory deteriorating?" "If I don't remember taking my medication today, does that mean I didn't actually take it, or that I took it and just forgot?").

Less research has been conducted on the aspect of metamemory concerned with general knowledge of how memory works. As described above, these general beliefs can also have profound consequences for individuals' behavior and for society as a whole. Although the two components of metamemory—awareness of one's own memory and general knowledge about memory processes—are clearly linked, the latter is more likely to be influenced by popular depictions of memory. There is a reciprocal relationship between memory myths and how popular media commonly portray memory phenomena.

Research on laypeople's knowledge of memory has addressed a number of different issues: memory accuracy and the role of emotion; repression, recovered memory, false memory, and hypnosis; memory loss as a result of brain damage or aging; memory in legal contexts, such as eyewitnesses and criminal suspects; and the popular notion of photographic memory, as well as its relationship to autism and savant syndrome and its implications for memory improvement. Nearly all of this research has focused on beliefs about a relatively small number of topics, depending on the researchers' particular research question. Future research should take a comprehensive approach to studying laypeople's knowledge and beliefs about memory, which would allow for an examination of which myths are more widely accepted than others and the relationship between knowledge of various topics. The survey described in chapter 1 indicated substantial variability in knowledge across different topical categories and positive but modest correlations among them. However, the survey included only college student participants, and it covered some topics (e.g., eyewitness memory) more extensively than others. A more diverse sample would permit a greater exploration of the role of individual differences. It would also be worthwhile to conduct developmental and longitudinal research, to examine the time course of memory myths.

Memory is a fascinating and intriguing topic. There are many possible reasons why: its variability across individuals, its existence in species besides humans, its intensely personal yet simultaneously social character, its obvious adaptive value in so many different contexts, its vibrant and unique phenomenological characteristics, and, in no small measure, its fallibility. Our fascination with memory means that there is an abundance of material in literature, film, and other entertainment media that treats the topic. That abundance is not likely to let up any time soon; if anything, it seems like the number of novels and films dealing with memory has increased in recent years. From an entertainment perspective, that is doubtless a good thing—memory makes for rich and varied characters and plot lines. From a scientific perspective, it is a little less clear. Although some popular portrayals get memory right to a reasonable degree of scientific accuracy, most of them perpetuate myths about how memory really works. In theory, we can learn just as much from these misleading portrayals as we can from the more accurate ones. The challenge is in being able to tell the difference, which most laypeople lack the expertise to do. Only time will tell whether, as the scientific understanding of memory advances and popular depictions of memory continue to proliferate, memory myths will wax or wane.

NOTES

1. I am grateful to an anonymous reviewer for suggesting this interpretation.

2. Fortunately, most of us do not have our memories scrutinized to the extent of Paul Ryan, Brian Williams, and other public figures. And fortunately for me, my marathon was long enough ago that I was unable to determine just how (in)accurate my remembered time really is—but it was definitely over 5 hours.

3. Although psychologists often (and rightfully) pride themselves on teaching students to think critically by exposing common assumptions about the mind and behavior to empirical scrutiny (e.g., Lilienfeld et al., 2010), training in many other subjects—other social and natural sciences, philosophy, and communications, to mention only a few—can doubtless be just as effective at teaching critical thinking. Many educational institutions also offer classes specifically on critical thinking, which teach it in a more direct manner. In addition, just as training in psychology lessens people's belief in psychological myths, training in other disciplines likely lessens people's belief in myths relevant to the discipline (e.g., courses in environmental science would presumably reduce the acceptance of myths related to climate change).

Appendix

Movies about Memory

Note. Year of release and leading actors in parentheses (see www.imdb.com); also noted if the original language is other than English. Several entries provided by Baxendale (2004) and Seamon (2015).

General Accuracy

Groundhog Day (2001; Bill Murray, Andie MacDowell)
Inside Out (2015, animated; Amy Poehler, Bill Hader, Lewis Black)
Limitless (2011; Bradley Cooper, Anna Friel)
Lucy (2014; Scarlett Johansson, Morgan Freeman)
Vantage Point (2008; Dennis Quaid, Forest Whitaker, Matthew Fox)

Repression/Trauma/Hypnosis/Recovered Memory

Amateur (1994; Isabelle Huppert)
Angel Eyes (2001; Jennifer Lopez, Jim Caviezel)
Dead Again (1991; Kenneth Branagh, Emma Thompson)
Gothika (2003; Halle Berry, Robert Downey Jr., Penelope Cruz)
Hellhole (1984; Judy Landers, Ray Sharkey)
Insaniac (2001; Robin Garrels)
Jacob's Ladder (1990; Tim Robbins)
Mister Buddwing (1966; James Garner, Suzanne Pleshette, Jean Simmons, Angela Lansbury)
Primal Fear (1996; Richard Gere, Laura Linney, Edward Norton)
Random Harvest (1942; Ronald Colman, Greer Garson)
Singing in the Dark (1956; Moyshe Oysher, Phyllis Hill, Joey Adams)
Shutter Island (2010; Leonardo DiCaprio, Mark Ruffalo, Ben Kingsley)
Snapdragon (1993; Steven Bauer, Chelsea Field, Pamela Anderson Lee)

Spellbound (1945; Gregory Peck, Ingrid Bergman)
Stir of Echoes (1999; Kevin Bacon)
Street of Memories (1940; Lynne Roberts, Guy Kibbee, John McGuire)
The Machinist (2004; Christian Bale, Jennifer Jason Leigh)
The Perks of Being a Wallflower (2012; Logan Lerman, Emma Watson)
Tommy (1975; Roger Daltrey, Ann-Margret, Elton John, Tina Turner)

Implants and Erasure

Assassin's Creed (2016; Michael Fassbender, Marion Cotillard, Jeremy Irons)
Criminal (2016; Kevin Costner, Ryan Reynolds, Gary Oldman, Tommy Lee Jones)
Dark City (1998; Kiefer Sutherland)
Eternal Sunshine of the Spotless Mind (2004; Jim Carrey, Kate Winslet, Kirsten Dunst, Elijah Wood)
Inception (2010; Leonardo DiCaprio, Joseph Gordon-Levitt, Ellen Page)
Johnny Mnemonic (1995; Keanu Reeves, Dolph Lundgren)
Memory (2007; Billy Zane)
Paycheck (2003; Ben Affleck, Aaron Eckhart)
Self/less (2015; Ryan Reynolds, Ben Kingsley)
Total Recall (1990; Arnold Schwarzenegger, Sharon Stone)
Total Recall (2012; Colin Farrell, Bokeem Woodbine, Bryan Cranston)
Transcendence (2014; Johnny Depp, Rebecca Hall, Morgan Freeman)

Retrograde Amnesia

Amateur (1994; Isabelle Huppert, Martin Donovan)
Anastasia (1956; Ingrid Bergman, Yul Brynner, Helen Hayes)
A Very Long Engagement (2004; French)
Cowboys and Aliens (2011; Daniel Craig, Harrison Ford)
Desperately Seeking Susan (1985; Rosanna Arquette, Madonna)
Finding the Way Home (1991; George C. Scott)
Garden of Lies (1915; Jane Cowl, William Russell)
I Love You Again (1940; William Powell, Myrna Loy)
Jason Bourne (2016; Matt Damon, Tommy Lee Jones, Alicia Vikander)
Kisses for Breakfast (1941; Dennis Morgan, Jane Wyatt, Shirley Ross)
Mulholland Drive (2001; Naomi Watts, Laura Harring, Justin Theroux)
Oldboy (2004; Korean)
Overboard (1987; Goldie Hawn, Kurt Russell)
Regarding Henry (1991; Harrison Ford)
Santa Who? (2000; Leslie Nielsen)
Shattered (1991; Tom Berenger, Bob Hoskins, Greta Scacchi)
Somewhere in the Night (1946; Nancy Guild, John Hodiak)
The Bourne Identity (2002; Matt Damon, Franka Potente, Chris Cooper)
The Bourne Supremacy (2004; Matt Damon, Franka Potente)
The Bourne Ultimatum (2007; Matt Damon, Joan Allen, David Strathairn)

The English Patient (1996, Ralph Fiennes, Juliette Binoche, Willem Dafoe)
The Forgotten (2004, Julianne Moore, Gary Sinise)
The Imaginarium of Doctor Parnassus (2009; Heath Ledger, Christopher Plummer)
The Jacket (2005; Adrien Brody, Keira Knightley, Daniel Craig)
The Long Kiss Goodnight (1996; Geena Davis, Samuel L. Jackson)
The Man without a Past (2003; Finnish)
The Majestic (2001; Jim Carrey)
The Matrimonial Bed (1930; Frank Fay, James Gleason, Lilyan Tashman)
The Return of the Soldier (1982; Julie Christie, Alan Bates, Glenda Jackson, Ann-Margret)
The Vow (2012; Rachel McAdams, Channing Tatum)
Trance (2013; James McAvoy, Vincent Cassel, Rosario Dawson)
Unknown (2006; Jim Caviezel, Greg Kinnear)
Waltz with Bashir (2008, animated; Hebrew)
X2: X-Men United (2003; Hugh Jackman, Patrick Stewart, Ian McKellen)
X-Men Origins: Wolverine (2009; Hugh Jackman, Liev Schreiber)

Anterograde Amnesia

Clean Slate (1994; Dana Carvey, James Earl Jones)
Fifty First Dates (2004; Adam Sandler, Drew Barrymore)
Finding Nemo (2003, animated; Albert Brooks, Ellen DeGeneres)
Finding Dory (2016, animated; Ellen DeGeneres, Albert Brooks)
Ghajini (2008; Hindi)
Memento (2000; Guy Pearce, Carrie-Anne Moss)
The Girl on the Train (2016; Emily Blunt)
The Lookout (2007; Joseph Gordon-Levitt, Jeff Daniels)
The Music Never Stopped (2011; Lou Taylor Pucci, J.K. Simmons, Julia Ormond)
Winter Sleepers (1997; German)

Alzheimer's Disease

A Moment to Remember (2004; Korean)
A Song for Martin (2001; Swedish)
Away from Her (2006; Julie Christie)
Before We Forget (2011; documentary)
Diminished Capacity (2008; Matthew Broderick, Virginia Madsen, Alan Alda)
Iris (2001; Judi Dench, Jim Broadbent, Kate Winslet)
Is Anybody There? (2008; Michael Caine)
Mr. Holmes (2015; Ian McKellen, Laura Linney)
Rise of the Planet of the Apes (2011; James Franco, Andy Serkis)
Safe House (1998; Patrick Stewart, Kimberly Williams, Hector Elizondo)
Still Alice (2014; Julianne Moore, Alec Baldwin)
The Notebook (2004; Ryan Gosling, Rachel McAdams, James Garner, Gena Rowlands)

Eyewitness Memory

Se souvenir des belles choses/Beautiful Memories (2001; French)
Anatomy of a Murder (1959; James Stewart, Lee Remick, Ben Gazzara)
Capturing the Friedmans (2003; documentary)
Eyewitness (1981; William Hurt; Sigourney Weaver)
Rashomon (1950; Japanese)
The Accused (1988; Kelly McGillis, Jodie Foster)
The Usual Suspects (1995; Kevin Spacey, Gabriel Byrne)
Witness for the Prosecution (1957; Tyrone Power, Marlene Dietrich)

Confessions

The Confession (1970; French)
The Confession (1999; Ben Kingsley, Amy Irving)
The Interrogation of Michael Crowe (2002; Ally Sheedy)
Under Suspicion (2000; Gene Hackman, Morgan Freeman)

Superior Memory

Little Man Tate (1991; Jodie Foster, Dianne Wiest)
Rain Man (1988; Dustin Hoffman, Tom Cruise)
Savant (1998; Rue DeBona, John Denver)
Searching for Bobby Fischer (1993; Joe Mantegna, Ben Kingsley)

Bibliography

Abel, A., & Bäuml, K.-H.T. (2013). Sleep can eliminate list-method directed forgetting. *Journal of Experimental Psychology: Learning, Memory, and Cognition, 39*, 946–952. doi: 10.1037/a0030529.

Abshire, J., & Bornstein, B.H. (2003). Juror sensitivity to the cross-race effect. *Law and Human Behavior, 27*, 471–480. doi:10.1023/A:1025481905861.

Acker, J.R., & Redlich, A.D. (2011). *Wrongful conviction: Law, science, and policy.* Durham, NC: Carolina Academic Press.

Alonzo, J.D., & Lane, S.M. (2010). Saying versus judging: Assessing knowledge of eyewitness memory. *Applied Cognitive Psychology, 24*, 1245–1264.

Alvarez, C.X., & Brown, S.W. (2002). What people believe about memory despite the research evidence. *The General Psychologist, 37*, 1–6.

Alzheimer's Association (2017). 2017 Alzheimer's Disease facts and figures. Retrieved from http://www.alz.org/facts/overview.asp.

American Psychiatric Association (2013). *Diagnostic and statistical manual of mental disorders* (5th ed.). American Psychiatric Publishing.

Anderson, C.A., Berkowitz, L., Donnerstein, E., Huesmann, L.R., Johnson, J.D., Linz, D., Malamuth, N.M., & Wartella, E. (2003). The influence of media violence on youth. *Psychological Science in the Public Interest, 4*, 81–110.

Anderson, M.C., & Levy, B.J. (2009). Suppressing unwanted memories. *Current Directions in Psychological Science, 18*, 189–194.

Anderson, M.C., & Levy, B.J. (2011). On the relationship between interference and inhibition in cognition. In A.S. Benjamin (Ed.), *Successful remembering and successful forgetting: A festschrift in honor of Robert A. Bjork* (pp. 107–132). New York: Psychology Press.

Anderson, N.D., & Craik, F.I.M. (2000). Memory in the aging brain. In E. Tulving & F.I.M. Craik (Eds.), *The Oxford handbook of memory* (pp. 411–425). Oxford: Oxford University Press.

Andrade, J. (1995). Learning during anaesthesia: A review. *British Journal of Psychology, 86*, 479–506.

Andrewes, D., & Gielewski, E. (1999). The work rehabilitation of a herpes simplex encephalitis patient with anterograde amnesia. *Neuropsychological Rehabilitation, 9,* 77–99.

Appleby, S., Hasel, L., & Kassin, S. (2013). Police-induced confessions: An empirical analysis of their content and impact. *Psychology, Crime & Law, 19,* 111–128.

Arizona v. Fulminante, 499 U.S. 279 (1991).

Aslan, A., & Bäuml, K.-H.T. (2013). Listwise directed forgetting is present in young-old adults, but is absent in old-old adults. *Psychology and Aging, 28,* 213–218. doi: 10.1037/a0031295

Avis, H.H., & Carlton, P.L. (1968). Retrograde amnesia produced by hippocampal spreading depression. *Science, 161,* 73–75.

Baddeley, A. (2013). Working memory and emotion: Ruminations on a theory of depression. *Review of General Psychology, 17,* 20–27. doi: 10.1037/a0030029.

Bahrick, H. P., Hall, L.K., & Berger, S.A. (1996). Accuracy and distortion in memory for high school grades. *Psychological Science, 7,* 265–271.

Baldacci, D. (2015). *Memory man.* New York: Grand Central Publishing.

Baldacci, D. (2016). *The last mile.* New York: Grand Central Publishing.

Balota, D.A., Dolan, P.O., & Duchek, J.M. (2000). Memory changes in healthy older adults. In E. Tulving & F.I.M. Craik (Eds.), *The Oxford handbook of memory* (pp. 395–409). Oxford: Oxford University Press.

Banaji, M.R., & Crowder, R.G. (2000). The bankruptcy of everyday memory. In U. Neisser & I.E. Hyman (Eds.), *Memory observed: Remembering in natural contexts* (2nd ed.) (pp. 19–27). New York: Worth [reprinted from *American Psychologist, 44,* 1185–1193)].

Bandura, A. (2006). Going global with social cognitive theory: From prospect to paydirt. In S.I. Donaldson, D.E. Berger, & K. Pezdek (Eds.), *Applied psychology: New frontiers and rewarding careers* (pp. 53–79). Mahwah, NJ: Erlbaum.

Bangerter, A., & Heath, C. (2004). The Mozart effect: Tracking the evolution of a scientific legend. *British Journal of Social Psychology, 43,* 605–623. doi: 10.1348/0144666042565353.

Baran, B., Wilson, J., & Spencer, R.M.C. (2010). REM-dependent repair of competitive memory suppression. *Experimental Brain Research, 203,* 471–477. doi: 10.1007/s00221-010-2242-2.

Barker, M.J., Greenwood, K.M., Jackson, M., & Crowe, S.F. (2004). Persistence of cognitive effects after withdrawal from long-term benzodiazepine use: a meta-analysis. *Archives of Clinical Neuropsychology, 19,* 437–454.

Baron, J. (2008). *Thinking and deciding* (4th ed.). New York: Cambridge University Press.

Barron, A.B.,& Brown, M.J.F. (2012). Science journalism: Let's talk about sex. *Nature, 488,*151–152. doi:10.1038/48 8151a

Bartlett, F. (1932). *Remembering.* Cambridge, UK: Cambridge University Press.

Bartlett, J.C. (2014a). The older eyewitness. In T.J. Perfect & D.S. Lindsay (Eds.), *The SAGE handbook of applied memory* (pp. 654–674). Los Angeles, CA: SAGE.

Bartlett, J.C. (2014b). True and false recognition of faces by young and old adults. In M.P. Toglia, D.F. Ross, J. Pozzulo., & E. Pica (Eds.), *The elderly eyewitness in court* (pp. 67–92). New York: Psychology Press.

Bartlett, J.C., & Memon, A. (2007). Eyewitness memory in young and older eye-witnesses. In R.C.L. Lindsay, D.F. Ross., J.D. Read, & M.P. Toglia (Eds.), *The handbook of eyewitness psychology (Vol. 2): Memory for people* (pp. 309–338). Mahwah, NJ: Erlbaum.

Baumann, M., Zwissler, B., Schalinski, I., Ruf-Leuschner, M., Schauer, M., & Kissler, J. (2013). Directed forgetting in post-traumatic-stress-disorder: A study of refugee immigrants in Germany. *Frontiers in Behavioral Neuroscience, 7* (Art. 94), 1–8. doi: 10.3389/fnbeh.2013.00094

Baumeister, R.F. (1998). The self. In D.T. Gilbert, S.T. Fiske, & G. Lindzey (Eds.), *The handbook of social psychology* (4th ed., Vol. 1, pp. 680–740). New York: McGraw-Hill.

Baxendale, S. (2004). Memories aren't made of this: Amnesia at the movies. *British Medical Journal, 329,* 1480–1483.

Bayley, J. (1999). *Elegy for Iris.* New York: St. Martin's Press.

Beaudoin, M., & Desrichard, O. (2011). Are memory self-efficacy and memory performance related? A meta-analysis. *Psychological Bulletin, 137,* 211–241. doi: 10.1037/a0022106.

Beaudry, J. L., Lindsay, R. C. L., Leach, A.-M., Mansour, J. K., Bertrand, M. I., & Kalmet, N. (2015). The effect of evidence type, identification accuracy, line-up presentation, and line-up administration on observers' perceptions of eyewitnesses. *Legal and Criminological Psychology, 20,* 343–364. doi: 10.1111/lcrp.12030

Beaulieu-Prévost, D., & Zadra, A. (2015). When people remember dreams they never experienced: A study of the malleability of dream recall over time. *Dreaming, 25,* 18–31. doi: 10.1037/a0038788.

Behrman, B.W., & Davey, S.L. (2001). Eyewitness identification in actual criminal cases: An archival analysis. *Law and Human Behavior, 25,* 475–491.

Behrman, B.W., & Richards, R.E. (2005). Suspect/foil identification in actual crimes and in the laboratory: A reality monitoring analysis. *Law and Human Behavior, 29,* 279–301. doi: 10.1007/s10979-005-3617-y.

Belleville, S., Gauthier, S., Lepage, E., Kergoat, M-J., & Gilbert, B. (2014). Predict-ing decline in mild cognitive impairment: A prospective cognitive study. *Neuropsy-chology, 28,* 643–652. doi: 10.1037/neu0000063.

Belleville, S., Gilbert, B., Fontaine, F., Gagnon, L., Ménard, E., & Gauthier, S. (2006). Improvement of episodic memory in persons with mild cognitive impairment and healthy older adults: Evidence from a cognitive intervention program. *Dementia and Geriatric Cognitive Disorders, 22,* 486–499. doi: 10.1159/000096316.

Belli, R.F. (2012). *True and false recovered memories: Toward a reconciliation of the debate.* New York: Springer.

Bennett, D.A., Schneider, J.A., Buchman, A.S., Barnes, L.L., Boyle, P.A., & Wilson, R.S. (2012). Overview and findings from the Rush Memory and Aging Project. *Current Alzheimer Research, 9,* 646–663.

Benson, D.F., & Geschwind, N. (1967). Shrinking retrograde amnesia. *Journal of Neurology, Neurosurgery and Psychiatry, 30,* 539–544.

Benton, T.R., McDonnell, S., Ross, D.F., Thomas, N., & Bradshaw, E. (2007). Has eyewitness research penetrated the American legal system? A synthesis of case history, juror knowledge, and expert testimony. In R.C.L. Lindsay, D.F. Ross., J.D. Read, & M.P. Toglia (Eds.), *The handbook of eyewitness psychology (Vol. 2): Memory for people* (pp. 453–500). Mahwah, NJ: Erlbaum.

Benton, T.R., Ross, D.F., Bradshaw, E., Thomas, W.N., & Bradshaw, G.S. (2006). Eyewitness memory is still not common sense: Comparing jurors, judges, and law enforcement to eyewitness experts. *Applied Cognitive Psychology, 20,* 115–130. doi:10.1002/acp.1171.

Beran, M.J., Brandl, J.L., Perner, J., & Proust, J. (2012). *Foundations of metacognition.* Oxford: Oxford University Press.

Bergen, P.S., Thompson, P.J., Baxendale, S.A., Fish, D.R., & Shorvon, S.D. (2000). Remote memory in epilepsy. *Epilepsia, 41,* 231–239.

Berk-Seligson, S. (2009). *Coerced confessions: The discourse of bilingual police interrogations.* Berlin: Walter de Gruyter.

Bermúdez-Rattoni, F., Miranda, M.I., & González, H.G. (2001). Cortical cholinergic modulation in memory formation. In P.E. Gold & W.T. Greenough (Eds.), *Memory consolidation: Essays in honor of James L. McGaugh* (pp. 185–199). Washington, DC: American Psychological Association.

Bernstein, D.M., & Loftus, E.F. (2009). How to tell if a particular memory is true or false. *Perspectives on Psychological Science, 4,* 370–374.

Berry, E., Kapur, N., Williams, L., Hodges, S., Watson, P., Smyth, G., ... & Wood, K. (2007). The use of a wearable camera, SenseCam, as a pictorial diary to improve autobiographical memory in a patient with limbic encephalitis: A preliminary report. *Neuropsychological Rehabilitation, 17,* 582–601. doi:10.1080/09602010601029780.

Billings, F.J., Taylor, T., Burns, J., Corey, D.L., Garven, S., & Wood, J.M. (2007). Can reinforcement induce children to falsely incriminate themselves? *Law and Human Behavior, 31,* 125–139.

Bjork, R.A. (2011). On the symbiosis of remembering, forgetting, and learning. In A.S. Benjamin (Ed.), *Successful remembering and successful forgetting: A festschrift in honor of Robert A. Bjork* (pp. 1–22). New York: Psychology Press.

Bjork, R.A., & Woodward, A.E. (1973). Directed forgetting of individual words in free recall. *Journal of experimental Psychology, 99,* 22–27.

Blair, I.V., Lenton, A.P., & Hastie, R. (2002). The reliability of the DRM paradigm as a measure of individual differences in false memories. *Psychonomic Bulletin & Review, 9,* 590–596.

Blandón-Gitlin, I., Sperry, K., & Leo, R. (2011). Jurors believe interrogation tactics are not likely to elicit false confessions: Will expert witness testimony inform them otherwise? *Psychology, Crime, and Law, 17,* 239–260.

Blazer, D.G., Yaffe, K., & Liverman, C.T. (2015). *Cognitive aging: Progress in understanding and opportunities for action.* Washington, DC: National Academies Press. Available at http://iom.nationalacademies.org/Reports/2015/Cognitive-Aging.aspx.

Block, S.D., Shestowsky, D., Segovia, D.A., Goodman, G.S., Schaaf, J.M., & Alexander, K.W. (2012). "That never happened": Adults' discernment of children's true and false memory reports. *Law and Human Behavior, 36,* 365–374. doi: 10.1037/h0093920

Bohannon, J.N. (1988). Flashbulb memories for the space shuttle disaster: a tale of two theories. *Cognition, 29*, 179–196. doi: 10.1016/0010-0277(88)90036-4.

Bonebakker, A.E., Jelicic, M., Passchier, J., & Bonke, B. (1996). Memory during general anesthesia: Practical and methodological aspects. *Consciousness and Cognition, 5*, 542–561.

Boovalingam, P., & Shah, N. (2013). Transient global amnesia. *Reviews in Clinical Gerontology, 23*, 189–195. doi:10.1017/S0959259813000063.

Borawick v. Shay, 68 F.3d 597 (2d. Cir. 1995).

Bornstein, B.H. (1995). Memory processes in elderly eyewitnesses: What we know and what we don't know. *Behavioral Sciences and the Law, 13*, 337–348.

Bornstein, B.H. (1998). The greatest memory teacher ever. *Applied Cognitive Psychology, 12*, 293–294.

Bornstein, B.H., & Greene, E. (2017). *The jury under fire: Myth, controversy, and reform.* New York: Oxford University Press.

Bornstein, B.H., Hullman, G., & Miller, M.K. (2013). Stress, trauma, and wellbeing in the legal system: Where do we go from here? In M.K. Miller & B.H. Bornstein (Eds.), *Stress, trauma, and wellbeing in the legal system* (pp. 293–309). New York: Oxford University Press.

Bornstein, B.H., Kaplan, D.L., & Perry, A.R. (2007). Child abuse in the eyes of the beholder: Lay perceptions of child sexual and physical abuse. *Child Abuse & Neglect, 31*, 375–391.

Bornstein, B.H., Liebel, L.M., & Scarberry, N.C. (1998). Repeated testing in eyewitness memory: A means to improve recall of a negative emotional event. *Applied Cognitive Psychology, 12*, 119–131.

Bornstein, B.H., & Muller, S.L. (2001). The credibility of recovered memory testimony: Exploring the effects of alleged victim and perpetrator gender. *Child Abuse & Neglect, 25*, 1415–1426.

Bornstein, B.H., & Robicheaux, T.R. (2009). Methodological issues in the study of eyewitness memory and arousal. *Creighton Law Review, 42*, 525–547.

Bornstein, B.H., & Zickafoose, D.J. (1999). I know I know it, I know I saw it: The stability of overconfidence across domains. *Journal of Experimental Psychology: Applied, 5*, 1–13.

Bothwell, R. K., Deffenbacher, K. A., & Brigham, J. C. (1987). Correlation of eyewitness accuracy and confidence: Optimality hypothesis revisited. *Journal of Applied Psychology, 72*, 691–695.

Bottoms, B.L., Golding, J.M., Stevenson, M.C., Wiley, T.R.A., & Yozwiak, J.A. (2007). A review of factors affecting jurors' decisions in child sexual abuse cases. In M.P. Toglia, J.D. Read, D.F. Ross, & R.C.L. Lindsay (Eds.), *The handbook of eyewitness psychology (Vol. 1): Memory for events* (pp. 509–543). Mahwah, NJ: Erlbaum.

Boyce, M., Beaudry, J., & Lindsay, R.C.L. (2007). Belief of eyewitness identification evidence. In R.C.L. Lindsay, D.F. Ross., J.D. Read, & M.P. Toglia (Eds.), *The handbook of eyewitness psychology (Vol. 2): Memory for people* (pp. 501–525). Mahwah, NJ: Erlbaum.

Boyle, P.A., Buchman, A.S., Wilson, R.S., Yu, L., Schneider, J.A., & Bennett, D.A. (2012). Effect of purpose in life on the relation between Alzheimer Disease pathologic changes on cognitive function in advanced age. *Archives of General Psychiatry, 69*, 499–506.

Boywitt, C.D., Kuhlmann, B.G., & Meiser, T. (2012). The role of source memory in older adults' recollective experience. *Psychology and Aging, 27*, 484–497. doi: 10.1037/a0024729.

Bradfield, A.L., & Wells, G.L. (2000). The perceived validity of eyewitness identification testimony: A test of the five *Biggers* criteria. *Law and Human Behavior, 24*, 581–594.

Brainerd, C.J., & Reyna, V.F. (2005). *The science of false memory*. New York: Oxford University Press.

Braun, K.A., Ellis, R., & Loftus, E.F. (2002). Make my memory: How advertising can change our memories of the past. *Psychology & Marketing, 19*, 1–23.

Brewer, N., & Burke, A. (2002). Effects of testimonial inconsistencies and eyewitness confidence on mock-juror judgments. *Law and Human Behavior, 26*, 353–364.

Brewin, C.R. (2007). Autobiographical memory for trauma: Update on four controversies. *Memory, 15*, 227–248.

Brewin, C.R. (2012). A theoretical framework for understanding recovered memory experiences. In R.F. Belli (Ed.), True and false recovered memories: Toward a reconciliation of the debate (pp. 149–173). doi:; 10.1007/978-1-4614-1195-6_5

Brigham, J.C. (2008). The role of race and racial prejudice in recognizing other people. In C. Willis-Esqueda (Ed.), *Motivational aspects of prejudice and racism* (pp. 68–110). New York: Springer. doi: 10.1007/978-0-387-73233-6_4.

Brown, R., & Kulik, J. (1977). Flashbulb memories. *Cognition, 5*, 73–99.

Brotons, M., & Koger, S.M. (2000). The impact of music therapy on language functioning in dementia. *Journal of Music Therapy, 37*, 183–195.

Brotons, M., & Marti, P. (2003). Music therapy with Alzheimer's patients and their family caregivers: A pilot project. *Journal of Music Therapy, 40*, 138–150.

Brundin, P., Pogarell, O., Hagell, P., Piccini, P., Widner, H., Schrag, A., … & Lindvall, O. (2000). Bilateral caudate and putamen grafts of embryonic mesencephalic tissue treated with lazaroids in Parkinson's disease. *Brain, 123*, 1380–1390.

Brunet, A., Orr, S.P., Tremblay, J., Robertson, K., Nader, K., & Pitman, R.K. (2008). Effect of post-retrieval propranolol on psychophysiologic responding during subsequent script-driven traumatic imagery in post-traumatic stress disorder. *Journal of Psychiatric Research, 42*, 503–506.

Buchman, A.S., Boyle, P.A., Yu, L., Shah, R.C., Wilson, R.S., & Bennett, D.A. (2012). Total daily physical activity and the risk of AD and cognitive decline in older adults. *Neurology, 78*, 1323–1329. doi:10.1212/WNL.0b013e3182535d35.

Bull, D.L. (1999). A verified case of recovered memories of sexual abuse. *American Journal of Psychotherapy, 53*, 221–224.

Bull, R., & Soukara, S. (2010). Four studies of what really happens in police interviews. In G.D. Lassiter & C. Meissner (Eds.), *Police interrogations and false confessions: Current research, practice, and policy recommendations* (pp. 81–95). Washington, DC: American Psychological Association.

Burgess, P., Sullivent, E.E., Sasser, S.M., Wald, M.M., Ossmann, E., & Kapil, V. (2010). Managing traumatic brain injury secondary to explosions. *Journal of Emergencies Trauma, and Shock, 3*, 164–172. doi: 10.4103/0974-2700.62120.

Bywaters, M., Andrade, J., & Turpin, G. (2004). Determinants of the vividness of visual imagery: The effects of delayed recall, stimulus affect and individual differences. *Memory, 12*, 479–488.

Cahill, L., Prins, B., Weber, M., & McGaugh, J.L. (1994). β-adrenergic activation and memory for emotional events. *Nature, 371*, 702–704.

Capaldi, E.J., & Neath, I. (1995). Remembering and forgetting as context discrimination. *Learning & Memory, 2*, 107–132.

Carey, B. (2008, December 5). H.M., an unforgettable amnesiac, dies at 82. *New York Times*. Available at http://www.nytimes.com.

Carpenter, S. (2001). Sleep deprivation may be undermining teen health. *APA Monitor, 32(9)*, 42. Available at http://www.apa.org/monitor/oct01/sleepteen.aspx.

Carroll, L. (1871/1960). *The annotated Alice*. New York: Meridian.

Casey, D.A., Antimisiaris, D., & O'Brien, J. (2010). Drugs for Alzheimer's Disease: Are they effective? *Pharmacy and Therapeutics, 35*, 208–211.

Ceci, S. J., & Bruck, M. (1995). *Jeopardy in the courtroom: A scientific analysis of children's testimony*. Washington, DC: American Psychological Association.

Ceci, S.J., & Friedman, R.D. (2000). The suggestibility of children: Scientific research and legal implications. *Cornell Law Review, 86*, 33–108.

Centers for Disease Control and Prevention (2015, September 3). Insufficient sleep is a public health problem. Retrieved from https://www.cdc.gov/features/dssleep/.

Centers for Disease Control and Prevention (2016, January 22). Rates of TBI-related emergency department visits, hospitalizations, and deaths—United States, 2001–2010. Retrieved from https://www.cdc.gov/traumaticbraininjury/data/rates.html.

Chabris, C.F. (1999). Prelude or requiem for the 'Mozart effect'? *Nature, 400*, 826–827.

Chartier-Harlin, M-C., Crawford, F., Houlden, H., Warren, A., Hughes, D., Fidani, L., … & Mullan, M. (1991). Early-onset Alzheimer's Disease caused by mutations at codon 717 of the β-amyloid precursor protein gene. *Nature, 353*, 844–846. doi: 10.1038/353844a0

Chase, W.G., & Ericsson, K.A. (1981). Skilled memory. In J. R. Anderson (Ed.), *Cognitive skills and their acquisition* (pp. 141–180). Hillsdale, NJ: Erlbaum.

Cheit, R.E. (2014). *The witch-hunt narrative: Politics, psychology, and the sexual abuse of children*. Oxford: Oxford University Press.

Chi, M.T.H., Glaser, R., & Farr, M.J. (1988). *The nature of expertise*. Hillsdale, NJ: Erlbaum.

Chojnacki, D., Cicchini, M., & White, L. (2008). An empirical basis for the admission of expert testimony on false confessions. *Arizona State Law Journal, 40*, 1–45.

Christianson, S.-Å. (1992). Emotional stress and eyewitness memory: A critical review. *Psychological Bulletin, 112*, 284–309.

Christianson, S.-Å., & Hübinette, B. (1993). Hands up! A study of witnesses' emotional reactions and memories associated with bank robberies. *Applied Cognitive Psychology, 7*, 365–379.

Chua, E.F., Pergolizzi, D., & Weintraub, R.R. (2014). The cognitive neuroscience of metamemory monitoring: Understanding metamemory processes, subjective levels expressed, and metacognitive accuracy. In S.M. Fleming & C.D. Frith (Eds.), *The cognitive neuroscience of metacognition* (pp. 267–291). Berlin: Springer-Verlag. doi: 10.1007/978-3-642-45190-4_12.

Clancy, S.A. (2005). *Abducted: How people come to believe they were kidnapped by aliens*. Cambridge, MA: Harvard University Press.

Clancy, S.A., McNally, R.J., Schacter, D.L., Lenzenweger, M.F. & Pitman, R.K. (2002). Memory distortion in people reporting abduction by aliens. *Journal of Abnormal Psychology, 111*, 455–461.

Clancy, S.A., Schacter, D.L., McNally, R.J., & Pitman, R.K. (2000). False recognition in women reporting recovered memories of sexual abuse. *Psychological Science, 11*, 26–31.

Clark, H.L., & Nightingale, N.N. (1997). When jurors consider recovered memory cases: Effects of victim and juror gender. *Journal of Offender Rehabilitation, 25*, 87–104.

Clark, S.E., & Loftus, E.F. (1996). The construction of space alien abduction memories. *Psychological Inquiry, 7*, 140–143.

Cleary, A.M., Brown, A.S., Sawyer, B.D., Nomi, J.S., Ajoku, A.C., & Ryals, A.J. (2012). Familiarity from the configuration of objects in 3-dimensional space and its relation to déjà vu: A virtual reality investigation. *Consciousness and Cognition, 21*, 969–975.

Clifasefi, S.L., Garry, M., & Loftus, E. (2007). Setting the record (or video camera) straight on memory: The video camera model of memory and other memory myths. In S. Della Salla (Ed.), *Tall tales about the mind and brain: Separating fact from fiction* (pp. 60–75). Oxford: Oxford University Press.

Clough, P.J., Earle, K., & Sewell, D. (2002). Mental toughness: The concept and its measurement. In I. Cockerill (Ed.), *Solutions in sport psychology* (pp. 32–43). London: Thomson Publishing.

Cohen, N.J., & Squire, L.R. (1980). Preserved learning and retention of a pattern-analyzing skill in amnesia: Dissociation of knowing how and knowing that. *Science, 210*, 207–210.

Colegrove, F.W. (1899). Individual memories. *American Journal of Psychology, 10*, 225–255.

Coluccia, E., Bianco, C., & Brandimonte, M.A. (2006). Dissociating veridicality, consistency, and confidence in autobiographical and event memories for the Columbia shuttle disaster. *Memory, 14*, 452–470.

Connolly, D.A., & Read, J.D. (2006). Delayed prosecutions of historic child sexual abuse: Analyses of 2064 Canadian criminal complaints. *Law and Human Behavior, 30*, 409–434.

Connolly, D.A., & Read, J.D. (2007). Canadian criminal court reports of historic child sexual abuse: Factors associated with delayed prosecution and reported repression. In Y. Orbach et al., *Child sexual abuse: Disclosure, delay, and denial* (pp. 195–217). Mahwah, NJ: Erlbaum.

Conway, M. (1995). *Flashbulb memories*. Brighton, UK: Erlbaum.

Conway, M., Anderson, S.J., Larsen, S.F., Donnelly, C.M., McDaniel, M.A., McClelland, A.G., ... & Logie, R.H. (1994). The formation of flashbulb memories. *Memory & Cognition, 22,* 326–343.

Conway, M., Justice, L., & Morrison, C. (2014). Beliefs about autobiographical memory. *The Psychologist, 27,* 502–505.

Corkin, S. (1968). Acquisition of motor skill after bilateral medial lobe-excision. *Neuropsychologia, 6,* 255–265.

Corkin, S. (2013). *Permanent present tense: The unforgettable life of the amnesic patient, H.M.* New York: Basic Books.

Corlett, P.R., Canavan, S.V., Nahum, L., Appah, F., & Morgan, P.T. (2014). Dreams, reality and memory: Confabulations in lucid dreamers implicate reality-monitoring dysfunction in dream consciousness. *Cognitive Neuropsychiatry, 19,* 540–553. doi: 10.1080/13546805.2014.932685.

Cosentino, S. (2014). Metacognition in Alzheimer's Disease. In S.M. Fleming & C.D. Frith (Eds.), *The cognitive neuroscience of metacognition* (pp. 389–407). New York: Springer.

Costanzo, M., Blandon-Gitlin, I., & Davis, D. (in press). The content, purpose, and effects of expert testimony on interrogations and confessions. In B.H. Bornstein & M.K. Miller (Eds.), *Advances in psychology and law* (Vol. 2). New York: Springer.

Costanzo, M., Shaked-Schroer, N., & Vinson, K.V. (2010). Juror beliefs about police interrogations, false confessions, and expert testimony. *Journal of Empirical Legal Studies, 7,* 231–247. doi: 10.1111/j.1740-1461.2010.01177.x.

Cowl, A.L., & Gaugler, J.E. (2014). Efficacy of creative arts therapy in treatment of Alzheimer's Disease and dementia: A systematic literature review. *Activities, Adaptation & Aging, 38,* 281–330. doi: 10.1080/01924788.2014.966547.

Crowder, R.G. (1992). Eidetic memory. In L.R. Squire (Ed.), *Encyclopedia of learning and memory.* New York: Macmillan.

Curci. A., & Luminet, O. (2009). Flashbulb memories for expected events: A test of the emotional-integrative model. *Applied Cognitive Psychology, 23,* 98–114.

Cutler, B.L., Berman, G.L., Penrod, S.D., & Fisher, R.P. (1994). Conceptual, practical and empirical issues associated with eyewitness identification test media. In D. Ross, J.D. Read, & M.P. Toglia (Eds.), *Adult eyewitness testimony: Current trends and developments.* New York: Cambridge University Press.

Cutler, B.L., Penrod, S.D. & Dexter, H.R. (1990). Juror sensitivity to eyewitness identification evidence. *Law and Human Behavior, 14,* 185–191. doi:10.1007/BF01062972.

Daglish, M.R., & Wright, P. (1991). Opinions about hypnosis among medical and psychology students. *Contemporary Hypnosis, 8,* 51–55.

Davidson, R.J. (1994). On emotion, mood, and related affective constructs. In P. Ekman & R.J. Davidson (Eds.), *The nature of emotion: Fundamental questions* (pp. 51–55). New York: Oxford University Press.

Davis, D., & Loftus, E.F. (2007). Internal and external sources of misinformation in adult witness memory. In M.P. Toglia et al. (Eds.), *Handbook of eyewitness psychology (Vol. 1): Memory for events* (pp. 195–237). Mahwah, NJ: Erlbaum.

Deckersbach, T., Moshier, S.J., Tuschen-Caffier, B., & Otto, M.W. (2011). Memory dysfunction in panic disorder: An investigation of the role of chronic benzodiazepine use. *Depression and Anxiety, 28*, 999–1007. doi: 10.1002/da.20891.

Deffenbacher, K.A. (2008). Estimating the impact of estimator variables on eyewitness identification: A fruitful marriage of practical problem solving and psychological theorizing. *Applied Cognitive Psychology, 22*, 815–826.

Deffenbacher, K.A., Bornstein, B.H., Penrod, S.D., & McGorty, E.K. (2004). A meta-analytic review of the effects of high stress on eyewitness memory. *Law and Human Behavior, 28*, 687–706.

Deffenbacher, K.A., & Loftus, E.F. (1982). Do jurors share a common understanding concerning eyewitness behavior? *Law and Human Behavior, 6*, 15–30. doi:10.1007/BF01049310.

Delaney, P.F., Goldman, J.A., King, J.S., & Nelson-Gray, R.O. (2015). Mental toughness, reinforcement sensitivity theory, and the five-factor model: Personality and directed forgetting. *Personality and Individual Differences, 83*, 180–184.

Della Salla, S. (1999). *Mind myths: Exploring everyday mysteries of the mind and brain.* Chichester, UK: Wiley.

Della Salla, S. (2007). *Tall tales about the mind and brain: Separating fact from fiction.* Oxford: Oxford University Press.

Della Salla, S., & Beyerstein, B. (2007). Introduction: The myth of 10% and other tall tales about the mind and the brain. In S. Della Salla (Ed.), *Tall tales about the mind and brain: Separating fact from fiction* (pp. xvii–xxxvii). Oxford: Oxford University Press.

Denny, E.R., & Hunt, R.R. (1992). Affective valence and memory in depression: Dissociation of recall and fragment completion. *Journal of Abnormal Psychology*, 101, 575–580. doi: 10.1037/0021-843X.101.3.575

Desmarais, S.L., Price, H.L., & Read, J.D. (2008). "Objection, your honor, television is not the relevant authority!" Crime drama portrayals of eyewitness issues. *Psychology, Crime and Law, 14*, 225–243. doi: 10.1080/10683160701652583.

Desmarais, S.L., & Read, J.D. (2011). After 30 years, what do we know about what jurors know? A meta-analytic review of lay knowledge regarding eyewitness factors. *Law and Human Behavior, 35*, 200–210.

Devenport, J.L., Kimbrough, C.D., & Cutler, B.L. (2009). Effectiveness of traditional safeguards against erroneous conviction arising from mistaken eyewitness identification. In B.L. Cutler (Ed.), *Expert testimony on the psychology of eyewitness identification* (pp. 51–68). New York: Oxford University Press.

Devenport, J.L., Stinson, V., Cutler, B.L., & Kravitz, D.A. (2002). How effective are the cross-examination and expert testimony safeguards? Jurors' perceptions of the suggestiveness and fairness of biased lineup procedures. *Journal of Applied Psychology, 87*, 1042–1054. doi: 10.1037//0021-9010.87.6.1042.

Dewhurst, S.A., Anderson, R.J., Cotter, G., Crust, L., & Clough, P.J. (2012). Identifying the cognitive basis of mental toughness: Evidence from the directed forgetting paradigm. *Personality and Individual Differences, 53*, 587–590. doi: 10.1016/j.paid.2012.04.036.

Diekelmann, S., Landolt, H.-P., Lahl, O., Born, J., & Wagner, U. (2008). Sleep loss produces false memories. *PLoS ONE, 3*(10), Article e3512. Retrieved from http://www.plosone.org/article/info%3Adoi%2F10.1371%2Fjournal.pone.0003512.

Diekelmann, S., Wilhelm, I., & Born, J. (2009). The whats and whens of sleep-dependent memory consolidation. *Sleep Medicine Reviews, 13*, 309–321. doi: 10.1016/j.smrv.2008.08.002.

Dietsche, B., Backes, H., Stratmann, M., Konrad, C., Kircher, T., & Krug, A. (2014). Altered neural function during episodic memory encoding and retrieval in major depression. *Human Brain Mapping, 35*, 4293–4302. doi: 10.1002/hbm.22475.

Dittrich, L. (2016). *Patient H.M.: A story of memory, madness, and family secrets.* New York: Random House.

Dobson, M., & Markham, R. (1993). Imagery ability and source monitoring: Implications for eyewitness memory. *British Journal of Psychology, 84*, 111–118.

Dorfman, J., Kihlstrom, J.F., Cork, R.C., & Misiaszek, J. (1995). Priming and recognition in ECT-induced amnesia. *Psychonomic Bulletin & Review, 2*, 244–248.

Dreisbach, G., & Bäuml, K.-H.T. (2014). Don't do it again! Directed forgetting of habits. *Psychological Science, 25*, 1242–1248. doi: 10.1177/0956797614526063.

Drizin, S.A., & Colgan, B.A. (2004). Tales from the juvenile confessions front. In G.D. Lassiter (Ed.), *Interrogations, confessions, and entrapment* (pp. 127–162). New York: Kluwer Academic.

Drizin, S.A., & Leo, R. (2004). The problem of false confessions in the post-DNA world. *North Carolina Law Review, 82, 891*–1007.

Drosopoulos, S., Schulze, C., Fischer, S., & Born, J. (2007). Sleep's function in the spontaneous recovery and consolidation of memories. *Journal of Experimental Psychology: General, 136*, 169–183. doi: 10.1037/0096-3445.136.2.169

Dube, E.F. (2000). Literacy, cultural familiarity, and "intelligence" as determinants of story recall. In U. Neisser & I.E. Hyman (Eds.), *Memory observed: Remembering in natural contexts* (2nd ed.) (pp. 426–443). New York: Worth.

Dubois, B., Feldman, H., Jacova, C., Cummings, J.L., DeKosky, S.T., Barberger-Gateau, P., ... & Scheltens, P. (2010). Revising the definition of Alzheimer's Disease: A new lexicon. *Lancet Neurology, 9*, 1118–1127.

Duff, M.C., Wszalek, T., Tranel, D., & Cohen, N.J. (2008). Successful life outcome and management of real-world memory demands despite profound anterograde amnesia. *Journal of Clinical and Experimental Neuropsychology, 30*, 931–945. doi: 10.1080/13803390801894681.

Dunlosky, J., & Metcalfe, J. (2009). *Metacognition.* Thousand Oaks, CA: Sage.

Dunlosky, J., & Nelson, T.O. (1992). Importance of the kind of cue for judgments of learning (JOL) and the delayed-JOL effect. *Memory & Cognition, 20*, 374–380.

Dysart, J.E., & Lindsay, R.C.L. (2007). Show-up identifications: Suggestive technique or reliable method? In R.C.L. Lindsay, D.F. Ross, J.D. Read, & M.P. Toglia (Eds.), *The handbook of eyewitness psychology (Vol. 2): Memory for people* (pp. 137–153). Mahwah, NJ: Erlbaum.

Dyson, S.C., & Barker, R.A. (2011). Cell-based therapies for Parkinson's disease. *Expert Review of Neurotherapeutics, 11*, 831–844.

Ebbinghaus, H. (1885/1964). *Memory: A contribution to experimental psychology* (H.A. Ruger, Trans.). New York: Dover.

Ehresman, C. (2014). From rendering to remembering: Art therapy for people with Alzheimer's Disease. *International Journal of Art Therapy, 19*, 43–51. doi: 10.1080/17454832.2013.819023

Eich, E. (2007). Context: Mood, memory and the concept of context. In H.L. Roediger, Y. Dudai, & S.M. Fitzpatrick, *Science of memory: Concepts* (pp. 107–110). New York: Oxford University Press.

Eich, E., & Metcalfe, J. (1989). Mood-dependent memory for internal versus external events. *Journal of Experimental Psychology: Learning, Memory, and Cognition, 15*, 443–455.

Eichenbaum, H. (2012). *The cognitive neuroscience of memory* (2nd ed.). New York: Oxford.

Einstein, G.O., & McDaniel, M.A. (2014). Prospective memory and aging: When it becomes difficult and what you can do about it. In T.J. Perfect & D.S. Lindsay (Eds.), *The SAGE handbook of applied memory* (pp. 37–58). Los Angeles, CA: SAGE.

Er, N. (2003). A new flashbulb memory model applied to the Marmara earthquake. *Applied Cognitive Psychology, 17*, 503–517.

Erdelyi, M.H. (1985). *Psychoanalysis: Freud's cognitive psychology*. New York: Freeman.

Erdelyi, M.H. (1994). Hypnotic hypermnesia: The empty set of hypermnesia. *International Journal of Clinical and Experimental Hypnosis, 42*, 379–390.

Erdelyi, M.H. (1990). Repression, reconstruction, and defense: History and integration of the psychoanalytic and experimental frameworks. In J.L. Singer (Ed.), *Repression and dissociation*. Chicago: University of Chicago Press.

Erdelyi, M.H. (2006). The unified theory of repression. *Behavioral and Brain Sciences, 29*, 499–551.

Ericsson, K.A. (2003). Exceptional memorizers: Made, not born. *Trends in Cognitive Sciences, 7*, 233–235. doi: 10.1016/S1364-6613(03)00103-7

Ericsson, K.A. (2006). The influence of experience and deliberate practice on the development of superior expert performance. In K.A. Ericsson, N. Charness, P. Feltovich, & R.R. Hoffman (Eds.), *Cambridge handbook of expertise and expert performance* (pp. 685–706). Cambridge, UK: Cambridge University Press.

Ericsson, K.A., & Chase, W.G. (1982). Exceptional memory. *American Scientist, 70*, 607–615.

Ericsson, K.A., Chase, W.G., & Faloon, S. (1980). Acquisition of a memory skill. *Science, 208*, 1181–1182.

Ericsson, K.A., Delaney, P.F., Weaver, G., & Mahadevan, R. (2004). Uncovering the structure of a memorist's superior "basic" memory capacity. *Cognitive Psychology, 49*, 191–237. doi: 10.1016/j.cogpsych.2004.02.001

Ericsson, K.A., & Faivre, I.A. (1988). What's exceptional about exceptional abilities? In L.K. Obler & D. Fein (Eds.), *The exceptional brain* (pp. 436–473). New York: Guilford.

Ericsson, K.A., & Kintsch, W. (1995). Long-term working memory. *Psychological Review, 102*, 211–245.

Ericsson, K.A., & Moxley, J.H. (2014). Experts' superior memory: From accumulation of chunks to building memory skills that mediate improved performance and learning. In T.J. Perfect & D.S. Lindsay (Eds.), *The SAGE handbook of applied memory* (pp. 404–420). Los Angeles, CA: SAGE.

Everaert, J., Duyck, W., & Koster, E.H.W. (2014). Attention, interpretation, and memory biases in subclinical depression: A proof-of-principle test of the combined cognitive biases hypothesis. *Emotion, 14*, 331–340. doi: 10.1037/a0035250.

Faigman, D.L., Blumenthal, J., Cheng, E., Mnookin, J., Murphy, E., & Sanders, J. (2014). *Modern scientific evidence: The law and science of expert testimony*. Eagan, MN: Thomson Reuters/West.

Faimon, B., O'Neil, K., & Bornstein, B.H. (2005). Recovered memory at trial: Effects of abuse type and manner of recovery. In L.M. Stoneham (Ed.), *Advances in sociology research, (Vol. 2)* (pp. 233–251). Hauppauge, NY: Nova Science Publishers.

Fawcett, J.M., Taylor, T.L., & Nadel, L. (2013). Event-method directed forgetting: Forgetting a video segment is more effortful than remembering it. *Acta Psychologica, 144*, 332–343. doi: 10.1016/j.actpsy.2013.07.005.

Feldman, H.H., & Jacova, C. (2005). Mild cognitive impairment. *American Journal of Geriatric Psychiatry, 13*, 645–655.

Feldman-Summers, S., & Pope, K. S. (1994). The experience of "forgetting" childhood abuse: A national survey of psychologists. *Journal of Consulting and Clinical Psychology, 62*, 636–639.

Fillmore, M.T., Kelly, T.H., Rush, C.R., & Hays, L. (2001). Retrograde facilitation of memory by triazolam: Effects on automatic processes. *Psychopharmacology, 158*, 314–321. doi: 10.1007/s002130100873.

Fischer, S., & Born, J. (2009). Anticipated reward enhances offline learning during sleep. *Journal of Experimental Psychology: Learning, Memory, and Cognition, 35*, 1586–1593.

Fisher, R.P., & Schreiber, N. (2007). Interview protocols to improve eyewitness memory. In M.P. Toglia, J.D. Read, D.F. Ross, & R.C.L. Lindsay (Eds.), *Handbook of eyewitness psychology, Vol. 1* (pp. 53–80). Mahwah, NJ: Erlbaum.

Fleming, S.M., & Dolan, R.J. (2014). The neural basis of metacognitive ability. In S.M. Fleming & C.D. Frith (Eds.), *The cognitive neuroscience of metacognition* (pp. 245–265). Berlin: Springer-Verlag. doi: 10.1007/978-3-642-45190-4_11.

Fleming, S.M., & Frith, C.D. (2014). Metacognitive neuroscience: An introduction. In S.M. Fleming & C.D. Frith (Eds.), *The cognitive neuroscience of metacognition* (pp. 1–6). Berlin: Springer-Verlag. doi: 10.1007/978-3-642-45190-4_1.

Foer, J. (2011). *Moonwalking with Einstein: The art and science of remembering everything*. New York: Penguin.

Forgas, J.P. (1995). Mood and judgment: The Affect Infusion Model (AIM). *Psychological Bulletin, 116*, 39–66.

Forgas, J.P. (2010). Affect in legal and forensic settings: The cognitive benefits of not being too happy. In B.H. Bornstein & R.L. Wiener (Eds.), *Emotion and the law: Psychological perspectives* (pp. 13–44). New York: Springer.

Forgas, J.P., Goldenberg, L., & Unkelbach, C. (2009). Can bad weather improve your memory? An unobtrusive field study of mood effects on eyewitness memory. *Journal of Experimental Social Psychology, 45*, 254–257.

Forgas, J.P., Vargas, P., & Laham, S. (2005). Mood effects on eyewitness memory: Affective influences on susceptibility to misinformation. *Journal of Experimental Social Psychology, 41*, 574–588.

Forrest, K., Woody, W. D., Brady, S., Batterman, K., Stastny, B., & Bruns, J. (2012). False-evidence ploys and interrogations: Mock jurors' perceptions of ploy type, deception, coercion, and justification. *Behavioral Sciences and the Law, 30*, 342–364.

ForsterLee, R., Horowitz, I.A., Ho, R., ForsterLee, L., & McGovern, A. (1999). Community members' perceptions of evidence: The effects of gender in a recovered memory civil trial. *Journal of Applied Psychology, 84*, 484–495.

Fournet, N., Roulin, J-L., Vallet, F., Beaudoin, M., Agrigoroaei, S., Paignon, A., ... & Desrichard, O. (2012). Evaluating short-term and working memory in older adults: French normative data. *Aging & Mental Health, 16*, 922–930. doi: 10.1080/13607863.2012.674487.

Frazier v. Cupp, 394 U.S. 731 (1969).

French, C.C., & Wilson, K. (2007). Cognitive factors underlying paranormal beliefs and experiences. In S. Della Salla (Ed.), *Tall tales about the mind and brain: Separating fact from fiction* (pp. 3–22). Oxford: Oxford University Press.

Frenda, S.J., Patihis, L., Loftus, E.F., Lewis, H.C., & Fenn, K.M. (2014). Sleep deprivation and false memories. *Psychological Science, 25*, 1674–1681. doi: 10.1177/0956797614534694

Freud, S. (1901/1960). *The psychopathology of everyday life.* New York: W.W. Norton.

Freud, S. (1928/1961). *The future of an illusion* (orig. published as *Die Zukunft einer Illusion*, J. Strachey, transl.). New York: W.W. Norton.

Freud, S., & Breuer, J. (1895/2000). *Studies on hysteria.* New York: Basic Books.

Friel, B. (1981). *Translations.* New York: Farrar, Straus and Giroux.

Friend, R. (1990). A puzzling misinterpretation of the Asch "conformity" study. *European Journal of Social Psychology, 20*, 29–44.

Frijda, N.H. (1994). Varieties of affect: Emotions and episodes, moods, and sentiments. In P. Ekman & R.J. Davidson (Eds.), *The nature of emotion: Fundamental questions* (pp. 59–67). New York: Oxford University Press.

Gafner, G. (2010). *Techniques of hypnotic induction.* Bethel, CT: Crown House Publishing.

Gais, S., & Born, J. (2004). Declarative memory consolidation: Mechanisms acting during human sleep. *Learning & Memory, 11*, 679–685. doi: 10.1101/lm.80504.

Gais, S., & Lucas, B., Born, J. (2006). Sleep after learning aids memory recall. *Learning & Memory, 13*, 259–262. doi: 1.1101/lm.132106.

Gallo, D.A. (2010). False memories and fantastic beliefs: 15 years of the DRM illusion. *Memory & Cognition, 38*, 833–848. doi:10.3758/MC.38.7.833.

Garde-Hansen, J., Hoskins, A., & Reading, A. (2009). *Save as ... digital memories.* New York: Palgrave Macmillan.

Garrett, B. (2010). The substance of false confessions. *Stanford Law Review, 62*, 1051–1119.

Garrett, B. (2011). *Convicting the innocent: Where criminal prosecutors go wrong.* Cambridge, MA: Harvard University Press.

Garry, M., Loftus, E.F., & Brown, S.W. (1994). Memory: A river runs through it. *Consciousness and Cognition, 3*, 438–451.

Garry, M., Loftus, E.F., Brown, S.W., & DuBreuil, S.C. (1997). Womb with a view: Beliefs about memory, repression and memory-recovery. In D.G. Payne & F.G. Conrad (Eds.), *Intersections in basic and applied memory research* (pp. 233–236). Hillsdale, NJ: Erlbaum.

Garry, M., Manning, C. G., Loftus, E. F., & Sherman, S. J. (1996). Imagination inflation: Imagining a childhood event inflates confidence that it occurred. *Psychonomic Bulletin & Review, 3*, 208–214.

Garven, S., Wood, J.M., & Malpass, R.S. (2000). Allegations of wrongdoing: The effects of reinforcement on children's mundane and fantastic claims. *Journal of Applied Psychology, 85*, 38–49.

Garven, S., Wood, J.M., Malpass, R.S., & Shaw, J.S. (1998). More than suggestion: The effect of interviewing techniques from the McMartin Preschool case. *Journal of Applied Psychology, 83*, 347–359.

Gauthier, S., Reisberg, B., Zaudig, M, Petersen, R.C., Ritchie, K., Broich, K., ... & Winblad, B. (2006). Mild cognitive impairment. *Lancet, 367*, 1262–1270.

Gay, P. (1988). *Freud: A life for our time.* New York: W.W. Norton.

Geda, Y.E., Topazian, H.M., Roberts, L.A., Roberts, R.O., Knopman, D.S., Pankratz, V.S., ... & Petersen, R.C. (2011). Engaging in cognitive activities, aging, and mild cognitive impairment: A population-based study. *Journal of Neuropsychiatry and Clinical Neuroscience, 23*, 149–154. doi: 10.1176/appi.neuropsych.23.2.149.

Genova, L. (2007). *Still Alice.* New York: Gallery Books.

Geraerts, E. (2012). Cognitive underpinnings of recovered memories of childhood abuse. In R.F. Belli (Ed.), *True and false recovered memories: Toward a reconciliation of the debate* (pp. 175–191). doi:; 10.1007/978-1-4614-1195-6_6.

Geraerts, E., Bernstein, D.M., Merckelbach, H., Linders, C., Raymaekers, L., & Loftus, E.F. (2008). Lasting false beliefs and their behavioral consequences. *Psychological Science, 19*, 749–753.

Geraerts, E., & McNally, R.J. (2008). Forgetting unwanted memories: Directed forgetting and thought suppression methods. *Acta Psychologica, 127*, 614–622. doi: 10.1016/j.actpsy.2007.11.003.

Geraerts, E., Raymaekers, L., & Merckelbach, H. (2008). Recovered memories of childhood sexual abuse: Current findings and their legal implications. *Legal and Criminological Psychology, 13*, 165–176.

Geraerts, E., Schooler, J. W., Merckelbach, H., Jelicic, M., Hauer, B. J. A., & Ambadar, Z. (2007). The reality of recovered memories: Corroborating continuous and discontinuous memories of childhood sexual abuse. *Psychological Science, 18*, 564–568.

Gerrans, P. (2014). Pathologies of hyperfamiliarity in dreams, delusions and déjà vu. *Frontiers in Psychology, 5* (Art. 97), 1–10. doi: 10.3389/fpsyg.2014.00097

Gerrie, M.P., Garry, M., & Loftus, E.F. (2005). False memories. In N. Brewer & K.D. Williams (Eds.), *Psychology and law: An empirical perspective* (pp. 222–253). New York: Guilford Press.

Gibbons, D.E., & Lynn, S.J. (2010). Hypnotic inductions: A primer. In S.J. Lynn, J.W. Rhue, & I. Kirsch (Eds.), *Handbook of clinical hypnosis* (2nd ed.) (pp. 267–291). Washington, DC: American Psychological Association.

Gibbs, R.B., Yu, J., & Cotman, C.W. (1987). Entorhinal transplants and spatial memory abilities in rats. *Behavioural Brain Research, 26*, 29–35.

Giles, D. (2003). *Media psychology*. Mahwah, NJ: Erlbaum.

Giles, D. (2010). *Psychology of the media*. New York: Palgrave Macmillan.

Golding, J.M., Dunlap, E., & Hodell, E.C. (2009). Jurors' perceptions of children's eyewitness testimony. In B.L. Bottoms, C.J. Najdowski, & G.S. Goodman (Eds.), *Children as victims, witnesses, and offenders: Psychological science and the law* (pp. 188–208). New York, NY: Guilford Press.

Golding, J.M., Sanchez, R.P., & Sego, S.A. (1996). Do you believe in repressed memories? *Professional Psychology: Research and Practice, 27*, 429–437.

Golding, J.M., Sanchez, R.P., & Sego, S.A. (1999). Age factors affecting the believability of repressed memories of child sexual assault. *Law and Human Behavior, 23*, 257–268.

Golding, J.M., Sego, S.A., & Sanchez, R.P. (1999). The effect of multiple childhood sexual assaults on mock-jurors' perceptions of repressed memories. *Behavioral Sciences and the Law, 17*, 483–493.

Golding, J.M., Sego, S.A., Sanchez, R.P., & Hasemann, D.M. (1995). The believability of repressed memories. *Law and Human Behavior, 19*, 569–592.

Goldstein, A.G., Chance, J.E., & Schneller, G.R. (1989). Frequency of eyewitness identification in criminal cases: A survey of prosecutors. *Bulletin of the Psychonomic Society, 27*, 71–74.

Gomes, C.F.A., Cohen, B.R., Desai, A., Brainerd, C.J., & Reyna, V.F. (2014). Aging and false memory: Fuzzy-trace theory and the elderly eyewitness. In M.P. Toglia, D.F. Ross, J. Pozzulo, & E. Pica (Eds.), *The elderly eyewitness in court* (pp. 137–166). New York: Psychology Press.

Gonsalves, B., Reber, P.J., Gitelman, D.R., Parrish, T.B., Mesulam, M.-M., & Paller, K.A. (2004). Neural evidence that vivid imagining can lead to false remembering. *Psychological Science, 15*, 655–660.

Goodman, G.S., Ghetti, S., Quas, J.A., Edelstein, R.S., Alexander, K.W., Redlich, A.D., … & Jones, D.P.H. (2003). A prospective study of memory for child sexual abuse: New findings relevant to the repressed-memory controversy. *Psychological Science, 14,* 113–118.

Gothard, S., & Ivker, N. (2000). The evolving law of alleged delayed memories of childhood sexual abuse. *Child Maltreatment, 5,* 176–189.

Gouvier, D.W., Prestholdt, P.H., & Warner, M.S. (1988). A survey of common misconceptions about brain injury and recovery. *Archives of Clinical Neuropsychology, 3,* 331–343.

Granhag, P., & Strömwall, L. (2004). *The detection of deception in forensic contexts*. Cambridge, UK: Cambridge University Press.

Granhag, P.A., Strömwall, L.A., & Hartwig, M. (2005). Eyewitness testimony: Tracing the beliefs of Swedish legal professionals. *Behavioral Sciences and the Law, 23*, 709–727. doi: 10.1002/bsl.670

Gray, B.B., & Mundell, E.J. (2013, November 14). FDA approves implanted brain stimulator for epilepsy. *HealthDay*. Available at http://consumer.healthday.com/cognitive-health-information-26/brain-health-news-80/fda-approves-implanted-brain-stimulator-for-epilepsy-682196.html

Greenberg, M., Dyen, S., & Elliott, S. (2013). The public's preparedness: Self-reliance, flashbulb memories, and conservative values. *American Journal of Public Health, 103(6)*, e85–91. doi: 10.2105/AJPH.2012.301198

Greene, E., & Bornstein, B.H. (2003). *Determining damages: The psychology of jury awards*. Washington, DC: American Psychological Association.

Griep, M.A., & Mikasen, M.L. (2009). *ReAction!: Chemistry in the movies*. New York: Oxford University Press.

Griggs, R.A. (2015). The disappearance of independence in textbook coverage of Asch's social pressure experiments. *Teaching of Psychology, 42*, 137–142.

Grisham, J. (2010). *The confession*. New York: Doubleday.

Gross, S.R., Jacoby, K., Matheson, D.J., Montgomery, N., & Patil, S. (2005). Exonerations in the united States 1989 through 2003. *Journal of Criminal Law & Criminology, 95*, 523–560.

Gruber, O., Zilles, D., Kennel, J., Gruber, E., & Falkai, P. (2011). A systematic experimental neuropsychological investigation of the functional integrity of working memory circuits in major depression. *European Archives of Psychiatry and Clinical Neuroscience, 261*, 179–184. doi: 10.1007/s00406-010-0165-3

Gudjonsson, G.H. (1984). A new scale of interrogative suggestibility. *Personality and Individual Differences, 5*, 303–314.

Gudjonsson, G. (2003). *The psychology of interrogations and confessions: A handbook*. Chichester, England: John Wiley and Sons.

Gudjonsson, G. (2010). The psychology of false confessions: A review of the current evidence. In G.D. Lassiter & C. Meissner (Eds.), *Police interrogations and false confessions: Current research, practice, and policy recommendations* (pp. 31–47). Washington, DC: American Psychological Association.

Gudjonsson, G., Sigurdsson, J.F., Einarsson, E., Bragason, O.O., & Newton, A.K. (2010). Inattention, hyperactivity/impulsivity and antisocial personality disorder: Which is the best predictor of false confessions? *Personality and Individual Differences, 48*, 720–724.

Guilmette, T.J., & Paglia, M.F. (2004). The public's misconceptions about traumatic brain injury: A follow up survey. *Archives of Clinical Neuropsychology, 19*, 183–189. doi: 10.1016/S0887-6177(03)00025-8.

Hambrick, D.Z., Salthouse, T.A., & Meinz, E.J. (1999). Predictors of crossword puzzle proficiency and moderators of age-cognition relations. *Journal of Experimental Psychology: General, 128*, 131–164.

Hamlat, E.J., Connolly, S.L., Hamilton, J.L., Stange, J.P., Abramson, L.Y., & Alloy, L.B. (2015). Rumination and overgeneral autobiographical memory in adolescents: An integration of cognitive vulnerabilities to depression. *Journal of Youth and Adolescence, 44*, 806–818. doi: 10.1007/s10964-014-0090-2.

Bibliography

Hansson, J-A., & Hagberg, B. (2005). Determinant factors contributing to variations in memory performance in centenarians. *International Journal of Aging and Human Development, 60*, 19–51. doi: 10.2190/WFUP-2J25-LWQF-PQ3W.

Harnishfeger, K.K., & Pope, R.S. (1996). Intending to forget: The development of cognitive inhibition in directed forgetting. *Journal of Experimental Child Psychology, 62*, 292–315. doi:10.1006/jecp.1996.0032.

Hasel, L., & Kassin, S. (2009). On the presumption of evidentiary independence: Can confessions corrupt eyewitness identifications? *Psychological Science, 20*, 122–126.

Hasselmo, M.E. (1999). Neuromodulation: Acetylcholine and memory consolidation. *Trends in Cognitive Science, 3*, 351–359.

Hausenblas, H.A., Campbell, A., Menzel, J.E., Doughty, J., Levine, M., & Thompson, J.K. (2013). Media effects of experimental presentation of the ideal physique on eating disorder symptoms: A meta-analysis of laboratory studies. *Clinical Psychology Review, 33*, 168–181.

Hawkins, P. (2015). *The girl on the train*. New York: Riverhead Books.

Heaps, C., & Nash, M. (2001). Comparing recollective experience in true and false autobiographical memories. *Journal of Experimental Psychology: Learning, Memory, & Cognition, 27*, 920–930.

Henkel, L.A. (2014). Memory trust and distrust in elderly eyewitnesses: To what extent do older adults doubt their memories? In M.P. Toglia, D.F. Ross, J. Pozzulo., & E. Pica (Eds.), *The elderly eyewitness in court* (pp. 232–262). New York: Psychology Press.

Henkel, L.A., & Coffman, K.J. (2004). Memory distortions in coerced false confessions: A source monitoring framework analysis. *Applied Cognitive Psychology, 18*, 567–588.

Henkel, L., Coffman, K., & Dailey, E. (2008). A survey of people's attitudes and beliefs about false confessions. *Behavioral Sciences and the Law, 26*, 555–584. doi: 10.1002/bsl.826.

Hennig-Fast, K., Meister, F., Frodl, T., Beraldi, A., Padberg, F., … & Meindl, T. (2008). A case of persistent retrograde amnesia following a dissociative fugue: Neuropsychological and neurofunctional underpinnings of loss of autobiographical memory and self-awareness. *Neuropsychologia, 46*, 2993–3005. doi: 10.1016/j. neuropsychologia.2008.06.014.

Herrmann, D., & Gruneberg, M. (2008). *SuperMemory II: The latest and best way to use memory successfully*. Strategic Book Publishing.

Hertzog, C., & Dixon, R.A. (1994). Metacognitive development in adulthood and old age. In J. Metcalfe & A.P. Shimamura (Eds.), *Metacognition: Knowing about knowing* (pp. 227–251). Cambridge, MA: MIT Press.

Hertzog, C., & Pearman, A. (2014). Memory complaints in adulthood and old age. In T.J. Perfect & D.S. Lindsay (Eds.), *The SAGE handbook of applied memory* (pp. 423–443). Los Angeles, CA: SAGE.

Hilts, P.J. (1995). *Memory's ghost: The nature of memory and the strange tale of Mr. M.* New York: Touchstone.

Hirst, W., Phelps, E.A., Buckner, R.L., Budson, A.E., Cuc, A., Gabrieli, J.D.E., … & Vaidya, C.J. (2009). Long-term memory for the terrorist attack of September 11:

Flashbulb memories, event memories, and the factors that influence their retention. *Journal of Experimental Psychology: General, 138*, 161–176.

Hodges, H., Allen, Y., Sinden, J., Mitchell, S.N., Arendt, T., Lantos, P.L., & Gray, J.A. (1991). The effects of cholinergic drugs and cholinergic-rich foetal neural transplants on alcohol-induced deficits in radial maze performance in rats. *Behavioural Brain Research, 43*, 7–28.

Hokkanen, L., Rantala, L., Remes, A.M., Härkönen, B., Viramo, P., & Winblad, I. (2003). Dance/movement therapeutic methods in management of dementia. *Journal of the American Geriatrics Society, 51*, 576–577.

Holcomb, M.J. & Jacquin, K.M. (2007). Juror perceptions of child eyewitness testimony in a sexual abuse trial. *Journal of Child Sexual Abuse: Research, Treatment, & Program Innovations for Victims, Survivors, & Offenders, 16*, 79–95. doi:10.1300/J070v16n02_05.

Holmes, D.S. (1990). The evidence for repression: An examination of sixty years of research. In J.L. Singer (Ed.), *Repression and dissociation* (pp. 85–102). Chicago, IL: University of Chicago Press.

Hooper, S.R. (2006). Myths and misconceptions about traumatic brain injury: Endorsements by school psychologists. *Exceptionality, 14*, 171–182. doi: 10.1207/s15327035ex1403_5

Horgan, A.J., Russano, M.B., Meissner, C.A., & Evans, J.R. (2012). Minimization and maximization techniques: Assessing the perceived consequences of confessing and confession diagnosticity. *Psychology, Crime & Law, 18*, 65–78. doi: 10.1080/1068316X.2011.561801

Horhota, M., Lineweaver, T., Ositelu, M., Summers, K., & Hertzog, C. (2012). Young and older adults' beliefs about effective ways to mitigate age-related memory decline. *Psychology and Aging, 27*, 293–304. doi: 10.1037/a0026088

Hornstein, S.L., Brown, A.S., & Mulligan, N.W. (2003). Long-term flashbulb memory for learning of Princess Diana's death. *Memory, 11*, 293–306.

Horselenberg, R., Merckelbach, H., & Josephs S. (2003). Individual differences and false confessions: A conceptual replication of Kassin and Kiechel (1996). *Psychology, Crime & Law, 9*, 1–8.

Hourihan, K.L., & Benjamin, A.S. (2014). State-based metacognition: How time of day affects the accuracy of metamemory. *Memory, 22*, 553–558. doi: 10.1080/09658211.2013.804091

Houston, K.A., Hope, L., Memon, A., Read, J.D. (2013). Expert testimony on eyewitness evidence: In search of common sense. *Behavioral Sciences & the Law, 31*, 637–651.

Houston, K.A., Meissner, C.A., & Evans, J.R. (2014). Psychological processes underlying true and false confessions. In R. Bull (Ed.), *Investigative interviewing* (pp. 19–34). New York: Springer. doi: 10.1007/978-1-4614-9642-7_2.

Howard, T., & Donnelly, S. (1999). The media and the brain. In S. Della Salla (Ed.), *Mind myths: Exploring popular assumptions about the mind and brain* (pp. 241–253). Chichester, UK: Wiley.

Hubbard, T.L. (2010). Auditory imagery: Empirical findings. *Psychological Bulletin, 136*, 302–329. doi: 10.1037/a0018436

Hudon, C., Belleville, S., & Gauthier, S. (2009). The assessment of recognition memory using the remember/know procedure in amnestic mild cognitive impairment and probable Alzheimer's Disease. *Brain and Cognition, 70*, 171–179.

Hughes, R.A., Barrett, R.J., & Ray, O.S. (1970). Retrograde amnesia in rats increases as a function of ECS-test interval and ECS intensity. *Physiology & Behavior, 5*, 27–30.

Hunt, E., & Love, T. (2000). The second mnemonist. In U. Neisser & I.E. Hyman (Eds.), *Memory observed: Remembering in natural contexts* (2nd ed.) (pp. 487–495). New York: Worth.

Hunt, M. (2007). *The story of psychology*. New York: Anchor Books.

Hunter, I.M.L. (1977). An exceptional memory. *British Journal of Psychology, 68*, 155–164.

Hupbach, A., & Sahakyan, L. (2014). Adaditional boundary condition for list-method directed forgetting: The effect of presentation format. *Journal of Experimental Psychology: Learning, Memory, and Cognition, 40*, 596–601. doi: 10.1037/a0034978.

Hux, K., Schram, C.D., & Goeken, T. (2006). Misconceptions about brain injury: A survey replication study. *Brain Injury, 20*, 547–553. doi: 10.1080/02699050600676784.

Hyman, I.E. (1994). Conversational remembering: Story recall with a peer versus for an experimenter. *Applied Cognitive Psychology, 8*, 49–66.

Hyman, I.E., & Billings, F.J. (1998). Individual differences and the creation of false childhood memories. *Memory, 6*, 1–20.

Hyman, I.E., Husband, T.H., & Billings, F.J. (1995). False memories of childhood experiences. *Applied Cognitive Psychology, 9*, 181–197.

Hyman, I.E., & Loftus, E.F. (2002). False childhood memories and eyewitness memory errors. In M.L. Eisen, J.A. Quas, & G.S. Goodman (Eds.), *Memory and suggestibility in the forensic interview*. Mahwah, NJ: Erlbaum.

Jager, T., Bazner, H., Kliegel, M., Szabo, K., Hennerici, M.G. (2009). The transience and nature of cognitive impairments in transient global amnesia: a meta-analysis. *Journal of Clinical & Experimental Neuropsychology, 31*, 8–19.

Jaffe, E. (2013). Building a fearless mind. *APS Observer, 26(8)*, 20–24.

James, S.D. (2011, September 28). Ex-football player's life is deleted by retrograde amnesia. *ABC News*. Available at http://abcnews.go.com/Health/football-player-scott-bolzans-life-deleted-irreversible-amnesia/story?id=14616045.

James, W. (1890). *Principles of psychology*. New York: Henry Holt.

Jelicic, M., Bonke, B., Wolters, G., & Phaf, R.H. (1992). Implicit memory for words presented during anaesthesia. *European Journal of Cognitive Psychology, 4*, 71–80.

Jelinek, L., Hottenrott, B., Randjbar, S., Peters, M.J., & Moritz, S. (2009). Visual false memories in post-traumatic stress disorder (PTSD). *Journal of Behavior Therapy and Experimental Psychiatry, 40*, 374–383. doi:10.1016/j.jbtep.2009.02.003

Jenkins, J.G., & Dallenbach, K.M. (1924). Obliviscence during sleep and waking. *American Journal of Psychology, 35*, 605–612.

Jin, Y-S., Ryan, E.B., & Anas, A.P. (2001). Korean beliefs about everyday memory and aging for self and others. *International Journal of Aging and Human Development, 52*, 103–113.

Johnson, M.K., Hashtroudi, S., & Lindsay, D.S. (1993). Source monitoring. *Psychological Bulletin, 114*, 3–28.

Johnson, M.K., Kahan, T.L., & Raye, C.L. (1984). Dreams and reality monitoring. *Journal of Experimental Psychology: General, 113,* 329–344. doi:10.1037/0096-3445.113.3.329.

Johnson, M.K., Raye, C.L., Mitchell, K.J., & Ankudowich, E. (2012). The cognitive neuroscience of true and false memories. In R.F. Belli (Ed.), *True and false recovered memories: Toward a reconciliation of the debate* (pp. 15–52). doi: 10.1007/978-1-4614-1195-6_2.

Joormann, J., Levens, S.M., & Gotlib, I.H. (2011). Sticky thoughts: Depression and rumination are associated with difficulties manipulating emotional material in working memory. *Psychological Science, 22,* 979–983.

Ju, Y.E., Lucey, B.P., & Holtzman, D.M. (2014). Sleep and Alzheimer disease pathology—a birectional relationship. *Nature Reviews Neurology, 10,* 115–119. doi: 10.1038/nrneurol.2013.269

Kang, J.E., Lim, M.M., Bateman, R.J., Lee, J.J., Smyth, L.P., Cirrito, J.R., ... & Holtzman, D.M. (2009). Amyloid-β dynamics are regulated by orexin and the sleep-wake cycle. *Science, 326,* 1005–1007. doi: 10.1162/science.1180962.

Kanno, H. (2013). Regenerative therapy for neuronal diseases with transplantation of somatic stem cells. *World Journal of Stem Cells, 5,* 163–171. doi: 10.4252/wjsc.v5.i4.163.

Kapur, N., & Abbott, P. (1996). A study of recovery of memory function in a case of witnessed functional retrograde amnesia. *Cognitive Neuropsychiatry, 1,* 247–258.

Kapur, N., Glisky, E.L., & Wilson, B.A. (2004). Technological memory aids for people with memory deficits. *Neuropsychological Rehabilitation, 14,* 41–60. doi: 10.1080/09602010343000138.

Karam, G., & Itani, L. (2014). Depression, anxiety, and memory impairment among geriatric inpatient subjects. *International Journal of Geriatric Psychiatry, 29,* 987–990. doi: 10.1002/gps.4127.

Kassin, S. (2007). Coerced-internalized false confessions. In M.P. Toglia, J.D. Read, D.F. Ross, & R.C.L. Lindsay (Eds.), *Handbook of eyewitness psychology (Vol. 1): Memory for events.* Mahwah, NJ: Erlbaum.

Kassin, S. (2015). The social psychology of false confessions. *Social Issues and Policy Review, 9,* 25–51.

Kassin, S.M., & Barndollar, K.A. (1992). The psychology of eyewitness testimony: A comparison of experts and prospective jurors. *Journal of Applied Social Psychology, 22,* 1241–1249. doi:10.1111/j.1559-1816.1992.tb00948.x.

Kassin, S.M., Ellsworth, P.C., & Smith, V.L. (1989). The "general acceptance" of psychological research on eyewitness testimony: A survey of the experts. *American Psychologist, 44,* 1089–1098.

Kassin, S.M., Drizin, S., Grisso, T., Gudjonsson, G., Leo, R., & Redlich, A. (2010). Police-induced confessions: Risk factors and recommendations. *Law and Human Behavior, 34,* 3–38.

Kassin, S.M., & Gudjonsson, G.H. (2004). The psychology of confessions: A review of the literature and issues. *Psychological Science in the Public Interest, 5,* 33–67.

Kassin, S.M., & Kiechel, K.L. (1996). The social psychology of false confessions: Compliance, internalization, and confabulation. *Psychological Science, 7,* 125–128.

Kassin, S.M., Leo, R.A., Crocker, C., & Holland, L. (2003). Videotaping interrogations: Does it enhance the jury's ability to distinguish between true and false confessions? Paper presented at the Psychology & Law International Interdisciplinary Conference, Edinburgh, Scotland.

Kassin, S., Leo, R., Meissner, C., Richman, K., Colwell, L., Leach, A.-M. & La Fon, D. (2007). Police interviewing and interrogation: A self-report survey of police practices and beliefs. *Law and Human Behavior, 31,* 381–400.

Kassin, S., Meissner, C., & Norwick, R. (2005). "I'd know a false confession if I saw one": A comparative study of college students and police investigators. *Law and Human Behavior, 29,* 211–227.

Kassin, S., & Neumann, K. (1997). On the power of confession evidence: An experimental test of the fundamental difference hypothesis. *Law and Human Behavior, 21,* 469–484.

Kassin, S., & Sukel, H. (1997). Coerced confessions and the jury: An experimental test of the "harmless error" rule. *Law and Human Behavior, 21,* 27–46.

Kassin, S.M., Tubb, V.A., Hosch, H.M., & Memon, A. (2001). On the "general acceptance" of eyewitness testimony research: A new survey of the experts. *American Psychologist, 56,* 405–416. doi:10.1037//0003-066X.56.5.405.

Kelley, C.M., & Jacoby, L.L. (2000). Recollection and familiarity: Process-dissociation. In E. Tulving & F.I.M. Craik (Eds.), *The Oxford handbook of memory* (pp. 215–228). Oxford: Oxford University Press.

Kendall-Tackett, K. A., Williams, L. M., & Finkelhor, D. (1993). Impact of sexual abuse on children: A review and synthesis of recent empirical studies. *Psychological Bulletin, 113,* 164–180.

Kensinger, E.A. (2008). Age differences in memory for arousing and nonarousing emotional words. *Journal of Gerontology: Psychological Sciences, 63B,* P13–P18.

Kensinger, E.A., & Schacter, D.L. (2006). When the Red Sox shocked the Yankees: Comparing negative and positive memories. Psychonomic Bulletin & Review, 13, 757–763.

Key, H.G., Warren, A.R., & Ross, D.F. (1996). Perceptions of repressed memories: A reappraisal. *Law and Human Behavior*, 20, 555–563.

Kirby, D.A. (2011). *Lab coats in Hollywood: Science, scientists, and cinema.* Cambridge, MA: MIT Press.

Klaver, J.R., Lee, Z., & Rose, V.G. (2008). Effect of personality, interrogation techniques and plausibility in an experimental false confession paradigm. *Legal & Criminological Psychology, 13,* 71–88.

Kleinsmith, L.J., & Kaplan, S. (1963). Paired-associate learning as a function of arousal and interpolated interval. *Journal of Experimental Psychology, 65,* 190–193.

Klemfuss, J.Z., & Ceci, S.J. (2012). Legal and psychological perspectives on children's competence to testify in court. *Developmental Review, 32,* 268–286.

Knapskog, A.-B., Barca, M.L., & Engedal, K. (2014). Prevalence of depression among memory clinic patients as measured by the Cornell Scale of Depression in Dementia. *Aging & Mental Health, 18,* 579–587. doi: 10.1080/13607863.2013.827630.

Kopelman, M.D. (1999). Varieties of false memory. *Cognitive Neuropsychology, 16,* 197–214.

Kopelman, M.D. (2002). Disorders of memory. *Brain, 125*, 2152–2190.

Kornell, N. (2011). Failing to predict future changes in memory. In A.S. Benjamin (Ed.), *Successful remembering and successful forgetting: A festschrift in honor of Robert A. Bjork* (pp. 365–386). New York: Psychology Press.

Kosslyn, S.M., Thompson, W.L., & Ganis, G. (2006). *The case for mental imagery.* Oxford: Oxford University Press.

Krackow, E., & Lynn, S.J. (2010). Event Report Training: An examination of the efficacy of a new intervention to improve children's eyewitness reports. *Applied Cognitive Psychology, 24*, 868–884. doi: 10.1002/acp.1594.

Kuhlmann, B.G., & Touron, D.R. (2012). Mediator-based encoding strategies in source monitoring in young and older adults. *Journal of Experimental Psychology: Learning, Memory, and Cognition, 38*, 1352–1364. doi: 10.1037/a0027863.

Kukucka, J., & Kassin, S. (2014). Do confessions taint perceptions of handwriting evidence? An empirical test of the forensic confirmation bias. *Law and Human Behavior, 38, 256–270.*

Lahl, O., Wispel, C., Willigens, B., & Pietrowsky, R. (2008). An ultra short episode of sleep is sufficient to promote declarative memory performance. *Journal of Sleep Research, 17,* 3–10.

Lamb, M. E., Hershkowitz, I., Orbach, Y., & Esplin, P. W. (2008). *Tell me what happened: Structured investigative interviews of child victims and witnesses.* New York: Wiley.

Lamb, M.E., Sternberg, K.J., Orbach, Y., Hershkowitz, I., & Horowitz, D. (2003). Differences between accounts provided by witnesses and alleged victims of child sexual abuse. *Child Abuse & Neglect, 27,* 1019–1031. doi: 10.1016/S0145-2134(03)00167-4.

Lampinen, J.M., Faries, J.M., Neuschatz, J.S., & Toglia, M.P. (2000). Recollections of things schematic: The influence of scripts on recollective experience. *Applied Cognitive Psychology, 14*, 543–554.

Lampinen, J.M., Neuschatz, J.S., & Cling, A.D. (2012). *The psychology of eyewitness identification.* New York: Psychology Press.

Lanciano, T., & Curci, A. (2012). Type or dimension? A taxometric investigation of flashbulb memories. *Memory, 20*, 177–188.

Lane, S.M., & Karam-Zanders, T. (2014). What do lay people believe about memory? In T.J. Perfect & D.S. Lindsay (Eds.), *The SAGE handbook of applied memory* (pp. 348–365). Los Angeles, CA: SAGE.

Lane, S.M., Roussel, C.C., Starns, J.J., Villa, D., & Alonzo, J.D. (2008). Providing information about diagnostic features at retrieval reduces false recognition. *Memory, 16*, 836–851.

Laney, C., Bowman Fowler, N., Nelson, K.J., Bernstein, D.B., & Loftus, E.F. (2008). The persistence of false beliefs. *Acta Psychologica, 129*, 190–197.

Laney, C., & Loftus, E.F. (2008). Emotional content of true and false memories. *Memory, 16,* 500–516.

Laney, C., & Loftus, E.F. (2010). Truth in emotional memories. In B.H. Bornstein & R.L. Wiener (Eds.), *Emotion and the law: Psychological perspectives* (pp. 157–183). New York: Springer.

Langlois, J.A., Rutland-Brown, W., & Wald, M.M. (2006). The epidemiology and impact of traumatic brain injury: A brief overview. *Journal of Head and Trauma Rehabilitation, 21,* 375–378.

Lassiter, G.D., Beers, M.J., Geers, A.L., Handley, I.M., Munhall, P.J., & Weiland, P. E. (2002). Further evidence of a robust point-of-view bias in videotaped confessions. *Current Psychology: A Journal for Diverse Perspectives on Diverse Psychological Issues, 21,* 265–288.

Lassiter, G.D., Geers, A.L., Handley, I.M., Weiland, P.E., & Munhall, P.J. (2002). Videotaped interrogations and confessions: A simple change in camera perspective alters verdicts in simulated trials. *Journal of Applied Psychology, 87,* 867–874.

Lassiter, G.D., & Irvine, A. (1986). Videotaped confessions: The impact of camera point of view on judgments of coercion. *Journal of Applied Social Psychology, 16,* 268–276.

Lassiter, G.D., Meissner, C.A., Ware, L.J., Marcon, J.L., & Lassiter, K.D. (2010). Introduction: Police interrogations and false confessions. In G.D. Lassiter & C. Meissner (Eds.), *Police interrogations and false confessions: Current research, practice, and policy recommendations* (pp. 3–7). Washington, DC: American Psychological Association.

Lassiter, G.D., Munhall, P.J., Geers, A.L., Weiland, P.E., & Handley, I.M. (2001). Accountability and the camera perspective bias in videotaped confessions. *Analyses of Social Issues and Public Policy, 1,* 53–70.

Lassiter, G. D., Ware, L.J., Lindberg, M.J., & Ratcliff, J.J. (2010). Videotaping custodial interrogations: Toward a scientifically based policy. In G.D. Lassiter & C. Meissner (Eds.), *Police interrogations and false confessions: Current research, practice, and policy recommendations* (pp. 143–160). Washington, DC: American Psychological Association.

Lassiter, G. D., Ware, L. J., Ratcliff, J. J., & Irvin, C. R. (2009). Evidence of the camera perspective bias in authentic videotaped interrogations: Implications for emerging reform in the criminal justice system. *Legal and Criminological Psychology, 14,* 157–170.

Lassiter, G.D., & Meissner, C.A. (2010). *Police interrogations and false confessions: Current research, practice, and policy recommendations.* Washington, DC: American Psychological Association.

Laub, C.E., Kimbrough, C., & Bornstein, B.H. (2016). Is an ear as good as an eye? Safeguards to help jurors use different kinds of identification testimony. *American Journal of Forensic Psychology, 34(2),* 33–56.

Laub, C.E., Maeder, E.M., & Bornstein, B.H. (2010). The influence of a psychology and law class on legal attitudes and knowledge structures. *Teaching of Psychology, 37,* 196–198. doi: 10.1080/00986281003626532.

Laurence, J.-R., Day, D., & Gaston, L. (1998). From memories of abuse to the abuse of memories. In S.J. Lynn & K.M. McConkey (Eds.), *Truth in memory* (pp. 323–346). New York: Guilford.

Lawson, R.B., Graham, J.E., & Baker, K.M. (2007). *A history of psychology: Globalization, ideas, and applications.* Upper Saddle River, NJ: Pearson/Prentice Hall.

Lee, Y.-S. (2013). Costs and benefits in item-method directed forgetting: Differential effects of encoding and retrieval. *Journal of General Psychology, 140,* 159–173.

Leichtman, M.D., & Ceci, S.J. (1995). The effects of stereotypes and suggestions on preschoolers' experiences. *Developmental Psychology, 31*, 568–578.

Leippe, M., & Eisenstadt, D. (2007). Eyewitness confidence and the confidence-accuracy relationship in memory for people. In R.C.L. Lindsay, D.F. Ross., J.D. Read, & M.P. Toglia (Eds.), *The handbook of eyewitness psychology (Vol. 2): Memory for people* (pp. 377–425). Mahwah, NJ: Erlbaum.

Leippe, M.R., & Romanczyk, A. (1987). Children on the witness stand: A communication/persuasion analysis of jurors' reactions to child witnesses. In S.J. Ceci, M.P. Toglia, & D.F. Ross (Eds.), *Children's eyewitness memory* (pp. 155–177). New York: Springer-Verlag.

Leo, R., & Liu, B. (2009). What do potential jurors know about police interrogation techniques and false confessions? *Behavioral Sciences and the Law, 27,* 381–399.

Leo, R., & Ofshe, R. (1998). The consequences of false confessions: Deprivations of liberty and miscarriages of justice in the age of psychological interrogation. *Journal of Criminal Law and Criminology, 88,* 429–496.

LePort, A.K.R., Mattfeld,, A.T., Dickinson-Anson, H., Fallon, J.H., Stark, C.E.L., Kruggel, F.R., … & McGaugh, J.L. (2012). A behavioral and neuroanatomical investigation of highly superior autobiographical memory. *Neurobiology of Learning and Memory, 98*, 78–92.

Levin, D.T., & Angelone, B.L. (2008). The visual metacognition questionnaire: A measure of intuitions about vision. *American Journal of Psychology, 121*, 451–472.

Levy, B.R., Ferrucci, L., Zonderman, A.B., Slade, M.D., Troncoso, J., & Resnick, S.M. (2016). A culture-brain link: Negative age stereotypes predict Alzheimer's Disease biomarkers. *Psychology and Aging, 31*, 82–88. doi: 10.1037/pag0000062.

Liberman, K. (1995). The natural history of some intercultural communication. *Research on Language and Social Interaction, 28*, 117–146. doi:10.1207/s15327973rlsi2802_2.

Light, L.L., & Singh, A. (1987). Implicit and explicit memory in young and older adults. *Journal of Experimental Psychology: Learning, Memory, and Cognition, 13*, 531–541.

Lilienfeld, S.O. (2007). Psychological treatments that cause harm. *Perspectives on Psychological Science, 2*, 53–70.

Lilienfeld, S.O., Lynn, S.J., Ruscio, J., & Beyerstein, B.L. (2010). *Fifty great myths of popular psychology: Shattering widespread misconceptions about human behavior.* Chichester, England: Wiley-Blackwell.

Lim, A.S.P., Kowgier, M., Yu, L., Buchman, A.S., & Bennett, D.A. (2013). Sleep fragmentation and the risk of incident Alzheimer's Disease and cognitive decline in older persons. *Sleep, 36*, 1027–1032.

Lin, W.-J., Kuo, Y.-C., Liu, T.-L., Han, Y.-J., & Cheng, S.-K. (2013). Intentional forgetting reduces the semantic processing of to-be-forgotten items: An ERP study of item-method directed forgetting. *Psychophysiology, 50*, 1120–1132. doi: 10.1111/psyp.12125.

Lindsay, D.S., & Read, J.D. (1994). Psychotherapy and memories of childhood sexual abuse: A cognitive perspective. *Applied Cognitive Psychology, 8*, 281–338.

Lindsay, D.S., & Read, J.D. (1995). "Memory work" and recovered memories of childhood sexual abuse: Scientific evidence and public, professional, and personal issues. *Psychology, Public Policy & Law, 1*, 846–908.

Lindsay, R.C.L. (1994). Expectations of eyewitness performance: Jurors' verdicts do not follow from their beliefs. In D.F. Ross, J.D. Read, & M.P. Toglia (Eds.), *Adult eyewitness testimony: Current trends and developments* (pp. 362–384). Cambridge, UK: Cambridge University Press.

Lindsay, R.C.L., Lim, R., Marando, L., & Cully, D. (1986). Mock-juror evaluations of eyewitness testimony: A test of metamemory hypotheses. *Journal of Applied Social Psychology, 16*, 447–459.

Lindsay, R.C.L. Ross., D.F. Read, J.D., & Toglia, M.P. (2007). *The handbook of eyewitness psychology (Vol. 2): Memory for people*. Mahwah, NJ: Erlbaum.

Lindsay, R.C.L., Wells, G.L., & Rumpel, C.M. (1981). Can people detect eyewitness-identification accuracy within and across situations? *Journal of Applied Psychology, 66*, 79–89.

Lineweaver, T.T., Berger, A.K., & Hertzog, C. (2009). Expectations about memory change across the life span are impacted by aging stereotypes. *Psychology and Aging, 24*, 169–176. doi: 10.1037/a0013577

Lineweaver, T.T., & Hertzog, C. (1998). Adults' efficacy and control beliefs regarding memory and aging: Separating general from personal beliefs. *Aging, Neuropsychology, and Cognition, 5*, 264–296.

Linton, M. (2000). Transformations of memory in everyday life. In U. Neisser & I.E. Hyman (Eds.), *Memory observed: Remembering in natural contexts* (2nd ed.) (pp. 107–118). New York: Worth.

Loftus, E.F., & Bernstein, D.M. (2005). Rich false memories. In A.F. Healy (Ed.), *Experimental cognitive psychology and its applications* (pp. 101–113). Washington, DC: American Psychological Association.

Loftus, E.F., & Ketcham, K. (1994). *The myth of repressed memory: False memories and allegations of sexual abuse*. New York: St. Martin's Press.

Loftus, E.F., & Loftus, G.R. (1980). On the permanence of stored information in the human brain. *American Psychologist, 35*, 409–420.

Loftus, E., Miller, D.G., & Burns, H.J. (1978). Semantic integration of verbal information into a visual memory. *Journal of Experimental Psychology: Human Learning and Memory, 4*, 19–31.

Loftus, E.F., & Pickrell, J.E. (1995). The formation of false memories. *Psychiatric Annals, 25*, 720–725.

Loftus, E.F., Weingardt, K.R., & Hoffman, H.G. (1993). Sleeping memories on trial: Reactions to memories that were previously repressed. *Expert Evidence, 20*, 50–59.

Logie, R.H., & Della Salla, S. (1999). Repetita (non) iuvant. In S. Della Salla (Ed.), *Mind myths: Exploring popular assumptions about the mind and brain* (pp. 125–137). Chichester, UK: Wiley.

Lonergan, M.H., Olivera-Figueroa, L.A., Pitman, R.K., & Brunet, A. (2013). Propranolol's effects on the consolidation and reconsolidation of long-term emotional memory in healthy participants: A meta-analysis. *Journal of Psychiatry Neuroscience, 38*, 222–231. doi: 10.1503/jpn.120111.

López-Lozano, J.J., Bravo, G., Brera, B., Dargallo, J., Salmeán, J., Uría, J., ... & CPH Neural Transplantation Group (1995). *Transplantation Proceedings, 27,* 1395–1400.

Lotterman, J.H., & Bonanno, G.A. (2014). Those were the days: Memory bias for the frequency of positive events, depression, and self-enhancement. *Memory, 22,* 925–936. doi: 10.1080/09658211.2013.856924.

Luria, A.R. (1987a). *The man with a shattered world: The history of a brain wound.* Cambridge, MA: Harvard University Press.

Luria, A.R. (1987b). *The mind of a mnemonist: A little book about a vast memory.* Cambridge, MA: Harvard University Press.

Luyten, P., Mayes, L.C., Fonagy, P., Target, M., & Blatt, S.J. (2015). *Handbook of psychodynamic approaches to psychopathology.* New York, NY: Guilford.

Lynch, S., & Yarnell, P.R. (1973). Retrograde amnesia: Delayed forgetting after concussion. *American Journal of Psychology, 86,* 643–645.

Lynn, S.J., Neuschatz, J., & Fite, R. (2002). Hypnosis and memory: Implications for the courtroom and psychotherapy. In M.L. Eisen, J.A. Quas, & G.S. Goodman (Eds.), *Memory and suggestibility in the forensic interview* (pp. 287–307). Mahwah, NJ: Erlbaum.

MacCoun, R.J. (2015). The epistemic contract: Fostering an appropriate level of public trust in experts. In B.H. Bornstein & A.J. Tomkins (Eds.), *Motivating cooperation and compliance with authority* (pp. 191–214). New York: Springer. doi: 10.1007/978-3-319-16151-8_9.

MacLeod, C.M., Jonker, T.R., & James, G. (2014). Individual differences in remembering. In T.J. Perfect & D.S. Lindsay (Eds.), *The SAGE handbook of applied memory* (pp. 385–403). Los Angeles, CA: SAGE.

MacLeod, M.D., & Hulbert, J.C. (2011). Sleep, retrieval inhibition, and the resolving power of human memory. In A.S. Benjamin (Ed.), *Successful remembering and successful forgetting: A festschrift in honor of Robert A. Bjork* (pp. 133–152). New York: Psychology Press.

Magnussen, S., Andersson, J., Cornoldi, C., De Beni, R., Endestad, T., Goodman, G.S., ... & Zimmer, H. (2006). What people believe about memory. *Memory, 14,* 595–613.

Magnussen, S., Safer, M.A., Sartori, G., & Wise, R.A. (2013). What Italian defense attorneys know about factors affecting eyewitness accuracy: A comparison with U.S. and Norwegian samples. *Frontiers in Psychiatry, 4,* 1–6. doi: 10.3389/fpsyt.2013.00028.

Maguire, E.A., Gadian, D.G., Johnsrude, I.S., Good, C.D., Ashburner, J., Frackowiak, R.S.J., & Frith, C.D. (2000). Navigation-related structural change in the hippocampi of taxi drivers. *Proceedings of the National Academy of Sciences, 97,* 4398–4403.

Maguire, E.A., Valentine, E.R., Wilding, J.M., & Kapur, N. (2003). Routes to remembering: The brains behind superior memory. *Nature Neuroscience, 6,* 90–95.

Maguire, E.A., Woollett, K., & Spiers, H.J. (2006). London taxi drivers and bus drivers: A structural MRI and neuropsychological analysis. *Hippocampus, 16,* 1091–1101. doi: 10.1002/hipo.20233.

Malloy, L., Shulman, E., & Cauffman, E. (2014). Interrogations, confessions, and guilty pleas among serious adolescent offenders. *Law and Human Behavior, 38,* 181–193.

Malpass, R.S., Tredoux, C.G., & McQuiston-Surrett, D. (2007). Lineup construction and lineup fairness. In R.C.L. Lindsay, D.F. Ross, J.D. Read, & M.P. Toglia (Eds.), *The handbook of eyewitness psychology (Vol. 2): Memory for people* (pp. 155–178). Mahwah, NJ: Erlbaum.

Manson v. Braithwaite, 432 U.S. 98 (1977).

Marek, G.R. (2000). Toscanini's memory. In U. Neisser & I.E. Hyman (Eds.), *Memory observed: Remembering in natural contexts* (2nd ed.) (pp. 508–511). New York: Worth.

Maren, S. (2011). Seeking a spotless mind: Extinction, deconsolidation, and erasure of fear memory. *Neuron, 70,* 830–845.

Marin-Garcia, E., Ruiz-Vargas, J. M., & Kapur, N. (2013). Mere exposure effect can be elicited in transient global amnesia. *Journal of Clinical and Experimental Neuropsychology, 35,* 1007–1014.

Mazzoni, G., Loftus, E.F., & Kirsch, I. (2001). Changing beliefs about implausible autobiographical events: A little plausibility goes a long way. *Journal of Experimental Psychology: Applied, 7,* 51–59.

Mazzoni, G., & Lynn, S.J. (2007). Using hypnosis in eyewitness memory: Past and current issues. In M.P. Toglia J.D. Read, D.F. Ross, & R.C.L. Lindsay (Eds.), *Handbook of eyewitness psychology, Vol. 1* (pp. 321–338). Mahwah, NJ: Erlbaum.

Mazzoni, G., & Memon, A. (2003). Imagination can create false autobiographical memories. *Psychological Science, 14,* 186–188.

McAuliff, B.D., & Bornstein, B.H. (2012). Beliefs and expectancies in legal decision making: An introduction to the special issue. *Psychology, Crime & Law, 18,* 1–10.

McAuliff, B.D., & Kovera, M.B. (2012). Do jurors get what they expect? Traditional versus alternative forms of children's testimony. *Psychology, Crime & Law, 18,* 27–47.

McCauley, M.R., & Parker, J.F. (2001). When will a child be believed? The impact of the victim's age and juror's gender on children's credibility and verdict in a sexual-abuse case. *Child Abuse & Neglect, 25,* 523–539.

McConkey, K.M., & Sheehan, P.W. (1995). *Hypnosis, memory, and behavior in criminal investigation.* New York: Guilford.

McDaniel, M.A., & Einstein, G.O. (2007). *Prospective memory: An overview and synthesis of an emerging field.* Thousand Oaks, CA: Sage.

McDaniel, W.F. (1988). The behavioral influences of brain tissue transplants following hippocampal or cerebral cortex injuries. *Medical Science Research, 15,* 435–439.

McGaugh, J.L. (2000). Memory—a century of consolidation. *Science, 287,* 248–251.

McNally, R.J. (2003). *Remembering trauma.* Cambridge, MA: Harvard University Press/Belknap Press.

McNally, R.J. (2004). Is traumatic amnesia nothing but psychiatric folklore? *Cognitive Behaviour Therapy, 33,* 97–101.

McNally, R.J. (2005). Debunking myths about trauma and memory. *Canadian Journal of Psychiatry, 50,* 817–822.

McNally, R.J. (2012). Searching for repressed memory. In R.F. Belli (Ed.), *True and false recovered memories: Toward a reconciliation of the debate* (pp. 121–147). doi:; 10.1007/978-1-4614-1195-6_4

McNally, R.J., Lasko, N.B., Clancy, S.A., Maclin, M.L., Pittman, R.K., & Orr, S.P. (2004). Psychophysiological responding during script-driven imagery in people reporting abduction by space aliens. *Psychological Science, 15*, 493–497.

McWilliams, J. (2015, Summer). The examined life: A meditation on memory. *The American Scholar*, 18–30.

Meeter, M., Murre, J.M.J., Janssen, S.M., Birkenhager, T., & van den Broek, W.W. (2011). Retrograde amnesia after electroconvulsive therapy: A temporary effect? *Journal of Affective Disorders, 132*, 216–222.

Mehr, S.A. (2015). Miscommunication of science: Music cognition research in the popular press. *Frontiers in Psychology, 6:988*. doi: 10.3389/fpsyg.2015.00988

Meissner, C.A., Russano, M.B., & Narchet, F.N. (2010). The importance of a laboratoary science for improving the diagnostic value of confession evidence. In G.D. Lassiter & C. Meissner (Eds.), *Police interrogations and false confessions: Current research, practice, and policy recommendations* (pp. 111–126). Washington, DC: American Psychological Association.

Meissner, C.A., Sporer, S.L., & Schooler, J.W. (2007). Person descriptions as eyewitness evidence. In R.C.L. Lindsay, D.F. Ross, J.D. Read, & M. Toglia (Eds.), *Handbook of eyewitness psychology (Vol. 2): Memory for people* (pp. 1–34). Mahwah, NJ: Erlbaum.

Memon, A., Meissner, C. A., & Fraser, J. (2010). The cognitive interview: A metaanalytic review and study space analysis of the past 25 years. *Psychology, Public Policy, and Law*, 16, 340–372.

Memon, A., & Thomson, D. (2007). The myth of the incredible eyewitness. In S. Della Salla (Ed.), *Tall tales about the mind and brain: Separating fact from fiction* (pp. 76–90). Oxford: Oxford University Press.

Memon, A., Zaragoza, M., Clifford, B.R., & Kidd, L. (2010). Inoculation or antidote? The effects of cognitive interview timing on false memory for forcibly fabricated events. *Law and Human Behavior, 34*, 105–117.

Merckelbach, H., Smeets, T., Geraerts, E., Jelicic, M., Bouwen, A., & Smeets, E. (2006). I haven't thought about this for years! Dating recent recalls of vivid memories. *Applied Cognitive Psychology, 20*, 33–42.

Merikle, P. M., & Daneman, M. (1996). Memory for unconsciously perceived events: Evidence from anesthetized patients. *Consciousness and Cognition, 5*, 525–541.

Metcalfe, J., & Shimamura, A.P. (1994). *Metacognition: Knowing about knowing*. Cambridge, MA: MIT Press.

Meyersburg, C.A., Bogdan, R., Gallo, D.A., & McNally, R.J. (2009). False memory propensity in people reporting recovered memories of past lives. *Journal of Abnormal Psychology, 118*, 399–404.

Mickes, L. (2015). Receiver operating characteristic analyses and confidence-accuracy analysis in investigations of system variables and estimator variables that affect eyewitness memory. *Journal of Applied Research in Memory and Cognition, 4*, 93–102.

Milner, B. (1971). Interhemispheric differences in the location of psychological processes in man. *British Medical Bulletin, 27*, 272–277.

Mineka, S., & Sutton, S.K. (1992). Cognitive biases and the emotional disorders. *Psychological Science, 3*, 65–69.

Mitchell, K.J., & Johnson, M.K. (2009). Source monitoring 15 years later: What have we learned from fMRI about the neural mechanisms of source memory? *Psychological Bulletin, 135*, 638–677.

Mitchell, M.B., Miller, L.S., Woodard, J.L., Davey, A., Martin, P., Poon, L.W., & Georgia Centenarian Study (2013). Norms from the Georgia Centenarian Study: Measures of verbal abstract reasoning, fluency, memory, and motor function. *Aging, Neuropsychology, and Cognition, 20*, 620–637, doi: 10.1080/13825585.2012.761671

Morgan, C. A., Hazlett, G., Doran, A., Garrett, S., Hoyt, G., Thomas, P., ... & Southwick, S.M. (2004). Accuracy of eyewitness memory for persons encountered during exposure to highly intense stress. *International Journal of Law and Psychiatry, 27*, 265–279. doi: 10.1016/j.ijlp.2004.03.004

Moriarty, L. (2009). *What Alice forgot*. New York: Berkley Books.

Mullet, H.G., Scullin, M.K., Hess, T.J., Scullin, R.B., Arnold, K.M., & Einstein, G.O. (2013). Prospective memory and aging: Evidence for preserved spontaneous retrieval with exact but not related cues. *Psychology and Aging, 28*, 910–922. doi: 10.1037/a0034347.

Myers, J.E., Redlich, A., Goodman, G., Prizmich, L., & Imwinkelried, E. (1999). Jurors' perceptions of hearsay in child sexual abuse cases. *Psychology, Public Policy, & Law, 5*, 388–419. doi:10.1037//1076-8971.5.2.388

Nachson, I., Read, J.D., Seelau, S.M., Goodyear-Smith, F., Lobb, B., Davies, G., Glicksohn, J., Lifschitz, M., & Brimacombe, E. (2007). Effects of prior knowledge and expert statement on belief in recovered memories: An international perspective. *International Journal of Law and Psychiatry, 30*, 224–236.

National Research Council (2014). *Identifying the culprit: Assessing eyewitness identification*. Washington, DC: National Academies Press.

National Sleep Foundation (2017). Teens and sleep. Retrieved from http://sleepfoundation.org/sleep-topics/teens-and-sleep.

Neal, T.M.S., Christiansen, A., Bornstein, B.H., & Robicheaux, T.R. (2012). The effects of mock jurors' beliefs about eyewitness performance on trial judgments. *Psychology, Crime & Law, 18*, 49–64.

Neath, I., & Surprenant, A.M. (2015). *Human memory* (3rd ed.). Cengage Learning.

Neil v. Biggers, 409 U.S. 188 (1972).

Neisser, U. (2000a). Snapshots or benchmarks? In U. Neisser & I.E. Hyman (Eds.), *Memory observed: Remembering in natural contexts* (2nd ed.) (pp. 68–74). New York: Worth.

Neisser, U. (2000b). Memorists. In U. Neisser & I.E. Hyman (Eds.), *Memory observed: Remembering in natural contexts* (2nd ed.) (pp. 475–478). New York: Worth.

Neisser, U. & Harsch, N. (1992). Phantom flashbulbs: False recollections of hearing the news about Challenger. In E. Winograd and U. Neisser (Eds.), *Affect and accuracy in recall* (pp. 9–31). New York: Cambridge University Press.

Neisser, U., & Hyman, I.E. (2000). *Memory observed: Remembering in natural contexts* (2nd ed.). New York: Worth.

Neisser, U., Winograd, E., Bergman, E.T., Schreiber, C.A., Palmer, S.E., & Weldon, M.S., (1996). Remembering the earthquake: Direct experience vs. hearing the news. *Memory, 4,* 337–357.

Nelson, T.O., & Narens, L. (1990). Metamemory: A theoretical framework and new findings. In G. Bower (Ed.), *The psychology of learning and motivation* (Vol. 26). New York: Academic Press.

Nelson, T.O., & Narens, L. (1994). Why investigate metacognition? In J. Metcalfe & A.P. Shimamura (Eds.), *Metacognition: Knowing about knowing* (pp. 1–25). Cambridge, MA: MIT Press.

Neuschatz, J.S., Lampinen, J.M., Preston, E.L., Hawkins, E.R., & Toglia, M.P. (2002). The effect of memory schemata on memory and the phenomenological experience of naturalistic situations. *Applied Cognitive Psychology, 16,* 687–708. doi: 10.1002/acp.824.

Neuschatz, J.S., Wetmore, S.A., Key, K., Cash, D., Gronlund, S.D., & Goodsell, C.A. (2016). A comprehensive evaluation of showups. In M.K. Miller & B.H. Bornstein (Eds.), *Advances in psychology and law* (Vol. 1, pp. 43–69). New York: Springer.

New Jersey v. Henderson, 208 N. J. 208, 27 A. 3d 872 (2011).

Newman, L.S., & Baumeister, R.F. (1996). Toward an explanation of the UFO abduction phenomenon: Hypnotic elaboration, extraterrestrial sadomasochism, and spurious memories. *Psychological Inquiry, 7,* 99–126.

Niedzwienska, A., Neckar, J., & Baran, B. (2007). Development and validation of the Implicit Memory Theory Scale. *European Journal of Psychological Assessment, 23,* 185–192. doi: 10.1027/1015-5759.23.3.185.

Nilsson, L-G., Bäckman, L., Erngrund, K., Nyberg, L., Adolfsson, R., Bucht, G., ... & Winblad, B. (1997). The Betula prospective cohort study: Memory, health and ageing. Aging, *Neuropsychology and Cognition, 4,* 1–32.

Nisbett, R.E., & Wilson, T.D. (1977). Telling more than we can know. *Psychological Review, 84,* 231–259.

Niven, C.A., & Murphy-Black, T. (2000). Memory for labor pain: A review of the literature. *Birth, 27,* 244–253. doi: 10.1046/j.1523-536x.2000.00244.x.

Noel, A., Quinette, P., Hainselin, M., Dayan, J., Viader, F., Desgranges, B., & Eustache, F. (2015). The still enigmatic syndrome of transient global amnesia: Interactions between neurological and psychopathological factors. *Neuropsychology Review, 25,* 125–133. doi: 10.1007/s11065-015-9284-y.

Noel, M., Taylor, T.L., Quinlan, C.K., & Stewart, S.H. (2012). The impact of attention style on directed forgetting among high anxiety sensitive individuals. *Cognitive Therapy and Research, 36,* 375–389. doi: 10.1007/s10608-011-9366-y.

Nolen-Hoeksema, S. (2000). The role of rumination in depressive disorders and mixed anxiety/depressive symptoms. *Journal of Abnormal Psychology, 109,* 504–511. doi: 10.1037/0021-843X.109.3.504.

Noon, E., & Hollin, C. R. (1987). Lay knowledge of eyewitness behaviour: A British survey. *Applied Cognitive Psychology, 1,* 575–593.

Noonan, D. (2014, November). Total recall: For the first time, two pioneering neuroscientists have implanted a memory of an event that never happened. *Smithsonian*, 48–53.

Norcross, J.C., & Karpiak, C.P. (2012). Clinical psychologists in the 2010s: 50 years of the APA Division of Clinical Psychology. *Clinical Psychology: Science and Practice, 19*, 1–12.

O'Connor, M., Lebowitz, B.K., Ly, J., Panizzon, M.S., Elkin-Frankston, S., Dey, S., … & Pearlman, C. (2008). A dissociation between anterograde and retrograde amnesia after treatment with electroconvulsive therapy: A naturalistic investigation. *Journal of ECT, 24*, 146–151.

Odinot, G., Wolters, G., & van Koppen, P.J. (2009). Eyewitness memory of a supermarket robbery: A case study of accuracy and confidence after 3 months. *Law and Human Behavior, 33*, 506–514. doi: 10.1007/s10979-008-9152-x.

Ofshe, R., & Watters, E. (1994). *Making monsters: False memories, psychotherapy and sexual hysteria*. New York: Scribner's.

Ogawa, Y. (2009). *The housekeeper and the professor* (trans. S. Snyder). New York: Picador.

O'Jile, J.R., Ryan, L.M., Parks-Levy, J., Gouvier, W.D., Betz, B., Haptonstahl, D.E., & Coon, R.C. (1997). Effects of head injury experience on head injury misconnceptions. *International Journal of Rehabilitation and Health, 3*, 61–67.

O'Kane, G., Kensinger, E.A., & Corkin, S. (2004). Evidence for semantic learning in profound amnesia: An investigation with patient H.M. *Hippocampus, 14*, 417–425.

Okdie, B.M., Ewoldsen, D.R., Muscanell, N.L., Guadagno, R.E., Eno, C.A., Velez, J.A., … & Smith, L.R. (2014). Missed programs (you can't TiVo this one): Why psychologists should study media. *Perspectives on Psychological Science, 9*, 180–195.

Oliveira, A.A., & Hodges, H.M. (2005). Alzheimer's Disease and neural transplantation as prospective cell therapy. *Current Alzheimer Research, 2*, 79–95.

Ost, J., Costall, A., & Bull, R. (2001). False confessions and false memories: A model for understanding retractors' experiences. *Journal of Forensic Psychiatry, 12*, 549–579.

Ost, J., Wright, D.B., Easton, S., Hope, L., & French, C.C. (2013). Recovered memories, satanic abuse, Dissociative Identity Disorder and false memories in the UK: A survey of clinical psychologists and hypnotherapists. *Psychology, Crime & Law, 19*, 1–19. doi: 10.1080/1068316X.2011.598157.

O'Sullivan, M., Frank, M.G., Hurley, C.M., & Tiwana, J. (2009). Police lie detection accuracy: The effect of lie scenario. *Law and Human Behavior, 33*, 530–538. doi: 10.1007/s10979-008-9166-4

Packer, S. (2012). *Cinema's sinister psychiatrists: From Caligari to Hannibal*. Jefferson, NC: McFarland & Co.

Palombo, D.J., McKinnon, M.C., McIntosh, A.R., Anderson, A.K., Todd, R.M., & Levine, B. (2016). The neural correlates of memory for a life-threatening event: An fMRI study of passengers from flight AT236. *Clinical Psychological Science, 4*, 312–319. doi: 10.1177/2167702615589308.

Papailiou, A.P., Yokum, D.V., & Robertson, C.T. (2015). The novel New Jersey eyewitness instruction induces skepticism but not sensitivity. *PLoS One 10(12):e0142695*. doi: 10.1371/journal.pone.0142695.

Park, A. (2016). Alzheimer's from a new angle. *Time, February 22–29*, 64–70.

Parker, E.S., Cahill, L., & McGaugh, J.L. (2006). A case of unusual autobiographical remembering. *Neurocase, 12*, 35–49. doi: 10.1080/13554790500473680.

Parkin, A.J. (1997). *Memory and amnesia: An introduction* (2nd ed.). Oxford, UK: Blackwell.

Parry, L., & O'Kearney, R. (2014). A comparison of the quality of intrusive memories in post-traumatic stress disorder and depression. *Memory, 22*, 408–425. doi: 10.1080/09658211.2013.795975

Pastötter, B., Kliegl, O., & Bäuml, K.-H.T. (2012). List-method directed forgetting: The forget cue improves both encoding and retrieval of postcue information. *Memory & Cognition, 40*, 861–873. doi: 10.3758/s13421-012-0206-4

Patel, S.N., Clayton, N.S., & Krebs, J.R. (1997). Hippocampal tissue transplants reverse lesion-induced spatial memory deficits in zebra finches (taeniopygia guttata). *Journal of Neuroscience, 17*, 3861–3869.

Patihis, L., Frenda, S.J., LePort, A.K.R., Petersen, N., Nichols, R.M., Stark, C.E.L., McGaugh, J.L., & Loftus, E.F. (2013). False memories in highly superior autobiographical memory individuals. *Proceedings of the National Academy of Sciences, 110*, 20947–20952. doi: 10.1073/pnas/1314373110.

Patihis, L., Ho, L.Y., Tingen, I.W., Lilienfeld, S.O., & Loftus, E.F. (2014). Are the "memory wars" over? A scientist-practitioner gap in beliefs about repressed memory. *Psychological Science, 25*, 519–530. doi: 10.1177/0956797613510718.

Pauly-Takacs, K., Moulin, C.J.A., & Estlin, E.J. (2011). SenseCam as a rehabilitation tool in a child with anterograde amnesia. *Memory, 19*, 705–712. doi: 10.1080/09658211.2010.494046.

Pawlenko, N.B., Safer, M.A., Wise, R.A., & Holfeld, B. (2013). A teaching aid for improving jurors' assessments of eyewitness accuracy. *Applied Cognitive Psychology, 27*, 190–197. doi: 10.1002/acp.2895.

Payne, J.D., Tucker, M.A., Ellenbogen, J.M., Wamsley, E.J., Walker, M.P., Schacter, D.L., & Stickgold, R. (2012) Memory for semantically related and unrelated declarative information: The benefit of sleep, the cost of wake. *PLoS ONE, 7(3)*: e33079. doi:10.1371/journal.pone.0033079.

Peace, K.A., & Porter, S. (2004). A longitudinal investigation of the reliability of memories for trauma and other emotional experiences. *Applied Cognitive Psychology, 18*, 1143–1159.

Peace, K.A., Porter, S., & ten Brinke, L. (2008). Are memories for sexually traumatic events "special"? A within-subjects investigation of trauma and memory in a clinical sample. *Memory, 16*, 10–21.

Peek, F., & Hanson, L.L. (2008). *The life and message of the real Rain Man: The journey of a mega-savant*. Port Chester, NY: Dude Publishing.

Pendergrast, M. (1996). *Victims of memory: Sex abuse accusations and shattered lives*. Hinesburg, VT: Upper Access Books.

Penrod, S.D., & Bornstein, B.H. (2007). Methodological issues in eyewitness memory research. In R.C.L. Lindsay, D.F. Ross, J.D. Read, & M. Toglia (Eds.), *Handbook of eyewitness psychology (Vol. 2): Memory for people* (pp. 529–556). Mahwah, NJ: Erlbaum.

Perillo, J. T., & Kassin, S. M. (2011). Inside interrogation: The lie, the bluff, and false confession. *Law and Human Behavior, 35*, 327–337.

Peter-Derex, L., Yammine, P., Bastuji, H., & Croisile, B. (2015). Sleep and Alzheimer's Disease. *Sleep Medicine Reviews, 19*, 29–38.

Peters, M.J.V., Horselenberg, R., Jelicic, M., & Merckelbach, H. (2007). The false fame illusion in people with memories about a previous life. *Consciousness and Cognition, 16*, 162–169.

Petiau, C., Onen, H., Delgado, A., & Touchon, J. (2013). Exploring sleep-related outcomes in patients with mild to moderate Alzheimer's Disease initiating acetylcholinesterase inhibitor therapy: The Morpheus survey. *International Journal of Geriatric Psychiatry, 28*, 654–659.

Pezdek, K., Blandón-Gitlin, I., & Gabbay, P. (20006). Imagination and memory: Does imagining implausible events lead to false autobiographical memories? *Psychonomic Bulletin & Review, 13*, 764–769.

Pezdek, K., Finger, K., & Hodge, D. (1997). Planting false childhood memories: The role of event plausibility. *Psychological Science, 8*, 437–441.

Pezdek, K., & Stolzenberg, S.N. (2013). Are individuals' familiarity judgments diagnostic of prior contact?" *Psychology, Crime & Law, 19*, 1–13.

Phelps, E.A. (2012). Emotion's impact on memory. In L. Nadel & W.P. Sinnott-Armstrong (Eds.), *Memory and law* (pp. 7–26). Oxford: Oxford University Press.

Phillips v. Gelpke, 190 N.J. 580, 921 A.2d 1067 (2007).

Pickel, K., Warner, T., Miller, T., Barnes, Z. (2013). Conceptualizing defendants as minorities leads mock jurors to make biased evaluations in retracted confession cases. *Psychology, Public Policy, and Law, 19*, 56–69.

Pigott, M.A., Brigham, J.C., & Bothwell, R.K. (1990). Field study of the relationship between quality of eyewitnesses' descriptions and identification accuracy. *Journal of Police Science and Administration, 17*, 84–88.

Pillai, J.A., Hall, C.B., Dickson, D.W., Buschke, H., Lipton, R.B., & Verghese, J. (2011). Association of crossword puzzle participation with memory decline in persons who develop dementia. *Journal of the International Neuropsychological Society, 17*, 1006–1013.

Piolino, P., Hannequin, D., Desgranges, B., Girard, C., Beaunieux, H., … & Eustache, F. (2005). Right ventral frontal hypometabolism and abnormal sense of self in a case of disproportionate retrograde amnesia. *Cognitive Neuropsychology, 22*, 1005–1034. doi: 10.1080/02643290442000428.

Piper, A., Lillevik, L., & Kritzer, R. (2008). What's wrong with believing in repression? A review for legal professionals. *Psychology, Public Policy & Law, 14*, 223–242.

Piper, A., Pope, H.G., & Borowiecki, J.J. (2000). Custer's last stand: Brown, Scheflin and Whitfield's latest attempt to salvage "dissociative amnesia." *Journal of Psychiatry & Law, 28*, 149–213.

Pitman, R.K. (2011). Will reconsolidation blockade offer a novel treatment for post-traumatic stress disorder? *Frontiers in Behavioral Neuroscience, 5* (Art. 11), 1–2. doi: 10.3389/fnbeh.2011.00011

Plassman, B.L., Langa, K.M., Fisher, G.G., Heeringa, S.G., Weir, D.R., Ofstedal, M.B., ... & Wallace, R.B. (2007). Prevalence of dementia in the United States: The aging, demographics, and memory study. *Neuroepidemiology, 29,* 125–132.

Plassman, B.L., Langa, K.M., Fisher, G.G., Heeringa, S.G., Weir, D.R., Ofstedal, M.B., ... & Wallace, R.B. (2008). Prevalence of cognitive impairment without dementia in the United States. *Annals of Internal Medicine, 148,* 427–434.

Plassman, B.L., Langa, K.M., McCammon, R.J., Fisher, G.G., Potter, G.G., Burke, J.R., ... & Wallace, R.B. (2011). Incidence of dementia and cognitive impairment, not dementia in the United States. *Annals of Neurology, 70,* 418–426.

Plassman, B.L., Williams, J.W., Burke, J.R., Holsinger, T., & Benjamin, S. (2010). Systematic review: Factors associated with risk for and possible prevention of cognitive decline in later life. *Annals of Internal Medicine, 153,* 182–193.

Polusny, M.A., & Follette, V.M. (1996). Remembering childhood sexual abuse: A national survey of psychologists' clinical practices, beliefs, and personal experiences. *Professional Psychology: Research and Practice, 27,* 41–52.

Pomara, N., Facelle, T.M., Roth, A.E., Willoughby, L.M., Greenblatt, D.J., & Sidtis, J.J. (2006). Dose-dependent retrograde facilitation of verbal memory in healthy elderly after acute oral lorazepam administration. *Psychopharmacology, 185,* 487–494. doi: 10.1007/s00213-006-0336-0.

Poole, D. A., Lindsay, D. S., Memon, A., & Bull, R. (1995). Psychotherapy and the recovery of memories of childhood sexual abuse: U.S. and British practitioners' opinions, practices, and experiences. *Journal of Consulting and Clinical Psychology, 63,* 426–437.

Poon, L.W., Woodard, J.L., Miller, L.S., Green, R., Gearing, M., Davey, A., ... & Markesbery, W. (2012). understanding dementia prevalence among centenarians. *Journals of Gerontology: Series A: Biological Sciences and Medical Sciences, 67A,* 358–365.

Porter, S., & Peace, K.A. (2007). The scars of memory: A prospective, longitudinal investigation of the consistency of traumatic and positive emotional memories in adulthood. *Psychological Science, 18,* 435–441.

Porter, S., Yuille, J.C., & Lehman, D.R. (1999). The nature of real, implanted, and fabricated memories for emotional childhood events: Implications for the recovered memory debate. *Law and Human Behavior, 23,* 517–537.

Price, J., Mueller, M.L., Wetmore, S., & Neuschatz, J. (2014). Eyewitness memory and metamemory in older adults. In M.P. Toglia, D.F. Ross, J. Pozzulo., & E. Pica (Eds.), *The elderly eyewitness in court* (pp. 167–191). New York: Psychology Press.

Price, P.C., & Stone, E.R. (2004). Intuitive evaluation of likelihood judgment producers: Evidence for a confidence heuristic. *Journal of Behavioral Decision Making, 17,* 39–57.

Principe, G.F., & Smith, E. (2008). The tooth, the whole tooth and nothing but the tooth: How belief in the Tooth Fairy can engender false memories. *Applied Cognitive Psychology, 22,* 625–642. doi: 10.1002/acp.1402

Quinette, P., Guillery-Girard, B., Dayan, J., de la Sayette, V., Marquis, S., … & Eustache, F. (2006). What does transient global amnesia really mean? Review of the literature and thorough study of 142 cases. *Brain, 129*, 1640–1658. doi: 10.1093/brain/aw1105

Rabinowitz, D. (1990, May). From the mouths of babes to a jail cell. *Harper's, 280(1680)*, 52–63.

Ramachandran, V.S., & Brang, D. (2008). Synesthesia. *Scholarpedia, 3(6)*: 3981. Available at http://www.scholarpedia.org/article/Synesthesia. doi: 10.4249/scholarpedia.3981

Ramirez, S., Liu, X., Lin, P-A., Suh, J., Pignatelli, M., Redondo, R.L., … & Tonegawa, S. (2013). Creating a false memory in the hippocampus. *Science, 341*, 387–391.

Ratcliff & Lassiter (2010). The hidden consequences of racial salience in videotaped interrogations and confessions. *Psychology, Public Policy and Law, 16*, 200–218. doi:10.1037/a0018482

Read, J.D., & Desmarais, S.L. (2009). Lay knowledge of eyewitness issues: A Canadian evaluation. *Applied Cognitive Psychology, 23*, 301–326. doi: 10.1002/acp.1459

Read, J.D., Connolly, D.A., & Welsh, A. (2006). An archival analysis of actual cases of historic child sexual abuse: A comparison of jury and bench trials. *Law and Human Behavior, 30*, 259–285. doi: 10.1007/s10979-006-9010-7.

Reardon, M.C. & Fisher, R.P. (2011). Effect of viewing the interview and identification process on juror perceptions of eyewitness accuracy. *Applied Cognitive Psychology, 25*, 68–77. doi: 10.1002/acp.1643

Reder, L.M., Oates, J.M., Dickison, D., Anderson, J.R., Gyulai, F., Quinlan, J.J., … & Jefferson, B.F. (2007). Retrograde facilitation under midazolam: The role of general and specific interference. *Psychonomic Bulletin & Review, 14*, 261–269.

Redlich, A.D. (2004). Mental illness, police interrogations, and the potential for false confession. *Law & Psychiatry, 55*, 19–21.

Redlich, A.D., & Goodman, G.S. (2003). Taking responsibility for an act not committed: The influence of age and suggestibility. *Law and Human Behavior, 27*, 141–156.

Reisberg, D. (2014). *The science of perception and memory: A pragmatic guide for the justice system.* New York: Oxford University Press.

Reisberg, D., & Heuer, F. (2007). The influence of emotion on memory in forensic settings. In M.P. Toglia, J.D. Read, D.F. Ross, & R.C.L. Lindsay (Eds.), *Handbook of eyewitness psychology (Vol. 1): Memory for events* (pp. 81–116). Mahwah, NJ: Erlbaum.

Reppucci, N.D., Meyer, J., & Kostelnik, J. (2010). Custodial interrogation of juveniles: Results of a national survey of police. In G.D. Lassiter & C. Meissner (Eds.), *Police interrogations and false confessions: Current research, practice, and policy recommendations* (pp. 67–80). Washington, DC: American Psychological Association.

Rhodes, M.G., & Anastasi, J.S. (2012). The own-age bias in face recognition: A meta-analytic and theoretical review. *Psychological Bulletin, 138*, 146–174.

Rihm, J.S., Diekelmann, S., Born, J., & Rasch, B. (2014). Reactivating memories during sleep by odors: Odor specificity and associated changes in sleep oscillations. *Journal of Cognitive Neuroscience, 26*, 1806–1818. doi: 10.1162/jocn_a_00579

Rimland, B. (1978). Savant capabilities of autistic chidren and their cognitive implications. In G. Serban (Ed.), *Cognitive defects in the development of mental illness* (pp. 43–65). New York: Brunner/Mazel.

Robson, D. (2014, July 22). Can you learn in your sleep? *BBC Online*. Available at http://www.bbc.com/future/story/20140721-how-to-learn-while-you-sleep.

Roediger, H.L., III, & McDermott, K.B. (1995). Creating false memories: Remembering words not presented in lists. *Journal of Experimental Psychology: Learning, Memory, and Cognition, 21*, 803–814.

Roediger, H.L., III, Wixted, J.H., & DeSoto, K.A. (2012). The curious complexity between confidence and accuracy in reports from memory. In L. Nadel & W.P. Sinnott-Armstrong (Eds.), *Memory and law* (pp. 84–118). Oxford: Oxford University Press.

Roh, J.H., Huang, Y., Bero, A.W., Kasten, T., Stewart, F.R., Bateman, R.J., & Holtzman, D.M. (2012). Disruption of the sleep-wake cycle and diurnal fluctuation of β-amyloid in mice with Alzheimer's Disease pathology. *Science Translational Medicine, 4*, 150ra122. doi: 10.1126/scitranslmed.3004291.

Roh, J.H., Jiang, H., Finn, M.B., Stewart, F.R., Mahan, T.E., Cirrito, J.R., ... & Holtzman, D.M. (2014). Potential role of orexin and sleep modulation in the pathogenesis of Alzheimer's Disease. *Journal of Experimental Medicine, 211*, 2487–2496. doi: 10.1084/jem.20141788.

Rönnlund, M., Nyberg, L., Bäckman, L., & Nilsson, L-G. (2005). Stability, improvement, and decline in adult-life development of declarative memory: Cross-sectional and longitudinal data from a population-based sample. *Psychology and Aging, 20*, 3–18.

Ros, L., Ricarte, J.J., Serrano, J.P., Nieto, M., Aguilar, M.J., & LaTorre, J.M. (2014). Overgeneral autobiographical memories: Gender differences in depression. *Applied Cognitive Psychology, 28*, 472–480. doi: 10.1002/acp.3013.

Rosenbaum, R.S., Köhler, S., Schacter, D.L., Moscovitch, M., Westmacott, R., Black, S.E., ... & Tulving, E. (2005). The case of K.C.: Contributions of a memory-impaired person to memory theory. *Neuropsychologia, 43*, 989–1021. doi:10.1016/j.neuropsychologia.2004.10.007.

Ross, D.F., Dunning, D., Toglia, M.P., & Ceci, S. (1990). The child in the eyes of the jury: Assessing mock jurors' perceptions of the child witness. *Law and Human Behavior, 14*, 5–23. doi:10.1007/BF01055786.

Ross, D.F., Jurden, F.H., Lindsay, R.C.L., & Keeney, J.M. (2003). Replications and limitations of a two-factor model of child witness credibility. *Journal of Applied Social Psychology, 33*, 418–431.

Ross, L. (1977). The intuitive psychologist and his shortcomings: Distortions in the attribution process. *Advances in Experimental Social Psychology, 10*, 174–221.

Rubin, D.C., & Berntsen, D. (2007). People believe it is plausible to have forgotten memories of childhood sexual abuse. *Psychonomic Bulletin & Review, 14*, 776–778.

Rush, R.A., & Clark, S.E. (2014). Social contagion of correct and incorrect information in memory. *Memory, 22*, 937–948. doi: 10.1080/09658211.2013.859268.

Russano, M.B., Meissner, C.A., Narchet, F.M., & Kassin, S.M. (2005). Investigating true and false confessions within a novel experimental paradigm. *Psychological Science, 16*, 481–486.

Ryan, E.B. (1992). Beliefs about memory changes across the adult life span. *Journal of Gerontology, 47*, P41–P46.

Ryan, E.B., & Kwong See, S. (1993). Age-based beliefs about memory for self and others across adulthood. *Journal of Gerontology, 48*, P199–P201.

Ryan, E.B., Jin, Y-S., & Anas, A.P. (2009). Cross-cultural beliefs about memory and aging for self and others: South Korea and Canada. *International Journal of Aging and Human Development, 68*, 185–194. doi: 10.2190/AG.68.3.a.

Ryan, L.M., & Warden, D.L. (2003). Post concussion syndrome. *International Review of Psychiatry, 15*, 310–316.

Sacks, O. (1998). *The man who mistook his wife for a hat and other clinical tales.* New York: Touchstone.

Sacks, O. (2007). *Musicophilia: Tales of music and the brain.* New York: Knopf.

Salthouse, T.A. (1991). *Theoretical perspectives on cognitive aging.* Hillsdale, NJ: Lawrence Erlbaum Associates.

Santucci, A.C., Kanof, P.D., & Haroutunian, V. (1991). Fetal transplant-induced restoration of spatial memory in rats with lesions of the nucleus basalis of Meynert. *Journal of Neural Transplantation, 2*, 65–74.

Schacter, D.L. (1987). Implicit memory: History and current status. *Journal of Experimental Psychology: Learning, Memory, and Cognition, 13*, 501–518.

Schacter, D.L., Chamberlain, J., Gaesser, B., & Gerlach, K.D. (2012). Neuroimaging of true, false, and imaginary memories: Findings and implications. In L. Nadel & W.P. Sinnott-Armstrong (Eds.), *Memory and law* (pp. 233–262). Oxford: Oxford University Press.

Schacter, D.L., Harbluk, J.L., & McLachlan, D.R. (1984). Retrieval without recollection: An experimental analysis of source amnesia. *Journal of Verbal Learning and Verbal Behavior, 23*, 593–611.

Schacter, D.L., & Slotnick, S.D. (2004). The cognitive neuroscience of memory distortion. *Neuron, 44*, 149–160.

Schmolck, H., Buffalo, E.A., & Squire, L.R. (2000). Memory distortions develop over time: Recollections of the O.J. Simpson verdict after 15 and 32 months. *Psychological Science, 11*, 39–45.

Schooler, J.W., Bendiksen, M., & Ambadar, Z. (1997). Taking the middle line: Can we accommodate both fabricated and recovered memories of sexual abuse? In M.A. Conway (Ed.), *Recovered memories and false memories: Debates in psychology* (pp. 251–292). Oxford: Oxford University Press.

Schreiber, N., Bellah, L.D., Martinez, Y., McLaurin, K.A., Strok, R., Garven, S., & Wood, J.M. (2006). Suggestive interviewing in the McMartin Preschool and Kelly Michaels daycare abuse cases: A case study. *Social Influence, 1*, 16–47.

Schwartz, B.L. (2014). *Memory: Foundations and applications* (2nd ed.). Thousand Oaks, CA: Sage.

Schwender, D., Madler, C., Klasing, S., Peter, K., & Pöppel, E. (1994). Anesthetic control of 40-Hz brain activity and implicit memory. *Consciousness and Cognition, 3*, 129–147.

Scoboria, A., Mazzoni, G., Kirsch, & Milling, L.S. (2002). Immediate and persisting effects of misleading questions and hypnosis on memory reports. *Journal of Experimental Psychology: Applied, 8*, 26–32.

Seamon, J. (2015). *Memory and movies: What films can teach us about memory.* Cambridge, MA: MIT Press.

Seamon, J.G., Philbin, M.M., & Harrison, L.G. (2006). Do you remember proposing marriage to the Pepsi machine? False recollections from a campus walk. *Psychonomic Bulletin & Review, 13*, 752–756.

Semkovska, M., Noone, M., Carton, M., & McLoughlin, D.M. (2012). Measuring consistency of autobiographical memory recall in depression. *Psychiatry Research, 197*, 41–48. doi: 10.1016/j.psychres.2011.12.010

Shah, D.V., Rojas, H., & Cho, J. (2009). Media and civic participation: On understanding and misunderstanding communication effects. In J. Bryant & M.B. Oliver (Eds.), *Media effects: Advances in theory and research* (3rd ed.) (pp. 207–227). New York: Routledge.

Shaked-Schroer, N., Costanzo, M., & Berger, D.E. (2015). Overlooking coerciveness: The impact of interrogation techniques and guilt corroboration on jurors' judgments of coerciveness. *Legal and Criminological Psychology, 20*, 68–80. doi: 10.1111/lcrp.12011.

Shannon, T.E., & Griffin, S.L. (2015). Managing aggression in global amnesia following herpes simplex encephalitis: The case of E.B. *Brain Injury, 29*, 118–124. doi: 10.3109/02699052.2014.954623.

Sharman, S.J., & Powell, M.B. (2013). Do cognitive interview instructions contribute to false beliefs and memories? *Journal of Investigative Psychology and Offender Profiling, 10*, 114–124. doi: 10.1002/jip.1371.

Simon, C.W., & Emmons, W.H. (1955). Learning during sleep? *Psychological Bulletin, 52*, 328–342.

Simon, C.W., & Emmons, W.H. (1956). Responses to material presented during various levels of sleep. *Journal of Experimental Psychology, 51*, 89–97.

Simon, D.J. (2012). *In doubt: The psychology of the criminal justice process.* Cambridge, MA: Harvard University Press.

Simons, D.J., & Chabris, C.F. (2011). What people believe about how memory works: A representative survey of the U.S. population. *PLoS ONE, 6(8)*: e22757. doi: 10.1371/journal.pone.0022757.

Slater, A. (1994). *Identification parades: A scientific evaluation.* Police Research Award Scheme. London: Police Research Group, Home Office.

Smith, R.E., & Hunt, R.R. (2014). Prospective memory in young and older adults: The effects of task importance and ongoing task load. *Aging, Neuropsychology, and Cognition, 21*, 411–431. doi: 10.1080/13825585.2013.827150.

Snowdon, D. (2001). *Aging with grace: What the Nun Study teaches us about leading longer, healthier, and more meaningful lives.* New York: Bantam Books.

Sobin, C., Sackeim, H.A., Prudic, J., Devanand, D.P., Moody, B.J., & McElhiney, M.C. (1995). Predictors of retrograde amnesia following ECT. *American Journal of Psychiatry, 152*, 995–1001. doi: 10.1176/ajp.152.7.995.

Somaiya, R. (2015, February 4). Brian Williams admits he wasn't on copter shot down in Iraq. New York Times. Retrieved at http://www.nytimes.com/2015/02/05/business/media/brian-williamsapologizes-for-saying-he-was-shot-down-over-iraq.html.

Souchay, C. (2007). Metamemory in Alzheimer's Disease. *Cortex, 43*, 987–1003.

Soukara, S., Bull, R., Vrij, A., Turner, M., & Cherryman, J. (2009). What really happens in police interviews of suspects? Tactics and confessions. *Psychology, Crime & Law, 15*, 493–506. doi: 10.1080/10683160802201827.

Spellman, B.A., Tenney, E.R., & Scalia, M.J. (2011). Relying on other people's metamemory. In A.S. Benjamin (Ed.), *Successful remembering and successful forgetting: A festschrift in honor of Robert A. Bjork* (pp. 387–407). New York: Psychology Press.

Sporer, S.L., & Martschuk, N. (2014). The reliability of eyewitness identifications by the elderly: An evidence-based review. In M.P. Toglia, D.F. Ross, J. Pozzulo., & E. Pica (Eds.), *The elderly eyewitness in court* (pp. 3–37). New York: Psychology Press.

Sporer, S. L., Penrod, S., Read, D., & Cutler, B. (1995). Choosing, confidence, and accuracy: A meta-analysis of the confidence–accuracy relation in eyewitness identification studies. *Psychological Bulletin, 118*, 315–327.

Squire, L.R., Cohen, N.J., & Zouzounis, J.A. (1984). Preserved memory in retrograde amnesia: Sparing of a recently acquired skill. *Neuropsychologia,22*, 145–152.

Squire, L.R., & Zouzounis, J.A. (1988). Self-ratings of memory dysfunction: Different findings in depression and amnesia. *Journal of Clinical and Experimental Neuropsychology, 10*, 727–738. doi: 1068-8634/88/1006-0727

Standing, L.G., & Huber, H. (2003). Do psychology courses reduce belief in psychology myths? *Social Behavior and Personality, 31*, 585–592.

State v. Hurd, 86 N.J. 525, 432 A.2d 86 (N.J. 1981).

State v. Michaels, 136 N.J. 299, 642 A.2d 1372 (1994).

Steblay, N.K., Dietrich, H.L., Ryan, S.L., Raczynski, J.L., & James, K.A. (2011). Sequential lineup laps and eyewitness accuracy. *Law and Human Behavior, 35*, 262–274. doi: 10.1007/210979-010-9236-2.

Steblay, N., Dysart, J., Fulero, S., & Lindsay, R. C. L. (2003). Eyewitness accuracy rates in police showup and lineup presentations: A meta-analytic comparison. *Law and Human Behavior, 27*, 523–540. doi:10.1023/A:1025438223608.

Steblay, N.K., Wells, G.L., & Douglass, A.B. (2014). The eyewitness post identification feedback effect 15 years later: Theoretical and policy implications. *Psychology, Public Policy & Law, 20*, 1–18.

Steel, E., & Somaiya, R. (2015, February 10). Brian Williams suspended from NBC for 6 months without pay. *New York Times*. Retrieved at http://www.nytimes.com/2015/02/11/business/media/brian-williams-suspended-by-nbc-news-for-six-months.html?_r=0.

Stickgold, R., & Walker, M.P. (2007). Sleep-dependent memory consolidation and reconsolidation. *Sleep Medicine, 8*, 331–343.

Stickgold, R., & Walker, M.P. (2013). Sleep-dependent memory triage: Evolving generalization through selective processing. *Nature Neuroscience, 16*, 139–145.

Stone, W., & Rosenbaum, J. (1988). A comparison of teacher and parent views of autism. *Journal of Autism and Developmental Disorders, 18*, 403–414.

Stovall v. Denno, 388 U.S. 293 (1967).

Stromeyer, C. (2000). An adult eidetiker. In U. Neisser & I.E. Hyman (Eds.), *Memory observed: Remembering in natural contexts* (2nd ed.) (pp. 503–507). New York: Worth.

Sullivan, T. (2012). A compendium of state and federal statutes, court rulings, departmental practices, national organizations' policy statements, and law review articles regarding electronic recording of custodial interviews of felony suspects. *Judicature, 95*, Whole No. 5.

Sumner, J.A., Mineka, S., Adam, E.K., Craske, M.G., Vrshek-Schallhorn, S., Wolitzky-Taylor, K., & Zinbarg, R.E. (2014). Testing the CaR-FA-X model: Investigating the mechanisms underlying reduced autobiographical memory specificity in individuals with and without a history of depression. *Journal of Abnormal Psychology, 123*, 471–486. doi: 10.1037/a0037271

Suzuki, M., Kanamori, M., Watanabe, M., Nagasawa, S., Kojima, E., Ooshiro, H., & Nakahara, D. (2004). Behavioral and endocrinological evaluation of music therapy for elderly patients with dementia. *Nursing and Health Sciences, 6*, 11–18.

Svoboda, E., & Richards, B. (2009). Compensating for anterograde amnesia: A new training method that capitalizes on emerging smartphone technologies. *Journal of the International Neuropsychological Society, 15*, 629–638. doi:10.1017/S1355617709090791.

Swift, T.L., & Wilson, S.L. (2001). Misconceptions about brain injury among the general public and non-expert health professionals: An exploratory study. *Brain Injury, 15*, 149–165.

Takahashi, M., Shimizu, H., Saito, S., & Tomoyori, H. (2006). One percent ability and ninety-nine percent perspiration: A study of a Japanese memorist. *Journal of Experimental Psychology: Learning, Memory, and Cognition, 32*, 1195–1200. doi: 10.1037/0278-7393.32.5.1195.

Talarico, J.M., & Rubin, D. (2003). Confidence, not consistency, characterizes flashbulb memories. *Psychological Science, 14*, 455–461.

Talarico, J.M., & Rubin, D. (2007). Flashbulb memories are special after all: In phenomenology, not accuracy. *Applied Cognitive Psychology, 21*, 557–578.

Tariot, P.N., Farlow, M.R., Grossberg, G.T., Graham, S.M., McDonald, S., Gergel, I., & Memantine Study Group (2004). Memantine treatment in patients with moderate to severe Alzheimer Disease already receiving donepezil: A randomized controlled trial. *JAMA, 291*, 317–324.

Technical Working Group on Eyewitness Evidence (1999). *Eyewitness evidence: A guide for law enforcement.* Washington, DC: National Institute of Justice.

Tekcan, A.I., Ece, B., Gülgöz, S., & Er. N. (2003). Autobiographical and event memory for 9/11: Changes across one year. *Applied Cognitive Psychology, 17*, 1057–1066.

Tenney, E.R., MacCoun, R.J., Spellman, B.A., & Hastie, R. (2007). Calibration trumps confidence as a basis for witness credibility. *Psychological Science, 18*, 46–50.

Thomas, A.K., & Loftus, E.F. (2002). Creating bizarre false memories through imagination. *Memory & Cognition, 30*, 423–431.

Thomas, K. (1971). *Religion and the decline of magic: Studies in popular beliefs in Sixteenth and Seventeenth Century England.* London: Weidenfeld and Nicolson.

Thompson, C.P., Cowan, T.M., & Frieman, J. (1993). *Memory search by a memorist.* Hillsdale, NJ: Erlbaum.

Thompson, N. (2012, September 3). Paul Ryan's marathon: Everyone else remembers his or her time. *The New Yorker.* Available at http://www.newyorker.com/news/news-desk/paul-ryans-marathon-everyone-else-remembers-his-or-her-time.

Toglia, M.P., Read, J.D., Ross., D.F., & Lindsay, R.C.L. (2007). *The handbook of eyewitness psychology (Vol. 1): Memory for events.* Mahwah, NJ: Erlbaum.

Tollestrup, P.A., Turtle, J.W., & Yuille, J.C. (1994). Actual victims and witnesses to robbery and fraud: An archival analysis. In D.F. Ross, J.D. Read, & M.P. Toglia (Eds.), *Adult eyewitness testimony* (pp. 144–160). Cambridge: Cambridge University Press.

Tomes, J.L., & Katz, A.N. (1997). Habitual susceptibility to misinformation and individual differences in eyewitness memory. *Applied Cognitive Psychology, 11,* 233–251.

Tracy, P.E. (2003). *Who killed Stephanie Crowe? The anatomy of a murder investigation.* True Crime Publications.

Treffert, D.A. (1989). *Extraordinary people: Understanding savant syndrome.* New York: Ballantine Books.

Treffert, D.A. (2010). *Islands of genius: The bountiful mind of the autistic, acquired, and sudden savant.* London: Jessica Kingsley Publishers.

Treffert, D.A., & Christensen, D.D. (2005). Inside the mind of a savant. *Scientific American, 293(6),* 108–113.

Tulving, E. (1985). Memory and consciousness. *Canadian Psychology, 26,* 1–12.

Tyler, T.R., & Huo, Y.J. (2002). Trust in the law: Encouraging public cooperation with the police and courts. New York: Russell Sage Foundation.

Underwager, R., & Wakefield, H. (1998). Recovered memories in the courtroom. In S.J. Lynn & K.M. McConkey (Eds.), *Truth in memory* (pp. 394–434). New York: Guilford.

United States v. Ash, 413 U.S. 300 (1973).

Valentine, T., Davis, J.P., Memon, A., & Roberts, A. (2012). Live showups and their influence on a subsequent video line-up. *Applied Cognitive Psychology, 26,* 1–23. doi: 10.1002/acp.1796

Valentine, T., & Mesout, J. (2009). Eyewitness identification under stress in the London Dungeon. Applied Cognitive Psychology, 23, 151–161. doi: 10.1002/acp.1463.

Valentine, T., Pickering, A., & Darling, S. (2003). Characteristics of eyewitness identification that predict the outcome of real lineups. *Applied Cognitive Psychology, 17,* 969–993. doi: 10.1002/acp.939

Van Daele, T., Griffith, J.W., Van den Bergh, O., & Hermans, D. (2014). Overgeneral autobiographical memory predicts changes in depression in a community sample. Cognition and Emotion, 28, 1303–1312. doi: 10.1080/02699931.2013.879052.

Van Wallendael, L.R., Cutler, B.L., Devenport, J., & Penrod, S. (2007). Mistaken identification = erroneous conviction? Assessing and improving legal safeguards. In R.C.L. Lindsay, D.F. Ross, J.D. Read, & M.P. Toglia (Eds.), *Handbook of eyewitness psychology.* Mahwah, NJ: Erlbaum.

Villalobos, J.G., & Davis, D. (2016). Interrogation and the minority suspect: Pathways to true and false confession. In B.H. Bornstein & M.K. Miller (Eds.), *Advances in psychology and law* (Vol. 1, pp. 1–41). New York: Springer.

Viswesvaran, C., & Schimdt, F.L. (1992). A meta-analytic comparison of the effectiveness of smoking cessation methods. *Journal of Applied Psychology, 77*, 554–561.

Vrij, A., Granhag, P.A., & Porter, S. (2010). Pitfalls and opportunities in nonverbal and verbal lie detection. *Psychological Science in the Public Interest, 11*, 89–121.

Wade, K.A., Garry, M., Read, J.D., & Lindsay, D.S. (2002). A picture is worth a thousand lies: Using false photographs to create false childhood memories. *Psychonomic Bulletin & Review, 9*, 597–603.

Wagenaar, W.A. (1986). My memory: A study of autobiographical memory over six years. *Cognitive Psychology, 18*, 225–252.

Wagenaar, W.A., Groeneweg, J. (1990). The memory of concentration camp survivors. *Applied Cognitive Psychology, 4*, 77–87.

Walker, L.E.A., Robinson, M., Duros, R.L., Henle, J., Caverly, J., Mignone, S., ... Apple, B. (2010). The myth of mental illness in the movies and its impact on forensic psychology. In M.B. Gregerson (Ed.), *The cinematic mirror for psychology and life coaching* (pp. 171–192). New York: Springer. doi: 10.1007/978-1-4419-1114-8_9.

Walsh-Childers, K., & Brown, J.D. (2009). Effects of media on personal and public health. In J. Bryant & M.B. Oliver (Eds.), *Media effects: Advances in theory and research* (3rd ed.) (pp. 469–489). New York: Routledge.

Wamsley, E., Donjacour, C. E., Scammell, T. E., Lammers, G. J., & Stickgold, R. (2014). Delusional confusion of dreaming and reality in narcolepsy. Sleep, 37, 419–422.

Warden, D. (2006). Military TBI during the Iraq and Afghanistan wars. *Journal of Head Trauma Rehabilitation, 21*, 398–402.

Warner, T.C., & Pickel, K.L. (2010). Camera perspective and trivial details interact to influence jurors' evaluations of a retracted confession. *Psychology, Crime & Law, 16*, 493–506. doi: 10.1080/10683160902926158.

Watson, S.J. (2011). *Before I go to sleep.* New York: HarperCollins.

Wearing, D. (2006). *Forever today: A true story of lost memory and never-ending love.* Corgi Books.

Weaver, C.A. (1993). Do you need a "flash" to form a flashbulb memory? *Journal of Experimental Psychology: General, 122*, 39–46.

Wells, G. L., & Lindsay, R.C.L. (1983). How do people infer the accuracy of eyewitness memory? Studies of performance and a metamemory analysis. In S.M.A. Lloyd-Bostock & B.R. Clifford (Eds.), *Evaluating witness evidence* (pp. 41–55). Chichester, U.K.: John Wiley & Sons.

Wells, G. L., Lindsay, R.C.L., & Tousignant, J.P. (1980). Effects of expert psychological advice on human performance in judging the validity of eyewitness testimony. *Law and Human Behavior, 4*, 275–286.

Wells, G. L., Memon, A., & Penrod, S. D. (2006). Eyewitness evidence: Improving its probative value. *Psychological Science in the Public Interest, 7*, 43–75.

Wells, G.L., & Quinlivan, D.S. (2009). Suggestive eyewitness identification procedures and the supreme court's reliability test in light of eyewitness science: 30 years later. *Law and Human Behavior, 33*, 1–14. doi: 10.1007/s10979-008-9130-3.

Wells, G.L., Steblay, N.K., & Dysart, J.E. (2014). Double-blind photo lineups using actual eyewitnesses: An experimental test of a sequential versus simultaneous lineup procedure. *Law and Human Behavior*.

Werner, C.A. (2011). *The older population: 2010*. Washington, DC: U.S. Census Bureau. Available at https://www.census.gov/prod/cen2010/briefs/c2010br-09.pdf.

Werner-Seidler, A., & Moulds, M.L. (2014). Recalling positive self-defining memories in depression: The impact of processing mode. *Memory, 22*, 525–535. doi: 10.1080/09658211.2013.801494.

Wetmore, S., Neuschatz, J., & Gronlund, S. (2014). On the power of secondary confession evidence. *Psychology, Crime and Law, 20,* 339–357.

Wilding, J.M., & Valentine, E.R. (1997). *Superior memory*. Psychology Press.

Willer, B., Johnson, W.E., Rempel, R.G., & Linn, R. (1993). A note concerning misconceptions of the general public about brain injury. *Archives of Clinical Neuropsychology, 8*, 461–465.

Williams, J.M.G., Barnhofer, T., Crane, C., Hermans, D., Raes, F., Watkins, E., & Dalgleish, T. (2007). Autobiographical memory specificity and emotional disorder. *Psychological Bulletin, 133*, 122–148. doi:10.1037/0033-2909.133.1.122.

Williams, J.M.G., Teasdale, J.D., Segal, Z.V., & Soulsby, J. (2000). Mindfulness-based cognitive therapy reduces overgeneral autobiographical memory in formerly depressed patients. *Journal of Abnormal Psychology, 109*, 150–155.

Wilson, B.A., & Wearing, D. (1995). Prisoner of consciousness: A state of just awakening following herpes simplex encephalitis. In R. Campbell & M.A. Conway (Eds.), *Broken memories: Case studies in memory impairment* (pp. 14–30). Oxford: Blackwell.

Wilson, R.S., Boyle, P.A., Yu, L., Barnes, L.L., Schneider, J. A., & Bennett. D. A. (2013). Life-span cognitive activity, neuropathologic burden, and cognitive aging. *Neurology, 81*, 314–321.

Wise, R.A., Pawlenko, N.B., Safer, M.A., & Meyer, D. (2009). What U.S. prosecutors and defence attorneys know and believe about eyewitness testimony. *Applied Cognitive Psychology, 23*, 1266–1281. doi:10.1002/acp.1530.

Wise, R.A., & Safer, M.A. (2004). What U.S. judges know and believe about eyewitness testimony. *Applied Cognitive Psychology, 18*, 427–443. doi:10.1002/acp.993.

Wise, R.A., Safer, M.A., & Maro, C.M. (2011). What U.S. law enforcement officers know and believe about eyewitness factors, eyewitness interviews and identification procedures. *Applied Cognitive Psychology, 25*, 488–500.

Witztum, E., Margalit, H., & van der Hart, O. (2002). Combat-induced dissociative amnesia: Review and case example of generalized dissociative amnesia. *Journal of Trauma & Dissociation, 3*, doi: 10.1300/J229v03n02_03.

Wixted, J.T. (2004). On common ground: Law of retrograde amnesia. *Psychological Review, 111*, 864–879.

Wixted, J.T., Mickes, L., Clark, S.E., Gronlund, S.D., & Roediger, H.L. (2015). Initial eyewitness confidence reliably predicts eyewitness identification accuracy. *American Psychologist, 70*, 515–526.

Wixted, J.T., Read, J.D., & Lindsay, D.S. (2016). The effect of retention interval on the eyewitness identification confidence-accuracy relationship. *Journal of Applied Research in Memory and Cognition, 5*, 192–203.

Wixted, J.T., & Wells, G.L. (in press). The relationship between eyewitness confidence and identification accuracy: A new synthesis. *Psychological Science in the Public Interest.*

Wood, J.M., Bootzin, R.R., Kihlstrom, J.F., & Schacter, D.L. (1992). Implicit and explicit memory for verbal information presented during sleep. *Psychological Science, 3,* 236–239.

Wood, N.E., Rosasco, M.L., Suris, A.M., Spring, J.D., Marin, M-F., Lasko, N.B. ... & Pitman, R.K. (2015). Pharmacological blockade of memory reconsolidation in posttraumatic stress disorder: Three negative psychophysiological studies. *Psychiatry Research, 225,* 31–39. doi: 10.1016/j.psychres.2014.09.005

Woodward, A.E., & Bjork, R.A. (1971). Forgetting and remembering in free recall: Intentional and unintentional. *Journal of Experimental Psychology, 89,* 109–116.

Woody, W.D., & Forrest, K.D. (2009). Effects of false-evidence ploys and expert testimony on jurors' verdicts, recommended sentences, and perceptions of confession evidence. *Behavioral Sciences and the Law, 27,* 333–360.

Woody, W., Forrest, K., & Yendra, S. (2014). Comparing the effects of explicit and implicit false-evidence ploys on mock jurors' verdicts, sentencing recommendations, and perceptions of police interrogation. *Psychology, Crime and Law, 20,* 603–617.

Woollett, K., Glensman, J., & Maguire, E.A. (2008). Non-spatial expertise and hippocampal gray matter volume in humans. *Hippocampus, 18,* 981–984. doi: 10.1002/hipo.20465

Woollett, K., & Maguire, E.A. (2009). Navigational expertise may compromise anterograde associative memory. *Neuropsychologia, 47,* 1088–1095. doi: 10.1016/j.neuropsychologia.2008.12.036

Worthen, J.B., & Hunt, R.R. (2011). *Mnemonology: Mnemonics for the 21st century.* New York: Psychology Press.

Wright, D.B., & McDaid, A.T. (1996). Comparing system and estimator variables using data from real lineups. *Applied Cognitive Psychology, 10,* 75–84.

Wright, D.B., Memon, A., Skagerberg, E.M., & Gabbert, F. (2009). When eyewitnesses talk. *Current Directions in Psychological Science, 18,* 174–178.

Wright, D.B., & Sladden, B. (2003). An own gender bias and the importance of hair in face recognition. *Acta Psychologica, 114,* 101–114.

Wright, L. (1995). *Remembering Satan: A tragic case of recovered memory.* New York: Vintage.

Wylie, L., Patihis, L., McCuller, L., Davis, D., Brank, E.M., Loftus, E.F., & Bornstein, B.H. (2014). The misinformation effect in elderly witnesses. In M.P. Toglia, D.F. Ross, J. Pozzulo, & E. Pica (Eds.), *The elderly eyewitness in court* (pp. 38–66). New York: Psychology Press.

Yaffe, K., Falvey, C.M., & Hoang, T. (2014). Connections between sleep and cognition in older adults. *The Lancet Neurology, 13,* 1017–1028.

Yapko, M.D. (1994). Suggestibility and repressed memories of abuse: A survey of psychotherapists' beliefs. *American Journal of Clinical Hypnosis, 36,* 163–171.

Young, W.C., Sachs, R.G., Braun, B.G., & Watkins, R.T. (1991). Patients reporting ritual abuse in childhood: A clinical syndrome. Report of 37 cases. *Child Abuse & Neglect, 15,* 181–189.

Yuille, J.C., & Cutshall, J.L. (1986). A case study of eyewitness memory of a crime. *Journal of Applied Psychology, 71,* 291–301.

Zhang, W., Wang, P.-J., Sha, H., Ni, J., Li, M., & Gu, G. (2014). Neural stem cell transplants improve cognitive function without altering amyloid pathology in an APP/PS1 double transgenic model of Alzheimer's Disease. *Molecular Neurobiology, 50,* 423–437. doi: 10.1007/s12035-014-8640-x.

Zimmerman, M.E., Bigal, M.E., Katz, M.J., Brickman, A.M., & Lipton, R.B. (2012). Sleep onset/maintenance difficulties and cognitive function in nondemented older adults: The role of cognitive reserve. *Journal of the International Neuropsychological Society, 18,* 461–70.

Index

A Very Long Engagement, 86
Visitors, 132
The Vow, 87

Waltz with Bashir, 86
Watson, S.J., xxix
Wearing, Clive, 111–12, 116, 118, 127, 130n1

What Alice Forgot, 87, 102
The White Hotel, 37
The Who, 37, 61, 62–63n1
Williams, Brian, 49–51, 63n4, 237, 244n2
Williams, Tennessee, 37
working memory, 33, 77, 110, 126, 137–38, 215, 222

About the Author

Brian H. Bornstein is professor of psychology and courtesy professor of law at the University of Nebraska-Lincoln; previously he was in the Psychology Department at Louisiana State University. He received his MA and PhD in Psychology from the University of Pennsylvania, and a Master of Legal Studies from the University of Nebraska-Lincoln. Dr. Bornstein's research efforts focus primarily on the reliability of eyewitness memory and how juries make decisions, for which he has received funding from the National Science Foundation, the National Institute of Justice, and other organizations. He teaches courses on human memory, eyewitness memory, jury decision making, and history of psychology. He has written or edited 17 books and approximately 160 scientific articles and book chapters. He is the coeditor of the NYU Press Psychology & Crime book series and the Springer Advances in Psychology & Law book series. Dr. Bornstein has received the College of Arts & Sciences Award for Outstanding Research and Creative Achievement in the Social Sciences from the University of Nebraska-Lincoln and the Outstanding Teaching and Mentoring Award from the American Psychology-Law Society. He has a wonderful wife and two amazing daughters.